LORD KABIR

LORD KABIR

LORD KABIR

SHARAN MALHOTRA

CBS PUBLISHERS & DISTRIBUTORS
4596/1-A, 11 Darya Ganj, New Delhi - 110 002 (India)

S.K. Publications
2 Canal Road, Vijay Nagar, Delhi 110 009, India

© 2000 by Science of Spirituality
   4S/175 Naperville Rd., Naperville, IL 60563, U.S.A.

ISBN : 81-239-0684-6

All rights reserved. No part of this publication may be reproduced, stored in a retrieval system, or transmitted in any form or by any means, electronic, mechanical, photocopying, recording, or otherwise, without the prior written permission of the publishers.

Production Director : Vinod Jain

Printed in India

Published by :
Satish Kumar Jain for CBS Publishers & Distributors,
4596/1-A, 11 Darya Ganj, New Delhi 110 002 (India)

Printed at :
Tara Art Printers, Noida, U.P.

LORD KABIR

LORD KABIR

SHARAN MALHOTRA

CBS PUBLISHERS & DISTRIBUTORS
4596/1-A, 11 Darya Ganj, New Delhi - 110 002 (India)

S.K. Publications
2 Canal Road, Vijay Nagar, Delhi 110 009, India

© 2000 by Science of Spirituality
   4S/175 Naperville Rd., Naperville, IL 60563, U.S.A.

ISBN : 81-239-0684-6

All rights reserved. No part of this publication may be reproduced, stored in a retrieval system, or transmitted in any form or by any means, electronic, mechanical, photocopying, recording, or otherwise, without the prior written permission of the publishers.

Production Director : Vinod Jain

Printed in India

Published by :
Satish Kumar Jain for CBS Publishers & Distributors,
4596/1-A, 11 Darya Ganj, New Delhi 110 002 (India)

Printed at :
Tara Art Printers, Noida, U.P.

DEDICATION

This little volume is humbly
dedicated to Almighty God,
all Masters working through Him,
and to my Beloved Master,
His Holiness
Sant Kirpal Singh Ji Maharaj,
Who kindly bestowed on me the
Gift of Holy Naam,
the Eternal Water of Life,
and to the Gracious Master,
Sant Darshan Singh Ji Maharaj,
at Whose Lotus Feet
I Experienced
the Sweet Ecstasy of Divine Love,
and to the Revered Living Master,
Sant Rajinder Singh Ji Maharaj,
Who is keeping aloft
the Torch of Spirituality.

FOREWORD

This auspicious year marks the Sixth Birth Centenary (1398-1998) of Sant Kabir. It is a great joy to see such a wonderful book, expounding on the life and Teachings of this Great Saint. His timeless words reflect the presentation of Spirituality in its simplest form, as an Eternal and Unchangeable Truth.

Kabir Sahib came to present to the world an in-depth and analytical study of the most ancient science that the world has ever known. It is the study of the Inner Self, which is a science of practical analysis, in the pursuit of which one obtains self-knowledge and God-realization, through the Grace of Almighty God and the Living Master. Never before had these Teachings been presented so openly to humanity in general.

Sant Kabir came at a very critical time in history. India was in the grip of chaotic conditions. Religion itself had degenerated into formalism, and people were losing faith in its meaningless rituals. In this period of darkness and confusion, Sant Kabir provided the Divine Light. Preaching the Love of God and the Love of human unity, He taught that everyone is born equal: none is high and none is low. In essence, Sant Kabir taught the Universal religion of 'man'. His aim was to reform religion, and to lift it from the complexity of theoretical, formal rites to the simplicity of practical Experience.

Overflowing with the Love and Glory of Almighty God, Sant Kabir taught the 'Inner Life' of the spirit, offering the Water of Life and the Bread of Life (Holy Naam) to the hungry souls of humanity. He said that once having partaken of this, nothing else remains to be received. The Divine Light that had manifested within Him, guided whoever came to His Lotus Feet.

Intoxicated with the Love of the Lord, in His All-Pervading Grace, Sant Kabir remained always in a state of perpetual ecstasy and inebriation. He ascribed this to Spiritual discipline and regular meditation, which results in progress on the Spiritual Path.

His disciples came from far-off places such as Iran, Afghanistan, Central Asia, as well as from all over India. They included the 'high-caste' Brahmins as well as the 'low-caste' Sudras, the Sufis, the Muslims, and a complete diversity of people, knit together like so many pearls on a string of Love.

Sant Kabir radiated Love and Light to the world for 120 years, remaining the very essence of humility. His followers dedicated themselves as humble servants of God, worshipping the Lord in the simplicity of the Inner Self.

The timeless words of Sant Kabir are as true today as they have been throughout the ages. Let us strive to live up to the Highest Spiritual Ideal, which is ensouled and exemplified within His verses. The purpose of celebrating the birth anniversary of a Great Saint is to remind us of His Teachings and His Ideals, thereby pursuing the Higher Purpose of the human life.

It is my hope and prayer that the Message of Sant Kabir will encourage the reader to follow in His footsteps, thereby making one's own life sublime, a fitting Tribute to His Sweet Memory.

December 1998   Rajinder Singh

CONTENTS

	DEDICATION	i
	FOREWORD	iii
1.	INTRODUCTION	1
2.	A SHORT BIOGRAPHY OF SANT KABIR	32
3.	INDIA AT THE TIME OF SANT KABIR	64
4.	CREATION OF THE WORLD	73
	#4-1 The Formation of Creation	74
	#4-2 Akaal and Kaal	82
	#4-3 Dharam Rai	84
	#4-4 How Kaal Rules Over His Domain	86
	#4-5 Karma (The Law of Action and Reaction)	93
5.	THERE IS A GREAT NEED OF SPIRITUALITY	110
	#5-1 Illusion (The Long Sleep of the Soul)	117
	#5-2 The Futility of Outer Worship	182
	#5-3 The Mind and its Desires	223
	#5-4 Fear and Fearless	243
	#5-5 The Effects of Association with Worldly People	257
	#5-6 Untrue Masters	260

6. THE SOUL'S RELATIONSHIP WITH GOD — 282

- #6-1 First Separation From God — 289
- #6-2 Sweet Is Thy Will — 291
- #6-3 The True Temple of God — 295
- #6-4 Sweet Praises of God — 302
- #6-5 The Four Categories of 'Ram' — 311

7. TRUE WORSHIP — 315

- #7-1 All Humanity Is One — 321
- #7-2 Human Body is the Golden Opportunity to Meet God — 324
- #7-3 Helping Factors For Spiritual Progress — 342
- #7-4 Discrimination (The Fifth Element) — 353
- #7-5 Prayer — 358
- #7-6 Bhairag (Detachment) — 371
- #7-7 Humility — 379
- #7-8 Divine Love — 392

8. THE TRUE MASTER — 400

- #8-1 The Master Makes People Into True Human Beings — 429
- #8-2 The Unbounded Grace of the Master — 441
- #8-3 Sharan (Surrender to the Master's Will) — 450
- #8-4 Satsang (The Master's Holy Discourse) — 455
- #8-5 Faith in the Master — 469
- #8-6 Seva (Selfless Service to the Master) — 475
- #8-7 Bhakti (Devotion to the Master) — 479
- #8-8 Puja (Worship of the Master) — 485
- #8-9 Bireh (The Longing and Pining of Separation) — 488
- #8-10 Sweet Praises of the Master — 504

9.	**THE HOLY NAAM**	**522**
#9-1	Dying While Living (First-Hand Experience of the Light and Sound of God)	537
#9-2	Simran (Repetition of the Names of God)	548
#9-3	Dhyan (Contemplation of the Master's Radiant, Effulgent Form)	565
#9-4	Shabd (The Divine Sound Current)	569
#9-5	The Inner Realms PART ONE	578
	PART TWO	585
#9-6	How This Science Can Be Obtained	594
10.	**SANT KABIR'S VERSES**	**605**
	Original Hindi-Punjabi Text	

BIBLIOGRAPHY　　667

GLOSSARY　　669

BIOGRAPHIES　　683

CHAPTER 1

INTRODUCTION

The religious literature of mediaeval India was mostly chanted. It spread across the country on the lips of the devotees and the wandering ascetics who walked from region to region, or met in conventions of 'holy men' on the banks of sacred rivers, where the chief activity was the singing of these *Bhajans* (hymns). This tradition still flourishes today. One can move among *Sadhus* (wandering monks) or groups of singers in villages, and hear versions of songs from Kabir Sahib that have been passed from generation to generation for centuries.

In His verses, Kabir Sahib primarily addresses the audience, making the reader central. Nearly everyone in North India is familiar with expressions such as "Kabir says, Listen brother Sadhu!" or "Listen, O Saints!" This is His trademark, and is a remedy to wake people up and affect them to listen to His wisdom.

His hymns left a deep impression for centuries to follow, touching the hearts and minds of the masses. Many of the Priests, Ministers, and other religious leaders of the day must have found it difficult to believe that a low-caste person, such as Kabir Sahib, had acquired the highest Spiritual Knowledge, when they themselves knew very little about the Scriptures or high philosophical thoughts, despite all their bookish learning. Yet the message of Sant Kabir's Love and devotion has transcended all castes and creeds, rites and rituals, in all times and in all climes, remaining eternally fresh and soul-stirring. There could be many a scholar who has read all the Scriptures, but only rarely will there be a person of True Spiritual Knowledge!

Sant Kabir uses down-to-earth metaphors and various everyday symbols in His observations of humanity at large. He remains quite indifferent to any traditional manners of regulated society and religion. He urges His followers to arise from their Spiritual slumber and behold the Glorious, Resplendent face of the Beloved. In many different ways, He makes use of various symbols of nature that refer to man's eternal search. For example, He says that the oyster, although residing in the ocean, is 'thirsty' for that *Special Drop of Rain* that will transform it into a Pearl. He also talks about the legendary bird called the *'Hans'*, that can separate milk from water, and He asserts that similarly a person of True Knowledge can know the Real from the unreal.

Another metaphor that is frequently used in His verses is that of a drop of water and the Ocean. In the ordinary state of Consciousness, the person sees himself merely as a drop of water. In a Spiritually Exalted State, however, one also sees the Ocean that is inherent in that drop, for the very gist of the Ocean is contained within the drop. Likewise, when the drop ultimately merges with the Ocean, it becomes the very Ocean itself and cannot be differentiated from it. In this state of unity, there is no more a condition of 'I' and 'Thou'.

Sant Kabir says that Consciousness permeates all Creation. The devotee attempts to be aware of this Cosmic Consciousness through meditation and prayer. Often this new 'Awakened' state has been described as being of Supreme Bliss, like waking up from a long, deep slumber. This is accessible only when the Eye of the soul, also known as the *Third Eye* (located behind and between the two eyebrows), is opened, and one sees the unity of man and Almighty God. This Awakened Eye discovers the Presence of God permeating everywhere. The drop is merged into the Ocean and the Ocean is submerged in the drop. All thoughts of the lover and the Beloved, the subject and the Object are gone. They are as One. There is a new awareness of an eternally still, whole, Oneness.

Sant Kabir teaches and emphasizes this unity of God and all Creation. He tells us that the different appellations of God are only expressions of one and the same Truth. According to Sant Kabir, it matters little by what Name one calls God, for He is one God for one humanity and everyone is a child of that same one God.

Of course, all these assertions and Experiences which speak of God and the seeker as One, had in the time of Sant Kabir a certain aura of heresy about them. He alone, dared to speak the Truth and also had the courage to suffer its consequences, particularly in those days when any attack on established religion was deemed as the worst type of heresy. His revolutionary ideas created much opposition and several attempts were made to humiliate Him, all successfully overcome through miraculous events which took place out of the great Love and mercy of Almighty God.

Sant Kabir's Teachings are a source of inspiration, and a revelation of new socio-ethical values. He is the forerunner of a new culture based on human equality and justice in all spheres of life. He is an ardent opponent of any practice which differentiates between man and man. He speaks about the unity of the entire Creation, proclaiming that the Hindu God called *Ram*, and the Muslim God called *Allah,* are actually One. He expresses intense concern for the oppressed and the exploited, invoking His devotees to *re-form* and *transform*. He advocates a mutual respect for the customs, rituals and beliefs of the two main religions existing at those times, namely *Hinduism* and *Islam*, although He has an aversion to all ceremonies and the like conducted in the Name of God and religion. He is against such customs as they leave little freedom to the individual person and keep him bound to the world and its affairs. Many customs had become so much a part of religion and tradition, that any step taken against them was considered blasphemy.

In His writings, Sant Kabir uses two main images which stand out prominently. One is of **the bride** (the soul) **and the Eternal Bridegroom** (Almighty God), which become as a metaphor for the union of man with God. The other image is of **music**. Kabir Sahib says that all Creation is full of Music: *it is all Music*. He perceives the Unstruck Music of the Infinite everywhere, and says again and again that this Celestial Music can be heard by everyone regardless of age, health, gender, occupation, nationality, or creed.

This Divine Sound Current is a Mystical Vibration audible only to the one who has succeeded in arousing his soul from the eternal slumber of the world. It is a revelation of God, which is given deep in the quietness of the human spirit. Sant Kabir pictures it as an *arrow* discharged by the Master, which pierces the very depths of the heart and opens the Inner (Third) Eye to the Experience of the Divine Light of God. He says, "Without hearing this Divine Sound of God, it is all utter darkness!"

Sant Kabir says that the Holy Word, this Divine Sound Current, also known as the *Holy Naam* or the *Five Holy Melodies*, is within man and cannot be found in the Scriptures. These Divine Sounds are Inner Spiritual Emanations from the Supreme Father and are the Essence of all Creation. There is no parallel in this world to which this Divine Sound can be compared, for it is a Soundless Sound, an unspoken Word, emanating throughout all Creation. He says, "It is through this Holy Naam that all Creation is made, is sustained and changes."

Accordingly, this Heavenly Melody is the Master's thought, or Attention. It is the expression of God's Truth, which is imparted to the individual by the Living Spiritual Master. All that concerns God is this Holy Naam or Divine Sound Current. The Holy Naam embraces all that is Truth, all that expresses the nature of God, the Names of God, and the means of attaining Him. Sant Kabir indicates that there is no salvation without God's Holy Naam, and in all humbleness He constantly refers to Himself as being nothing more than 'God's Slave'.

A significant portion of His verses emphasize the need for a living Teacher, a *Sat Guru*, a True Master. "Creed, class, or religious heritage count not at all in the Court of the Lord, and have no bearing whatsoever on one's Spiritual Journey. Holy Scriptures, ethical Teachings, or long discourses alone cannot carry the soul back to merge in the Lord."

He emphasizes again and again the dire importance of seeking a True Master. "So long as the True Master is not found, the Inner Secret of the Pathway to God remains hidden. The Master holds the Inner Key, and shows the Way to the soul's Real Home through the Holy Naam. This Holy Naam is also known as the Divine Sound Current emanating from the Pure Spiritual Regions of Almighty God, ever beckoning mankind to come back to its True Home."

This Holy Naam, however, can be seen only with the Inner Eye, and heard with the Inner Ear. For this reason, Sant Kabir says that the guidance of an earthly Guru is indispensable and invaluable, because only the One Who Himself has Experience, Enlightenment, and union with God, is competent to pass on to others the Blessings that He

Himself has received. But Sant Kabir cautions that great care must be given in choosing a Master, so that a false teacher may be avoided, and the human birth does not go to waste. He outlines several qualities or characteristics that one might discern a true Master. For example, a true Master lives on His own earnings; He shares with the needy and the oppressed whatever He has; He does not charge any fee for His Divine Teachings of Truth; He does not perform any miracles for the purpose of impressing seekers; He does not advocate outer rites and rituals of established religions; and He has Love for all and embraces all as Children of One God.

The importance and necessity of the Master for Sant Kabir is such as to cause Him to put forth the fundamental questions of life and death, and human destiny. He says, "When one touches the True Guru's Feet, he can humbly bow and ask to have explained the meaning and purpose of the origin and destruction of the soul and the world."

"When the True Master is found," He continues, "He must be treated with great respect and reverence, for He is the Guide that holds the Key to unlock the Door of Divinity. The Spiritual Charging of His Holy Naam is the *gate-pass* leading to the Lane of God. The Guru alone is competent to grant the seeker a first-hand Experience of the Divine Light and Sound."

Sant Kabir affirms Almighty God's activities of creating and sustaining the Creation. The Supreme Being is a participant in every aspect of the life of the entire universe, but human understanding is, naturally, severely limited to only worldly knowledge. Kabir Sahib emphasizes that Almighty God is far beyond the human intellect, and man just cannot comprehend His eternal and supreme, infinite existence. God is without beginning, beyond time and space, ever constant. Sant Kabir beholds God manifested everywhere in all Creation. God is portrayed as being not only Omnipotent and Omniscient, but also Omnipresent.

He often elaborates on this theme of God's Omnipresence and condemns the narrow-mindedness of the Hindus and Muslims in trying to keep God confined to their respective places of worship. He asserts that God is universal and is present everywhere, but that His true abode is within the human heart. Through Divine Grace alone, Almighty God makes Himself available to human beings, coming within the compass of mortal understanding and experience by taking a human form. Almighty God becomes immanent in order that human beings might Know Him, and thus by Knowing Him enter into union with Him. It is only by this immanent aspect that a person can thus Know God, for only man can be a teacher of man.

Sant Kabir advocates *Bhakti*, or Loving Devotion to God, through the guidance of this Living Master. He speaks of repeating the Holy Names of God, as given through the *Godman*. This Living Master has Himself traversed the Higher, Inner Spiritual Realms, and can take the soul back to its True Home in the purely Spiritual Region, known as *Sach Khand* (the Fifth Inner Spiritual Region).

It is the Master's Attention, His Divine Charging of these Holy Names of God, that stills the mind of the seeker, and helps him to concentrate at the focal point between and behind the two eyes, thereby assisting the disciple to realize his union with God. Sant Kabir says, however, that the repetition of the Holy Names of God must not be mere lip service. It must be done with the tongue of the soul, which is the attention.

Sant Kabir tells us how the Master 'awakens' the Power of Discrimination and perception in man. He says, "He who hears and responds to the Master's instructions begins to comprehend the *Divine Shabd* (the Holy Word, or Naam) made manifest in all Creation." This response takes the form of adoring Love, or devotional worship. Slowly but surely, the seeker becomes cleansed of his impurities, and grows progressively nearer to the Eternal One. Ascending to Higher and yet Higher levels of Spiritual Realms, the devotee finally reaches the ultimate union with Almighty God, in which all earthly bonds are dissolved and the endless Cycle of death and rebirth is at long last brought to an end.

Sant Kabir's ideal is a perfected man clothed in the personality of a Saint, who lives to Enlighten man as to the method of Divine Living. This is His unforgettable and timeless Message. Kabir Sahib Himself is the personification of such a Saint. To Him, the Guru or the Master is the Real Teacher of man, Who has perfected Himself through self-knowledge. There is no other Way open for mankind, except to follow the Saint's pattern of life.

However, the Master, according to Sant Kabir, is no renouncer of the world, nor a dabbler in mere metaphysical speculation. He lives in the world with full awareness, but does not belong to it. This sense of living in the world, and yet being non-worldly in attachment, awakens the person of the senses and desires, and instructs him to live a full life without the entanglement of the many and diverse strings attached to it, which keep pulling him in all directions.

"This world is both a revelation of God," says Sant Kabir, "and also a snare of the Negative Power." What ultimately matters is the individual's attitude to it. The Creation as a whole can either be man's ally or his enemy. Everything is from God, because He is the sole Creator, but the awareness of God with which people are Blessed by the Master, determines either their salvation or transmigration. The most fundamental thing that is needed is purity of heart, for God dwells within the heart of the devotee. Sant Kabir, therefore, advocates a change of heart and mind for progress on the Inner Spiritual Path.

How does God communicate with man? Sant Kabir says that God reveals His Truth in and through the Divine Sound Current, the Holy Naam, and the Master. Furthermore, he who perceives this Truth will find salvation. The Truth may be here for all to grasp, but few there are who do in fact lay hold of it. Why are there so few? Those who, in their previous existence have lived lives of relative merit, acquire the Grace of God to enable them to recognize the Truth. Divine Grace is a Godly Gift. God's Grace, however, is not ultimately dependent on the merit of the soul in this or in any prior existence.

"With the unbounded Grace of God," says Sant Kabir, "is the True Master found. One is liberated by the Master's Grace. Where there is the Grace of God, Divine Love is Experienced. By the Grace of the Master, the innermost being is touched by Divine Love. In such companionship, there can be no death of the soul."

The aim and object of all religions is to take the soul back to its Source. Kabir Sahib says that the True Master knows of all the Higher Spiritual Stages, including the numerous pitfalls and temptations on the upward Journey within, and makes these known to the devotee. From one step to another, the soul beholds wondrous sights and sounds which cannot be described in any human language. In fact, there are no words to even remotely convey any semblance.

He emphasizes that the True Religion of humanity is a wholly inward Experience with one-pointed attention. Sant Kabir Himself lived in the city of Benaras, considered by many to be sacred, a place of learning from very ancient times, where great importance was attached to ancestry of caste, Scripture, ceremony, and ascetic practice.

"But," He says, "of what value is all this book-learning, reading and memorizing, of listening to the Vedas and Puranas? What avails all this effort, if the Divine Experience is not attained?"

He presents the Path of the Holy Word of Almighty God in a simple, clear, more direct appeal than had ever been done before. His approach to the problem of life is based totally on His religious thought. He is a sharp assessor of human values, and His guidelines on the basic principles of life can assist everyone in the right pursuit of his ultimate Goal.

He emphasizes humility, honesty, compassion, and speaking with a sweet tongue. He instructs humanity to rise above selfishness and ego, and to become *human in the truest sense of the word*. This can only happen through the guidance of a True Master, because there is Divine Radiation and Charging in His physical Company. "Sitting in His Holy Presence, the mind becomes still." All worries of this world and its problems leave off, and one is filled with peace and Love.

Sant Kabir attacks the attitude of a society infected by the vicious disease of the caste system. Originally, classification was based on profession, but later this grouping became hereditary, a superficial division of mankind into high and low distinctions. He condemns the folly of social inequality and the resulting injustices inflicted upon mankind in the name of caste.

"The rules of caste are definitely a hindrance in the worship of Almighty God," He affirms. He makes those who believe in the law of the caste feel the significance of a Living Faith in God, in comparison to a dead belief in classification. All humanity before God is equal. He points out that instead of helping humanity, the caste system is an obstruction to its progress. All human souls should be free of rank because all people are made of the same Essence as God. The Unity of God is symbolic of the oneness of the people in God's Creation, and Sant Kabir preaches the equality of all beings.

He says, "Everyone is born the same way, and therefore all have the same privileges from God." He encourages all to rise above these limiting distinctions which only form barriers between man and man.

The higher class believed that they were the only 'pure' ones, the rest of society being 'impure'. Sant Kabir, however, declares that the determination of purity and impurity lies not in the social position determined at birth, but rather in the condition of the individual's mind. He goes on to ridicule idolatry and any worship of likeness. He rejects bathing at places of pilgrimage as being completely ineffective to scrub away the defilement of this material world. Salvation is not to be found in these outer ascetic practices, such as abandoning the world to pursue a solitary path of escapism, or the life of a mendicant; rather a disciplined life is affirmed.

"Thus", He says, "all these Ascetics and Yogis wander about in vain." He insists that the Way of Truth consists of living in the world and fulfilling all responsibilities of life in the world; yet remaining unaffected by its material and sensual attractions. He uses the conventional figure of the lotus flower, that lives with its roots firmly planted deep down in the mud, while its pristine flower gently floats on top of the water, to illustrate this detachment. He says that the beauty of the lotus is in no way diminished by the filthy water in which it may dwell, nor by the mud in which it takes root.

Sant Kabir speaks strongly against useless idol-worship, belief in the various incarnations of God, vain notions of gaining bliss in heaven by taking ritual baths in so-called 'sacred' rivers, and the like. He equally chastises the orthodox adherence to places of worship, meaningless rituals and rites, and unending superstitions. Besmearing the body with ashes, keeping fasts, going on pilgrimages, wearing rosaries, and repeating God's Name loudly are all ridiculed in His sacred verses. He is a bitter critic and opponent of sectarianism and narrow-minded creeds; instead emphasizing intense Love towards the Supreme Being.

He denounces hoarding or any show of wealth. He preaches simplicity and contentment, and believes that everyone should do honest physical work, not stealing nor coveting another's property. The practice of the marriage dowry is also condemned by Sant Kabir. People were selling their sons and daughters in marriage as if marriage was a trade thriving in money, not a relation of love. He says that this has put a stigma on human values and it degrades society in general.

Sant Kabir encourages many similar reformations in the society. For example, He totally rejects the concept of the system of *Sati* (the voluntary or forced suicide of the widow at the time of her husband's cremation).

Although Kabir Sahib propagated His Teachings, He did not leave any Sect after Him. He condemns the founding of Sects, for He sees no need for such a course. He lays emphasis on leading a simple, fruitful life, full of honest toil. According to Him, only devotion with a pure and upright heart will achieve Union with the Divine.

"Without purification of the heart, pilgrimage to places of worship is of no avail. Ceremonies and rituals, forms and practices, as prescribed by the Priests, take one's attention away from realizing the Presence of God everywhere. These are useless contrivances to deceive man, and to dissuade him from following the Path of Divine Life. God is not to be found in a particular man-made object of any religion. The search for Almighty God is the search within, and one must first realize his true self. Man has already the Divine Perfection within, but he is not aware of it. Man is God, and God is man." Again and again, Kabir Sahib refers to the Lord that resides within, for the very Essence of God Himself is the soul, or spirit, that enlivens the physical body.

He teaches that true religion can be found in the inward disciplines of Love, Faith, mercy and humility, expressed in righteous and compassionate deeds, as well as service to mankind. He preaches the religion of God for the good of humanity, and as a man of God, He refuses to label this Way of life with a specific name, and to divide it into segments of denominational character.

He points out that it is the intense longing of the devotee that qualifies him to attain Enlightenment. This is a one-pointed search, which entails a great deal of sacrifice and perseverance. It is a constant day and night pursuit. The Path is arduous and the way is beset with the five vices of Lust, Anger, Greed, Attachment, and Ego. These are like the predators of life, and one must constantly be on guard against them. God has mercy on the sincere seeker after Truth, and makes provision for him to go to a Teacher, a True Master.

It is only by God's unbounded Grace that one can reach the Goal. Divine Bliss is enchanting, but is not easy to attain. "It asks for a heavy price", says Sant Kabir, "at times even for the *head* of the seeker!" This entails casting out one's ego and replacing it with the virtues of humility and compassion.

Divine Love is the basic ingredient of devotion to the Master, and Love plays the most vital part in the union of the soul with the Supreme Soul. In order to develop true and deep Love for God, one has to cleanse his mind and heart (which is the Seat of God as well as of the soul in the body). Unless the person restrains his mind and abandons the five evil tendencies, he will easily fall prey to negative forces both inside and out, and thereby will lose the chance of uniting his soul with God.

This Divine Love to which Sant Kabir refers again and again, is not the same 'Love' symbolism which is associated with human physical love. Rather it is the pangs of separation from the Beloved and longing, of pining for the Loved One, the pathetic torment of the exiled soul which has not yet obtained the beatific Vision of the Divine Beloved. The soul yearns to be constantly in communion with Almighty God.

Kabir Sahib often uses the symbolism of the village girl (represented by the soul) who is married in childhood, but who reaches adolescence without ever having met her earthly husband. She longs for the meeting which would consummate the union and at last make her a happy wife. Child marriages were customary in those days, although the couple would live together only after maturity.

Sant Kabir has brought to light the tragic situation of the soul who, though already belonging to the Eternal Husband (Almighty God), has not yet been able to 'meet' Him. But since the Divine Spouse is always present within, the fault lies with the soul itself, since it is the impurity of its Love that makes the soul Spiritually 'blind'. The senses are continuously turning the attention outward, away from God into the world and they in turn drag the mind away from the Path Godwards. The mind, in turn, pulls the soul along with it into the outer attractions.

In other verses of Sant Kabir, reference is made to the *Papiha,* which is a 'rainbird'. In Hindu lore, the Papiha thirsts for the first raindrops from Heaven. Since it will drink no other liquid, it would rather die than drink other than the pure rainwater. Sant Kabir uses this image to represent the soul, longing to be united with the Lord. It is said that the pathetic cry of the Papiha is *'Piu! Piu!'* ('Beloved! Beloved!')

'Love' is a popular theme of Sant Kabir. Although it can be an overused word in all languages, it is easy to assume that one appreciates its full meaning. It must, however, be realized that there are many different kinds of love: a mother's love, a love of one's country, romantic love, and then there is God's Love, which is Infinite, unconditional and ever-flowing. It is this 'Love' of which Sant Kabir speaks. It is not the 'love' that ordinary people comprehend. This is a much higher form of Divine Love.

Sant Kabir dismisses much that He considers irrelevant to the Experience of Love, such as idol-worship, rosary beads, chanting, rituals, debating, pilgrimages, and bathing in holy rivers for purification. Instead He speaks of the yearning, the pining, and the longing to behold the Inebriated, Glorious Face of the Beloved. The voice of Sant Kabir reflects the Eternal seeking of mankind since time immemorial. Sant Kabir's *Divine Love Songs*, for that is what they are, inform us that the Beloved for Whom He searches and glimpses, is not new nor is He distant. Almighty God is very near; and He is ever present, eternal. He is for anyone to see if only he would *open his Inner Eye and Behold!*

Sant Kabir's verses are recited even to this day with a zeal and affection that is comprehended only by those who understand this type of Love. He says quite simply, "O dear friend, to be a man of knowledge, one needs to realize only one word: *LOVE!*" The very relationship between God and man, according to Sant Kabir, is Divine Love.

In this connection, He uses the analogy of the Husband-wife relationship, with God being the Eternal Husband to Whom the devoted soul (which is the wife) is attached by Love, trust and implicit obedience. The Lord is the only Groom and everyone else is His bride. Kabir Sahib says, "I have been betrothed to the One indestructible Lord." For lovers, actually there are only two states of being: either they are in union, or they are separated from each other.

There is a certain sweet irony about this image of the human soul pining for her Lover, Who is actually hers all along but

Who is, nevertheless, 'far away' if He remains unknown and unseen. In the many stories of Divine Love, union of the lovers is doomed to be interrupted by numerous forces and is ultimately foiled. Just as the theme of some human lovers finding their meeting possible only after death, a certain 'dying' is inferred in the yearning of the self for the Overself. The Lovers die without a meeting on the earthly Plane, but their Love survives, eternally, at another place. To be liberated from the Cycle of birth and rebirth, one must face a necessary 'Death'. What is implied is that on the Spiritual Journey, the hidden Self needs to be awakened and 'given birth'. The attention, therefore, 'dies' to the outer attractions of this world. The layers of the self (coverings such as Ego, Greed, Lust, etc.) in whose presence little else can be perceived, require to be taken off and discarded.

Kabir Sahib's yearning for His Beloved is all-consuming. For Him, the True Lover has a pact with 'death'. He is ready to sacrifice his all, to be united with his Beloved. Sant Kabir gives the example of the soldier who goes to the battlefield never to return until the victory is his, inspired by such worldly ambitions as power, pride and wealth.

"However, anyone who undertakes the Spiritual Journey", Sant Kabir explains, "has to engage in a perpetual battle. The devotee has everything at stake and if he stumbles, he falls into pieces." Often the lover is not aware of the price that these lofty aspirations must exact. Kabir Sahib's 'night' is the long night of suffering of the soul, knowing that without undergoing this 'suffering', no one can hope to see the Face of the Beloved. And Sant Kabir's Beloved is the King of the 'Night of Anguish'. Fortunately Almighty God, in His great Mercy, understands the great pain that resides in the heart of the sincere seeker and *He readily responds even to the quietest whispers of Love!*

In a simple and melodious manner, Sant Kabir reveals that His Love for the Divine Beloved is no sudden infatuation that in a moment of frenzy might transgress its limits. It remains strictly disciplined and fully respectful to the limit. Neither will it wither away nor become stale in the absence of the Beloved. This intensity of suffering can be comprehended, however, only by one who has gone through a similar experience of pain himself, and Sant Kabir's verses require the necessity at every step of seeing the Beloved through the eyes of the lover.

Kabir Sahib's constant appeal is that devotees of the Lord should live in the world and fulfill all the worldly duties and responsibilities connected with their relations, societies, communities, nations, as well as for the whole Creation. He emphasizes again and again *the transient nature of life*, with its Illusions and charms which bind the person to come again and again into the world, but which will not accompany him after his physical death.

Sant Kabir constantly emphasizes first-hand Experience, the 'real' rather than the 'theoretical'. The meaning and purpose of human existence centres in the Divine Existence of the Eternal One. Almighty God, Who has created everything, reveals Himself throughout His Creation. By Divine Grace alone, God communicates to man the Way of Salvation and calls forth that response which enables him to live up to that salvation. Man is constantly being deluded by the transitory attractions of this world and, tempted through the outgoing faculties, lives a life which binds him more firmly to the *Wheel of Transmigration* (Cycle of birth and rebirth through which the soul must pass to reap the rewards and punishments of its deeds).

Opposed to this destructible world, however, there stands the eternally constant God Almighty. If an individual's affections and attention are transferred from the world to his Beloved God, then the result is a relationship which endures for all eternity, and the person who is united with God in such a relationship participates in the Blessed Immortality of the Divine.

"Death is the only reliable companion in life", observes Sant Kabir. Since it is the one fact that people just don't want to hear, it is the constant subject to which He returns again and again. He Lovingly, and sometimes forcefully, turns everyone's eyes toward the inevitable destruction of the body. His aim is to wake everyone up, either by shaking them or by frightening them. It is a paradox that by denying death in life *(not learning to 'Die While Living'),* one is also denying Life *(the Eternal, Spiritual Life).*

Sant Kabir says, "Knowledge of the process of physical death and of Life into the Beyond gives the worldly life its urgency, and makes one not only honest but sincere, loving, and patient towards others. Death forces one to remember that he does not have forever to do his True Work of becoming One with God."

Physical life is so short and transient, and the soul has a limited number of precious opportunities, the foremost being the actual attainment of this human birth. Usually, however, after finally attaining the pinnacle of glory, this priceless Jewel of the human lifetime ends up being squandered. The entire life is spent pursuing money, power, and pleasure. Only when it is too late does one suddenly realize what has happened, and then again, many do not even wake up enough to be terrified at the last moment, or even to realize that there is a Higher Spiritual Life!

Therefore, Sant Kabir refers to Immortality as one of the ultimate values to be obtained. Meeting with the Oversoul is what He calls 'breaking away' from the ever-revolving Wheel of birth and death. He openly teaches that death is not something to be feared.

"Physical death comes to all," He points out, "but it can also bring Spiritual Birth to an Enlightened Soul." He has said that He welcomes physical death, for it is a source of great happiness to Him. Only at that time will He become One with His Beloved.

"That death which the world fears will become a source of joy, for it is by 'dying' (becoming 'dead' to the attractions of the physical world) that one can attain the Supreme bliss of God!"

He admonishes, "Wake up, dear friend! At the head of the bed stands *Kaal* (the Negative Power). Separated for aeons from Almighty God, how can you possibly sleep in peace?"

This, then, is Sant Kabir's 'religion'--pure, simple, and direct, totally stripped of all paraphernalia, formalism and confusion. Man is a Conscious entity, living in the ever-Presence of God. Thus, Divinity realized in the human heart gives a moral tone and a Spiritual spark to life. It is only through such Divine realization that mankind is enabled to establish a Spiritual relationship with all fellow-beings. This tie of human brotherhood is strengthened by the deepening of one's own Divine Faith.

In many verses, Sant Kabir stresses the importance of using the Power of Discrimination, with which man alone has been Blessed, and He has many methods to open up one's power of Discrimination. He questions relentlessly, probes with challenges, persuades with riddles exposing Truth, shocks with insults to the religious leaders, indeed all madmen who prevail in any position of power. His provocation often takes the form of questions, exposing the truth about blind actions and beliefs, in which the whole nature of mankind stands out starkly revealed.

Usually the reader, however, out of sheer conscience, will tend not to identify with the subjects, being more inclined to identify with Sant Kabir. When Kabir Sahib describes an amusing priest, we smile. When He reveals the astounding blindness of people who refuse to acknowledge the reality of death, we are amazed but, we argue, *these are not descriptions of us!* Gradually, however, something begins to gnaw at our Consciousness.

We slowly begin to realize the artificiality and phoniness of our gestures, in the voices of our 'friends', in the violence and corruption of our governments, of greed in the marketplace, and definitely in the meaningless rituals of our religions.

But the Greatness and Power of Sant Kabir is most revealed when His words begin to reverberate in our heart. Slowly, but surely, it begins to dawn upon us that we have been living our days behind different masks, different faces we put on to meet the various people in our daily lives. His is a constant effort to strip away these disguises, expose the lies, and to remove the blinkers with which we like to cover up our eyes.

Truth and True Words are not easy to recognize. It is equally difficult to acknowledge that there *just might be someone* who knows a little bit more of the Truth than we do. This calls for a special kind of listening and understanding which people are not generally accustomed to. When the faculty of listening is developed correctly, one is able to understand much more than just the meaning of the words being spoken. Hearing is just done with the ears, but *listening can only be done with the heart!*

Sant Kabir sees and observes a great deal of fraud and falsehood practised in the name of religion. He tries to emphasize the basic yearnings of man, the perpetual quest for internal peace and happiness, the frustrations of people functioning in a maladjusted society. When religions turn into ritualistic codes, and wherever there is a crisis between conscience and deed, Kabir Sahib's poetry serves as a great inspiration.

His Teachings give a new dimension to the religious life of mankind. They represent a kind of religious universalism that is unknown in the Spiritual history of the world. He tries to divert the attention of the people towards a religion of the Universal Path above the sectarian level, a Path which both the Hindus and Muslims and in fact all religions, can tread together in peace and harmony.

Sant Kabir reveals the True Religion of Humanity, which is an Inner Science, also known as the *Science of the Soul*. It is a Path which releases the soul from its bondage of aeons and aeons of *Karmas* (actions and reactions), and with the Grace of the Living Godman, permits it to have a Direct Contact with the *Oversoul* (Almighty God). Sant Kabir stresses living an ethical life, with Love for all mankind, indeed for all Creation, for Creation is made by Almighty God.

Kabir Sahib teaches and shows by giving His own example of how to live in this world. Most of the clergy live in monasteries and they stress celibacy. But Kabir Sahib, by His own example, shows how to live a family life while pursuing the Spiritual Goal. He earned His own livelihood by the profession of weaving cloth and then selling it in the market. Thus He fully demonstrated that living a family life is not a barrier to Spiritual progress. It is the purity of one's heart that guides the true devotee.

Sant Kabir teaches the two fundamental doctrines of *Karma* (the result of actions, being either good or bad), and the transmigration (or *Reincarnation*) of the soul into different life forms, the result of Karma. Accordingly, man is bound by his actions, and every act he does, is productive of future good or ill. Evil deeds destine a person to punishment by his being born in a lower form of life in his next birth ('chains of iron'). Good deeds (the 'chains of gold'), on the other hand, destine a soul to reap a reward of a stay in heaven, but in either case the weary, endless round of births and rebirths goes on until these chains of bondage (whether they be of iron or of gold) are cut through by the Grace of a True Master, and thus one achieves eternal salvation.

Sant Kabir is all things to all men: a Revolutionary Who speaks against the tyranny of the powerful and the privileged in favour of the down-trodden and the oppressed, for the 'untouchables', as well as for sincere Spiritual seekers. He is like a guiding Beacon Light in the dark and stormy night of this worldly life.

There have been universal attempts by all religions to claim Sant Kabir as one of their own. Muslims remember Him as *Kabir Shah* (the Great King), while the Hindus refer to Him as *Kabir Das* (Kabir, the Holy Servant). Sikhs and the Kabir-Panthis (followers of Kabir) often call Him as *Kabir Sahib*, or *Sant Kabir* (the Supreme Being). For the *Sufis* (who believe in a Living Master), Kabir is a *Pir* (Spiritual Master). The *Vaisnavas* (worshippers of Vishnu) refer to Him as a *Bhakta* (great Devotee of the Lord).

Nevertheless, for all the claims made about Him and the various titles bestowed, for the whole world and indeed for all Creation, He remains as the Great LORD KABIR! It is to the whole world that He addresses His profoundly simple Message of Divine Love. And He does so not in Sanskrit, the language of the academics and the Priests, but in the various colloquial dialects common to the places He visited. The verses of Sant Kabir are part of the folk-lore in India. They have been sung for six centuries in the fields, as well as in the Temples and Gurdwaras by peasants, scholars, and musicians alike.

CHAPTER 2

A SHORT BIOGRAPHICAL STUDY OF SANT KABIR

What an admirable life it must be, to live in this world just like us, but to reach the highest Spiritual Realms! Such a magnificent life was that of the Divinely Inebriated Personality known as **Param Sant Kabir Sahib**.

It was the very warm, quiet and auspicious night of the *Puran Mashi* (the full moon) on a Monday in the month called *Jeth* of the Indian calendar (which corresponds in the Christian calendar to the middle of May through to the middle of June) in the year 1398. The birds had long gone to rest, and the gentle breezes played soft music through the trees, gently rustling their leaves to play a sweet lullaby. The moon filled the air with a soft glow, while the stars overhead twinkled their excitement. The whole earth was hushed, holding its breath as if in anticipation of a paramount event.

It was sometime after the moon rose high and bright that Almighty God had compassion on mankind and clothed Himself in the human form, that He would act as a Saviour for the well-being and liberation of all Creation. In His great wisdom and mercy for all the separated souls hankering to once again be with their Supreme Father, Almighty God answered their heartfelt prayers, and gave His Beloved Son to all humanity. The first rays of Truth concerning the Reality of Life and Being shone forth, illuminating the darkness of this earthly existence.

Sant Kabir was born near Lahar Talao Lake in the outskirts of Varanasi (also known as Kashi, but now known as Benaras), in the Province of *Uttar Pradesh* in North-Eastern India. His father's name was *Noor Ali* (or 'Niru' for short), and His mother was called *Nima*. His parents were weavers, in the Muslim caste.

The happiness and beauty of the young Child fascinated all who saw Him. He was extremely charming, with bright eyes and sharp features. There was a wonderful glow on His face, such radiance and enchantment that enticed all without exception. He brought so much joy and peace into the house, that Niru and Nima felt honoured to be the parents of such an auspicious Child.

When the appropriate time came to name the little Baby, a *Qazi* (a Muslim Priest) was consulted, according to the custom. He solemnly opened the *Qur'an Shariff* (the Sacred Scriptures of the Muslims) in search of a proper name to confer upon the child. In quite a few attempts, he always found the name *'Kabir'*.

The name *'Kabir'* is of Arabic origin, and is derived from *'al-Kabir'*. It means *'Great'*, or *'The Most High'*, and is used as an honourable attribute of God. God is considered to be the only One Who is Great. Therefore, it is not the custom to bestow this type of name on an ordinary human being.

The astonished Qazi was most perplexed as he continued the search in vain. Every time he opened the Holy Book, only the name *'Kabir'* was found! What to do? No one could understand this!

Therefore, in the mercy and wisdom of *Sat Purush* (Almighty God), the Divine Light Lovingly and so Graciously descended upon this earth, and hence was given the auspicious and revered name *'Kabir', the Most High,* and indeed, the boy Kabir was to be the *Most High Guiding Light* amongst all men!

Even at an early age, the youth recited many hymns and quoted them with amazing appropriateness. Whatever decisions He took, bore the stamp of maturity. The elders were deeply impressed. Whoever saw Him, was completely won over by His youthful charm and holiness. He often spent a lot of time alone, lost in deep thought and meditation.

According to the custom prevailing at the time, the boy Kabir was engaged to be married at a very early age. Children were usually engaged like this early in life, and then formally married later when they had reached maturity. As the boy was growing up, however, His parents noticed that their

Son seemed very sad and pensive. They thought that if He was actually married, perhaps He might become happier.

Accordingly, when young Kabir attained the age of eighteen years, His mother and father consulted with the *Faqir* (Muslim Priest) to fix the date for the wedding. They also began to gather the needed items for the feasts that were to follow, requisites such as *ghee* (clarified butter), sugar, rice, and various grains.

During these days, Kabir Sahib's Uncle (who was named 'Kaka') purchased a cow from the market and brought it home to slaughter for the feasts. When the young Kabir learned about this, He was horrified and asked, "Dear Uncle, why did you bring this cow here?" The uncle replied, "I brought it for your wedding, because the guests won't be pleased if we don't serve them meat."

The boy pleaded, "O Uncle, please don't do like this! Please give this cow away to a *Brahmin* (Hindu Priest), but don't kill it!" He knew quite well that all Hindus regard cows as being sacred, and thus the cow would be saved.

However, the Uncle protested, "How will this occasion be fulfilled without a proper feast? So many people are coming, and we have to serve them what they are expecting to eat."

The young Kabir was horrified and asked, "Dear Uncle, why did you bring this cow here?" The uncle replied, "I brought it for your wedding, because the guests won't be pleased if we don't serve them meat." The boy pleaded, "O uncle, please don't do like this! Please give this cow away to a Brahmin, but don't kill it!"

The boy Kabir cradled the cow's head in His hands, and gently stroking it, He appealed to the Uncle. "Please listen to the many qualities of the cow. Each and every one of its hairs has so many gods and goddesses living in it. *Brahma* (God) lives in each and every vein of this cow. This is the same cow that gives us milk, and from this we make butter, yogurt, and cheese. Even its waste is burned as fuel, and is also used as plaster for our homes. It has so many good qualities that it should not be killed!"

It appeared as though the cow was actually smiling as it bathed in the waves of Love radiating from its young Saviour! With its big brown eyes, it looked fondly up into the sublime face of the young Boy.

Uncle Kaka, however, pointed out that he was only following the long-established custom of the family, which had become tradition by now for generations. The Child, however, persisted in objecting to this needless sacrifice. He urged him, "O Uncle, listen to me! You have brought this cow for my marriage. Why? Because you want the function to go well, but if I am not happy, then why even have this wedding? It is quite simple: I won't marry if you don't leave off this custom!"

The Uncle, then, had no choice but to agree with Kabir Sahib. Not only that, but the rest of the relatives also had to accede! They assured the boy that they would donate that cow in charity to a Brahmin. They also had to confirm that no meat would be served at the young Kabir's wedding.

Kabir Sahib, however, had *one further condition* for His marriage! He told them, "You have to make my in-laws agree that they, too, will not kill any animal with which to serve a feast of meat for their side of the relatives!"

Such strong-will and brave character was shown by this personality known as the young Kabir! He demonstrated Loving compassion and sympathy for all Creation, and taught a proper lesson to everyone about the value of God's Life! He pointed out to them that God's Power lives in each and every hair of every living being throughout all Creation. Only a Godman could even remember these things at the happy and busy time of His marriage!

Sant Kabir became a family man, with a wife named *Loi*, a son called *Kamal*, and a daughter named *Kamali*. By His own example, He showed that a family life of contentment and restraint need not interfere with one's Spiritual progress.

Kabir Sahib supported his family by weaving cloth, and then selling it in the market. He always lived on His own earnings, no matter how meagre they were! His income, obviously, was very limited, but He lived a humble life, with modest needs and simple food.

Sant Kabir was quite young when He started His Divine Mission, going from place to place and giving Holy Discourses. Some people would ask Him the question, "Who is your Guru? We want to know!" He didn't have the answer for this because as He Himself was all-knowing of all knowledge, He couldn't see anybody who could teach Him anything about Spirituality! He was a 'born Godman', a *Param Sant* (a Saint of the highest order) from birth.

Sant Kabir only needed the name of someone, so that whenever anyone would ask for the name of His Guru, He could say that "Yes, he is my Master!" What to do?

"Well," He thought, "I am a Muslim, born in a Muslim family. I also have a very large Hindu audience." Therefore, He thought that instead of having a Muslim *Faqir* as a Guru, He would adopt some Hindu person. The problem that lay before Him, however, was whose name could He adopt?

He decided upon *Ramanand*, who was a very popular figure amongst the Hindus. He knew, however, that Ramanand was strongly in favour of idol-worship with all its various rites and rituals. On top of that, Ramanand was quite rigid in his habit of avoiding the company of low-caste people. How was Sant Kabir to approach him? Kabir Sahib thought and thought what to do.

He knew that Ramanand lived very near the Ganges River, and He also knew that Ramanand went there early every morning for his bath. Thus, Kabir Sahib devised a strategy.

One morning, in the pre-dawn darkness, He quietly lay down across one of the steps leading down to the shore of the river where Ramanand was to come. It was difficult to see in the early morning mist, and as predicted, Ramanand tripped over the waiting Kabir Sahib. Naturally, when Ramanand's foot touched something on the step, he was startled and exclaimed his own Mantra of *'Ram! Ram!'* (O God! O God!) Kabir Sahib now had what He wanted! He quietly slipped away in the darkness, the mission accomplished!

Subsequently, whenever anyone asked who was His Guru, Kabir Sahib claimed that the Mantra had been given and that He, Kabir, was now a disciple of Ramanand. Naturally in a village there are no secrets, and word soon got around that Ramanand had accepted a low-caste Muslim as his devotee.

When this news reached Ramanand, however, he vehemently denied that he had accepted Kabir Sahib as his disciple! He called Kabir Sahib to come before him, and explain the meaning of this claim.

When Kabir Sahib arrived at the house of Ramanand, it happened that Ramanand was busy in performing *Puja* (worship) of his idols. There was a heavy curtain dividing the inner and outer courtyards of Ramanand's house. This barrier was evidently placed to avoid Ramanand having to look at a person of low caste. Kabir Sahib thus waited outside in the courtyard while Ramanand was inside completing his devotion.

All things needed for the ceremony were there but one thing, however, prevented Ramanand from continuing. Somehow he had forgotten to place the rosary around the neck of the idol before placing the crown on its head. The devotion could not be completed without this necklace, but once the devotion had commenced, it would be most disrespectful to first remove the headpiece and then place the rosary around the neck. A very big problem, indeed!

Meanwhile Kabir Sahib was sitting outside, but He suddenly called forth the solution. He told Ramanand to simply untie the knot of the beaded necklace and then retie it around the neck of the stone idol, thereby completing the Puja in full reverence!

Ramanand was amazed and flabbergasted how Kabir Sahib could even know about this predicament as He was sitting outside in the courtyard and Ramanand was inside the building! He instinctively knew that Kabir Sahib must have some kind of Spiritual Power, so he immediately asked his attendants to bring Kabir Sahib inside.

Ramanand asked Kabir Sahib to account for the claim of Guru-discipleship about which everyone in the city was talking, and Sant Kabir related the events which had taken place at the riverside early that same morning.

Ramanand suddenly realized what had happened. When he thought carefully about all these recent incidents, he was greatly impressed, and realized the Eminence of Kabir Sahib. Thereafter, Ramanand openly declared Kabir Sahib to be his disciple.

The fast-spreading tales of Sant Kabir's greatness were naturally resented by the fanatic Hindu and Muslim Priests, who kept the masses under their control through complicated rites and meaningless rituals. Using Sanskrit words in the language of ritual that only the Priests themselves could understand, these powerful Priests threatened excommunication from the Hindu Temples and the Muslim Mosques to

Kabir Sahib suddenly called forth the solution. He told Ramanand to simply untie the knot of the beaded necklace, and then retie it around the neck of the idol, thereby completing the Puja in full reverence!

anyone who dared to challenge their undisputed authority. Their sway on the people's minds (and pocketbooks!) was revealed by Sant Kabir for what it really was: a sham of hypocrisy and lies. These jealous Priests, therefore, watched for any chance to slander Kabir Sahib and to try to bring down His growing popularity and attraction amongst the masses.

The very idea that their business empire might be shaken down by a simple man with a low-caste status who dared to speak out the Truth, was simply intolerable, especially in an Age when such insolence was punishable by death! These fanatics were always on the watch for an opportunity to laugh at Sant Kabir, and to humiliate His mannerisms. They unduly criticized and slandered Him, and openly despised His Teachings, particularly since many of His Principles appeared to be so different.

From all established Sects, the leaders joined forces to counter His Divine influence. Those in authority could only see their source of income being jeopardized, as Sant Kabir exposed the futility of established rites and ritualistic customs, and the fakery and fraud of these Priests, who posed as the saviours of the people's souls.

Kabir Sahib loudly and fearlessly challenged the very heart of their established religions: the useless practices and meaningless ceremonies. His Words of Truth set off alarm bells in all formal institutions. However, His basic Teaching that one should find God within himself, rather than wasting his life in outer fruitless efforts, appealed to the masses, making them to question the very structure of the Temples, indeed even the very need of the Priest or the *Pir!* (Muslim term for Guru or Master).

Many plans were devised to humiliate Him. It is said that one day these same religious leaders announced that Sant Kabir was intending to hold a great religious feast, and all were welcome to attend. They invited on His behalf as many people as they could, from all over the area. When the day for the supposed feast arrived, hundreds flocked to His humble dwelling. When Sant Kabir saw so many people, He immediately realized this was another trick of those cruel Priests. Being a simple weaver, He had no money with which to entertain this multitude. He left everything in God's hands, and without anybody knowing that He had gone, he simply made Himself available on the other side of town all through the day.

Upon His return in the evening, He was surprised to learn that in all Love and mercy, the Lord Himself had manifested in the form of Sant Kabir, and had arranged a spectacular feast to feed each and every person that had come. All the people had eaten to their fill, and then had left highly praising the name of Kabir Sahib for His generous hospitality. Kabir

Sahib was amazed when He realized what had happened, that the Lord Himself had come in the physical form of Kabir and had served the entire feast!

He was filled with gratitude and joy, and exclaimed that it was all the unbounded Grace of the Lord in saving the honour of His humble Devotee! This incident thus went against those same persecutors, the very people who were trying their best to bring shame to the name of Kabir Sahib, and naturally they became even more enraged that this episode ended in such praise.

These same Brahmin and Muslim Priests, their hearts filled with only bigotry and narrow-mindedness, even dared to complain to *Sultan Sikandar Lodi* (the Muslim ruler of Benaras), putting poison into his ear so as to further propagate their cause. They tried all conceivable means to achieve their objectives. They protested that Sant Kabir was openly advising the people not to go to the Temples and Mosques, nor to listen to the Priests, whom He said were teaching wrong ways and useless rituals.

There are several stories of His having been brought before the Sultan, the various types of punishments that were inflicted upon Him, and His overcoming them by seemingly performing miracles. We can call them to be 'miracles', but they all were, of course, according to the Will and mercy of Almighty God for His Beloved Devotee.

Some of the religious leaders won the favour of the close associates of the Sultan, and even tried to use their influence and high position against Sant Kabir. One of the head persecutors was a very high political figure by the name of *Qasi Sheikh Taqqi,* who called himself to be a 'Spiritual' person. This Sheikh was of the belief that he had more authority than anybody else, so the Priests first brought their complaints to him. He, in turn, used his own influence to address the whole matter before the Sultan.

Naturally, when the Sultan heard all this ruckus, he decided to send guards to bring Sant Kabir before him to discuss the matter in more detail, but several hours passed before Sant Kabir actually appeared in the Court. This delay, of course, caused the Sultan to become quite annoyed, and he demanded of Kabir Sahib the reason for this undue delay in responding to the royal summons.

Sant Kabir calmly looked around the Court, at each and every person there, and then He replied that He had been engaged in watching a most wondrous spectacle. He proceeded to describe a most miraculous thing, saying that He had seen the eye of a needle, *through which a long line of camels was passing!*

Of course, everybody was flabbergasted, and scorned this supposedly ridiculous answer. When the laughter had died down, Sant Kabir then told them that the Path to Spiritual Realization (the eye of the needle) was very narrow, and they could not pass through with all their excess baggage of ego and pride!

He further asked them, "Consider the distance between the earth and the sky. How many camels and other creatures come and go?" By this, of course, He was informing them that without discovering the true meaning of taking birth in the human form, they will keep coming and going in the never-ending *Wheel of Transmigration* (Cycle of birth and rebirth).

Then Sant Kabir looked around the whole Court. "Which Holy Book", He sternly asked, "orders men to slaughter cows, goats, or fowl?" He pointed out to them that Dharam Rai punishes such killers. "There can be no escape from the reactions of these heinous deeds!"

The Sultan, of course, didn't know what to do. Whatever Lord Kabir said was absolutely accurate, and hit right to the point. The Sultan himself felt fully satisfied and convinced with these answers. He knew that Sant Kabir was speaking the Truth. Since no accusations could be proven, all charges against Kabir Sahib were duly dismissed, and He simply left the scene.

The persecutors, however, would not give up so easily. They were very upset with the Sultan's decision, but what could they do? Again and again, they returned to Sheikh Taqqi, accusing Sant Kabir of various crimes. They focused on His out-spoken denunciation of the external aspects of both Sects, including idol worship, various rituals, purification baths, fasts, pilgrimages, etc. They pointed out that Kabir Sahib was discouraging the people from attending the Temples and Mosques, and told of His claim that only a money business flourished there. They called His Teachings to be blasphemy, accused Him of being irreligious, and of keeping company with other such untouchables and outcasts, such as Ravi Das. They tried their best to influence the Sheikh to do something more to help their cause, and to rid Benaras of Sant Kabir once and for all!

Their unrelenting accusations during such a period of religious and political unrest in India brought matters to a crisis. Once more the soldiers were sent to bring Sant Kabir into the Court. When He arrived, this time He was ordered to bow before the Sultan, but Kabir Sahib just looked around, slowly, at all of them. He said gently, but firmly, that He bowed only to the Supreme King, Almighty God. Then He explained, "I talk about only one God. I am against your outer rituals of many

Kabir Sahib ultimately sank with the heavy weight of the chains. When He was no longer visible, His enemies rejoiced while His followers were totally overcome with grief and sorrow. However, the mood of the crowd on the riverbank changed markedly when the Divine Lord was suddenly seen floating upstream against the current, peacefully seated on a deer-skin, His chains having been broken by the waves! Such amazement! No one could believe his eyes!

deities and your false Ministers. You are misleading the people in all aspects of Spiritual matters."

Of course, the Sultan was not happy with any of these accusing words. Fuelled by protests coming from the various Priests, he felt he had no choice. The matter was becoming out of hand. The Priests were not relenting in the least, perhaps more fired up that now He was standing before them, and still bravely declaring a threat to their priestcraft.

The Sultan, therefore, decreed that by Imperial Order, Kabir Sahib was to be bound with heavy, strong chains and thrown into the Ganges River. And so, Sant Kabir was escorted to the riverside, bound hand and foot with heavy iron chains, and then cruelly dumped into the deep, fast-flowing river. His devotees tearfully and helplessly remained on the riverbank, wailing loudly at the thought of their Beloved Lord being treated so badly.

Kabir Sahib ultimately sank with the heavy weight of the chains. When He was no longer visible, His enemies rejoiced while His followers were totally overcome with grief and sorrow. However, the mood of the crowd on the riverbank changed markedly when the Divine Lord was suddenly seen floating upstream against the current, peacefully seated on a deer-skin, His chains having been broken by the waves! Such amazement! No one could believe their eyes! His devotees danced with joy and relief at this wondrous sight! The fires of growing despise and anger, however, burned even brighter in the hearts of these fanatics, as Sant Kabir calmly glided to shore and walked away. The guards just stood there, dumbfounded in disbelief!

After a few days, the Priests again began to present their vicious complaints to the Sultan. The previous incident had gone against them, and now the frenzy of defeat triggered a whole new enthusiasm for their protests.

Again the guards were called and once more Kabir Sahib was bound in heavy chains. This time he was bundled into an enormous basket, and then firewood was heaped up high all around Him. The wood was lit, and a huge fireball leaped up into the sky. His devotees again were left helplessly wailing while the Priests and Ministers breathed a sigh of relief that finally they were rid of Kabir Sahib.

However, as the onlookers watched intently, they were astounded to see the figure of a young man calmly standing in the middle of the flames. It was several hours before the fire had at last died down, and Sant Kabir walked out of the smouldering ashes, completely unharmed! Again He was triumphant as the crowds gasped in total awe and disbelief! The Priests were left to grumble amongst themselves, as once more Sant Kabir had overcome this adversity.

As the onlookers watched intently, they were astounded to see the figure of a young man, calmly standing in the middle of the flames. It was several hours before the fire had at last died down, and Sant Kabir walked out of the smouldering ashes, completely unharmed! Again He was triumphant as the crowds gasped in total awe and disbelief!

When the Sultan heard this latest news of Sant Kabir's miraculous escape from the raging fire, shock and fear gripped his heart. It slowly dawned upon him just how great a God-man was Sant Kabir! The Sultan realized that this was no ordinary man, and that He must be some Special Power. The Sultan did not have much time to ponder over this, however, and his fear did not last long, for the mob was rapidly growing as the Priests began to look for another excuse to really finish off Kabir Sahib.

They thought of a plan to present Sant Kabir in front of all the citizens as a true heretic, and total disbeliever. For a third time, the guards were called. They brought Him to a large open assembly ground, tied Him up again in the heaviest chains, this time from head to foot. There was no way to even remain standing with the weight of all these chains.

By this time, however, the maddening crowd had grown beyond control. The people were mostly made of religious fanatics, frightfully wild and unrelenting. Waving their fists into the air, they shouted in unison 'Infidel!' and 'Magician!' and demanded that an end should be put to Kabir Sahib once and for all. Therefore, it was arranged that a drunken elephant should come, put its foot upon Kabir Sahib, and trample Him finally to death!

The elephant was brought forward with great difficulty, as it was wild with intoxication and trumpeting loudly, swaying its trunk from side to side, its red eyes flashing with anger! Several men had to restrain the beast with chains tied to poles sunk deep into the ground. But to the utter amazement of all, this same animal could not be persuaded to go anywhere near the chained figure lying on the ground.

The elephant driver called out that there seemed to be a ferocious tiger in front of the elephant, frightening it away from Sant Kabir. Nobody else, however, could see this 'tiger', and the roar of the mob became even louder. Over the din of the crowd, the Sultan shouted that the elephant driver should try again, but the driver replied that he just could not control the animal.

The crowd was sure that some magic had been performed and they started to clamour 'Heretic!' and 'Disbeliever!' louder and louder, until the Sultan felt obliged to try something else. Just then the ruler himself also saw the tiger standing in front of the elephant! He began to realize his own foolishness in this matter. Sant Kabir was a Great Saint, and the Sultan suddenly understood what a heinous mistake he was committing. To the utter amazement of the crowd, as well as the Ministers and Priests, the Sultan suddenly fell at Kabir Sahib's Lotus Feet, crying to be forgiven!

The elephant driver called out that there seemed to be a ferocious tiger in front of the elephant, frightening it away from Sant Kabir. Nobody else, however could see this 'tiger', and the roar of the mob became even louder. Just then the Sultan himself also saw the tiger standing in front of the elephant.

Sant Kabir refers to these episodes in some of His verses and He comments, "They could not make me frightened, neither me nor my body. By my heart and soul, I am always with the Creator. No one can injure the One that God wants to be spared! Not a hair can be harmed, even if the whole world be against that One!"

Again and again Sant Kabir reveals **the unfathomable dimensions of His Greatness!** His devotees saw Him in His true glory, and their hearts overflowed with songs of praise and humble devotion. He says, "Love alone can knit the finite with the Infinite, the part with the Whole. He who lives in perpetual sweet remembrance of his very own Beloved, becomes transformed in His same Colour."

Sant Kabir says, "I have no friend or companion. My God and my Master are my only Friends! They look after me in the air, on land, and everywhere!"

When Kabir Sahib was approaching the end of His earthly life, He decided to leave the city of Benaras. It was commonly believed by many that Benaras was the most holy and auspicious place to die, and that whoever died within its boundary, invariably would go to heaven.

In spite of all these claims, however, Sant Kabir resolved to travel to *Mughar*, about 175 miles from Benaras. As opposed to Benaras, the city of Mughar was thought to be an extremely unfortunate place to end one's days. There is a story in the Ancient Books of the *Puranas* (Hindu Scriptures) that a certain King Dukash had called for a great feast in Mughar and had invited everyone to attend, with the exception of *Ganesh*, the son of *Avtar Shiva*. It is said that in great anger Ganesh put a curse on the city, that whoever died there would not only have to take another birth, but have to take on the form of a donkey. Those people who live in Mughar praise this same Ganesh in their Temples and houses, but due to this popular and dreaded belief, even they don't want to die in that city. They make every effort to leave it when their own end draws near. Therefore, in order to expose this story for the false superstition that it really was, Kabir Sahib knowingly left Benaras and settled in Mughar during His last earthly days.

Sant Kabir had an immense following of disciples and devotees, and when they came to know of His decision to leave Benaras, they flocked to Him in great multitudes. Huge crowds begged Him that they should all be allowed to accompany Him to Mughar, and in His great compassion, He granted this humble request. Many devotees lined the route throughout His journey, in order to greet Him and pay their respects. When *Raja Bir Singh*, the Hindu ruler of Benaras, heard that his Guru, Sant Kabir, would journey to Mughar, he also hastened there.

After days of travelling, Sant Kabir finally reached Mughar along with that huge number of followers. The city, however, just could not contain that many people. The crowds became so vast and their needs so great, that the nearby river dried up, resulting in an extreme shortage of water. To alleviate the great suffering of these devotees and to give them drinking water, in His great mercy Sant Kabir caused the river to flood again. It then became known as the *Ami River*, for the water that now flowed in it was cool and refreshing, like *Amrit* (Ambrosial Nectar from the Almighty).

Sant Kabir went straight to the banks of this River and occupied an abandoned hut. In the meantime, the Muslim ruler of the district in which Mughar was situated, a disciple by the name of *Newab Bijli Khan*, heard of the arrival of Sant Kabir. He also quickly made plans to journey to the city.

When Raja Bir Singh realized that now Newab Bijli Khan had arrived, he quickly sent for his army to come from Benaras. Secretly, he wanted to be the one who would have the honour of performing the Hindu last rites of death for the Holy Body when Sant Kabir would finally leave.

Naturally, when the Raja's large army arrived with all its noisy men, horses and camels, the Newab decided that he (the Newab) must have the Holy Body for disposal according to the Muslim rites, so he quickly called for his own troops. The city became even more strained at the seams, with these two huge legions of men. Raja Bir Singh intended to cremate the Body according to the Hindu religion, while the Nawab wished to bury It. Just see that both leaders, representing two different religions, remained very determined, and even vied for the privilege of claiming Sant Kabir as their own!

After a few days, when the time came for His final departure into the Lap of Almighty God, Sant Kabir instructed His disciples to remain outside the hut and not to disturb Him. Several hours passed and their Beloved Master did not come out. They called to Him, worried. There was no response, however. In great respect, they waited some more time before calling out again to Him. Again, no response.

Alarmed, they quickly opened the door but to their astonishment, there was nothing to be seen but a simple white sheet lying open on the ground. When it was gently lifted, to the utter amazement of all, only fresh, fragrant flowers were found underneath! Everyone was flabbergasted that the Body had disappeared! Sant Kabir's Holy Body was never seen again. He had attained the age of 119 years, 5 months, and 27 days.

To their astonishment, there was nothing to be seen but a simple white sheet lying open on the ground. When it was gently lifted, to the utter amazement of all, only fresh, fragrant flowers were found underneath! Everyone was flabbergasted that the Holy Body had disappeared!

In order to settle the matter of death rites, it was decided that Raja Bir Singh and his following would take half of the sheet and half of the flowers back to Benaras. There he cremated them according to the Hindu rituals and then buried the ashes at a Temple he constructed, what is now called *Kabir Chaura*.

On the other hand, according to the Muslim Faith the Nawab Bijli Khan buried his half right there in Mughar, where he built a Mosque. Both the Temple and the Mosque are still standing today in both cities.

Thus, even in death Sant Kabir substantiated to what He had dedicated His whole life: unveiling popular superstition, as well as useless external religious prejudice and meaningless rituals. In some of His verses, Sant Kabir states that it is not the place where a person lives and dies, but rather the relationship which he has with God which is the all-important thing.

There exist literally hundreds of collections of Sant Kabir's hymns, but there are several anthologies considered to be of greater importance. *The Bijak*, which means literally 'The Chart of Secret Treasures' represents the *Kabir-Panthi* (lit. 'The Followers of Kabir') tradition of Kabir's verses from Eastern Uttar Pradesh and Central India.

There is another compilation called *Kabir Granthavali*, (Lit. 'The Teachings of Kabir'), which was developed in Rajasthan and was compiled by the *Dadu Panth* (Lit. 'The Followers of Dadu Sahib', a sixteenth century Saint).

There is also another manuscript with the same title of *Kabir Granthavali* dated 1504, which is preserved in the archives of the Nagari Pracharini Sabha in Benaras. Its very existence indicates that this particular collection was made during Sant Kabir's lifetime, some fourteen years before He physically departed.

Another important collection of Sant Kabir's verses is found in a compilation by the poet *Rajab* of Rajasthan, himself a disciple of Dadu. The *Niranjani Sect* in Rajasthan also depends directly on the Teachings of Kabir.

Then there are the *Kabir Vachnavali* (Lit. 'The Book of Kabir's Teachings') and the *Kabir Shabdavali* (Lit. 'The Book of Kabir's Hymns'), and many, many more diverse compilations.

Sant Kabir travelled a great deal, and underwent many extended journeys to spread the message of Almighty God to all mankind. He visited many provinces of India including the Punjab, Uttar Pradesh, Bihar, Rajasthan, Gujarat, Madhya

Pradesh, Maharashtra, and Orissa. His verses include words from numerous languages and dialects, including Braj, Rajasthani, Punjabi, Marathi, Gujarati, Sanskrit, Persian, Arabic, Avadhi, and others. In some collections of His poems, it is suggested that He even travelled to Balakh, Bokhara, Baghdad, Mecca, and other places in the Middle East. But wherever He visited, He left a legacy rich in Sacred Hymns.

Still another collection of Sant Kabir's Banis was made during His lifetime, being gathered during His various meetings with *Guru Nanak Dev Ji* (1469-1539), another great Saint of India and a contemporary of Sant Kabir.

During the four extensive tours of Guru Nanak, lasting in total more than thirty years, throughout India and the Middle East, He (Guru Nanak) began to gather Banis of the previous Saints (whatever was available) including those of Sant Kabir, to which He added His own. This collection of Guru Nanak existed in two volumes, and was commonly known as the *Goindwal Pothis* (Books).

When He left the mortal frame in 1539, Guru Nanak Dev Ji left this two-volume anthology to His successor, *Guru Angad Dev Ji* (1504-1552), who then added His own verses to this same collection. Guru Angad Dev Ji also further simplified

---

* Gurbachan Singh Talib, "Sri Guru Granth Sahib", Punjabi University, India 1988

and codified the *Gurmukhi* script of Punjabi, and transcribed this entire collection into Gurmukhi.

The Third Guru, *Guru Amar Das Ji* (1479-1574) undertook (from 1570-1572) to compile the Goindwal Pothis into what became known as the *Adi Granth* (Lit. 'First Book'). He took these pre-existing hymns, added Banis of other Saints as well as His own, to make a total of 1,048 pages, with some of these pages knowingly left blank for the inclusion of verses by the later Gurus.

The next (fourth) compilation of the Adi Granth was completed by the fifth Guru, *Guru Arjan Dev Ji* (1563-1606) in 1603-1604 in the city of Amritsar. Guru Arjan Dev Ji set about the project of compiling the Granth in a very scientific way. He arranged the hymns in chronological order, and numbered them throughout the Book. He then arranged these verses according to *Rags* (musical settings) in order to inculcate certain moods expressed by the verses themselves. This version contained 1,430 pages, when completed.

The final (fifth) revision of the Adi Granth was redictated by *Guru Gobind Singh Ji*, using the basis and form of the Adi Granth, and it was now called the *Guru Granth Sahib* (Lit. 'The Teachings of the Saints').

It is interesting to note that at the beginning of each and every verse (and there are thousands of verses!) in the Guru Granth Sahib, it is written exactly the same thing:

"Ek Onkar,
Sat Naam,
Kartaa Purkh,
Nirbhao Nirvair,
Akaal Moorat,
Ajoonee Saibhang,
Guru Prashaad."

("There is but One Reality, the Unmanifest-Manifested; Ever-Existent, He is Naam (Conscious Spirit),
The Creator; pervading all;
Without fear; without enmity;
The Timeless; the Unborn and the Self-existent;
Complete within Itself.
Through the favour of His true Servant, the Guru,
He may be realized.
He was when there was nothing;
He was before all Ages began; He existeth now, O Nanak, And shall exist forevermore!") •

• Sant Kirpal Singh Ji Maharaj, "The Jap Ji: The Message of Guru Nanak", Kirpal Printing Press, India 1964.

Five hundred and forty-one verses written by Sant Kabir are included in the Guru Granth Sahib, covering all conceivable aspects of Spirituality and life in general. These verses are found in no less than seventeen different Ragas. This makes the Guru Granth Sahib one of the largest anthology of compositions by Sant Kabir. In this collection, the short poems are referred to as either *Shabds* or *Bani* (which are the utterances of the true Master), or as *Pauri* (lit. 'the rung of a ladder', in this case the Spiritual Ladder). Most of the Shabds of Sant Kabir are made of two to four stanzas, including a refrain, and each stanza is made of two short or two long lines rhyming together.

The Guru Granth Sahib is a unique Spiritual Book in the history of mankind. Perhaps the most notable subject of the entire collection is its underlying fundamental unity of all the religions and Spiritual Experiences. Through a careful study of this Granth, one can see the sociological, economic, and political conditions of the period between the 12th and the 17th centuries in India. It leads the reader to ponder intensely the fanatical clergy, the fake religious leaders, the absurd customs and superstitions that paralyze the Inner Spiritual growth of mankind.

Almighty God Himself made the Path to go back to Him, and this Way is also known as *the Word, the Holy Naam*, the *Shabd, Bani, Surat,* or *Kalma*. This Path already exists within each and every person, but it is hidden. To obtain this Way to God, one needs the assistance of a True Master, and then one must practice on the Direct Contact, the first-hand Experience that the Master bestows, and develop it further. For the physical life, one needs physical bread and water, but to know himself inwardly, he needs the Holy Naam, the Bread and Water of the Divine Life, which is the Holy Food for the soul.

If one wants to know the Truth, then he must go to Someone Who is Truth personified, a Godman, a True Master, a Saint, and then follow His guidance. This very body is the true Temple of God. God Himself resides in the body. If one knows himself, then he becomes full of Divine knowledge and he can obtain God. In the Spiritual world, Scriptures like the Guru Granth Sahib are Spiritual Treasures written by the True Masters, but they remain like closed books until the devotee opens them, reads them, and then abides by what they say. It remains for the seeker to live up to, and to develop what he has learned.

CHAPTER 3

INDIA AT THE TIME OF SANT KABIR

During the Middle Ages, India was divided into small kingdoms and feudal states. Due to this lack of common unity, the citizens of these small monarchies could not fight off the crushing waves of Muslim invaders that infiltrated the Northwest territories from Persia, Iran, and Afghanistan. The entire country and its people suffered greatly in every aspect, as the aggressors quickly took control of the various smaller governments, leaving them in factional chaos and literally tearing apart the whole country. Separate Muslim nations were established, and Persian quickly became the language of the court, the government, and the literature. While *Hinduism* had been India's major religion, along with several smaller dissident movements, such as *Jainism* and *Buddhism*, the new Muslim rulers soon spread their Faith of *Islam* throughout most of the country.

It should be noted that the general classification of 'Hindu' included an amalgam of many different smaller *castes*, from the very low to the middle, and then to the very high. However, Hinduism has traditionally divided its followers into four basic social orders.

1. The *Brahmins* are considered to be the highest caste, comprised generally of the Priests and *Pundits*, engaged in the study and teaching of Scriptures.
2. The *Ksatriyas* (the second highest caste) consist of fighting forces for purposes of defence.
3. The *Vaisyas* represent the third highest class of merchants and farmers.
4. The *Sudras* consist of those low class manual workers, which serve the foregoing three classes. This group is also widely known as the 'untouchables', and are excluded from the social and religious privileges of the general way of life known as *Hinduism*.

There were many further intricate sub-divisions within these four major castes. Although the Muslims themselves didn't prescribe to 'caste' *per se*, their major groups also consisted of numerous smaller sub-castes in a pattern similar to Hinduism.

The minds of the masses at this time had become utterly crippled by this caste system, to the extent that superstition and doubt were the rule of the day. In the name of religion and swayed by lust, greed and ego, all kinds of atrocities were being committed by those in authority. Mistrust and hatred prevailed throughout the land and people were rapidly losing faith in both their political, as well as religious, leaders. Religion itself had degenerated to a series of blind beliefs, superstitions, rites, and rituals. It was common for the populace to follow the practices of going to Temples or Mosques, worshipping idols, and other meaningless ceremonies according to the instructions of the powerful Priests and Ministers.

In Islam, the religious leaders are known as *Maulvis* and *Mulanas*, and in Hinduism they are the *Pundits* and *Brahmins*. They were not necessarily Blessed with the gift of Divinity. The extent of their Spiritual knowledge usually was obtained through the reading of books and Scriptures, or from lectures given by others. They had not solved the mystery of life and death themselves, and thus they had no practical Experience of the things they were preaching. Religion had become more and more complicated. Since the leaders could not explain Spirituality in its true sense, they invented an intricate network of words and customs, which totally confused the seekers who unfortunately came under their care while hoping for Spiritual Enlightenment. The ignorance of the Priests became hidden behind a veil of tedious ceremonies, which the devotees were expected to follow without question. The leaders were well-compensated for these so-called 'services', and thus religion became a paid profession. Blinded by greed and power, the Ministers of both Hinduism and Islam preached hatred against each other, totally forgetting the true spirit of religion, which is to realize the Fatherhood of God and the brotherhood of all humanity.

In the meantime, the Muslim conquerors began to gradually extend their influence, at first in Northern India and then throughout the length and breadth of most of the country from 1206-1525. As a result, large numbers of Hindus became converted to Islam, but mostly this happened at the point of the sword. As well, many concessions of both material and political natures were offered to help persuade this change. However, the Muslim rulers were very conscious of the separate identity needed to retain their political power and economic security, especially in a foreign land. As a result, the sharp distinction between the four castes continued, even among those recently converted to Islam.

The new Muslim rule suddenly reduced the political and economic predominance of the Hindu Brahmins, and now they were required to do many things, pay taxes for example, from which they had been previously exempt. Related to this was the inferior status accorded to non-Muslims by the *Shari'ah* (Islamic Law). Under the Shari'ah, a non-Muslim could not be accorded full status as a citizen of the State. Followers of the Islamic Faith were, on the other hand, given all kinds of preferential treatment, and it is of little wonder that Hindus found hardly any place in the higher offices of the administration.

The power and prestige of the Hindu Brahmins, however, remained indisputably great throughout most of this period of time, and the majority of India was still under the authority and influence of this priestcraft. However, when the Muslims began to desecrate the sacred Hindu temples, this political challenge now became a religious threat as well. The Muslims despised the Hindu practice of idol worship, and they began to force conversion to Islam. On the other hand, the Hindu laymen realized that if their own gods and goddesses could not protect the various places of worship from these conquerors, neither could they protect the devotees. Consequently, many Hindus began to question their beliefs in these stone idols and sacred paintings. In order to counter this new religious intimidation, the majority of the Hindu Brahmin leaders further tightened the ropes of their orthodoxy, and became even more dogmatic, obstinate, and narrow-minded.

Slowly, however, there began to develop some significant mixing of the two cultures, at first in such fields as music and literature, and later in dress, food, customs, speech, and art. In everything except the place of worship, the two communities gradually became somewhat interacted. Even the Muslim rulers themselves tried to bring their Hindu and Muslim subjects together in a somewhat unified Indian state, under this new 'Indo-Islamic' culture.

During this time, especially in the North of India, there was a conscious upsurge for freedom, both Spiritual and intellectual. The united front which Islam had attempted to present in a predominantly non-Muslim setting could not be maintained for long. The emergence of several dissenting Movements resulted from the excessive tyranny, oppression, and cruelty of the Muslim kings over their subjects. Among the forces which challenged the authority of the Muslim nobility were the Mystics of both the *Bhakti* and the *Sufi* schools of thought, as well as the *Yogis*.

Many of the *Bhakti* poets and teachers came from a diversity of backgrounds, most of them belonging to the less affluent classes, as did also the *Sufis*. The Bhaktis and the Sufis taught a Path of Love and devotion to One God, with meditation as the means of achieving rapturous Union with the Divine. They were devoted to their *Saints*, although such worship was looked upon by orthodox Islam as being none other than heresy.

However, the main appeal of these new Movements was their folk literature, consisting of poems composed in the local spoken dialects of the regions, using familiar themes of the common city and village life. These new reformers believed in the equality of all humanity, as all are God's living forms, and this was especially attractive to those aspiring for social equality. For both the Sufis as well as the Bhaktis, there was no difference between a Muslim and a Hindu. They both shunned all the meaningless rites and rituals at the level of the senses. They believed that God was not inseparable from the One Who had Himself merged with God (as a God-in-Man), and that God Himself could manifest here on earth in such a *Godman*, or a *Master*.

During this same period of history, the barbaric *Mughals* from China and Turkey began to infiltrate the northern frontiers of the Muslim dominions. The Hindus and the Muslims suddenly found themselves fighting shoulder to shoulder against these treacherous and brutal invaders. Political and social conditions sank to a new low, as the entire country became ransacked and looted. The various provinces found themselves fully independent, and a period of political instability, anarchy and turmoil prevailed over these small, regional kingdoms. The resulting Mughal Empire became firmly established in the North and Central regions, and it was to govern India for the next two hundred years (1526-1707).

It was during this very difficult period in India's history that Sant Kabir came on the scene. The *Sat Yuga* (Golden Age), with its emphasis on the Inner Life, had long disappeared. The *Kali Yuga* (Dark Age) had set in, with stress on the outer world and its attractions, dragging the people far away from the Spiritual vision of India's ancient enlightened souls, the *Rishis* and *Mahatmas*, who had emphasized the practical, esoteric side of Spirituality. Sant Kabir came at a time when the Hindus and the Muslims, who formed the major communities, were undergoing a period of great strife and turmoil, and were bitterly opposed to each other.

Sant Kabir, from whose lips flowed thousands of verses, gives the minutest details of the whole history of mankind, changing the lives of countless numbers of lucky souls with His Spiritual Message of the Oneness of all humanity. People commonly speak of 'Mystic India', for India is the home of Mysticism, but of all the Saints and Mystics that India has produced, perhaps Sant Kabir is the most well-known worldwide.

It is a tribute to His greatness that both Hindus and Muslims (the two main religions at that time) were amongst His followers, and even in today's time, each group proclaims that Sant Kabir belongs to their religion.

CHAPTER 4

CREATION OF THE WORLD

A large number of Sant Kabir's verses are written in the form of questions and answers between Himself and *Dharam Das* (one of Sant Kabir's major disciples) about the existence and formation of Creation. In His illustrious answers, Sant Kabir reveals how the souls are sent down from *Sat Purush* (Almighty God), and their long journey back Home.

#4-1 The Formation of Creation

First, Sant Kabir gives us an insight into the vast abode of Almighty God, from the highest Spiritual Region to the lowest. He states that in *Anami Lokh* (the Nameless Region), which is the Highest (Eighth) Spiritual Plane where Almighty God resides, there is no sun, no moon, no light, and no darkness.

He says, "There, God is in perpetual ecstasy and bliss, far above any kind of Deception or Illusion. The Lord is changeless and there is no other than Him. The Supreme Father is Knowing of all the knowing. No ordinary human being, however, can comprehend His limits because He is limitless."

Further down, Almighty God, in His own wisdom, created the Seventh Spiritual Region, known as *Agam Lokh* (the Inaccessible Region). Still further down, He created *Alak Lokh* (the Invisible, or Indescribable Region), the Sixth Spiritual Region of all Creation.

After this, the Lord made *Sach Khand* (the Imperishable Region of Truth), the Fifth Spiritual Region. It should be noted here that in all these afore-mentioned existing Regions, there is no matter of any kind. There is only All-Consciousness, and since this All-Consciousness consists of only one element, it never changes. It remains eternal, as opposed to Matter, which is made of more than one element. Thus, matter is continuously changing and is not permanent. Everything in the Creation below Sach Khand is made up of one or more of the following five elements: Earth, Air, Fire, Water, and Ether (also known as Discrimination).

Sant Kabir explains that since Almighty God was all alone, He wished to have some devotees (Lovers). He wanted to become many from One, so He created souls from His own Form and sent them down from the Higher Spiritual Regions into Sach Khand. Each soul was made of the same Essence as Almighty God. (For example, if a drop is taken from the Ocean, it is still part of the Ocean, and the qualities and the characteristics of the Ocean are reflected in each drop.) Since Almighty God is All-Consciousness, the soul retains this state of pure Consciousness. Sant Kabir says that in the Region of Sach Khand, the purity of the soul is such as to reflect the Godly Light of sixteen outer suns. The Divine Sound Current, which emanates from Almighty God in this Region, has a sound similar to the instrument known as the *Beena* (the bagpipe).

After that, God created *Par Brahm*, the Fourth Spiritual Region, further down. It is also known as *Bhanwar Gupha*, *Maha Sunn,* or the *Super Causal Region*. This Region is made of Consciousness with a fraction of matter being present. As the soul descended into this Spiritual Plane, a covering of that fraction of matter mixed up with the soul to give it the fine veil of the Super Causal body. As regards to the Celestial Music that resounds in this Region, Sant Kabir reveals that the Melody resembles that of the flute.

More further down God made *Brahmand*, the Third Spiritual Region, also known as the *Causal Region*, or *Dhaswan Dwar*. Sant Kabir has also called it as *Seth Sunn*. It consists of roughly half matter and half Consciousness, which gives the soul a covering not only of the Super Causal body, but also the Causal, as more and more matter has now mixed up with the soul. This Region is also known as the Original Home of the mind, because it is in this Region that the Causal mind becomes attached to the soul when it leaves on its descent.

Still yet further down, God made *Trikuti*, the Second Region, also known as *Sahansdal Kanwal*, or *Andh* (the *Astral Region*), consisting of even more matter with the balance made of Consciousness. Thus, the soul obtains a greater covering of matter, with the Astral body now added to the existing coverings of the Causal and Super Causal bodies. The Astral and the Causal minds also come along with the soul when it leaves this Stage.

The First Region, the *Pind* or the *Physical Region*, is mostly made of matter, with only a very small part being pure Consciousness (which is called as the soul or the spirit). This is the Region in which we live. When the soul descends into this Region, as it already has the coverings of the Astral, the Causal and the Super Causal bodies, it needs the Physical body in which to function on this Physical Plane. And of course, added to this are the Physical, the Astral, and the Causal minds.

Kabir Sahib says that all the gods, goddesses and Avatars who have come to this world, or who are in this world, such as *Shiva* and his son *Ganesh*, *Vishnu* and his son *Sanak*, *Sanand*, and *Mahesh*, *Brahm* and his sons, as well as *Ashtangi* (another name for *Maya*, the wife of *Kaal*), *Lakshmi*, *Parvati* (the wife of *Shiva*), and many others, even although they are all considered to be as gods and goddesses, they can only work in the lower first three Regions (the Physical, the Astral, and the Causal). These Regions are not made of pure Consciousness, but have some varying degrees of matter and Consciousness mixed together.

Sant Kabir, however, tells us that He alone was existing from the very beginning of Creation, at the time even before the three gods (*Brahma*, *Vishnu*, and *Shiva*) came into existence. These three Powers look after the affairs of the Creation, including Creation, Sustenance, and Destruction of the lower three Regions (namely, the Physical, the Astral, and the Causal). Because it is so difficult to comprehend with the limited human intellect just how long ago was this period of time, Sant Kabir illustrates His verses with the statement that at that time Brahma did not even have his crown, Vishnu did not have his *tikka* (sacramental mark on the forehead), and Shiva was not yet born.

Sant Kabir tells us that He (Kabir) came with the knowledge of the highest stage of *Sant Mat* (also known as *Surat Shabd Yoga*, or *Science of Spirituality*) at that time. He says that this Path Godwards existed so very long ago, even before these lower three Regions were made. From this statement, we can deduce that this Path was made by Almighty God Himself, and this is the one Way, and the only Way, back to God.

To put the time of Sant Kabir's own existence more into perspective, He has written that by the order of *Sat Purush* (Almighty God), He (Sant Kabir) appeared in God's Creation to spread the Nectar of the *Holy Naam* (the Holy Word), to awaken the souls as to the true nature of their Spirituality by the means of the *Sat Shabd* (Divine Sound Current), and to take them back to their true Home in *Sat Lokh* (the Region of Truth), at that period of time in the history of the earth before these Incarnations appeared. Sant Kabir says that at that time His Name was *Achint*, and before He had even descended into the Lower Spiritual Planes, He met at the top of the *Causal Plane* (Third Spiritual Region) with Dharam Rai. Dharam Rai performs his duties under Kaal. It is significant to note that neither Sant Kabir nor Dharam Rai had physically incarnated at this period in time.

During that meeting, Dharam Rai had revealed all his clever traps and myriad ensnarements designed to keep the souls ever bound and very busy in their *Karma* (a system of action and reaction, based on the *Law of Cause and Effect*). Sant Kabir cautioned Dharam Rai that no matter what the latter would do to entangle the souls, He (Sant Kabir) would break apart all these chains and release the poor souls from the hand of Kaal.

Sant Kabir emphasizes, "Whoever catches hold of the *Holy Shabd* of God (the God-into-manifestation Power; also known as the *Holy Word*, the *Sonorous Light*, the *Holy Naam*, or *Kalma*), will be liberated for all time and will go to the Region of *Sat Lokh*, or *Sach Khand*, which is the true Home of the soul."

Sant Kabir then tells us that *He physically incarnated in all the four Yugas*. At the time of His first physical appearance on the earth Plane, it was that period of history known as the *Sat Yuga* (the Golden Age). He says that His Name then was *Sat Sukrit*, and that He used to wear simple, wooden sandals upon His feet. By the order of Sat Purush, He went throughout the entire Creation, and began to awaken the souls slumbering in total forgetfulness as to their true Spirituality.

In the next Age, the *Treta Yuga* (the Silver Age), Sant Kabir was known as *Maninder*. He says that He came at that time to teach about the glory of Sat Purush, so that more souls should go back Home. The souls were very much caught up in the beauty of the world, with its various attractions and relations, not putting much attention as to the real Aim of taking the human birth. Sant Kabir tells us a little bit about Himself during this period of time, describing that He wore a type of thin shirt and carried a particular kind of bag on His shoulder.

He then says that for a third time He mercifully donned the human form in the *Dwapar Yuga* (the Copper Age), a very advanced Age materially, but not Spiritually. His name was *Karunamai*, and He has portrayed another and very different type of dress at that time. He says that He came to liberate the souls by making them realize the Holy Shabd, to make them aware of their Godly heritage, and to wake them up from an ever-deep sleep of Spiritual ignorance.

In this *Kali Yuga*, (the Dark Age), He says that He has Graciously incarnated once more, and now He is known as *Kabir*. He has come to make the souls more firm in the Holy Shabd, breaking the Illusions of the Negative Power through the

Divine Contact bestowed by the *True Master* at the time of Spiritual Initiation.

Sant Kabir tells us that in His great mercy for all Creation, He has been extensively going back and forth between all the *Khands and Brahmands* (the various Spiritual Regions) *not only before,* but also *during* the Creation of these Four *Yugas* (Spiritual Ages). Sant Kabir praises all of God's infinite Creation. God has cast Himself in millions of colours and forms, and yet each one of these is unique. His expanse of Creation spreads to infinity and eternity.

Sant Kabir advises the seeker after Truth that only the Holy Name of *Sat Purush* is the true Liberator. In His great mercy and compassion, the Perfect Master makes manifest within the soul of the devotee the Form of the *Holy Light and Sound of God.*

Kabir Sahib teaches the Path of *Sant Mat* (the *Way of the Saints*), which is the true Teachings of all the Saints, shorn of rites and rituals, and presented as an *Inner Spiritual Path.* He proclaims that the Perfect Master can show the devotee how to traverse into the Beyond and gain the Kingdom of God, which is the soul's eternal birthright.

#4-2 Akaal and Kaal

Sant Kabir says that both *Akaal* (the Positive Power) and *Kaal* (the Negative Power), were made by Sat Purush to look after the Creation. *Akaal* is a Sanskrit word meaning 'without Kaal', and denotes 'eternity' or 'timelessness'. It is beyond Time and Space, and therefore the hours, days, years, and Ages have nothing to do with this Power. Being Eternal, this Power resides over the Pure Spiritual Regions from Sach Khand upwards, and is far beyond the reach of Kaal. The Regions of Sach Khand and upwards are the Regions of All-Consciousness, and are totally void of any kind of matter. They are pure Spiritual Regions, unlike the domain of Kaal (from the Fourth Spiritual Region and downwards), which contains matter in varying degrees.

Kaal has his abode in the Fourth Spiritual Plane (the Super Causal). This is the Region where some matter, albeit very little, is present. Kaal's domain extends as well downwards throughout the lower three Regions (the Causal, the Astral and the Physical). Each of these Regions in descending order contains more and more matter until the Physical Plane is reached, where there is mostly matter and very little Consciousness. Kaal is responsible for the sustenance and the control of the souls in all these Regions.

Akaal, the Positive Power, has many Agents to help look after the Creation, and among these Agents is *Kaal*, also known as *Kaal Purush*. Kaal, in turn, has two Powers to assist him in this matter. They are known as *'Time'* and *'Space'*. Time, as it is, brings forth changes, and Space thereby helps to spread the Creation ever outward and downward. We also learn that wherever there is any amount of matter, even a tiny bit as is in the Fourth Region, that Region eventually undergoes a *Grand Dissolution* at the end of a certain period of time.

Kaal Niranjan is the full name of the Negative Power, but it is generally shortened to just *Kaal*. *Niranjan* means 'beyond Illusion', and *Kaal* means 'Time' because he is the creator of Illusion, and Illusion relies on Time for its subtle effect. Each of Kaal's universes is under the jurisdiction of a ruler, and each ruler has three Forces, or Powers, for assistance: *Brahma* (the Creator), *Vishnu* (the Sustainer), and *Mahesh*, or *Shiva*, (the Destroyer). These administrators work under Kaal. Each universe, therefore, contains a *Brahma*, a *Vishnu*, and a *Mahesh*, all under the administration of *Kaal*, who is, furthermore, supervised by *Akaal*.

Time has nothing to do with Akaal. Akaal is beyond Time and Space because Kaal has no connection with Kaal. Therefore all the ages, years, months, days, minutes and seconds merge in its eternal existence.

#4-3 Dharam Rai

Sant Kabir explains that *Dharam Rai* administers to the three worlds of the Physical, the Astral, and the Causal. The word 'Dharam' means 'righteousness', or 'a mode of life', and 'Rai' means 'King'. Accordingly, Dharam Rai dispenses justice (the King of Justice!) according to the *Dharma* (rules and regulations) of this Creation. He is also known as the *Agent of Death*, *Yam Raj*, and *Kaal Purush*. Sant Kabir says that those people who do not have a True Living Master, all go at the time of their physical death, to the Court of Dharam Rai to render an account of their good and bad deeds. Under God's Order, Dharam Rai administers this reconciliation, but he does so very impartially.

Sant Kabir issues a caution concerning the everyday deeds that one commits during his lifetime. "When Dharam Rai asks for a reckoning of the account, there shall be a heavy balance against thee. The five evils (lust, anger, etc.) that have plagued thee all through life shall run away, and thou shalt have to take responsibility for their evil deeds." He explains that various hells have been made for the sinners, and the heavens exist as a reward for those with meritorious deeds. However, after the soul's allotted time in the region of hell or heaven is over, the soul has to once again go back into the *Wheel of Transmigration* (the Cycle of birth and death), and once more take birth in some physical form.

Dharam Rai is assisted by *Yamas*, or *Yam Doots* (Ambassadors of Death), who pull the soul out of the body at the time of physical death and drag it to Dharam Rai. Sant Kabir tells us that there are fourteen of these Representatives of Death to assist Dharam Rai at the time of the person's physical death, and there can be no possibility of escape from them. Dharam Rai has a very grave temperament, for he thinks in the minutest detail what is right and what is wrong, in order to pass fair judgement in his Court.

Kabir Sahib has said that since the dawn of Creation, people have been so caught up in their worldly work, so engrossed in the 'busy-ness' of their families and the attractions of this life that they have little, if any, time to ponder over the direction that their life is going. "The Name of the Lord is thus set aside. The worldly work never gets finished; yet people are frantically running here and there, trying to complete everything. All are carrying heavy burdens of worthless activities, knowledge, and desires."

The soul has become totally helpless, not fully realizing its situation, although it does comprehend sometimes that it is not happy. It generally becomes sad, for example, when the body is sick or a loved one dies. Sometimes, however, in the midst of all this rush and pomp of everyday life, one is suddenly dragged to the Court of Dharam Rai for the reckoning of his account, and there is no time to make amends for any wrongdoing committed during the physical life.

The mind continuously has more and more new desires, and tries its best to gratify them. It is entirely forgetful of the day of reckoning when the soul will be summoned to the court of Dharam Rai. The poor soul is constantly being dragged helplessly by the mind outwards into the mire of this world. Sant Kabir says that one might try to cover his sins, but "Everything is revealed at the time of physical death, when one is asked to account for his deeds. The entire statement of one's thoughts, words, and deeds which occurred all through his life will be laid bare, but there will be no one to vouch for the soul!"

#4-4 How Kaal Rules Over His Domain

Each Region under Kaal is eventually destroyed (as a *Dissolution*) after an allotted period of time, due to the effects of Time and Space (i.e. after each of the Four Yugas, or Ages, have passed). In addition, these Regions collectively undergo a *Grand Dissolution* after another period of time has passed. Kaal has the whole Creation of the lower three Regions under his command, and therefore he is also referred to as *Kaal Purush* (Lord of the three Regions).

Every soul in these lower three Regions is under the control of its own individual body, whether it be of Physical, Astral, or Causal material. Kaal wants all the souls to remain separated from their Supreme Lord (so that his domain continues to be populated), and he is assisted in this objective by his wife, commonly called *Maya* (Illusion).

Maya is another Power created by Sat Purush (Almighty God). Through Illusion, Kaal created three Forces, known as *Brahma* (the Creator), *Vishnu* (the Sustainer), and *Mahesh*, or *Shiva* (the Destroyer). They work under Kaal, ruling over the lower three Regions (the Physical, the Astral, and the Causal, respectively). Almighty God can see Brahma, Vishnu, and Shiva but they are not capable, however, of seeing Him.

Kabir Sahib tells us that Kaal ordered *Maya* (who is not only the wife of Kaal, but also the mother of these three gods) never to reveal to her sons (these Powers) that Kaal is their father. He ordered Maya not to tell the secret of his existence to anyone.

"Furthermore," Sant Kabir continues, and this is a very important point, "Kaal does not want these Powers to know that Kaal himself was created by Sat Purush (Almighty God)."

Maya and her sons, Brahma, Vishnu, and Shiva were to go into the world and spread such Illusion over all, so as to prevent any soul from obtaining knowledge of Almighty God, because Kaal wanted the souls to remain in his domain, and not to know the Truth. This Illusion that spreads all over the world is not the Truth. It has all the magic of mirage!

Maya then told these three Powers to rule over the three Worlds. Kaal's system is such a drama, that Brahma, Vishnu, and Shiva actually believe that they are the gods of these lower three Regions. They only know these three Worlds, but nothing more beyond them.

Kaal has thus kept Brahma, Vishnu, as well as Shiva also in this Illusion. They know nothing beyond the third Spiritual Region, and fully believe that they are gods with great powers in themselves, as the Creator, the Sustainer, and the Destroyer. They have been led to understand that they alone have the Power to keep everything (in these lower three Regions) under their control. Kaal reasoned that this is the only way that these Powers would stay under his regulation, and maintain these Regions on his own behalf.

Kabir Sahib explains that these three Regions are established in the domain of Kaal as follows:

1. *Pind*, which consists of the Physical body and the Physical Region.
2. *Andh*, which consists of the Astral body and the Astral Region.
3. *Brahmand* which consists of the Causal body and the Causal Region.

Kaal, however, has one major limitation in his regulation. He cannot create nor destroy any soul anywhere in his domain because the soul, being immortal, is made of the same Divine Essence as God. Therefore it belongs to God, and ultimately it has to go back to God. The soul is given a physical body when it enters the Physical Region, according to the desires and attention of the previous life, and then that same body is returned to that Region after the allotted period of time is over. The same thing is true with the Astral and the Causal bodies. Not only that, but the Physical, the Astral and the Causal minds have to be returned as well. Of course, this only happens as the soul rises up and passes through the different Spiritual Regions. As the soul passes through the Astral Region, for example, the Astral mind and the Astral body are left behind. As the soul rises through and crosses the Causal Region, the Causal mind and body remain there, and now the soul, free at last of the mind and body coverings, forges ahead, undeterred.

"It is the desire of Kaal to keep everybody in his domain", explains Sant Kabir, "because the charm of this Creation is that souls remain to inhabit it." Therefore Kaal does his best that the people should continue to be entangled in an intricate web of Delusion, Illusion, doubt, superstition, rites, rituals, and in fact anything that would even remotely appeal to the mind and the five outgoing senses. Thus, the soul should never realize its real self.

From time to time Kaal has sent other agents, called *Avatars*, to this world. They are all incarnations of Brahma (the Creator), and Vishnu (the Sustainer). These Avatars come on behalf of Kaal to administer justice, to put people on to the right path, and to punish the wicked. In short, they do everything to make the world run smoothly, but the Avatars themselves are not allowed to know anything beyond the Third Region (Causal Region).

The Negative Power can also take on the form of other Powers which incarnate seemingly as 'protectors' of the souls, and they appear to 'conquer' demons and other lower Powers to 'save' mankind. All of them come to the Physical level either from the Second Region (Astral), or from the Third (Causal). Many types of dramas are performed in the Physical Region in order to woo the souls, that they should then begin to worship these 'saviours'. "The outcome of all this," says Sant Kabir, "is that the deluded souls end up again in the Cycle of

Transmigration, with no hope of a way out beyond the Region from which the Powers themselves originate."

Sant Kabir explains fully how Kaal sustains these Regions under his domain, and then destroys them after a certain period of time has passed. These Regions are under the continual effects of the past, present, and future, and they revolve around the Four *Yugas* (Ages). The years, months, weeks, days, hours, and seconds are the divisions of all these Yugas. Each Yuga is of a certain length and when one Yuga draws to a close, the dawn of the next one occurs.

The first Age, or Yuga, was the *Sat Yuga* (the Age of Truth, also called the Golden Age). Life at that time in the Physical Region was so good that the souls didn't understand that they were actually trapped in this Region with its myriad attractions. The souls could have returned to their true Home very easily if they had wanted to, but very few actually wished to.

The *Treta Yuga* (the Silver Age), was the second Age. Avatar Vishnu incarnated as King Ram Chandra of the great epic *Ramayana* during this period in time. People in this Age were still not fully aware of the necessity of going quickly back Home, due to the diverse attractions and pleasures of this time. As a result, again very few wished to leave the Physical Region.

The third Age was the *Dwapar Yuga* (the Copper Age). Vishnu incarnated as Avatar Krishna during this Age. It was a highly technical and material Age, but ended in catastrophe when the *Mahabharata War* was fought by people who came to India from all parts of the world. A nuclear war resulted, which devastated India, and all civilization as we know it, was totally obliterated within eighteen days.

The present Age is the *Kali Yuga* (also known as the Dark, or Iron, Age). Nowadays people hardly live up to 100 years, but they generally are more Spiritually Awakened and understand more readily about the 'long slumber' of the soul. Only in this Age have significant numbers of people followed the great Masters.

Sant Kabir tells us that besides other duties, the main work of Kaal is to see that no one escapes from his domain. Kaal accomplishes this by controlling all living beings through one or the other of the five senses (Sight, Hearing, Taste, Touch, and Smell). These senses, in turn, give expression to the five evil tendencies of lust, anger, etc. All living beings have forgotten their Origin and their true Home, and thus wander about lost in Delusion. Kaal makes the souls worship him by employing the clever traps of Holy Scriptures, the rites of pilgrimages, fasting, rituals of penance, various types of worship, sacrifices, rules and formalities, austerities, friends, family and other relations, and boundless entanglements of pleasures such as sight, hearing, and taste.

As an example, Sant Kabir reveals that the *Four Vedas* (the most ancient of the Hindu Scriptures) actually were given by Kaal for the sole purpose of consoling the souls whenever they would feel the separation from God. The Vedas do give out theoretical knowledge of the various rites of Hinduism, but if someone carefully reads through them, he will understand that they do not offer any practical Way out from the Cycle of Transmigration. The seeker literally becomes bogged down in these intricate rituals which lead nowhere. Sant Kabir says, "The person's mind is quite happy to follow these practices because they keep the mind busy, but the soul itself receives absolutely no comfort from this!"

#4-5 Karma: The Law of Action and Reaction

Kabir Sahib fully illustrates the *Law of Karma* (the Law of Action and Reaction) and all its implications. He says, "Karma is anything that takes the mind and attention away from Almighty God, and binds it to something else." He cautions that every person claims that he knows all about Karma, but actually it is a rare soul who truly understands its theory.

Karma is a system of action and reaction which causes continual wandering in the Cycle of Transmigration, making an unending chain of cause and compounded effect. It is the result of a thought, a word, or a deed. Each of these has the potential to come to fruition, not only in this very lifetime, but even in lives to come. Karma has been further classified by Sant Kabir into three categories:

1. *Sanchit* (stored) Karmas, which are Karmas from the soul's past lives, the good and bad deeds earned in all the previous existences. The soul knows nothing about them. The Master takes over these Karmas from the devotee when he comes under His Divine protection. The Master, however, cautions the devotee not to incur any new Karmas.

2. *Pralabdha* (fate or destiny) Karmas, are that portion of the Sanchit Karmas which make up the living present. The present life is just an unfolding of these predestined Karmas, with which the soul comes into the world at the time of its birth into the human body. The Pralabdha Karmas determine the person's life form (body), the place where he is supposed to be born, the state of his health and wealth, his name and fame, and so on. A person has no control over them, and their effects can be borne either with smiles or tears. The Master does not eliminate these Karmas, because if He did so, there would be no more purpose of the devotee continuing his present physical life. (It is only in the physical body that

the soul can undergo the effects of these Karmas.) The Master, however, is so Gracious and Loving, that He often 'tones down' the stinging outcome of these Karmas. The effect of the 'gallows', for example, might become reduced to a 'pinprick'.

3. *Kriyaman* Karmas are those 'free' Karmas, of which one is at liberty to perform in this present earthly existence. These Karmas will determine the soul's future. Kabir Sahib tells us that the soul is mostly bound in this present existence due to the Pralabdha Karmas, but one is also somewhat free (about 25% free) to determine the actions he will perform in this lifetime, which thereto lay the foundation for the future. Due to the person's intellect (the Power of Discrimination), he can choose what is right and wrong, and thereby select the Path that will facilitate his return to the Creator, rather than a return to this physical existence.

The Law of Karma is very simple. *"As ye sow, so shall ye reap!"* It can be compared to a farm where the farmer reaps the harvest, which in turn gives him grain to eat. Then he sows the seeds for the next crop, but at the same time he stores away some of the last crop as a reserve. Soon the second crop is ready to be harvested, and meanwhile the farmer sows the seeds for the third crop.

Similarly, the seeds of good or bad actions are sown in this lifetime and the resulting Karmas are reaped in this, the next, or subsequent lives. One accumulates too many Karmas (reactions) to be paid off in a single lifetime and just like the farmer with leftover grain, these 'extra' Karmas are stored for the future. Kabir Sahib comments that man becomes caught in a web of Illusion due to his own foolishness and carelessness which leads to these different Karmas. However, there is hope, as also it is mentioned that the person can transcend this net if he realizes his own predicament, and makes an effort to withdraw his attention from worldly pleasures and objects.

Each person, continuously with each and every breath, is becoming more and more entangled in the web of Karma which keeps him in perpetual bondage. Sant Kabir says that this Wheel of birth and rebirth turns slowly, but ceaselessly. He says that whatever Karmas one is making, nothing can cancel them, except by repaying them. That person alone who makes the Karmas is the one who has to undergo the results, as reactions. Sant Kabir says that it is such an amazing thing that the mind never comprehends this, but instead thinks that this world will go on forever and ever. Man is totally oblivious to the fact that a reconciliation for the account of his deeds will ever take place!

Generally, people say that others cause their troubles, but that success they have themselves achieved. Actually, whatever happens in life is part of the chain of one's actions, part of his Karmas. The day that the person accepts and experiences total responsibility for himself, a transformation begins to take place within. Everyone completely forgets that he has sown the seeds when the fruits begin to appear. No one worries about another. Each is concerned with his own self. Each person, therefore, must seek out the thread of his own actions. One must recognize and accept quietly the reactions and results of his own past actions. It makes no sense to produce fresh ills, while repaying the fruit of past actions.

Man is Blessed with the gift of Discrimination and with intellect, which in turn give him the Power to determine what is right and wrong, and thereby he can make or mar his future as he wishes. When one develops detachment from the attractions of this world, an opportunity is provided to escape, as it were, from this Cycle of Transmigration. Therefore, the person with Discrimination will carefully weigh the consequences of his every thought, word, and deed.

Sooner or later, one's desires are fulfilled and when one experiences the inevitable consequences of those desires, their attractions wane. Sometimes the reactions are pleasant, sometimes unpleasant, but usually we find that they are unsatisfying and not worth the effort spent on them. The glitter and glamour of the world are outlived by experience, which is a theme of many of Sant Kabir's Discourses. Everyone forgets that an account has to be rendered for all his actions. People go on blindly spinning the web of Karma around and around the soul, but still they find no happiness. The soul has had a long affiliation with the mind, which in turn is under the tremendous influence of Illusion. This combination of association makes people to commit all manner of sins. One must, however, beware: the Agent of Death cannot be bribed, and the Karmic laws cannot be defied.

Once, a follower of Sant Kabir came to Him, and with all humbleness asked the question, "Please, O Merciful One! Expound on this: why did Almighty God send the souls to this earth? Why does the person have to take birth, die and then come back again? Please explain thy Secret knowledge of God, O Lord! Please have mercy on me and put me into the right Path, which will take me to the doorstep of Almighty God, so that my fears of this Deception and Illusion will vanish. Please cut the bondage of attachment to this world."

In great mercy and compassion, Sant Kabir explained that due to thoughts, words, and deeds of the present life, plus the actions that one has done in previous lives, the person comes back into a body again and again to reap the reactions of those thoughts, words, and deeds. For example, every day thousands of cattle are slaughtered, and uncountable thousands of sheep, fowl and fish shriek in anguish as their throats are cut or wrung, but there is no one to listen to their cries of terror and pain.

"Once they might have been human beings, maybe even kings or emperors, but now today they are cows, chickens, or beasts of burden, such as donkeys or camels, forced to carry heavy loads long past the point of exhaustion. Now they are reborn as animals, birds, and fish for the wrong they did to others while they themselves were in the human body!" What can man possibly do himself about all the Karmas accumulated during the past hundreds of lives?

The person keeps indulging in outer desires connected with this world, and immerses in them. He doesn't even try to cut those bonds, nor does he come to the True Master. Instead, the person is busy day and night trying to alter that course to which he is foredoomed, and he pays no attention to accomplishing what he is free to bring about. He should try not to remain under the effects of Illusion. For example, the span of his life is predetermined, and he becomes rich or poor, dies and is reborn, suffers pain or feels happy according to his inflexible Karmas. He should not brood over it, but instead attend to his main Task and true Aim of taking birth in the noble human form.

Sant Kabir further clarifies that some people have been provided beautiful silken clothes and nice beds by the Creator to make for themselves a comfortable life, while others can hardly make their ends meet, living day to day, wondering where their next meal will come from. This is all due to their previous deeds.

Sant Kabir reminds us that salvation does not connote the accumulation of nice clothes or a nice house. He explains, "O my dear friend! Don't be jealous and concerned about this. Don't envy others' possessions! This is all due to peoples' good actions done in previous lives--the theory of Karma."

"Man has lost his Inner Spiritual Sight, and cannot see the Radiant, Divine Light of God." For this reason Sant Kabir says that man is Spiritually 'blind', and he thus tumbles helplessly through the *Cycle of 8.4 Million Species* (the Wheel of Transmigration). After an almost endless length of time in diverse inferior kinds of bodies, at last he reaches the pinnacle and incarnates as a human being. Even at this stage he is not saved, as the pleasures of the senses combined with his desires continually pull him into activities reflecting the fulfillment of all these wants. Precious time is frittered away, day after day, hour after hour, totally wasted on endless appetites of one kind or the other.

"Nothing happens of its own accord," Kabir Sahib gently reminds us. "All the pains and pleasures of life are the result of one's own actions, and all actions must have their reactions. Every action is indelibly recorded by the sub-Conscious mind. The general run of life is thus determined before one is born."

Sant Kabir fully illustrates that after the Creation was made, souls were sent down to the Physical Plane. A soul would arrive with the physical body, as well as the five outgoing senses of Sight, Hearing, Taste, Touch, and Smell. On top of all that, the physical body also had the physical mind, with its five Karma-making faculties of Lust, Anger, Greed, Attachment, and Ego.

When the soul, as Consciousness or Spirit, is in the First Region of the physical senses, the physical body continuously makes actions day and night through the mind. Every action (whether of thought, word, or deed) that the soul makes in this physical body, through the mind and its outgoing senses, has a reaction. Sant Kabir says that if, for example, one uses violence in an unjust or cruel way, that person will have to answer to Dharam Rai in reconciliation of this anger at the time of that person's physical death. This will, in turn, ultimately result in some Karma for the soul to suffer in a future physical body. "Anger," He points out, "is like a dream because it is not Truth." One moment it is not there, and after another moment it again shall not be there.

Another example that Sant Kabir uses is of desire. Desire causes a reaction of greed, and then with greed comes ego, etc. These outgoing faculties can perform both good and bad acts. However, the physical body has to reap the result of all these actions (whether good actions or bad actions), and they are all accounted for, each and every second. Day and night, the soul becomes the slave of these outgoing faculties and the senses. The soul is made impure due to its attachment with matter, which exists throughout the lower four Spiritual Regions in varying degrees.

In other words, this total mesh web is made by worldly Illusion. It is an intricate, extremely complicated entanglement in which the body keeps dying, taking rebirth in another form to reap whatever reactions were made from the previous actions, and then dying again to take rebirth again in perhaps yet another form to reap the new compounded reactions, and so on and so forth.

Sant Kabir continues in His explanation of Karma. He says, "The world has been created and destroyed countless numbers of times." He tells us that we have existed in it throughout the ages, treading the Wheel of Transmigration and incarnating as minerals, plants, worms, insects, reptiles, birds, or animals. Even vegetables and plants have souls; however in a latent form.

Having birth in the human form is something very precious and rare. He says, "Once the soul has taken birth in the human body, it may not necessarily obtain the human body again. If the soul performs wrong deeds while in the human body, then it might fall to a lower level of species in a subsequent birth. It will have to reap the Karmas made as a result of those bad deeds. It might have to again go through the Cycle of 8.4 million species of forms."

Sant Kabir has written a verse comparing a fully ripened fruit that falls to the ground and cannot be reattached to the branch again. "In the same way," He says, "once the soul has fallen from the high status of the human birth, it takes a long time to get again the human birth. It just might never again obtain the human form." Lord Kabir makes us aware that it is only the result of very good Karma that one is able to obtain the precious Boon of the human form.

He tells us that the entire Creation is divided amongst many, many forms of species. All souls in the Creation are involved in the various stages of the ever-revolving Wheel of births and rebirths. The soul can spend aeons and aeons of years (many, many lives!) to evolve through all of them, working its way up again to the human form.

He explains that Creation has been divided into the following 8,400,000 species:

(i)   3,000,000 types of plants, grass, vegetables, trees, fruits, etc.,

(ii) 2,700,000 types of insects, rodents, reptiles, etc.,

(iii) 1,400,000 types of air creatures, including bats, birds, etc.,

(iv) 900,000 types of water creatures, including fish, whales, and all marine life, etc. and,

(v)   400,000 types of animals, humans, gods, goddesses, demons, spirits, fairies, ghosts, lower Powers, higher Powers, Rishis, Munis, and Yogis, etc. over which the human body is supreme.

Sant Kabir reveals that in every species where the soul takes birth, it faces great misery, pain and suffering, because this Physical Region is the Realm of all misery. Its myriad attractions drag the mind and the senses away from any thoughts of a Higher Spiritual Life and the Way back to God, and keep the soul engrossed in the worldly busy-ness. There is no one to listen to the soul's agonizing cries of anguish and great distress, as it roams from one form to another.

After endless wanderings, it may be born as a human, but then the mind and the senses stand ever ready to again deceive it. The soul has totally forgotten its previous births and consequently keeps doing wrong deeds, which in turn keep bringing the soul back again and again into these lower forms. However, if the soul did remember these things, it would shudder in horror, and would not continue to do them. The outcome would be that eventually the soul would wind up all its Karma, thereby having the chance to escape from Kaal.

Sant Kabir explains that the law of nature is such, that as one thinks, so he becomes. He gives the example that if one thinks ill of others, naturally the result bounces back to him as the reaction of those bad thoughts. He says that people have no right to judge another fellow human being, because the whole world is caught in this web.

He illustrates that if someone speaks ill of a person, naturally the speaker is taking the ills of the other person. In other words, one is putting his full attention on that other person, and thereby he also suffers that person's ills. He is freely putting the burden of the other man's dirt on himself. This is the subtle workings of the Law of Action and Reaction. Kabir Sahib says that person is just like a washerman, cleaning away the sins of others.

In the Cycle of Transmigration, all living forms pass from one level of creation to the next one according to the results of their thoughts, words, and deeds. However, Sant Kabir makes us aware of yet another Wheel working in this material world, the *Law of Evolution*. The basis of determining the value of evolution depends upon matter and intellect. The factor that usually determines the worthiness (value) of the body, is the amount of the intellect (with its greater power of the Wakefulness of the spirit) that it possesses.

He says that man is at the highest part of the ladder of life, with all five Elements (Earth, Air, Water, Fire, and Ether or Discrimination) in full activity. The animals have the fifth Element of Ether (Discrimination) dormant, and are thus placed next in value. The birds consist of three active Elements (Water, Fire and Air), and therefore are of even lesser position. Lesser still is the value of forms with two active Elements (Earth and Fire), such as insects and reptiles. Still lesser yet are the forms of vegetation, such as plants and fruits with only the one Element of Water being active, and all the other four as dormant. Thus, vegetarian and fruitarian diets are the least pain-producing and the least Karma-producing diets, suitable for man at the top of the list of beings in God's Creation.

There is a story to illustrate the Law of Action and Reaction. *Ramanand* was a learned Hindu philosopher who settled in Benaras at the time of Sant Kabir. He was very well known, and had a large following, who respected him greatly. However, during his last earthly days, Ramanand became very sad and pensive. When Sant Kabir saw this solemn condition, He was moved to inquire as to the reason for such disheartenment.

With a very heavy heart, Ramanand answered, "Well, whenever I remember how I am going to die, the fear of public humiliation and dishonour grips me and makes my heart so sad. I become filled with deep remorse for my past deeds." With tears in his eyes, he told Sant Kabir the following story.

"In my previous life, I have very cruelly killed someone. I tied him up with rope, and dragged him behind my horse through the streets of the city until he was dead. In this very lifetime and for this horrendous deed, I have to pay back in a similar way to that very person. He is also alive in the human body at this time, and he happens to occupy a very high post in the king's court. I know my end will occur in the same way, and that person has to drag me behind his horse until I die. This is the only way that this dreadful Karma can be finished. Such a terrible thought, that my life is going to end in this manner, and I will have to suffer thus, brings untold sorrow into my heart. I tremble from head to foot at the very thought of it. I don't know what to do, and I am in a very pitiful state, as my time to leave draws quite near."

Sant Kabir could not help but feel pity for Ramanand, and He told him, "I will see as to what I can do for you in this matter."

Sant Kabir went to visit that same minister, but somehow the man was not at home. He tried to meet with him several times, but this man seemed to be avoiding Him. Actually, this minister had performed some great devotion in a former life and as a result, he had the Power to know of his own previous happenings. He was already aware of the events which were to unfold in this lifetime.

Finally, Sant Kabir was able to meet with that man, and He told him about Ramanand's story. Sant Kabir humbly requested that minister to kindly forgive Rananand. The minister ultimately agreed with Sant Kabir saying, *"Because You have come to me*, I will not drag him through the streets the way he did to me. I will forgive him for that, but he will be killed by me!"

Kabir Sahib went back to Ramanand and told him what the man had said. Ramanand folded his hands towards the heavens, and sighed deeply, feeling very much relieved in his heart that he would not suffer the disgrace and dishonour of being dragged behind a horse.

Some time later, war broke out in that very district, and of course the same minister was fighting for the king. During the battle, that minister was quite near Ramanand's house, and Ramanand was ultimately killed with the minister's spear. Thus, with the Grace of Sant Kabir, this Karmic reaction was finally finished only in this manner, and Ramanand was spared the humiliation of being dragged throughout the streets.

Sant Kabir tells us, in summary, that the main events of one's life are the results of past actions, and this is the debt that stands before us. "Like a debtor, one should be happy when the debt is being paid off." Sometimes, however, the debt is painful to repay. It is difficult to remain calm when one is in calamity, but if the person understands the reason for the adversity, it helps then to have the strength to bear it bravely.

Sant Kabir gives many examples, saying that sometimes it happens that a person is unhappy about his lot and he suffers greatly, which is the result of the seeds he has sown in the past. On the other hand, another person is happy and seemingly successful. Sant Kabir says that this is due to his past Karmas, but that same person might be ruining his future life. One must think carefully in his heart of hearts *what the intentions truly are* in any action. Any thought passing through the mind, will eventually escape as a word, and the harvest of this careless seed will be reaped in due time. Sant Kabir warns, "Be careful! Even seeds which are *sown in secret* will also sprout forth!"

CHAPTER 5

THERE IS A GREAT NEED OF SPIRITUALITY

People all over the world have great tension and worry, but they feel even more restless and unhappy when they discover that material objects can bring comfort to the body, but absolutely no peace to the soul. Sant Kabir tells us that the soul is a Conscious entity and cannot receive comfort from any material article. All the mighty efforts of science and technology have not been able to bring happiness to the people. The more man advances materially, the more he finds himself drifting into a state of continual restlessness and despair. Obtaining worldly possessions only brings grief and sorrow, and the person ends up indulging in pride and greed. Not only that, but then he has to guard all these possessions!

This is the *Kali Yuga* (Dark Age) of high scientific and technological advances; yet Sant Kabir says that man has made little, if any, progress towards the discovery of the basic Truths of his life and the after-life. Most people are, as He terms it, *'Spiritually blind'*. This does not mean that the person is without eyes, but rather that his Inner Eye (The Third, or Single Eye) is not yet opened to reveal the Inner Mysteries of the Divine Light and Sound.

There is a very interesting story about *Hazrat Ibrahim Adham*, the King of Balkh-Bokhara (now in Afghanistan). He was following the Spiritual Way of life, regularly seeking the company of the holy men in his kingdom. However, being a king, he was surrounded by much wealth and luxury, so much so that he slept on a bed full of fresh, fragrant rose petals.

One night, as he was preparing to retire for the night, he heard a noise on the palace roof. He immediately went up there, but found nothing. Suddenly a man appeared, dressed in very simple clothes, and he began to approach the king.

The king was startled at first to see someone, and wondered who could this man be? He asked him, "What do you want?"

The man stated that he was searching for his lost camels. The king was flabbergasted and amazed to think that someone might expect to find his camels on the top of a palace roof! How possibly could this be? How could anyone even *think* such a thing? *"But in the same way, how possibly can you realize God in your soft bed of flowers!"* the man replied.

This remark came as a shock to the king. He was dumbfounded, and he had no answer. The man had disappeared before he could think of any reply. That made him ponder what was this all about, and what strange words had he heard tonight! He thought and thought over it, and then suddenly he realized that what he wanted to achieve, could not be obtained in the way of life that he was leading.

His angle of vision immediately began to change. He inquired all over his kingdom for someone who could help him to solve the mystery of life and death, but alas! Nobody could complete his inquiries. No matter who he asked or where he travelled, the king could not quench his thirst. Eventually he came all the way to India where he began a long search of many cities, until at long last he reached the Great Saint, Kabir Sahib.

The king was flabbergasted and amazed to think that someone might expect to find his camels on the top of a palace roof!

"But in the same way, how possibly can you realize God in your soft bed of flowers!" the man replied.

This world is a place of suffering and pain; yet man exclaims, "Sweet is this life! Who knows of any other?" Were the person to carefully ponder his condition, he would hasten to save himself and ensure that he would not have to keep coming and going in this physical body.

Kabir Sahib says, "If one looks around at all the world, he would find that no one is really happy." Everyone in this world is sad and worried. "I went everywhere, from North to South, from East to West, but everyone I met was full of sorrow and unhappiness. *I have not seen even one person who is truly happy!*" Some are unhappy because they have no money, or due to some disease, many grieve for their spouse, parents, or children. Possessions can vanish overnight, the health fails, the supply of wealth disappears, the children present all kinds of problems, or the unhappy spouse complains. One finds no peace within, although God is present in him, because there are a number of worldly things present. Everyone's ambitions, hopes and dreams seem unstable and frustrating. All mankind suffers with one thing or another. There appears to be an atmosphere of depressing gloom.

"Except for the Godman, no one is without worry and fear," says Sant Kabir. As more and more of the material objects take over one's life, the voice of Spirituality becomes less and less. In this resulting chaos, people's souls tend to be very restless. There may be tremendous inventions and accomplishments of great commendation, but there have not been any achievements whatsoever in the arena of knowledge of the soul. The great ocean depths have been explored and the highest mountains have been climbed, but very few have cared to find their own Truth.

God showers His Unbounded Grace on all alike, just like the rain falls the same everywhere. The valleys, however, get filled up because they are 'empty', whereas the mountains remain dry, filled up as it were, with themselves. The more life changes, the greater is man's restlessness, and as science advances faster and faster, more changes come. Especially in the large cities, nothing remains the same even for a few days.

How can anything which is perishable even hint evidence of the Imperishable? On the other hand, Sant Kabir knew the subtle art of reading that which is not written. Many of the world's Scriptures have already been lost and many more will be lost, but the Truth will remain the same forever. Those Who know about God become silent. If They have written anything, it is always pointing towards the Silence within.

Sant Kabir explains that in order to have true knowledge, one must know himself. "Even if a person were to gain everything in the world and then have the knowledge of it all, if he doesn't know his own soul, *he knows nothing and his life has been wasted!"*

A person may have all the outer knowledge, but he has no information about the soul. Man does not know about the soul, its identity or its source. On the basis of knowing the soul, one acquires the knowledge about how the whole Creation is working. Sant Kabir explains that people are restless and worried, because they are separated from God. Man has forgotten about the Fatherhood of God and the brotherhood of his fellow-beings. A person who is not aware of the true value of himself is the most foolish person. People spend their precious breath to obtain power and fame, but all to no purpose.

With all his wits about him, man is blindly groping in the dark and cannot find the Way of Light. He turns to his preachers and religious teachers to no avail. Sant Kabir pointedly asks, "How possibly can the illiterate person teach others to become literate? How can one who is Spiritually blind himself lead others to the Light? The Priests and other Preachers only try to guess the Inner Secrets of the Holy words. People carelessly follow those who have no Practical Experience of the Creator."

When the True Master comes into this world, He offers right understanding to the people as long as He is in the physical body, but after the passing of this Blessed Soul, the populace once again by sheer habit, falls back into its careless, worldly ways.

Sant Kabir says that the mind is constantly wasting away its priceless moments through the sense enjoyments. "People kill time!" The spirit is not yet the master of the house in which it lives.

He continues, "The person wastes his total life and then he dies, thinking that this is the ultimate life for him to enjoy. Some people feel that enjoyment in life is to be intoxicated with drink, and to eat the best possible foods (the Epicurean belief of 'Eat, drink, and be merry!') but these same people totally forget that they will die one day. Man thinks that he has won everything in this world by having all kinds of riches and luxuries, but he loses all when he leaves them behind at the time of death! Even the body itself is lost, because the physical body which has been loaned by Kaal at the time of one's birth, has to be returned."

Sant Kabir explains these temporal ways of people. "The whole world keeps saying that this possession belongs to me, me, and only me!" This is *my* spouse, this is *my* car, *my* house, *my* land! "But this kind of person never actually fulfills any of his desires, because they keep growing by leaps and bounds." The more a person has, the more he wants. Desires grow greater by attachment to these material things. In his quest to gain more and more, man loses himself in them, forgetting totally himself and the Overself, Almighty God.

Sant Kabir points out that as long as one says "This is mine!" none of the Real Work gets done. On the contrary, when all of the "Mine! Mine!" is finished, then the Lord Himself looks after all the needs of the devotee. The person then becomes more pure, and God gives him the Inner knowledge of the Beyond, granting him salvation from life and death. Sant Kabir reiterates this, saying that the person who gives up all desires, and detaches himself from the worldly attractions while living in this world, is the only one who can know the Truth and the Creator.

He uses the illustration of a person's ship crossing the Ocean of worldly existence and says, "Whoever wins in the worldly way will sink, and whoever loses (turns away from) the world will, with the Grace of the Master, cross over this Ocean of worldly mirage. Thus, one should direct his attention all the time towards God or the Master "

#5-1 Illusion: The Long Sleep of the Soul

Sant Kabir defines *Illusion* as being something that seems to be there, but is not. It is a Deception, a mirage. As long as one is in the material, physical body, that is called *being in the clutches of desire and its attractions*, because the physical body has the five sense organs of the eyes, ears, nose, mouth, and skin. From these outgoing faculties, the attention gets drawn to the outside attractions, opening the way for desire. In turn, a passion of 'wanting' things comes about, bringing with it greed, attachment, and ego.

With reference to worldly attachments, Sant Kabir explains that since birth, many mirages have enveloped the person, and with age this covering of Illusion gets thicker and more dense. Desire literally overpowers him until it becomes his owner, because day and night he is engulfed in this 'wanting'. All of this put together, is called *Maya*, or Illusion. Maya engages all the person's attention only in thinking about worldly attractions. Sant Kabir says, "It is like a vicious circle where Illusion remains always as the dearly beloved, and the person who was indulging in the attractions of Illusion, goes into hell."

Maya (Illusion) is in direct connection with the five senses and the five outgoing faculties. They are grouped together, and they work together. Kabir Sahib explains that even with all that, Illusion does not leave the person as long as he is in the physical body. Illusion becomes the 'winner' over him, by not allowing him to direct his attention inward to realize God.

Sant Kabir says that on the other hand, Maya stands at the threshold of the Saint, begging His forgiveness, and seeking His mercy and Grace. "Maya requests forgiveness, even rubbing its nose on the ground in supplication."

This is a very subtle thing to understand. Actually Illusion, is like a position, occupied by a god or a goddess (lower than the human body on the scale of the species). Just like the person occupying the post of a prime minister gets replaced after a period of time, that soul who is occupying the post of 'Maya' also departs, and another soul then takes over that post. Illusion is, therefore, just a 'job' position for a soul doing its work under Kaal.

In the same way, the souls that occupy the posts of Brahma, Vishnu, and Shiva also work under Kaal, but the names of those posts never change. When their time is finished, another Brahma replaces the first Brahma, another Vishnu replaces the first Vishnu, and so on. Sant Kabir says that actually Illusion prays day and night to the Living Master that somehow it should obtain a human body, because only in the human body can the soul occupying this position of Illusion come under the protection of the Living Master, and go back unto God.

In many, many verses, Sant Kabir reveals how the whole world is hopelessly caught in the web of this Maya. The world is but a dream seen with open eyes, because one's involvement is so intense that he forgets himself. The attention can work, unfortunately, only in one direction. It is quite a pitiful state of the soul that is described, telling how the precious life given by Almighty God is shamelessly frittered away. Nearly everyone throws their life away, needlessly on mere trifles.

Sant Kabir says that the first twelve years (the childhood) of the person's life are just spent in playing, without even a thought of the Creator. The next thirty years are indulged in outer gatherings, possessions of the world and fulfilling desires of children, spouse, parents, friends, and career. Immersed in name and fame, the person has totally forgotten that one day he must die, and he has never remembered God at all. Thus, *people actually forget to remember God!* Most of a person's life has passed, by the time he realizes that he will not live forever! People live as if they are never going to die.

Whoever is constantly aware of death, however, cannot forget God. The earth is a resting place only. Where was the person before birth and where will he be after death? This party on earth lasts only for a few days; yet in this short span, people cling to things that are, and also to things that are not. They clutch not only wealth and possessions, but also their dreams, hopes, and desires. The person worries about the past, the present, and the future. If he were to carefully look into his mind, he would find that it is filled with anxieties that no longer exist. Something that happened ten years ago still rankles in his heart. Or perhaps he is thinking about something that may happen ten years from now.

Thus, his worries and anxieties increase many times in this way. And for whom does he worry? For the husband, the wife, the relations, the children, the parents, the friends that one just happens to meet on life's journey. People involve themselves completely in them, and take upon themselves all sorts of anxiety on their behalf. All these outer affairs, when the real concern of recalling one's true Home is never pondered!

The world will be taken away from the person, but the web of his actions will remain with him. He will die, but the world will no longer be for him. However, whatever he did in the world will follow him just like shadows. His actions will hound him for infinite births. When a person dies, his dreams remain behind, but all that he did in these dreams will go along with him. In this bargain, many things turn out to be expensive. If the person were to keep in his mind that the world is only a resting place for a short time, then almost all of these actions would stop by themselves.

Nobody can be one's very own in this world. All unions here are false meetings. Separation is the Truth, but these meetings are nothing more than dreams. The only true union can be with God. Sant Kabir says that one can only be the bride of Ram (God). There alone will the thirst be quenched and the anguish of separation ended. But before that happens, the worry and unrest will continue.

Sant Kabir has painted a vivid picture of the whole world asleep--the rich, the poor, those who are intellectual and those who are illiterate, because they have no awareness of themselves. Each man's soul is at the mercy of the mind, which is itself at the mercy of the senses, which in turn are being dragged around by the sense-enjoyments.

Kabir Sahib tells us that those who pursue the intellect lose themselves even more than the others, for although the masses are lost in the senses, yet through the intellect one can get more deeply involved in both the senses as well as the intellect. On the other hand, it is only the intellect that can help one to understand the true state of affairs, which is that the soul is a Conscious entity, and that the greatest aim as human beings is to realize oneself and God. The true aim of the soul is to rejoin the Lord.

A person is rich only if he can take something with him after death. However, anything that can be measured by volume or weight cannot be taken along after death. Whatever can be measured is prone to disintegration. It is temporary and an Illusion. When one has wealth or position, he can be measured and valued, such as a person worth a million dollars, or a person who is a president. But how can one determine the value of someone who has nothing except God?

Both the mind and Maya, the main ingredients of the world of Illusion, are one. The outside world is the measure, and the inside mind is the measurer. The person sees with his physical eyes only what he can evaluate. Everyone knows that meditation leads to bliss, but this happiness has no market value. It cannot be sold or bought. In their own way, people always want to know the price of what they can attain in this world, and the same applies to the Spiritual arena, but the joy experienced during meditation cannot be measured in the world of value and price.

Sant Kabir emphasizes many times that one can only learn about the Inner Truth from Someone Who has Experienced the Spiritual Reality Himself. One cannot be awakened by someone who is himself sleeping. Only an Awakened Soul can awaken others. "Father or mother cannot assist you; nor can friends and relations. They may suffer in sympathy with you, but they cannot help you, for they are also fast asleep, and are being helplessly looted just like you."

Wealth and wisdom offer no relief, for this is the general condition of the scholarly and the illiterate, the rich and the poor. People don't realize that God lives right within the human body. The Spiritually 'blind' one does not know it, because he is caught in the delusion of Deception.

Kabir Sahib says that "Everyone is sleeping in a drugged state." People lose their most valuable possessions, and tragically do not even realize that this is happening. They are so engrossed in the worldly enjoyments that whatever knowledge of righteousness they might have gained, is quickly pushed aside.

Wherever He went, Sant Kabir saw that everyone was busy only in the hustle and bustle of this world. He saw many different towns and scenes, but they were all without the remembrance of God. He concludes that without seeing any true devotee with the constant Sweet Remembrance of God, it was all just like a wilderness for Him. "When people are in the Temple, they are different from when they are in their shop. In the Temple, tears of adoration are shed, unlike the behaviour of people in everyday life."

He comments on this as follows, "A hut where the fragrance of Love is immense, and where the Remembrance of the Saint exists, is the most adorable place, pious and clean. On the other hand, if there are beautiful palaces without Love, and without the sweet remembrance of *Hari* (the Creator), those places should be put to fire because all bad things are being done there. Let those places be burnt, where the Holy Name of God is not practised!"

Divine Love exists between the soul and God. In Love, one forgets everything. Wherever one talks of God, that very place becomes like a garden. If there is no remembrance of the Lord, that place remains a jungle. One who is tied up in the affairs of the world cannot ascend to the Higher Spiritual level.

Kabir Sahib continues. "As long as one has no recognition of the Godman, the senses and the mind cannot be stilled. When one comes to the Master Who gives the Recognition of God, then that person becomes free from the attachment of all these sorrows. Those people who do rituals, rites, and blind dogmas indulge in sorrow and pain all through their lives. They are the ones who never come to the Master."

Sant Kabir is describing the Reality of this world, about life and death, and how the *Jiva* (the embodied soul) lives and then dies, and ultimately is reborn again, a process which has been going on for aeons of years. That person keeps dying and taking birth again, and then dying only to again take birth. That unlucky soul has not come into contact with the human Pole where God is manifested as the Master. Those people never finish their endless desires, which usually grow more and more as life goes on. Actually, those same people work very hard in order to realize those ambitions.

When some of the desires are fulfilled, the person gets so much engrossed in the love of those desires as possessions, that he subsequently becomes attached to them. In other words, his give-and-take, his debit-and-credit, grows by his actions and the resultant reactions, in thought, word and deed, and this keeps bringing him back into the world. It is the law of nature that as one thinks, so he becomes. One goes where he is attached, regardless of whether he goes into a human body or an animal body.

He compares the body to be like a prison for the soul, which is confined in it like a bird in the cage. The bird does not know better and loves the cage, and sings its praises constantly, as well as sweet songs of attachment to the earth. If, however, the bird tastes the Truth and the cage is shattered, then it is free to fly away to its Real Home in Sach Khand. Those are the most rare and fortunate ones who escape from this world of Illusion. As long as one does not drink of this Divine Nectar, the Wheel of Birth and Death will go on revolving endlessly, and liberation from this prison-house of the body will be no more than an empty dream.

Kabir Sahib tells us that when one sleeps soundly, often he has dreams, and they seem so real that when he gets up in the morning, he can't imagine that it was only a dream. It is hard to differentiate whether it was real or not. In a similar way, everyone forgets all about the Story of Life which is just like a dream. He says that man has gotten into the state of only a dream, but he must realize that it is not Reality.

Sant Kabir tells us repeatedly that the knowledge of the soul is far away from the knowledge of the mind and the intellect. Spiritual knowledge cannot be known by the mind, because it is not a subject of hearing and listening. It is the definite subject of Seeing and Experiencing for oneself. The soul needs that Divine Connection with the Oversoul.

One must catch hold of the Truth, which is the Ultimate Goal. It is necessary to go into the study of this, in order to fully understand it, and then to practice on it. All other efforts are useless, Kabir Sahib reveals, because reading all the Scriptures and doing their recommended rites and meaningless rituals will not vanquish the five deadly foes. Reading outer books only serves to keep one away from Truth and Reality, because the mind becomes busy in these outer methods. Sant Kabir says very firmly, "When the mind and the intellect become still, then the soul can have the Divine Darshan of Almighty God."

The soul cries out that the worldly Delusions have stolen all the internal wealth of the awakened intellect, and from that intellect the soul would have Loved its Creator. Illusion has also taken away the ability to think clearly; otherwise the soul would have realized the knowledge of the Beyond. Kabir Sahib illustrates this condition of the person and how Illusion, attachment, and desire do all kinds of trickery.

"What a pity that the moth knows that if it goes towards a burning lamp, it will be burned, but the fatal attraction of that fire emits such an irresistible pull that even knowing that it is going to die, still it goes determinedly into the flames. God has given man a gift of the intellect, to decide what is right and what is wrong, but even knowing that he lives in a perishable world, he plans for *the forever*." Such is the Illusion of life!

He says that in exactly the same way, the love between man and woman creates lust, and then attachment is born, each one being possessive of the other. Gold (possessions) and relations let man totally forget his Higher Self, just like the moth forgets his death in the attraction of the fire. These are the things that will become the cause of his 'death'. Without man taking any advantage of this invaluable earthly life granted by God for the purpose of obtaining the Supreme Inner Treasure, the opportunity of his lifetime becomes lost. If one comes to the Master, and that only happens with the Grace of Almighty God, that Godman will put him in His Lap and take him across the worldly Ocean of Illusion.

Kabir Sahib also illustrates the grand Illusion of life as seen through the eyes of a mother. She happily observes her child growing day by day, but does not realize that the very child to whom she is loving and cherishing, will one day be taken away. Yama (the Agent of Death) overlooks all this, and just laughs at her simple ignorance, because he knows that eventually the child will be his 'food' to eat (meaning that the child will remain under the great influence of Illusion which is created by Kaal). The mother is not aware that day by day, the child's life is *reducing*. She does not know that the child, instead of adding anything to his age, is really losing it year by year. The child is actually becoming younger day by day, rather than becoming older!

Death gives its first knock on the day of one's birth. The day Brahma started his work, Shiva started his also. Sant Kabir points out that God is forgotten to him who does not remember death. Death should be the focal point of one's life, for there is nothing more certain than death. At the time of death, all events pass before the person, just like a dream. Did he really live, or was it just a dream? *It is truly a dream, but dreamed with open eyes!* It is a dream because it is a state of imagination: it consists of thoughts, and thoughts are nothing but Illusion. The characteristic of a dream is that it is here one moment, and gone the next, and at the time of death, all is lost! All Power fails at the moment of death, and this is why people make such efforts not to remember death.

In this world, nothing is one's own: everything belongs to the Almighty. What is there, then, to accompany the person? The moment that the soul leaves the body, the earthly possessions become of no consequence. Sant Kabir says that most people are so much engrossed in the web and clutches of Illusion, they find that they are unable to make their own family and friends happy. This 'wanting' of more and more possessions, and its resultant general dissatisfaction seem to be like a circle, with no way out.

He says that people care the least for the higher values in life, and He notes that Spiritual ignorance comes to kings and paupers alike. Both wail that they do not have sound sleep due to worldly disturbances and unfulfilled desires. "In Spiritual ignorance, one cannot sleep in peace." This disease will remain, however, as long as one does not go inside.

Sant Kabir gives many examples of worldly Delusion. He says, "Life and wealth are like the sunshine which continuously changes its path according to the direction of the sun. In the same way, the condition of man is that one moment he is happy when things go according to his plan, but the rest of the time he is miserable. All through life he is in this pursuit, wasting his precious time by chasing after worldly things, which bring him no happiness. What good is it if one loses his life pursuing temporary worldly objects?"

He continues, "I have not seen anyone who has taken the human birth and is happy. Whoever has the body, is not happy. Whoever I saw, was sad and sorrowful. Everyone is unhappy on account of either the physical body, illness, want of money, or the cruelty of the mind."

"Therefore," He asks, "what shall I pray for, when nothing is permanent? What shall I ask of God? We are in a place that is not our own. Nothing here is lasting, not even the body we have been given." Kabir Sahib says that our body is made of matter, which is perishable. People don't want to realize that one day the body will die. He gives the example that just like music that is hidden in the strings of an instrument; yet melodies flow when the strings are touched. In the same way, one cannot see Almighty God residing in the body, and yet the Lord is present in each and every atom of Creation.

He says very simply that if one prays for heaven or for the realm of Shiva, it will all be a waste of time and life. Why? Because "neither Shiva nor *Indra* (the King of Heaven) have seen the Truth of God." If one truly wants the Treasure of Divinity in himself and to know about God, he should renounce all attachments and surrender himself to the Godman. Then he will have the Power to know himself and God.

Kingdoms and riches, along with their resulting attachments and bonds, do not help anybody at the end of life. The warrior on the battlefield, however, will reach the Ultimate Truth because he is willing to stake his all. He isn't afraid of danger. It is impossible for this warrior to forget death: it stands at his door every moment. And he who remembers his death, begins to be reminded of God also. Remembrance of God is the only antidote to the remembrance of death. It is, but natural, to remember God when the thought of death grabs hold of someone. He who flees is defeated already, because he has not accepted the challenge. A true warrior enters right into the heart of danger. Where death stands lurking, he accepts the invitation.

Again and again Sant Kabir says, "My brother! Listen carefully! Money, possessions, and properties will never give you any peace, because they are made of Illusion. Why do you pray for worldly attachments, which will never help you? Rather they won't let you go inwards, becoming a great source of sorrow. Go inward and find the Treasure of God lying latent right in your body. Catch hold of that with the Grace of the Master, and then this Treasure will bring you great peace. Your coming and going in the world will be ended forever."

Another example that He uses is that of the bird called the *Hans* (Swan) in Indian mythology. It is a very respected and glorified bird, which is the symbol of the pure, immortal soul. Sant Kabir illustrates that the *Hans* is representative of the soul, which ultimately merges back into its Source, Almighty God. "O man! The body will become food for Kaal. The *Hans* (the immortal soul) lives forever, but the perishable body will go into the mouth of Kaal."

The Saints come to warn mankind not to become entangled in this land of Kaal, the Negative Power. None of the activities that man does in this world are of any real benefit. They only serve to earn money for one's family and to fulfill the inclinations of worldly pleasures, but one knows in his heart of hearts that nothing will go with him. He can take nothing along with him when he leaves. The only activity of lasting value is the Spiritual practice revealed by a Master. Two things alone are one's permanent companions: the Master and His Gift of the Holy Naam.

Sant Kabir describes the worldly relations one has with his body and its surroundings, such as father, mother, brothers, sisters, friends, and other relatives. He maintains that one has made his own world with these people, and this is the Illusion, or mirage, of life. They are created around him, along with other worldly attachments, such as possessions.

Kabir Sahib asks, "To whom does the son belong, and to whom does the father belong? All these relations are linked with us only for their own selfish ends. None of them belong to us. Neither mother, father, brother, sister, wife, nor husband will accompany us at the time of our death. We feel that our relatives are our very own, but we forget totally that the body is not even our own. All human relationships must terminate at the grave. The dying person's soul departs alone and unbefriended. Such is the outcome of all this worldly love and ambition!"

Sant Kabir says that when someone close to us dies, we say that we have lost a worldly possession (my mother, my friend, etc.), not understanding that all these worldly relations as well as all possessions are transitory. We are totally engrossed in this worldly life of our belongings, properties, wealth, families, appetites for material progress, and position in life.

"If we look around us," He continues, "we find that most of our interests and contacts are all perishable. When circumstances change for the worst, often our friends and relatives desert us. So long as we are prosperous, people are drawn to us for their own selfish reasons, but these same people abandon us when fortune no longer smiles. They do not keep company with us all the time, and most of them leave us during the middle of our lives. Even those who are considered most sincere leave us at the time of our physical departure from this world."

Lord Kabir advises us to look still more closely. "If one reflects further, it will be found that even this body, which we consider to be our very own, leaves us at the time of death. How can anything which is of a temporary nature give eternal peace and bliss? That can only come from something that is Conscious."

He continues, "Attachments become the cause of all our sorrows and they make our life miserable day and night. The Lord is our Creator, Who is the All-in-All, the Enticer, the Sat Guru, without Whom we cannot have peace and contentment in us. After knowing ourselves and having the Nectar of His Holy Naam, we cannot live for even a moment without Him. This is a true fact and the Truth of all the Truths, that He is in our body and this is the only place we can find Him. After having the Grace of the Master, we cannot bear to be separated from Him."

Kabir Sahib says that day and night the person wastes his breaths, which are priceless. How beautifully He tells that Almighty God has granted man a golden chance in the human birth to know himself and to go back to God, but how cleverly the Negative Power, in the form of Illusion, steals from his precious breaths.

Sant Kabir describes how the Negative Power exerts control over the five senses, and they in turn drag the attention out into this world of Illusion. The sense of Sight drags the attention outwards and creates inclinations, which in turn create lust. Kabir Sahib gives us the worldly example of how the elephant hunter makes a paper decoy in the form of the female elephant, knowing that the male will run blindly to it in the hope of fulfilling his lustful cravings. The male then falls into a deep trap and for the rest of his life, he is a slave under the iron goad.

In a similar way, the monkey comes into the web of the hunter (which is the mind), even though he knows that he will get caught and remain a slave for the rest of his life. The hunter puts a few pieces of *gram* (roasted chick peas) into a large earthenware pot with a small opening. The monkey comes and because gram is his favourite food, he puts his hand into the pot to grasp them. However, with his fist full of the grams, he finds that now he cannot pull his hand out of the pot. In greed, he won't let go of the grams and yet he cannot pull out his fist. The mind is so strong in greed for that food that he cannot resist holding onto his prize, and for this he pays the price and gets caught! For the rest of his life, he is a slave to his captor and is made to dance from house to house for a few pennies.

Then Kabir Sahib gives the example of how the parrot is caught. The hunter has a reed trap in which he puts its favourite food. As soon as the parrot enters the trap to eat, it is caught, but with the parrot's movement, the food falls down. The hunter usually keeps the trap above some water and when the parrot looks down and sees this, its fear of falling into the water keeps it there. Actually it is able to fly away, but greed and subsequent fear make it paralyzed, and thus it becomes caught.

"That soul which keeps itself lost in the nine portals of the body, can never realize Eternal bliss." In other words, all the senses are so strong that they cannot easily come under control at all, unless one prays from the core of his heart. "The prayer is heard if it comes from the core of the heart. The person turns towards the Godman, and with His Grace, becomes fearless."

Kabir Sahib describes and unfolds the nature of the mind, how one has come under the clutches of Illusion of the senses and attachment. "We want all kinds of worldly things so that we can have a comfortable life, but we are not aware that God Almighty watches us every moment, and He knows what is best for us. When we demand all these worldly enjoyments, we do not know what we are asking from God. These things sometimes affect in reverse, becoming the cause of our sorrows." He is describing our helplessness in asking for things from the Creator. He says that we should humbly request God to "Please give us whatever is best for us!"

"God resides in us but we do not put any thought towards Him, not realizing that He is in us. We forget Him totally.

Instead, we bring all these petty, perishable things in front of us. There is no way that God, the Creator, will manifest in us because we cannot see Him in our present condition. It seems that the more we desire happiness in this world, the more we feel disappointed. The reason for this is that the real happiness is within us. All joy and peace lie within. The pleasures and comforts of this world last only for a short time--as long as our attention is linked with them, but if our soul is free from the influence of the mind and the senses, it will gain communion with God, Who is All-Powerful. Only then can it attain everlasting happiness."

The ego spreads its net of hopes ever before the person, drawing him further and further onwards. The person tries to cover his weaknesses and hide his faults. The public face of a so-called 'successful' person is different from his private face. He is smiling and laughing in public, but alone in his own room, he cries. After attaining all, there is still no satisfaction. One can only be satisfied if God is pleased with him. A person attaining everything, remains yet unhappy. True happiness, therefore, has nothing to do with who one is or what he possesses. Rather, it has everything to do with one's connection with the Supreme Lord, his relationship with Almighty God. Having the Grace of God, decides whether one has attained favour in His eyes. When one sees God working everywhere, then he has attained His Grace. Never for a single moment is He out of the heart's remembrance.

Sant Kabir says that everyone, everywhere, is in a state of continuous Delusion. This Delusion begins with a misconception of the permanence of the human body. When the person, by a practical process of self-analysis, gets an actual out-of-body Experience, then he knows that the body is not something permanent, and that it has to be vacated one day, whether his soul wants to leave it or not. When a person dies, however, Illusion right away leaves because the body is no longer functioning, and thus the sense organs no longer work. The source of the body's Power, which is the soul or the Consciousness, has left.

"Ever ready to let man forget his death is the mind!" This pitiful condition of humanity in the world is described by Sant Kabir. He says that everyday we see people being buried or burnt to ashes. "These bodies are the same ones who used to eat rich delicacies, without even giving a thought as to the other world."

He asks, "O man! What are you doing in slumber? Rise up, awake, and sing the praises of the Lord! Do His Simran! The day is coming when you are going to sleep and won't get up again."

Lord Kabir reminds the people again and again that this life span has to finish one day, sooner or later. Each breath brings one closer to the great final change called death. He says that just as a bird makes its nest only for the time being and then leaves, in the same way, one's own life span is not permanent or eternal.

He intensely describes one's physical condition in old age, when tears start falling from the eyes. The person feels repentant, but now there is no time to make amends. It is too late! Sant Kabir says, "O unfortunate Jiva (soul). You cannot speak now, at the end of your life. The thin Thread of Light that connects the physical body with the soul (the *Silver Cord*) has been broken, and the *Hans* (the soul) has flown away."

He, whose home is in the grave, should be crying over the fear and pain of death! "You should wake up and get up! From Whom you are separated, you should be hankering to again become as One. You should understand these noble things. Awaken from this slothfulness, and become more Conscious!"

He says, "Day by day, hour by hour, time is being wasted. The body begins to crumble. Death stalks like a hunter and a murderer. The Lord of Death is counting each and every day, every hour of the hour! He sees that your life is reducing by sickness and weakness. Death *will* come, and you will be yanked out of the body. You will be dragged to the Court of Dharam Rai and asked to account for your deeds! At that time, whoever can tell you of a Way to Salvation?"

Sant Kabir then speaks to a certain category of people who have much wealth and status. "You have so much pride that you think yourself to be great, just like you are working for the king's court. Your ego makes you act as if you are drunk, but you are in fact very arrogant, falling badly when you see a beautiful woman, or gold. No doubt you have obtained these things, but at the cost of the Real Aim of your life, which is to know God, and to have humility. The possessions you have gathered are not going to stay with you forever, and in time they will leave you, or you will be made to leave them. Therefore, you should not have any pride in these things!"

He further says to them, "O ignorant people! What have you earned all your life? Your earnings are not true. They are full of greed, because you have constantly lied and you are full of ego. Your life has consisted of running around in the Illusion of the world. This is the way you have spent your precious breaths. The clock is ticking away and in the end, the Lord of Death will snatch you. O naive person! The Yam Doots will drag you out of the body, and take you to Dharam Rai, where you will undergo terrible punishment according to your deeds! You have lived a life of four days, and you have seen and done all the worldly things. You have gathered a lot of possessions, but nothing will you take along!"

He reveals that the human body is alive as long as the Life Impulse, which is the soul, stays in it. People respect the body as long as it is functioning but when the soul leaves, that body is worth nothing. Sant Kabir gives the description that as long as the wick is in the lamp, and the lamp has oil, it will burn. The 'wick' of course, is the soul, the 'lamp' represents the body, and the 'oil' describes the breath of life.

He continues, "When the wick burns, it can give Light and Power to the entire human body." As long as this is happening, the person can understand and Discriminate the difference between right and wrong. When the oil slowly, slowly finishes and the wick is burned out, the soul leaves and then the body dies, just like the lamp turns off. The gist of this allegory is that the soul is the Light and the soul is the Power. The soul is the Essence of God Himself.

"O Man! As long as there is day (Light) in you, take advantage of that. Consider this very seriously. After the soul leaves, nobody will keep the body even for a moment. This is the only time and the golden opportunity given to you to recognize yourself and the Oversoul. This body is loved and respected by your parents, spouse, and children, but after the Reality is gone and the true Spirit has left the body, then there is nothing but sorrow remaining for them. Whoever has obtained God while in the body, when he dies, there is no sorrow of any kind. He departs very happily because he knows that he is going into the Lap of God."

Sant Kabir asks if there is anybody who can save man from death? But the answer is, "No, none." Man is afraid of death, the last enemy, for several reasons. In the first place, he does not know what death is. Secondly, he has not learned to 'Die While Alive', in the terminology of the Saints. Thirdly, he does not know where he is going after death. Sant Kabir explains that death is just a gateway to life eternal. The soul goes from the Physical world to the Astral.

He describes this world to be like a play of the Negative Power and ultimately everyone, whether child, youth, or aged, has to leave the very body in which he lives. Naturally, all the attachments and treasures which have been gathered such as possessions, kith and kin, relations, friends, and even the body itself, everything is left behind. Yama comes when the life of the person is finished. It doesn't matter if that person is a king or a pauper. Yama takes him away to *Dharam Rai* for reward or punishment according to the person's good and bad deeds.

Sant Kabir advises, "You must come to the Master and remember God; otherwise you are going to be looted half-way." And then He proceeds to tell us what happens after death. "Just see the play of the Negative Power! See what the *Yam Doots* (the Messengers of Death) do to the soul who has not come to the Sat Guru. At the time of death, those Yam Doots drag the soul out of the body, but on the way to Dharam Rai, that soul becomes hungry and thirsty. These scheming Yam Doots provide food and drink, but demand in return the merit of some of the person's good deeds. As a result, all or most of the soul's good merits are looted, and the soul is left with only its bad deeds to present to Dharam Rai. There is absolutely no one to vouch for the soul at that time. Those Agents of Death knowingly take a long time to bring the soul to Dharam Rai for judgement, so that they have time to do their mischief. These are all horrible tricks of the Negative Power."

"Man only wakes up when the merciless iron rod of the Agent of Death strikes him on the head! If one does only bad deeds and keeps his attention always in this world, the Yam Doot will come with his dreaded club, grasp him by the hair, and drag his soul out of the body. The soul, however, is very attached to the body and doesn't want to leave, but the Yam Doot mercilessly yanks out the soul. No one can overcome him. *Even just to see him, the soul begins to tremble!*" No one ever 'awakens' without a blow. True knowledge, however, becomes the 'hammer' that can break the impeding ego into pieces!

Sant Kabir goes on to describe those unlucky people who have not come to the Perfect Master. They tremble in their shoes, terrified at the thought of death. They keep coming and going in this world, never finishing their true Aim in life, because they have not used their Power of Discrimination to realize God. They have forgotten that death ultimately has to come, but they don't have an inkling of Reality and they don't know the Truth of the Holy Naam. "When the devotee practices on the Celestial Music (the Sound Current) and adopts the Teachings of the Master, that Divine Sound (the Unstruck Melody) takes away his fear of death forever."

The Master assures man that he does not die. The process of the physical death of the body is not the death of the soul. The devotee of the Master has an additional concession: the Master comes to take charge of his soul at the time of his physical death. That lucky soul is not met by the Yam Doots, and he happily leaves his body, soaring with the Master into the Beyond. Ultimately the soul realizes its Divine Nature, and sees its Oneness with Almighty God. The Beloved Master accompanies that lucky soul, both here and in the hereafter.

Sant Kabir goes on to refer to a bad habit that many people have. This is the tendency to slander others and gossip about them in thought, word, and deed. He warns, "Even remembering others in this way, one is continuously taking the fires of their sorrows and troubles on his own head. The result is that one is just making his own life more miserable than it already is." When one speaks wrongly of others, one's own credit of goodness flows to the person being wronged. Naturally, the credit balance of good deeds eventually becomes bankrupt, as the person continues to defame others.

Kabir Sahib, acknowledging the soul's terrible plight, prays to Almighty God to have mercy on the whole of humanity. He sees that Delusion has betrayed mankind, and He implores, "O God! You have put a cover of Illusion on people. How possibly can people know You? Please take this cover away, so that mankind can know the Reality. If You don't take it away, how can people even recognize this Delusion?"

He gives the example that everyday in the village, people make butter in their homes. But how does one obtain butter from the milk? If milk is examined, one can never imagine that there is butter in that liquid. The answer is that one has to first churn the milk. In other words, one has to take the Practical Experience from the Scriptures (which are considered as the milk), and bring it into one's life. When the milk is churned, that will produce cream. It means that now one is physically practising what those Holy Books say, not that the person is only reciting from them. People need to receive something practical out of the Books, and then bring this true meaning into their lives.

Continuing on the theme of Illusion, Sant Kabir says that after churning this cream, the butter will come up. In other words, the fruit of one's Spiritual exercises comes by first churning from milk to cream, and then churning the cream into butter. Thereby, the person has got the gist out of the milk. He has now truly realized what the Religious Books are saying. That is why the Masters have said that an ounce of practice is worth tons of theory; otherwise, if one only recites theory for thousands of lifetimes, he will not receive anything.

Sant Kabir says that while in the physical body, the soul's intellect becomes defiled and entangled in the web of Illusion. The soul has forgotten God, and now it has ended up in this pitiful condition. The attention, day and night, becomes fixed solely on worldly desires. The person thinks only about this world and its affairs. Even in dreams, he acts out the fantasies of his desires for wealth and health.

Kabir Sahib is explaining the real condition of the world. He is telling the truth, that everyone is busy day and night, working to improve his status and fame, along with his relationship to the world. He keeps on gathering those worldly things to which he is attached, totally forgetting what will happen to everything when he will suddenly die and leave this body.

Sant Kabir often reminds people that the Lord of Death is not far away to take the soul out of the body. He pointedly asks if one has ever wondered about this body that he wears so proudly. "This body is getting older day by day. Anything that you wear for some time, grows old and tears of itself. So also the body will wear out in due course of time. Why are you so terribly proud of it? One day you have to leave it."

He continues, "O naive person! You are living in a house *which is made of nothing but sand!*"

One of the most amazing facts of human life, and the biggest Delusion of all, is that although one sees people dying all around him, he forgets about his own death. He thinks that he himself shall never have to leave the body. He buries their dead bodies or lights the fire himself, and yet he feels that he is singularly immune to this ordeal.

Sant Kabir advises, "Do not be proud of your body, of the little bones knit together, with just a covering of skin over them. Soon you shall desert it, just like the snake sheds its skin. The life is so short and the body shall just be cast off. What is the body after all? It is only dust, and *unto dust it shall return!*"

Kabir Sahib says that when the Hindus cremate their dead, the body turns into dust. That very same body which was admired so much, becomes just like a heap of ashes. The Muslims, on the other hand, bury their dead and the small ants eat up that beautiful body which used to be highly praised by the people.

He continues, "Your own children will become frightened of seeing your dead body. People will say, 'Hurry up, and take away this corpse!' and without wasting any time, they will take it quickly to the graveyard. Just think! Your own wife who lived with you for many, many years, will see you off at the doorstep, and the rest of your relatives will only see you to the graveyard." (It was the custom at that time that the wife would only accompany the body to the front door, and the male relatives would then carry the body to the gravesite.)

Sant Kabir reminds us that death is inevitable and everyone is going to die for sure. "The world is not going to remember anyone for very long," He cautions. He vividly describes that when the person leaves the body at the time of death, all possessions, treasures, wealth, friends and relatives are left here. The person departs empty-handed.

Giving an example from history, He says that "Lanka (an island south of India) was made of gold, but what did poor Ravan (the King of Lanka) take with him when he left the body?" Sant Kabir emphasizes that outer things have a relationship only with the body, and they must remain here because the body stays here.

"The thief called *Death* carries away in an instant what the fool had been guarding as his own, all through life! There have been so many kings and wealthy people, but they have taken nothing along with them at the time of their physical departure!" All relationships end at the time of death. Sant Kabir compares this to somebody leaving his village. "The person takes nothing, and no one with him. Once he departs, he is ultimately forgotten!"

"Worldly attachments are false and transient. Consider a landowner or a farmer with huge fields of abundant crops. If a drought comes or a fire, all the crops (the person's possessions) are valueless. If a family person abruptly meets with an accident, the family is left utterly alone. A sudden collapse of one's bubble, and he is powerless to do anything!" This is a fact that Sant Kabir is describing, and this is the sad condition of the whole world!

He continues, "This world is so temporary, and all therein die in the same way without any true accomplishment in the field of Spirituality." He sees everyone departing without attaining the true Aim of life, which is self-knowledge and God-realization.

Sant Kabir says to the person, "You have had time in this physical body to complete all your worldly duties. Day by day you are becoming old. Your intellect is not giving you full cooperation. Sometimes you remember things, but sometimes not. Your beautiful eyes are now tired of seeing the world, and your ears are weary of listening to it. Your once-beautiful body has become fragile, and is breaking down. If you think with your God-given sense and intellect, you will discover that you have been covered by Illusion. Your whole life has been spent in looking after worldly responsibilities so successfully. Unfortunately, you have not thought that you might have to leave the body some day."

Sant Kabir is pointing out, "O foolish Person! You have not realized that you have not done anything for the soul, or spirit, which lives in the body. You have never even imagined about this, and you are not aware how pitiful it is that you have wasted your life unnecessarily. You have lost both yourself and your true Aim in this world in your grand forgetfulness that this world will not go along with you. It is just like you are hitting your own foot with an axe, in utter foolishness!"

He continues, "This kind of person doesn't even visit the house where the Saints discourse on God! Instead, he lives only with thieves and persons of evil and worldly ways. He becomes full of lust, anger, greed, desire and jealousy. Not even in a dream can that person practice any compassion, piety, nor any kind of service for the Master."

Sant Kabir says that the house where there is no regard nor interest to know about, or do service for God or the Saint, is considered to be just like a cremation ground, where ghosts and demons dwell. "In other words, maybe you have performed so well all your duties towards your family and this world, but if you have not known your Inner Self (the soul), all your hard efforts to do good in this world are of no consequence. The world for you will finish abruptly with the end of this physical life!"

If it was possible to find true and everlasting happiness in the pleasures of this world, man would never even think about the Lord. People, however, know that they cannot find happiness here. If one looks to the richest person in the world, the healthiest person in the world, a person of great name and fame, is he happy? Perhaps he will be among the most unhappy and miserable ones. Sant Kabir says that unless the soul returns to the Lord, it can never have true peace.

Actually Sant Kabir is describing humanity at large. One's whole world of friends and relations is drowning in the clutches of this worldly mirage. Illusion works like a chilling poison all through life. Instead of being embedded with God's Love, man has filled his body with the evil of desire. Sant Kabir says that throughout the person's life, he keeps going deeper and deeper into this 'wanting of things', thinking that this is the Way to Reality!

Kabir Sahib cautions that everything in Illusion is constantly changing. It is never static or permanent. "As well," He continues, "anything that has a stomach to fill, is Spiritually asleep under the effects of this Deception. Everything is forgotten when the stomach is in question!" This means that all principles are cast aside in consideration of satisfying one's appetite. He says that some people have actually used the Holy Scriptures to earn their living, reciting a few verses here and a few verses there, all in the name of selfishness and greed! These people promise salvation in return for money! He comments, "People love to engage for the whole day in religious disputes, but *they are themselves totally devoid of the Love of God!*"

Sant Kabir uses just about all the imagery that one can think of, telling about the palmists, the fortune tellers, the astrologers; those who know grammar or other languages, and those people who know all the worldly lower Mantras, like mesmerism, black magic, and spells; the emperors and kings who always have many attendants around them; those who dip themselves in perfumes; and still others who boast that they know the Scriptures such as the four *Vedas*, the eighteen *Puranas*, and the *Simritis*, or even the many other subjects of study. Kabir Sahib says that at the end of all this pursuit, they themselves cannot avoid the ultimate death, which patiently awaits each and every person.

He says, "Death has fallen on the whole world, and even the doubting scholars are included in its list. Fear of death, however, does not come near the true devotee who worships God with Love and devotion."

Sant Kabir is describing the distressing condition of how most people pass their time. He says that since birth, people have been involved only in performing worldly duties and obligations. Kaal ordered Maya to go into the world to spread superstitious beliefs that would entangle mankind, to such an extent that now no one truly wants to go back to his Eternal Home. These superstitions are based on questions, fear, ignorance, and suspicion. Everyone is content to exist in this world of pain and sorrow, enticed by the fleeting attractions of the sense pleasures. This is Kaal's vast net to keep the souls captive in his dominions.

Day and night man has used his eyes and ears, and taken so much work from his body to perform certain duties towards his children, parents, friends, and relatives. He has always worked according to the dictates of the mind, and its endless sea of waves.

Sant Kabir comments that, "On whatever people focus their attention, that becomes embedded in the mind. Even when people close their eyes or fall asleep, they keep seeing the same impressions that they have gathered during their wakeful hours. These perceptions make life appear to be superficial."

Kabir Sahib is Lovingly advising people to leave off the temporary pleasures which are obtained from the senses and attachments to the Illusionary world, because there is death in this Illusion. People think that the outer world of the senses is the sole Reality, but this outer world is just a part of the realm of Illusion, being bound by time and subject to its effects.

One's whole life is spent in pursuit of one thing or the other. People are seeking power and wealth for either themselves or their relations. Those in pursuit of intellectual knowledge, are only seeking outer knowledge. All of this cannot help in Spiritual matters, for it will not accompany the soul beyond the grave.

Despite all this emptiness in every aspect, however, man continues to gather all the knowledge of the world throughout his life, so that he can live comfortably and successfully. Sant Kabir says, "Year after year the person has worked for others. Although now he is tired and exhausted from toiling to serve his family and friends, no one remains with him. One by one, they have all left. Either the friends and relations have run away for one reason or another, or else they have died!"

Sant Kabir also talks about attachment, saying that whoever comes into its web, finds it extremely difficult to break free. "It is only a rare person, the Saint, who can recognize attachment for what it really is. The whole world is very much absorbed in this."

He says that attachment is such a great Illusion that not only humans, but also the gods and goddesses from the Nether (lower) Worlds, as well as the Rishis and the Munis, are all under its clutches. "This," He says firmly, "I have seen. In this river of attachment, they keep drowning. It is a brave person who goes against this stream and fights with it. All those who do penance by reading Scriptures are drowned in the net of attachment. The Deception of attachment is everywhere."

No matter whether one is in youth, middle or old age, all have fallen into the snare of attachment to this worldly world and its relations, objects, and even this body. Sant Kabir says, "Now the end condition is coming, when the person is about to die, and death is sitting at the door, like a cat looking at the mouse and licking its lips."

He has also compared the qualities of ego and pride to common dogs. "Whoever makes these 'dogs' into friends, they (the dogs) lick his face because they like that person, and want to involve him at every moment. However, if you make them into the enemy and try to avoid them, they only growl at you. Don't go into the lane where they live, and you won't get bitten!"

Sant Kabir also advises, "Omit ego and pride from your heart. Get rid of them from your body. Don't lower the value of your beautiful face by losing it to pride and ego. Wherever there is pride, there are all kinds of sorrows, questions and superstitions involved. Sadness also comes along with it and this eats up the people. If you have given up all your possessions, but you have not cast out ego, the same ego will loot you and eat you up. Ego has made even the famous Rishis and Munis come under its spell."

Some people try different methods, like narcotics and alcohol, to induce a state of intoxication, thinking that this will afford them some peace of heart. In reference to this Sant Kabir says, "If you drink of this, but you have not had the sweet taste of the Holy Naam (the Holy Word), it will only further lower your Consciousness. Even a tiny Experience of true Love obtained from the Master, will provide what these intoxicants cannot."

There are many types of intoxication in this world. Pride of worldly knowledge is one of them, and Sant Kabir has illustrated this with a story of a very proud and clever young man by the name of *Sarvanand*, who claimed that he had achieved the acme of perfection in the field of Spiritual discussion. This young man enjoyed having debates with other Pundits, and winning over them. He especially liked arguing about religious subjects with the various heads of religions, for he was very learned in all the Holy Books. Wherever he went, he took along his many books. He felt that no one could beat him in debate, so he insisted that people call him '*Sarbajeet*', a name which means 'winner of all'.

One day, he went to see his mother. Puffed up with pride, he did not even pay his respects to her, which is a common courtesy according to Indian culture. Unfortunately, worldly knowledge often encourages pride.

When he entered the house, she called him by his nickname, but since he was completely taken over by his ego, he became upset and told her, "Dear mother, please don't call me by that name. You know that I am such a learned and important man. The entire world is calling me *Sarbajeet*. Everybody respects me like anything because I know so much more than other people. I am always victorious and I have asked everybody to call me Sarbajeet. You should please also call me by that name!"

His mother was very wise, and she understood that he had gone astray with pride, being heavily weighed down with his learning. Only humbleness brings one closer to God. She was a devotee of the Great Kabir Sahib, and she wished her son to come to the correct Path. She lovingly and patiently said, "My dear son, go to Kabir Sahib and discuss Spirituality with Him. If you gain victory over Him, then I will certainly call you by the name Sarbajeet."

The boy immediately put all his Scriptures in a big cart and set out for Kabir Sahib's house. Saints, of course, know what is in each person's heart, and Kabir Sahib immediately understood the purpose of Sarbajeet's visit. The Saint, however, welcomed him and the proud, arrogant young man explained why he had come, mentioning some of the names of the Pundits he had defeated.

Kabir Sahib said very humbly, "Dear friend, let us not waste our time arguing. You are such a learned Pundit. Write down whatever you want and I will sign it. Then you can take it back to your mother." So, happily Sarbajeet wrote down that Sarbajeet has won and Kabir has lost! He told Kabir Sahib to sign the sheet, and the Saint did so.

The boy ran back to his mother, and flourished the paper at her. "Look mother! I have defeated Kabir Sahib and He has given me a certificate!" The mother took the paper, but when she had read it, she exclaimed, "What is this? You had better read it to me!" The proud son became flabbergasted when he saw the paper. He could not believe his eyes because he found the words written, "*Sarbajeet has lost and Kabir has won!*"

In a somewhat faltering voice he said, "Mother, there seems to be some mix-up, but no matter. I will go back and have it written again!" So he dashed off again to Kabir Sahib and told

Him that there had been an error. "Sir, there seems to have been some little mistake. Could the paper please be written again?"

"Yes, by all means!" agreed Kabir Sahib. "Write whatever you want and I will sign it." And again Sarbajeet wrote on the paper that Sarbajeet has won, and Kabir has lost. He wrote very carefully and when he had finished, he read it slowly three times. "Yes! Now it is correct!" he said to himself, and Sant Kabir signed it.

He hurried home to his mother, brandishing the paper in his hand. "Mother! I have the correct paper this time!" She took it, but again it said something else. *"Sarbajeet has lost and Kabir has won!"* He was in total shock! He gasped, "Mother, there is no possibility of a mistake. This time I have read it several times before Kabir Sahib signed it!"

He blamed himself again for a silly error twice made. He could not understand what had happened! Actually, his heart was startled and his ego had become quite a bit down by now. He thought to himself that there must be something more to these events, but he could not understand.

In a very quiet and humble tone, he told his mother that he would go once more to get the right paper. When he arrived for the third time at Kabir Sahib's house, Sarbajeet was ready to listen to Kabir Sahib. In a rather humble tone Sarbajeet related, "Sir, in my heart I know that the first time I came to You, the paper was written correctly. Even the second time, it was right! Kindly explain to me the true meaning of this."

Kabir Sahib was prepared to open Sarbajeet's eyes to the Truth. The Master never belittles a person, but with Love and compassion He makes him understand. Sant Kabir explained, "O Learned Pundit! How can you and I think alike? I say everything on the basis of my personal Experience, and you say everything on the basis of bookish knowledge. Spirituality is not a matter of intellect. Whatever I talk about, *I have seen with my own eyes* and Experienced for myself! Whatever you say, either you have read in the Scriptures, or have heard about it from other people."

Kabir Sahib further told the young man, "I say whatever I have seen with my own eyes, but you speak whatever you have read in the books. I undo the knots of Illusion and doubt of these talks, but you tie them again, creating suspicion and Deception. I instruct the people to stay awake, but you tell them to sleep. I advise them to go further into Spirituality, but you say not to delve into the Inner meanings. Whatever you have not Experienced for yourself, you are guiding them as to what you have only learned from others, or according to your intellect. This is a true example of falsehood!"

When it finally dawned on Sarbajeet that he was in the August Presence of the Great Sant Kabir, he bowed down to His Lotus Feet, begging for Inner knowledge. The Great Saint explained to him that no amount of learning from books could bring a person closer to God. One has to have a Direct Connection with the Divine Light and Sound Current under the Benign Guidance of the Living Master. In this way, the soul receives a Direct Experience of the God Power, and under the Loving Master's Divine Protection, at last the soul reaches its true Home.

How can one who has never seen anything reveal the Inner Truth to others? So, one must keep the Company of He Who has gained knowledge through Experience. Reading, writing, and thinking are all at the level of the intellect, so one must rise above these in order to have some Experience of God. *A Saint is One Who has Seen the Lord!* Therefore, if one sits with the Saint, he will also be able to understand God, and ultimately to be One with Him. This subject is known only by an Enlightened Soul, not by an intellectual. Only a Realized Soul can tell others how He became One with God, and He can Guide many more to also attain Him. The man who cannot see, will say that these things do not exist, but He Who Sees, can take people by the hand and show them first-hand.

There are many other types of pride including that of good health, body, mind, position of power and possessions, which

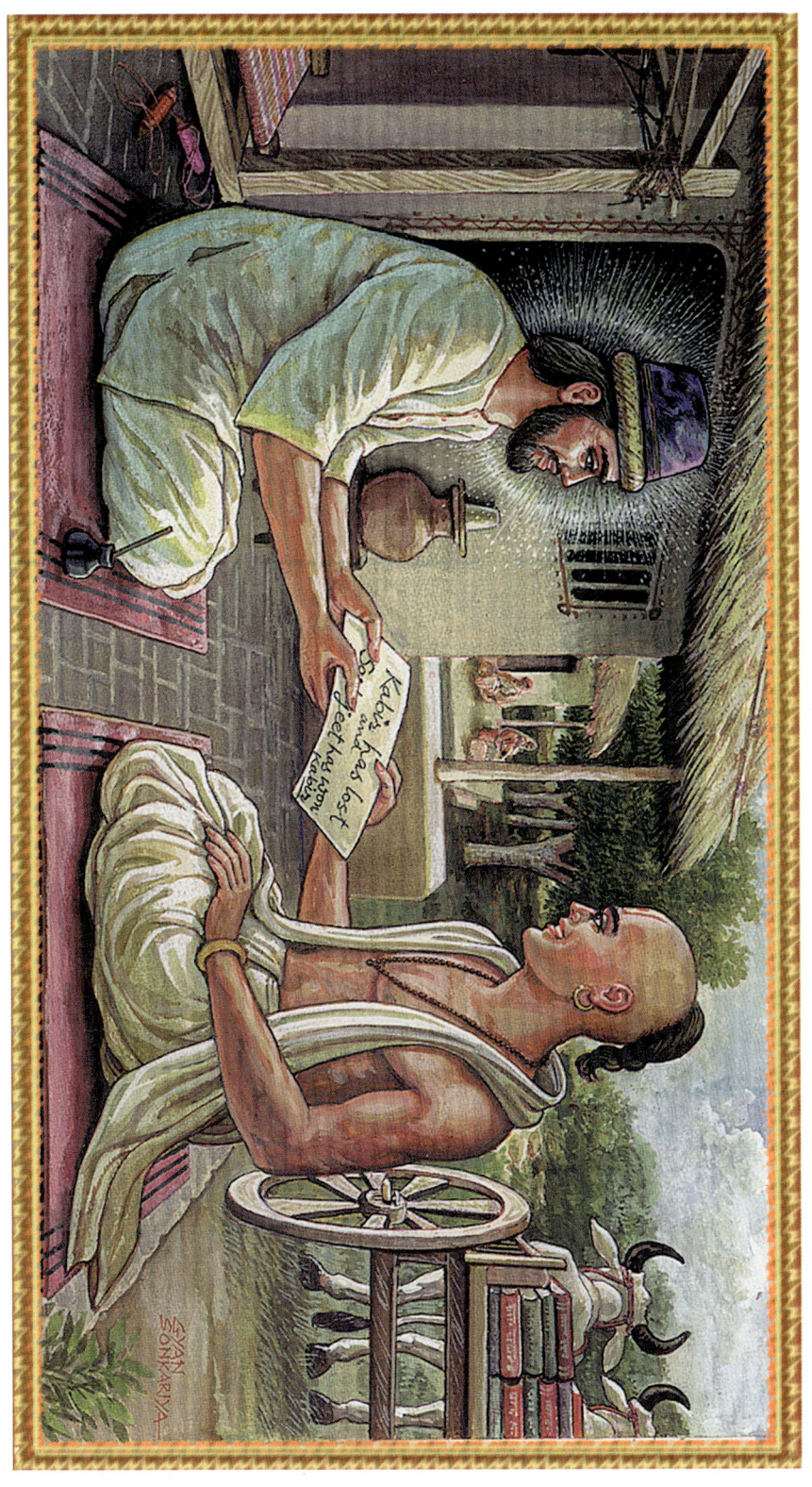

Sant Kabir said very humbly, "Dear friend, let us not waste our time arguing. You are such a learned Pundit. Write down whatever you want and I will sign it. Then you can take it back to your mother." So happily Sarbajeet wrote down that Kabir has lost and Sarbajeet has won!

make people blind in their intoxication. Knowledge makes people puffed up because their ego inflates. Still again, power of authority corrupts the mind and the body. How possibly can a person come out of a state of authority, to listen attentively to the Holy Sound Current, and to become One with God?

Kabir Sahib continues to discuss the fragile condition of the human body, and says that time is slipping by so quickly. He compares the condition of the body to 'the stars that vanish in the morning sky.' When day breaks, all the stars seem to fade away, dwarfed by the brightness of the morning sun. People don't even realize where the stars have gone.

"In the same way, the life is passing and day by day, hour by hour, time is being wasted. No one can realize where the time has gone. Death stalks like a hunter and a murderer." In other words, death slowly comes upon the person by stealth, never leaving him for a moment, always hovering around his head, waiting for its chance.

Sant Kabir discusses the delicateness of the human body very simply in layman's language so that everybody can understand. Giving examples found in the village life, He describes a clay water pot that will eventually fall and crumble with continued use.

Exactly this is the condition of one's own body. "The body becomes, with time, quite brittle. The vision and hearing deteriorate, and the person cannot even walk properly. The body begins to crumble with age, but the person doesn't even realize this. When man becomes very feeble in health, he tries to somehow regain the strength he enjoyed in youth, but the essence of time and tide don't wait for him." The times have not changed, but time is running out!

Continuing on the theme of how short life truly is, Sant Kabir states very clearly that, "Each and every breath without *Simran* or the thought of God, is just wasted. Looted by the thieves of desire, attachment and Illusion, the condition in health eventually comes that the head starts to shake. Suddenly the person realizes that absolutely, surely, he is going to die and now he suddenly remembers that he never sought the Company of the True Master. What will happen now? When he was young, he gave it no thought. What possibly can be done at this stage, for now it is too late!"

Even royalty, with their grand umbrellas flapping overhead, were at last buried under the earth. The Truth is there: the body must die eventually. "Those who possessed millions, have departed bare-footed and empty-handed." They took absolutely nothing with them. Sant Kabir strongly advises everyone to contemplate this.

"It is no good that at the end of one's life he leaves this body and other treasures, just like a gambler who ultimately leaves the place of gambling empty-handed. The worldly and perishable treasures have to be left behind. Only the true Treasure of the Holy Naam can be taken along when the soul leaves the body at the time of physical death."

It is quite shocking when Sant Kabir describes the true condition of the world, saying that, "At the time of death, right from the moment the soul leaves the body, the friends and relatives will fight for, and try to grab all that material wealth which the person had laboriously gathered together by any means!" Furthermore, He points out that "To what avail is knowledge of this Divine Love to the scholar, king or landlord? They are so puffed up in their ego of possession and power, that they would not be affected in the least by this type of Love!"

"O Foolish One! Why do you have such ego in you? You have totally forgotten that when you came into the Creation of this world, your little body being formed by Almighty God, you were held upside down for 10 months in the fire-like womb of the mother. You promised, *O God! Save me from the hell of this fire! I will always remember Thee!*"

Then Sant Kabir reminds the person, "O brother! God came to your rescue! His Divine Light filled your little body with

Love and ecstasy, and you remembered only Him all the time! But now you have totally forgotten Almighty God, the Creator. You are too busy in gathering the perishable treasures and possessions of the world!"

He continues, "The pearls of wisdom have been scattered on the way, but the Spiritually 'blind' person cannot pick them up!"

There is a story of King Bir Singh Baghela, who was the ruler of a state near Benaras. He had recently built a beautiful, new palace and was very proud of its magnificent construction. Accordingly, he invited everyone, including Sant Kabir, to come and admire it. All were welcome. Lavish meals were prepared and festive decorations were seen to be hanging everywhere. Everybody walked throughout the entire palace, praising its stunning design and strong architectural lines. Such beautiful applications of expensive marbles and inlays had never before been seen.

The King walked with Sant Kabir, pointing out the strong supporting walls, the expensive materials, and how much wealth had been poured into its construction. "No expense has been spared," stated the King. In all the admiring crowd, however, Sant Kabir alone remained serious and pensive, and naturally the king was very much puzzled at His silence.

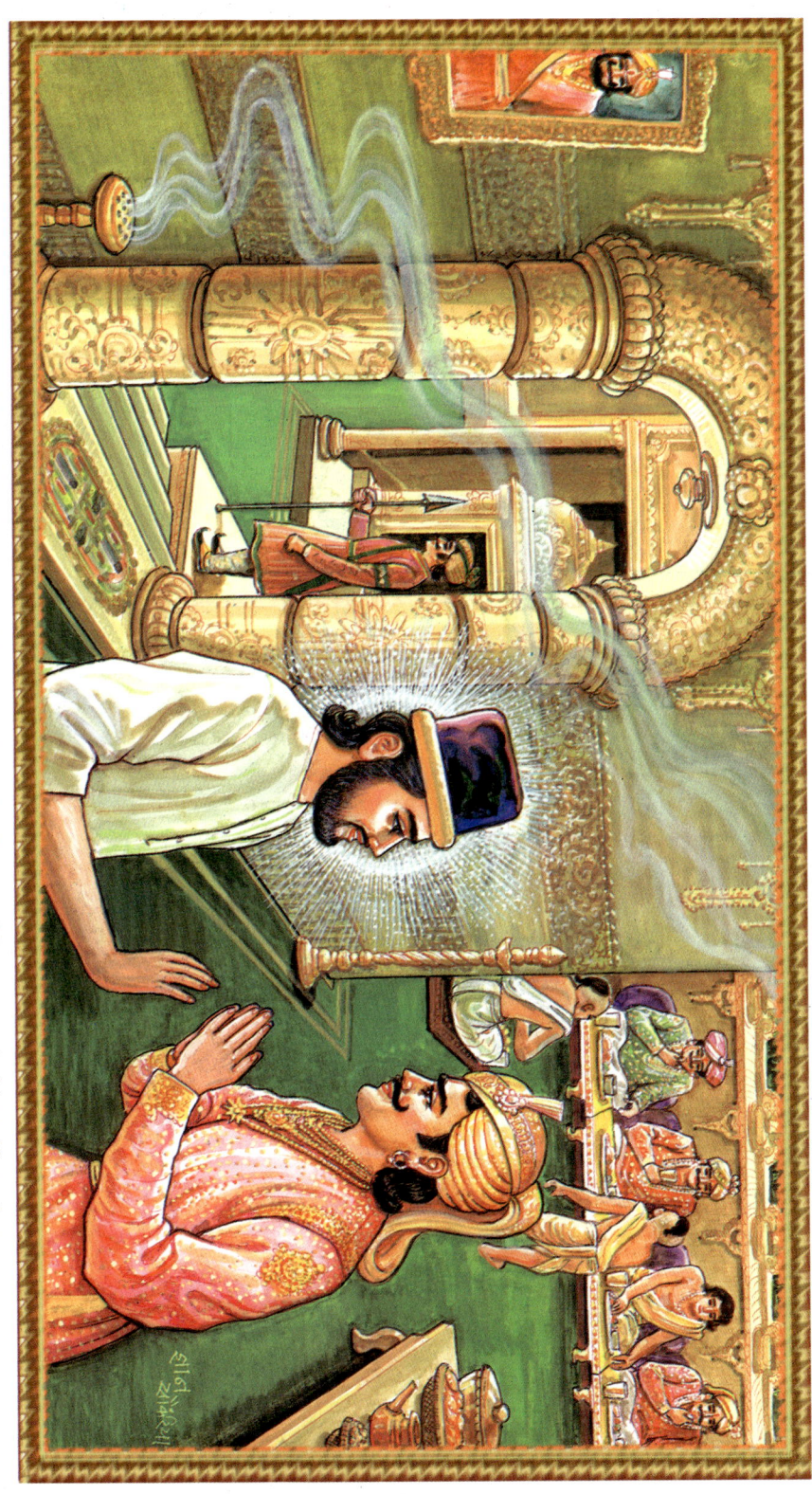

When Kabir Sahib was coming out of the front door, the King could not contain himself any longer and inquired if He had liked the castle. Sant Kabir replied that it was indeed impressive, but it was too bad that the person who had built it was not going to live in it!

When Kabir Sahib was coming out of the front door, the King could not contain himself any longer and inquired if He had liked the castle. Sant Kabir replied that it was indeed impressive, but it was too bad that the person who had built it was not going to live in it!

The King, of course, was stunned and flabbergasted at this answer. Kabir Sahib then kindly explained to him that the edifice would eventually crumble, because it was made of matter and would not stand forever. Secondly, the one who had built it would, before long, have to leave it.

Seeing that He had the full attention of the King, and that he was in a receptive mood, Sant Kabir then explained that everything returns to dust after a period of time, and in the same way, whoever has taken the physical birth must eventually die.

Later, after everyone had left, the King reflected deeply on what Sant Kabir had told him, and he realized that yes, indeed, *this is true!* The King sought out Lord Kabir, and eventually became one of His devoted disciples.

In reflecting upon the temporary and transient nature of this world, Kabir Sahib prays to God, "O my Supreme Lord! What should I ask Thee to give me? There is nothing I can ask of Thee, because nothing in this world is permanent. Before my very eyes, the world is disappearing! It is all temporary and transient. Nothing is lasting."

All the beautiful forms which the eyes behold, all the enticing sounds with which the ears are fascinated, are born of dust. They are made of mud and clay that must soon vanish, and be no more! Unfortunately, everyone is under a grand delusion that this enchanting world is forever and ever!

Sant Kabir has also discussed the dreadful reactions of the very heavy Karmas that some people have carried over from their past lives. He says, "Those people become so much attached to the world, that they are unable to even think any Godly thought! Just see the trickery of the mind, that it entangles the worldly person so much in Deception and Illusion! That kind of person does not like Bhakti because it doesn't appeal to him. He quickly runs away from it." Sant Kabir compares that kind of person to a fly who is used to going into filth. Even such a captivating fragrance as the sandalwood tree cannot attract the fly.

Sant Kabir discusses another type of Illusion, that of selfishness. He says that some people indulge in bad deeds all their lives, with never a thought of serving humanity. He says in His verses that He even carried a drum on His shoulders and played it for emphasis, but wherever He went, He saw that people are only for their own selves and their own needs. In conclusion, He announces that no one is truly a friend of anyone else.

At best, each person is concerned with only his own family, but people do not truly care about anyone else. He says that people need to be more interactive with others, and to share in their pain and sorrow. Selfish people live only for themselves, gathering and stealing things. "They are fully in the clutches of attraction, under the influence of desire and greed so much so that they totally forget their true Aim of taking the human birth."

Sant Kabir also gives a vivid illustration of greed. He says, "If you take a skull and put it on the ground, and then put all the treasures of the three worlds (the lower three Regions of the Physical, the Astral, and the Causal) inside, it can never be filled." This is how many articles in this world are considered to be 'treasures', and also this example shows the extent of human greediness. The person's desires and dreams can never be fulfilled, even in all the three worlds.

The human qualities of respect and self-esteem disappear when greed is on the horizon. Whenever one asks Almighty God for material things, that person is just considered to be dead and finished. "Regardless of how many ways one tries to get his desires fulfilled, there is no fruit of contentment. The greedy person keeps gathering money or treasures but in the end, the Thief of Death takes it away in a moment!"

By way of explanation for this, Sant Kabir tells us that the soul is at the mercy of the mind, living ultimately under its rule. People indulge in good or bad actions, performing pious or sinful deeds, according to the whim and dictates of this mind. When the time of a person's death draws near, a painful realization comes upon him. Suddenly he is remorseful and repentant, but it is too late! What is the use of wailing at that point? When the time of physical departure comes, the Agents of Death quickly appear and drag the soul to the Court of Dharam Rai, the Lord of Judgement. The soul is confronted with an account of its deeds, and called upon to receive the reward or punishment for the same.

"The whole world", Kabir Sahib says, "is the helpless prey of cunning Kaal. Some people he rapidly devours (they become lost in the attractions of the world); others he playfully holds in his lap. Those who have not realized the mystery of the Holy Naam return to the earth again and again. Entangled in the Illusions of the world, they keep weeping over their hopeless destiny." There appears to be no way out of this dilemma!

With a view to making people aware of these shortcomings, Kabir Sahib advises the evil tendencies that have to be discarded in order to make Spiritual progress. He says that the first one to be cast out is *lust*. In a broad sense, lust may include all desires and outward tendencies of the mind. Lust is most alluring with its manifold promises, which turn out to be false and deluding. Lust can degrade a person to a level worse than a beast! Sant Kabir says that under the sway of lust, the Power of Discrimination becomes clouded and the intellect dulled. When lust attacks, the attention falls down, whereas the purpose of meditation is to bring it up to the eye-focus. He advises that lust should be replaced with the qualities of restraint and purity.

The second enemy of Spiritual progress is *anger*. Its quality is to cause confusion, to scatter the attention of the mind, and to keep a condition of enmity brewing. It destroys peace, breeds hatred and turns hearts into enemies. It fosters destruction and wipes out everything that is noble. Sant Kabir recommends that anger be replaced with the merits of forgiveness and patience. Anger is a great hindrance to Spiritual progress, and must be harnessed in order to concentrate the spirit.

"If one has anger, that will bring hundreds of thousands of bad deeds along with it. When the Illusion of anger comes in the person, whatever good deeds are done, all will go wasted due to these other related tendencies. The person with anger brings fire all around him from the ten directions. That person can only quench his thirst and cool that kind of heat in the Holy Company of the Saint."

He continues, "Bad words are the worst of all. They can make another person's body burn into ashes. They are like a nail going into the heart of the other. The wound they make lasts forever, and does not heal. That person will remember those bad or harsh words all through life, and won't forget what was wrongly said. The Saint always has a cooling breeze raining down like Divine Amrit Water. His sweet words work like a balm soothing the lacerated hearts, whereas harsh words are like arrows going through the ears, making small holes as they spread throughout the body."

The third passion to be discarded is *greed*. Sant Kabir advises that contentment should take the place of greed. However good a man may be, if he is greedy, the whole world despises him. On the other hand, a grateful heart invites the unbounded Love of Almighty God.

Kabir Sahib tells us that the fourth inclination is *attachment*, which chains the soul to this earth Plane. When one's Inner Eye opens, Discrimination easily replaces attachment.

The fifth evil tendency is *ego*, which arrests the Inner progress by keeping the attention a captive of the mind and the senses, and away from the True Master. Kabir Sahib says that people wander about, lost in 'I-ness'. But when the Inner Eye is opened, the person shall be in the realm of 'Thou-ness'. That person then says, "God is the only Giver and I am like a beggar. I am Thy humble slave. Kindly keep me always with Thee!" Ego is considered to be the most difficult of all the tendencies to cast out, but eventually with persistence, humility can replace ego.

Sant Kabir reveals the despair of the soul when it becomes aware of its weakness under the influence of the senses. He tells us about the supplication of the soul at the time of the body's physical death. The soul prays, "O Almighty God! Is there anyone who can save me from the sorrow of this ego, which fights with me day and night, and won't let me think calmly? My desires give me even more pain. I don't know how I can spend my life in this world! When I was not yet born, I was in the ecstasy of God's Light in the womb of my mother. I remember the time that I was the one, Loved by my true Beloved God. But since I came into this world, the five evil tendencies have shrouded me. Day by day, I am suffocated and dragged by them to the ultimate death of this body. The price that I am paying for this suffering, is that they want me to lose this priceless life of the human body and my golden chance to know God, and in this failure, I become just as the rest of the world. It is a pity that I paid the price: I sold myself to these five evils, and they have looted me. Now I see that the whole world is false, like a mirage, and I realize that both desire and Illusion have congealed me in this existence."

Almighty God has, however, provided Discrimination to each and every soul. With this intellect, one can determine what is right and wrong; yet still the person does wrong things! The Delusion that he will live forever takes him to his death without his obtaining true Salvation. The whole aim of taking the human birth is to enable the person to find his True Father and Creator while in the physical body.

Sant Kabir reminds us about all of this with utmost Love and compassion, because He is the One Who knows and understands that the souls are caught in this web of Illusion. With Graciousness and humbleness, He gives out the Message of God in so many different ways, to remind all humanity not to get captured in the snare of attachment.

Continuing His discussion of Illusion, Sant Kabir points out that the rules of the caste system pose a definite hindrance on the Spiritual Path. "In the search for Truth, one should not be concerned with race, religion, nor any social order. The real problem before everybody is that of finding God. People are all worshippers of the Reality that is One, pervading everywhere. Mankind is seeking after God--the One God of the entire Universe, Who is the same God for the learned and the unlearned, the rich and the poor, the young and the old.

This Goal has nothing to do with one's religion. God is One and only One, and all Creation is His worshippers. All of God's Creation has a right to meet God!"

In reference to His own status as a weaver in a society that places such a vocation next to that of the street-sweepers and garbage collectors, Kabir Sahib says, "Everybody laughs at my low caste but I am eternally grateful because in this same caste, I have worshipped the Beloved Creator. In whatever caste one meditates on the Lord, that is the true Caste."

Caste itself should not be a bar to Spirituality. The Saint is indifferent to these outer labels, for God Himself has no caste or status of being high or low. No one is worthy, no one is unworthy. Almighty God bestows His bounteous gifts on all alike, for all come from Him, and ultimately all will merge into Him again. He gives out His Love unconditionally.

These such petty things are of no import in the realm of Spirituality. If it is God Who has created all things great and small, then no one is big, no one is small, because all are His Creations. Whoever has made the tiny ant and also the mighty elephant, is One. If the Creator is One, then who is greater and who is lesser?

Once there was a Faqir by the name of *Jahan Gasht Shah,* who had recently arrived in India. He had visited a number of places and had met many holy men in his search for Truth. Hearing of the great fame of Kabir Sahib, he made a plan to meet Him. Sant Kabir knew that although this man was searching for Truth, he still possessed certain deep-rooted prejudices which would present a hindrance to his Spiritual progress.

Subsequently, when the day arrived that the man would visit Him, Sant Kabir ordered that a pig should be tied near the doorway of His own simple house. According to the Islamic tradition, the pig is considered to be the most unclean of all animals. Those following this religion do not eat pigs, and abhor even being in close proximity to them.

Obviously, when the Faqir reached the door of Sant Kabir, and saw the pig, he immediately started to leave in disgust, but Sant Kabir called him back. The man asked the Saint why He allowed this animal, considered to be very dirty and unlawful, to be tied up at His door.

Sant Kabir replied, "I have kept this unlawful thing *outside my house*, but you have kept what is unlawful and unholy (hatred, anger, jealousy, etc.) *in your heart!*" The Faqir then felt ashamed of all his sinful deeds, and realizing the Truth in Sant Kabir's words, eventually became His disciple.

There is another story that shows the rigidity of the caste system. Once there were two Brahmin brothers by the names of *Tatva* and *Jiva* living in Gujarat (a state in Western India). They had been in search of Truth all their lives, and had dedicated themselves to serving many Sadhus and other holy men who came on pilgrimage to a nearby place. Nonetheless, they were unable to find a True Master for their own selves.

There happened to be a small banyan tree near their house, which began to wither and die. Despite the best efforts of the two brothers to revive it, the beautiful tree eventually became very dry.

In those days, people commonly walked from place to place, and therefore it was the custom to remove one's dirty shoes, and wash the feet before entering a building. The two brothers devised a plan that they would water their dying banyan tree with the same water which had been used to wash the feet of each Sadhu who visited them. They vowed to accept as their Master only that Sadhu whose 'foot nectar' would make the tree sprout again.

They tried this test on many a Sadhu, but the tree remained dead. The brothers then realized that not every Sadhu was a True Master with the Highest Teachings, and they did not want to waste their lives by following an untrue Master.

They prayed from their hearts that one day a True Saint would come and visit them. When the sincere seeker prays from the depths of his heart, that cry is bound to be heard by the Creator.

Sure enough, one day Sant Kabir arrived at their door. Tatva and Jiva sprinkled the roots of that dying tree with the same water that had washed His Lotus Feet and lo! Within a couple of days, the tree started to grow again, and then it began to sprout green leaves. The brothers felt great relief that at long last their earnest prayers had been answered. They ran as fast as they could to Sant Kabir Who was still in Gujarat. They fell at His Blessed Feet, begging for the Boon of Spiritual Initiation.

Naturally Tatva's and Jiva's caste-fellows, the Brahmins, became outraged that these brothers had taken a low-caste Muslim as their Master, which in those days was considered horrendous. Just imagine the rigid insistence by Brahmin castes on the rules of ritual pollution! These brothers were declared to be outcasts, and the high priests decreed that no one should have any association with them. They were immediately shunned by everyone in their village. This was distressing because one of the brothers had a daughter of marriageable age and the other had a son, but no one from the village would allow their own children to become a suitable match for these outcast children.

Tatva and Jiva knew that the high priests of the community were not likely to grant them any kind of reprieve, so they decided to visit Sant Kabir and explain the whole situation to Him. He listened patiently and then advised them to go back to their town, and announce that their son and daughter would be married together. He then smiled and assured them that everything would be alright.

The brothers duly returned home to begin the preparations for the wedding. However, when the Brahmins learned what Tatva and Jiva planned to do, they became even more outraged! What Sant Kabir had proposed was a marriage between parallel cousins, the children of two brothers, which was not acceptable within their religion.

According to the advice of Sant Kabir, the brothers explained that since the Brahmins would not allow them to marry their children within the community, they were left with no alternative. In the end, their fellow Brahmins submitted and allowed them to marry their children within the village. The ban was lifted, and the brothers were no more ostracized.

Tatva and Jiva then returned to Sant Kabir to get His permission for this change of plans. Sant Kabir told them to accept this offer, but also to impose the condition that their caste-fellows accept the true Path of Bhakti. After debating the issue for some time, some of the Brahmins agreed. Just see, even some of the staunchest Brahmins became the devotees of Sant Kabir during these times of such persecution of the lower-caste people.

Further on the topic of Illusion, Sant Kabir says that it is like an ugly devil, but in the eyes of the world, the ways of Illusion are the fairest and most beloved of all. He continues, "There are thousands and thousands of different attractions and shows in the world, just waiting to ensnare the senses. Just like there are different traps in the jungle to catch birds and animals, Illusion has so many unseen and unique tricks to lure the unwitting souls."

He says, "O man! You are seized by death and have fallen into a deep well. This Illusion easily wiles everyone in a great Deception, just like the parrot is easily captured in the reed trap."

There are many ambushes made by Kaal to keep the souls imprisoned in his domain. For example Sant Kabir tells us that it is Brahma who made the various Scriptures such as the Smritis, the Vedas, the Shastras and the Puranas. The souls become stuck fast in the study of these, memorizing, interpreting, and reciting them endlessly. Eventually people begin to worship the Holy Books, even bowing down to them. By doing like this, *these people are actually worshipping Kaal,* because through him all of those Scriptures were made! Sant

Kabir says, "All become deluded in this world, and no one knows the Secret of Sat Purush."

He points out that if the study of these Books was sufficient for liberating oneself, then *Ravan* (the King of Lanka) would have been liberated long ago, for he was considered to be the best scholar of the Vedas. But study is quite different from the right pursuit and having the Living Experience. By recitation and repetition of Scriptures, the soul may find out about going within, but it cannot get that Divine Contact with the Almighty needed to actually go within.

Kabir Sahib says that when one uses his Power of Discrimination to know what is right and wrong, only then will he know all the secret tricks of Maya. The Master progressively reduces this fear of Deception in the devotee as he begins to learn the Truth.

Kabir Sahib sees this pitiful scene of the world and implores, "O Man! See inward! Come inward! And when you do, the Simran of the Godman's Life-Giving Impulse will liberate you from the trickery of bondage, and the aeons and aeons of years you have been under its clutches."

The mind, of course, is the major obstacle and Illusion has put a beautiful covering on top of it. Sant Kabir is advising the people that if anyone has any kind of desire in his heart to obtain worldly things, regardless of the ritual and the intention that one does to attain them, all efforts are wasted.

Lord Kabir says that one should praise the Lord, the Creator, Who gives the Life-Impulse to all, regardless of whether one is Hindu or Muslim, rich or poor. "Almighty God permeates all!" He says, "Come to the Lord, and don't run around in the outer Illusion of the world. Nobody has obtained God in this way and nobody ever will!"

#5-2 The Futility of Outer Worship

Sometimes, it seems that the only thing left in religion in these days, is just to learn the history of it, read all the Scriptures and then to be able to quote from them. People talk about the various outer rituals, and argue with each other between the new and the old knowledge of religion, and then they try to bring new ways of religion into the old. Every religious belief thinks that their Way is true, and better than the others.

The effect of this, is that people put faith in their religious Books or in the past Prophets, and the Priests and Ministers begin to sell the Holy Name of God by creating complicated rituals. They knowingly put fear and suspicion into the people's minds about these outer methods, compelling everyone to believe that this is the true religion, and the only Way back to God.

Sant Kabir points out, "Don't say that the religious Books are false! They are not saying anything wrong. What is false, is the person who doesn't realize and understand the Truth contained in them!" People read Scriptures thinking that true knowledge can only be gained by this reading, but they don't bring these Teachings into their practical lives.

The fault lies not with the religious sects and societies which have provided people with the knowledge of the Way Godwards, but one has to come into contact with Someone Who has Himself found God, and Who can explain the true import of the Scriptures. To think that a person without Inner knowledge can interpret the Scriptures is as ridiculous as saying that a child in the first grade can understand advanced algebra, but this is not possible. His intellect is not developed up to that higher level.

The gist of most Scriptures is only concerned with practical living in this world. The *Dharmas* (moral and religious rules and regulations) and Commandments are there in these Books, but they lead one to worship only up to that point. The reader, however, does not obtain the Divine One from Whom the gods and goddesses are getting their Power. The Scriptures only lead the people to worship the Holy Books, but not to the Source of the Power behind these Books. That is why Sant Kabir illustrates again and again that bookish knowledge leads one nowhere.

He says that even if the religious leaders are able to tell people about the Experiences of the Godmen Who came in the past, they cannot give the devotees any first-hand Practical Experience to gain salvation. The followers and even the leaders themselves cannot realize the Spiritual Truth, and the Kingdom of God that is described in these Holy Scriptures.

In their own ignorance of the Truth, these leaders don't tell the people that God is the Oversoul, of Whom the true Worship is to become One with this Truth. The observance of certain rituals all through life is generally what is considered to be 'religion', but this leads absolutely nowhere. Unfortunately, this is all that the Ministers and Priests can offer their congregations. In this way, religion fails the people.

Sant Kabir teaches that to be uttering various *Mantras* (Prayers) in different manners, thinking that this is the only Way to know the Oversoul, is of no help in controlling one's thoughts and restraining the evil tendencies which affect everyone at every moment throughout life. All the outer symbols are just that, symbols of the Journey Godwards, but people grasp these symbols to their heart, as if these objects were the actuality.

Many customs have been carried forward without any true meaning to them. For example, the wearing of certain clothes such as robes or hats in various colours, or observing certain days as being more lucky than others, using numbers as lucky symbols, the use of incense, bowing down before idols, offering food to pictures and statues, chanting, using different positions of the body or even motions of the arms and hands, all are useless in helping one to draw aside the veil of Illusion and to come closer to knowing himself.

Sant Kabir says that *Brahma* made the four Vedas, but Brahma himself did not reveal the secret of how to obtain salvation. These Scriptures guide the reader in only the performance of outer rituals, but the Way of liberation is not mentioned at all! The result is that the person ends up worshipping Brahma! In these Books, Brahma advises that people should give to charities and do other types of *Seva* (selfless service), but in fact he (Brahma) has not even the foresight of his own end!

How can one who has no knowledge of his own death, possibly counsel others about it, or even about the life after death? None of the gods and goddesses, including Shiva and Ganesh, have any knowledge of the Beyond, because *they themselves cannot go into the Beyond!*

Sant Kabir illustrates that Kaal ordered Maya never to reveal to Brahma, Vishnu and Shiva that Kaal is their father. As a result, these gods themselves cannot go higher than Brahmand, the Causal Region.

Sant Kabir says that when someone does outer rituals and sings prayers to God (or to someone whom he has not seen), his attention might dwell for a few moments on that, but soon the attraction fades away. Sant Kabir compares this to the *Kasumbha* colour (a pale saffron colour). This is a very temporary colour and fades quickly, but in comparison the true Grace of the Master's Holy Naam is permanent and eternal.

"The Master dyes us in the permanent Colour of the Holy Naam, and takes us across the Ocean of Illusion to become One with Him. The Colour of the Holy Naam is so permanent that it will not fade away. It will last forever!"

Due to a lack of realized souls who Spiritually know themselves and can truly assist others in this dilemma, people are generally stuck in the different sects with their rules and regulations, which do not teach the person to go inward and reach the Kingdom of God. The leaders only instruct in the outer teachings, consisting of the performance of certain rituals which confuse the person, and keep him away from the Reality. These outer practices teach people to spend their precious life in singing hymns, turning the wooden beads on

When so much time had passed, and still Kabir Sahib had not returned with the milk, Ramanand sent some of his disciples to find out what had happened. Their eyes opened wide in astonishment when they found Kabir Sahib sitting on the ground beside the dead cow, with a pile of grass and bucket nearby!

their rosaries, and shouting prayers to the Lord, all of which take the soul absolutely nowhere.

"One has to learn how to close down the impressions of the outer world, which bombard from every direction. When the person goes within, he discovers for himself infinite happiness and profound peace."

Sant Kabir points out that whatever is contained in the religious Books and Holy Scriptures is not the Holy Naam itself, but is only a *description* of it. These Books serve a useful purpose, in that they induce one to tread the Path. However, just as medical books contain prescriptions but not the actual medicine, so too, the Scriptures contain the description *but not the Holy Naam itself!* One's appetite cannot be appeased, for example, by only reading cookbooks. The person has to actually do the cooking. Similarly, one's Spiritual hunger cannot be satisfied by only reading descriptions of the Path. *He must also tread the Path himself!*

There were many occasions when Ramanand himself was influenced by Kabir Sahib's superior insight. One day Ramanand wanted cow's milk for a certain ritual to honour departed relatives. As part of this ceremony, the people prepare a feast of the foods that the departed person especially liked to eat when he was alive. The people believe that this special food will go to the dead person. Usually rice pudding made with milk would be one of the dishes.

Therefore, Ramanand sent Kabir Sahib to fetch the required milk. Sant Kabir, however, went and placed a vessel beside a cow that had just died and He started to gather grass for her to eat. The cow did not oblige, neither by producing milk nor by eating.

When so much time had passed and still Kabir Sahib had not returned with the milk, Ramanand sent some of his disciples to find out what had happened. Their eyes opened wide in astonishment when they found Kabir Sahib sitting on the ground beside the dead cow, with a pile of grass and a bucket nearby!

"What is this?" they asked. They were flabbergasted that somebody actually believed that a dead cow could produce milk!

In return, Sant Kabir asked them that if the dead cow cannot give milk, how possibly can the dead relatives, in whose memory this function was taking place, eat that specially prepared food! Sant Kabir's logic is unique and His wit is razor-sharp. He makes use of this unconventional humour to expose the hypocrisy and Illusion that permeate religion.

Whenever Godmen come, They always teach the people to leave the pride of belonging to a religion, and to rise above their Spiritual egoism, which comes about due to narrow-mindedness and Illusion. Kabir Sahib says that wherever selfishness and ego exist, there are religious scorpions who hover around, making the people divided and ready to fight with each other. These religious fanatics have only false pretences and deceptive promises to mislead their followers and keep them in total confusion. On the other hand, the Divine Intoxication of the Godman is the same for all, no matter to which sect one belongs. Anybody can drink from the Master's Fountain of Divine Elixir.

Sant Kabir emphasizes again and again that until the person, with full attention, doesn't turn inward and attach himself to the Creator and know His Qualities and His Power, all outer efforts are wasted. All rituals, the outward observances of religions and the righteous modes of life, are of no avail. God is a limitless and very subtle Ocean. Until silence and stillness do not come in a person, he cannot listen to and catch hold of, the Shabd Sound Current. In the quietness and stillness of the heart can be found the Reality of God. The Experience of God, Who is all-stillness and Who is forever, cannot be had by the intellect.

Sant Kabir says that the soul can have the Experience of God only when one inverts himself, because the Lord is away from the clever mind and its scheming intellect.

In another verse, Kabir Sahib is speaking to a *Yogi*. Most of the Yogis observe all the outer rites and rituals. For example, they wear big, thick earrings, they have a sack hanging from their shoulder, and they carry a begging bowl in their hand. Sant Kabir advises the Yogi, "Change what you are doing. Instead of wearing earrings, just close up the ears."

He continues, "O Yogi, make your ears closed to the worldly sounds of talk and gossip. The bag you carry should be used to collect the Grace of the True Master and when you have this Grace, then you can use the bowl to hold your intellect (the Power of Discrimination). Make the body as a begging bowl and fill it with nothing but the Name of the Lord. If you do these things, then you will have earned the title of being called a true Yogi. When your daily life is filled with honest living with a portion of the earnings going to charity, when you fulfill your worldly duties and responsibilities, observe chastity, keep away from anger and observe Spiritual discipline in your life, then when you sit for meditation and recite His Holy Name, you are fit and deserving to receive Grace and attention in abundance from the Master. You will become a true devotee of the Lord!"

Sant Kabir also refers to the Yogi's habit of shouting loudly the name of God, but "Only repeating this name or that, without any actual Contact with the Named One, is of no avail. If one were to become rich only by calling for riches, then there would hardly be anyone left who is poor!"

The Yogis have another ritual of rubbing ashes on their bodies, thinking that in this way they are washing themselves clean of any sins. Sant Kabir advises them, "If you want to put something on your body, rub the attention on the Oversoul, thereby becoming more pious. Direct your concentration towards your own Consciousness and become One with God. The ashes are outer and will not have any affect. They will wash off, but if you bring your attention upwards, this will be the 'attention' that you are rubbing on your body." Merely smearing ashes on the body is of no avail. He advises to let meditation be the sacred ashes, and to besmear the body with this meditation.

Another practice of the Yogis was to wander from village to village. About this, Sant Kabir tells them sternly, "Instead of wandering foolishly around from one village to the other, doing whatever your mind dictates and calling yourself as a Sadhu, go to the True Master and He will give you His Grace. He will make you understand the Truth of the God-World. His Charging of the Five Holy Words will become embedded in your heart, soul, and mind."

"When you have done all these things, then sit down for meditation. In the stillness, you will rise above the body consciousness. Your meditation will be unique and fruitful! Then you are doing your Real Work in this world. O listen, devotees! The Radiation of the Godman will engulf you and work like a protective hedge of Grace, to encompass you all around. The Spiritual Path has many turns and twists, but the True Master can take the devotee through in no time!"

Sant Kabir continues further, speaking now as a true Devotee of God. "For this Nectar of God, I have done all outer rituals such as travelling on pilgrimages and fasting, and I have performed many different Yogas, including various breathing exercises, but I have not found that special Goblet of Nectar which I drank when I reached the True Master. Now my mind, body, and soul continuously drink that Nectar day and night. I am in ecstasy, and I am becoming more and more pure. This is the only true Nectar of Nectars, the Wine of Wines of the Creator. God is the ultimate Truth and the outer wines (liquor) are false. This one given by the True Master is the Truth."

Regarding the ritual of turning the rosary beads, Sant Kabir says, "People generally have a string of wooden beads which they show off to the world. They move the beads, one by one, and say prayers, but in their heart of hearts there is no Sweet Remembrance of the Holy Name of God. Having only

Sant Kabir just put His Godly hand on the head of the nearby buffalo and asked, "Listen, buffalo! Why are you just standing there and not saying anything? Hurry up and recite some lines of the Vedas!" The buffalo then began to speak! Everyone was astonished!

remembrance with wooden beads will bring no result. By the use of beads we only please ourselves through mental satisfaction, but if we were to make the mind into a big bead, then an Inward Light would Dawn!"

If the mind is not engaged in the Remembrance of the Lord, the telling of beads can become a ritual, a dead habit. Sant Kabir tells an amusing tale that the rosary became angry and said, "Why do you keep turning me up and down? Turn the beads of your heart and I will bring you to God!"

Beads are intended to remind the mind to keep alive the memory of God, but counting the beads with the mind running amuck is a useless ritual. Telling beads is a practice to be done on the Plane of the senses, but God is beyond this 'seeing and thinking'. The person may even break his back bowing in the Temples, but if his obeisance is not directed towards Almighty God, it is of no avail. Whenever and wherever one bows, it should always be at His Lotus Feet.

There is a sacred bathing place named *Totadari*, on the way to *Rameshvar*, a city in the extreme South of India. It is said that one day Sant Kabir and some disciples arrived at Totadari, leading a buffalo that carried their supplies of blankets and cooking materials. Living here were mostly high-class Brahmins, who were very careful to observe all the strict rules of caste purity in bathing, cooking, and eating.

They were so rigid that if even the shadow of a low-caste person fell on their cooking place or materials, they would not eat from that place, but would choose another one.

These Brahmins knew that Kabir Sahib belonged to the 'low caste', according to them, but since they had also heard about His Spiritual Greatness, they were afraid to come forth and speak frankly. In their heart of hearts, they really wanted Him to sit in a separate food line, but they realized that to insist on this would be impolite.

They quickly devised what they thought would be a clever plan to exclude Him from the place where they would sit and eat. They declared that whoever could recite from the Vedas could sit and eat in their line, but whoever was not able to recite, should sit apart. They thought that naturally since 'low-caste' persons had no right to recite the Vedas, this would solve their problem. All the Brahmins began to recite a few lines.

Finally, Sant Kabir's turn came. He just put His Godly hand on the head of the nearby buffalo and asked, "Listen, buffalo! Why are you just standing there and not saying anything? Hurry up and recite some lines of the Vedas!" The buffalo then began to speak! Everyone was astonished! They quickly realized the greatness of Sant Kabir, and found themselves shamed. They begged Him to kindly forgive them.

The Brahmins planned a trick to keep Sant Kabir apart from them, but to no avail! When it became time to eat, in all His Godly wisdom, Kabir Sahib was seen sitting between each and every orthodox Brahmin!

Godmen always have a Special Aura, a Distinctive Personality blended with Divine Charismata that others are drawn to Them and instinctively bow down.

On another occasion and in a different city, Sant Kabir was with other Brahmins who similarly also wished to keep Him out of their eating line. What to do? They didn't want to even touch Him, because He belonged to the 'lower' caste! One can only imagine how they would feel to eat with Him! They were sure that they would be ruined! They could not just say "No!", but this was the voice of all the Brahmins in thinking this way.

They also planned a similar trick to keep Him apart from them, but to no avail! When it became time to eat, in all His Godly wisdom, Kabir Sahib was seen sitting between each and every orthodox Brahmin! The Master Power is Omnipresent, and He is the only One who can become from One to Infinity. No one can comprehend His immense Power. He has all the attributes of Almighty God. Of course, the Brahmins felt ashamed to see this Power of Kabir Sahib manifested in such a manner, and they all bowed down to Him.

Sant Kabir tells us that amongst some people, it is the custom to fast in the daytime for one month of the year. They fully believe that by following this ritual, they will attain a level of purity which would be pleasing to God. However, at night, Kabir Sahib points out, these same people do not hesitate to butcher cows and eat their meat! Such grotesque deeds done in the name of ritual sacrifice!

"On one hand, they say they are worshipping the Creator through their fasting but on the other, they are murdering His Creation. Now tell me, how possibly can the Lord be happy about this?"

The Master explains that the diverse rules and regulations of all the different *Isms* (religions) are due to the various countries having distinct climates. For example, in countries where there is a shortage of water, it is the prescribed custom that the devotee should just wash his face and hands with sand, and then sit for prayer. In those countries where water is in abundance, people are expected to take a full bath before prayer. These are only outer rituals with the aim to make the person wide awake and alert for prayer, but in the eyes of God these rituals *per se* have no importance. These methods are only meant to cleanse the body, but they cannot make the soul pure.

While observing rituals with their many different formalities, it sometimes appears that one ritual is better than another. Actually rituals are born after the real Saint leaves the physical body. No Saint knowingly makes a ritual!

Sant Kabir points out that very few rituals have any deep Spiritual meaning, and most of them just further bind the follower in worldly attachment and Illusion. Originally, many rituals and ceremonies had a purpose and a meaning behind them, but their meanings became lost with the passage of time. For example, in most of the Churches and Temples, various candles are lit. Originally the purpose behind this was to remind the people that there is Light within the Consciousness, so that the devotee may try to see that Light within himself. If the person starts lighting candles but forgets altogether why the candles are being lit, then the ritual of lighting candles is absolutely of no use.

Many rituals come into being due to the narrow-mindedness of the Priests and Ministers, who just want to keep the followers under their own strict control. Sant Kabir very clearly states that these preachers and priests put such complicated conditions on the meeting with Almighty God, that the aspiring devotees become totally confused. "But carefully following rules and regulations will not bring one even a little bit closer to God. The outer rituals of religion cannot make a difference in the Way Godward, because the soul is One with Almighty God, being of the same Essence as the Lord."

Every religion starts as a Way to bring people into Spirituality so that liberation can be achieved, but it ends up just being a cage of narrow-mindedness, rituals, fanaticism, bigotry, and superstition. Even going to the Temple or Mosque has become a social obligation. Sant Kabir says that people love and respect their own religious places of worship and Books, but due to narrow-mindedness, they have hatred for the Books and religions of others, and even for the people who worship in these other religions!

"Forgetting the real knowledge, people become chained by the bonds of their own little religious communities and rituals. Slowly, but gradually, they drift farther away from the true meaning of religion." It is the desire to know God that makes people come under the clutches of the Priests and Ministers, who in turn advise these same people to worship idols and do all outer rituals.

One cannot easily get out from the clutches of desire. Sant Kabir says that these desires eat up one's precious life, and in this respect He says that it is similar to a female snake which eats its own eggs. "Similarly, the same empty rituals and outer formalities, 'eat' up the person day and night!"

He shows us that the preachers, with their communities and rituals, have made religion only for these outer practices. The rituals work just like chains and bonds, and the other religions, sects, and communities easily form the reason to fight with each other. Becoming enemies, they drift far away from the true meaning of religion for humanity.

Sant Kabir reminds us that when the soul comes into the human body, its real and only work is to become One with God, to have the purity and Love of God, and to Love His entire Creation. Somehow, exactly the reverse is happening. People allow themselves to become the enemies of each other, and thus man breaks away from the Truth, which is God.

The preachers are supposed to be Lovers of God, but instead they become leaders of small communities and sects, congealing themselves and everyone else in their own way. Sant Kabir illustrates that the leaders make the people of this world to break away from God, and all that they know is right in their own hearts, falling in Love with worldly desires and turning against others.

Various holy people, such as Yogis, Rishis and others, gave out methods by which the souls could be taken up to the same Spiritual Region to wherever the leaders had attained themselves. Just like in a school, a student who has attained up to the level of Grade 10 can only instruct others up to that level, not at the difficulty of the college level. The Teachings became preserved in their own Scriptures, and as long as the devotees followed instructions, they received some Spiritual progress.

In due course of time, however, those leaders left the earth Plane and the followers ultimately left off the Inner practices, thereby totally forgetting about the Inner Way of Spirituality. Over more time, they began to adopt various outer rites, rituals, and ceremonies, becoming satisfied only with these methods.

Religious Teachings can be divided into two parts. The first part is objective, consisting of the outer rituals such as the worship of idols and photographs, the reading of Scriptures, pilgrimages, various fasts, charity, and chanting. The second part is subjective, which is concerned with the Inward Spiritual practices. Here, Spiritual Realization has a direct relationship with the soul and the development of Inner Truth.

Sant Kabir states that "Rites and rituals don't lead anywhere inside." They may cultivate emotion or create a certain type of atmosphere around the person, but there is always the danger that one might become a slave to those rituals, and then this in turn becomes a detriment to any Spiritual progress.

Kabir Sahib advises, "O Please, my friend! Wake up! You are wastefully consuming your breath and these breaths are very priceless. O wake up! Cast out all doubts and Illusions. Discard all bookish knowledge by throwing it into the water. Lose it and then forget about it. You must attach your heart and soul, but not the intellect, towards the Lord. Intellect and cleverness don't help one to attain the Lord."

There are fifty-two letters and sounds in the *Sanskrit* alphabet. "The whole Creation of the three worlds is contained in these words. However, these words will perish when man leaves the body, because the human life ends when the soul leaves the body. For that person, this physical life has ended, but the Eternal Word (the Holy Naam, Sound Current) is not to be found within these fifty-two sounds. The Holy Naam which leads to salvation is not a spoken or written letter. It belongs to the language of the heart, and is Eternal." Kabir Sahib says that in that place where there is no speech and no thought, the mind does not even exist. "There, one can find the Holy Name of God."

Sant Kabir explains that each human breath is valued as the Three Regions combined. "Just consider then how ruthlessly the life is being wasted. Who knows when, or if, one will get this human birth again? The person spends all his life in a dream, misusing his time and ignoring the true purpose of life. What can be put to his credit of good deeds? At the time of physical death and the reconciliation of the account of his deeds, he will receive only the rewards (either good or bad) of his actions, but all of his deeds are motivated by the selfish desire for his own pleasure. People repeat mistakes again and again, and go on paying for them. These misdeeds may appear attractive from the level of the body, *but not from the level of the soul!*"

Sant Kabir says that people are, as it were, 'asleep' as regards the Reality within, because their Inner Eye has not yet been opened and they have not witnessed the Light of God. They have never risen above the body consciousness, and never seen through the *Single Eye*. This alone is the Way to pierce into the Beyond. He says that man is identified only with the body and its impressions, leading a superficial life on the Plane of the deadly senses.

"When one rises above body consciousness, he will find this physical frame to be as mere dust, a lump of clay." He compares this frame to the bellows of a blacksmith which breathe in and out, but are themselves lifeless. In reality, people are just like 'dead' because they are embedded in the world of men and matter, totally forgetting God. They are always engaged in their children, home, money, property, or fame. Even in sleep, they dream of the world. Sant Kabir advises that while going about one's work, the person should keep Almighty God in his mind, for then the Lord will be ever present by his side, ever ready to be his Saviour.

Kabir Sahib says that the Supreme Father, Almighty God, is the Nameless One. He is the Lighthouse for all Creation, and He is All in All. He doesn't belong specifically to any sect or religion. He is One and only One, and therefore all people are also one. Some people might shave their heads or leave their homes to do penance. However, even in the wilderness, one will count his money, and the faces of his relatives will ever be in front of him. One may be high in the mountains, but his attention will be at his home with his family.

Another person might be a Yogi, maybe somebody else this or that, but the true Caste of every person is only One. "Both the 'doer' of actions (i.e man, with God residing in his heart) and the Creator are One. He is the Giver and the Gracious One, and there is no difference between these Names. God, however, is without Name."

Kabir Sahib says that no matter what Name one gives to God, when that person with full heart remembers Him, Almighty God responds accordingly. Sant Kabir says that all of a person's questions and fears vanish when he Loves the One and Only God. God sees only the sincerity of the Love directed towards Him. Outer rites don't make any difference in one's meeting with Almighty God.

What should one offer to Almighty God to express thanksgiving? How shall one worship and adore Him? Flowers are plucked from His bushes--killed and then offered at the feet of some lifeless statue. No gift can ever be offered to the Creator of all. To understand that everything is His, is enough. As long as one feels that something belongs to his own self, then the purpose cannot be served. Everything is already His, even the very life itself is His! Whatever can be earned or gathered, seen or touched, is all His play.

When one realizes that everything is already His, there is no need to offer anything to Him. The flowers on the plants are already an offering to Him. Even the sun and the moon and the stars pay obeisance to Him. All of Creation stands offered at His Door. This is exactly the meaning of the word 'Lord'. He is the Lord of all!

What can the devotee speak, and in which language, so that God may Love him? Sant Kabir says to speak only the language of Love. Whatever one could possibly think or say or do, it is God Who thinks, speaks, and acts through him. No words can become prayers because all words are His. It is He Who is the Breath of all breath. Sant Kabir advises to repeat the Simran of the Lord's Holy Name. There is nothing else to be done.

"People know only the outer knowledge of the world and accept all of this readily, without having their own Divine Experience. The mind thus feels compelled to perform acts of devotion and worship. These outer practices keep one engaged in the world and its affairs, but they are not helpful in preparing the ground for Spirituality." One needs to feel totally dissatisfied with his worldly life, and then he begins to search for a Higher meaning to life.

All outward ablutions bring no transformation. At most, one will gain a little respect in the eyes of others, but the ego will ultimately try to make a mountain out of it. The ego won't stop recounting how many pilgrimages have been undertaken, how many fasts have been observed, how many hungry mouths have been fed by donations. One must not allow pride to creep in over the thought that he is a renunciate, or giving in charity, or doing this or that.

In the time of Kabir Sahib, there existed a popular belief that whoever died in the city of Benaras would go straight away to heaven. Benaras was supposed to be a very holy city near the Ganges River, and many Sadhus and other Spiritual persons lived there. People would come to that city, hoping that by taking a bath in the Ganges, they would obtain salvation.

This tradition was so appealing that people willingly went to Benaras when they were nearing the end of their lives. The Priests and Ministers would take advantage of this, telling the people that salvation would come to them if they would leave all their possessions to the Temples.

Sant Kabir even speaks about a famous 'saw' that was installed at Benaras, with the sole purpose of cutting off the heads of those willing to die early, and thus obtain salvation sooner! Naturally, all of their possessions would then be left to the people who performed this cutting service!

On the other side of the coin, in the city called Mughar (which is about eighty-five miles east of Lucknow and about fifteen miles west of Gorakhpur), it was popularly believed that whoever died there would have to take birth again, but it would be into the form of a donkey. The city of Mughar was established by Ganesh, one of the gods to whom the people pray.

Just see how contradictory this is! Mughar is supposed to be a blessed city, and just imagine what the clever priests made out of it, all in the name of religion! This, of course, was all myth. Kabir Sahib wanted to show people that it was just a hoax, a cruel and vicious rumour made out of greed. Therefore, when the time came that He should leave the earthly sojourn, Sant Kabir knowingly left Benaras and went straight to the city of Mughar.

He says, "The common people love to do these outer rituals, because this method satisfies the mind. Rituals are easy to do and keep the mind occupied. It is all a play of the mind. Some people pray to the gods and goddesses, such as *Lakshmi* (the goddess of wealth) so that they might have better health, and more money."

In other words, they pursue these rituals only for worldly gains. People are all chanting the praises of something or someone they have never seen. Some people send water to ancestors, some bathe in the Ganges to wash away sins, and still others sit before idols without any feeling of worship or adoration, merely to ask for worldly things.

Kabir Sahib unfolds this condition of the world, using the example that people worship stone idols, hoping to fulfill worldly desires, actually thinking that this is the way that they will attain salvation and Almighty God. They have never met these stone gods and goddesses in the physical form, and they are only vaguely described in the Vedas, the Shastras, and the Puranas.

People are losing this precious life by deluding themselves, even having different days of the week in which to observe fasting, and other days in which they worship the various gods and goddesses. They follow the lunar days, and schedule important events accordingly. Sant Kabir explains that all the days of the lunar cycle are good, and none is greater nor lesser in any sense of the word. Those are all the lucky days when true humanity lives and those fortunate souls do not waste any breath, or even a single moment, without the remembrance of God.

There is no way to fashion or mould God, because it is God Himself Who fashions people. How can the Absolute come out of insignificant human hands and be made into a stone form? He is too vast to contain in any building. He is blowing in the flowers, gurgling in the rivers, and shining from the stars in the sky. The whole of Creation is His domain.

People bathe in the sacred rivers, but the mind remains unwashed. They offer rituals in the Temples, but that is no cleansing. Flowers are also offered, but the people do not offer themselves. They give in charity, feed the poor and many other little 'religious' deeds, but they remain totally devoid of Love. Love arises from Experience, which suffuses the word with LIFE! The word 'water' in the dictionary cannot quench one's thirst. Similarly, one cannot understand the word 'Love' without actually Experiencing it!

Nevertheless, these meaningless rituals have been going on for thousands of years. Kabir Sahib, however, preaches one Truth, which is all God. God is the One Truth Who can grant salvation for life eternal, not these pieces of stone statues. God is complete in Himself. There is no need to create Him in statues, paintings, etc. He was when the statues were not, and He will still be when the idols are no more.

"The whole world is praying to idols and Scriptures, and whoever is putting all his faith in stones and in Scriptures thinks that just by reading books and worshipping idols that he will be saved. Do you think that these stones and books will help you when you are going to die, or when you are going to drown? They are themselves drowning! How can they possibly help you?"

In another verse, Sant Kabir says, "O learned person! The practical knowledge (which is learned from a True Master), is very important. If you compare that one gram of Practical compared with ten thousand grams of theoretical knowledge, still the one gram of Practical Inner knowledge is much higher than the outer."

Kabir Sahib points out that all outer rites and rituals pertain only to the body. There is no sense of kneeling, falling to the ground, crying, shouting, or wailing. That is not prayer. One needs only to wash the face or take a full bath before meditation, to ensure that he remains wide-awake and alert in order to put concentration for the sweet memory of the Lord. In the eyes of God, all these rituals have no importance, but in the eyes of the common worldly people, rituals and rules have even been granted a far higher place than that of the Greatness of God!

Kabir Sahib points out that people are *actually worshipping Kaal* in the form of gods, goddesses, idols, books, and photographs! They pray to Kaal through these things, hoping to obtain all manner of perishable, worldly objects in return. In the eyes of those people, Kaal becomes like a 'lord'. Sant Kabir emphasizes that when humanity has at long last taken the human birth, it is nothing short of shameful to see people worshipping in these wrong ways of meaningless rituals.

He also warns those who sacrifice living creatures, such as animals, believing that they will receive benefit for the offering. He asks, "How possibly will those people get a reward? Almighty God will be very unhappy with these deeds! Those people shall suffer tremendous consequences at the end of their life for these acts!" Sant Kabir issues a strict warning to those who partake of any kind of meat, fish or wine. He says that regardless of what kind, or how many pilgrimages, fasts, or daily rites that person performs, he will end up in hell as punishment for these evil deeds.

"Do not take the life of any living creature! If we have Love for God, then we must Love all His Creation." He gives the example, "The gentle goat eats only simple grass, but in the end, he gets skinned! *What will happen to those who eat the goat?*"

In many different ways, Kabir Sahib tries to teach humanity the knowledge of the Higher Self. Different angles of vision are presented, so that people can easily understand His meaning. He gives very humourous comparisons of those who are illiterate to those who consider themselves to be very learned. For example, He explains that one cannot know God by running around in a jungle without any clothes. "If people think that they can catch hold of God in this way, then all the animals would have long ago reached God!" He especially emphasizes this because nakedness was the practice of some ascetics.

Another example used is that a person cannot obtain God by wearing animal skins. There was a custom amongst the wandering mendicants to go about wrapped in deer hides. Kabir Sahib says that ultimately one must recognize God in one's own self, and the wearing of deer skin does not bring anyone closer to God. God is vibrating in each and every pore of the human body.

A third example given is the practice of shaving the head in order to find God. "If shaving the head would help one to find God, then all the sheep which get shorn every season and grow wool again, would have long ago obtained Enlightenment!"

Sant Kabir gives many, many examples of the foolishness that people follow in the name of religion. He tells about the mendicants who do not cut their hair or even comb it, allowing it to become terribly matted. He asks how possibly can this practice bring about liberation from the effects of the senses?

Without drinking the Nectar of God's Holy Name, one cannot have salvation in this way!

He very Lovingly explains that one's life has to be very simple. One must earn his own livelihood, and not beg for charity. "It would be better to stay hungry rather than to beg, for one cannot obtain God in this fashion. The rosaries and beads are useless and should be given up also, because one cannot obtain God by wearing them, or in saying prayers by turning the threaded beads. Aeons have passed in telling beads; yet the mind has not been changed."

He advises to cast off the wooden beads and take to the mental ones. The true rosary lies in the mind, and the rest is all a worldly show. When the beads are turned and the mind still wanders, then such outer deeds of merit are hollow. "How can God be found with an insensitive mind? The rosary makes its round in the hand and the tongue does the same by wagging in the mouth, but the mind keeps running out in ten directions-- such is not the remembrance of God!"

Sant Kabir says, "Listen furthermore! Don't come into the delusion of the four Vedas, the seven Simritis, and the eighteen Puranas. These were all created by the Avatars!" Then He gives the fact that all the gods and goddesses are also under the effects of Illusion. "Even Lakshmi and her husband *Vishnu*, have not understood or found Almighty God yet."

Kabir Sahib also discusses about the six *Chakras* (Centres of Energy) in the physical body. He tells us that each of them has a presiding deity. Everybody is familiar with them and many actually worship these gods and goddesses, but Sant Kabir says that man's soul is higher on the scale of Creation than these gods, to whom many offer their devotion.

He reminds us that with the advent of death, the body begins to die from the lower parts, and then upwards. Naturally, the first of these gods to perish is Ganesh, who is the presiding deity at the first *Guda Chakra Centre* (near the rectum).

Next to die is Brahma, who rules at the second *Indri Chakra* (near the regeneration area).

After that is Vishnu, who discharges his duties at the third *Nabhi Chakra* (near the navel).

Shiva resides at the fourth *Hirdey Chakra* (located near the heart).

And finally there is Shakti, who looks after the fifth *Kanth Chakra* (located near the throat region).

It is important to note that although these gods are contained within the human body, they occupy a place lower than where the soul sits. The soul dwells at the Third Eye, the Single Eye, and this place is called the Seat of the Soul.

Sant Kabir says, "What a pity that the soul, which is of a higher status, should pay homage to that which is lower than itself. If all these deities die before the total body is dead how, then, can they possibly be worthy of our worship?"

He tells us that any effort in praying to these gods and goddesses cannot assist one to come above the body consciousness. "Only when the soul comes up to the *Ajna Chakra*, the sixth Centre, the Region of *Jyot Niranjan*, at the Third Eye behind and between the two eyebrows, can it pass from the Physical into the Astral Region."

Lord Kabir explains many other outer rituals that people observe, such as looking for God on top of the hill, in the jungle, or at the various places of pilgrimage. The people who perform those rituals say that God lives here, or there. Years roll by and they keep on looking for God. Sant Kabir points out that it is not through acts of piety, or even exercises of restraint that one can find the Lord. The consequence of one's good or bad actions is a return to this world, *but not liberation from it!*

Salvation cannot be attained by visits to sacred places, fasting, ritual piety, and alms-giving. "If it were so, it would be very easy for the rich people and kings to win salvation, but liberation comes only through the practice of the Holy Naam."

All the external disciplines and good deeds do not grant Contact with God, nor do they lift the Inner Veil. These are only methods devised by Kaal *to keep the people away from God!* The attention becomes focused on these rituals, and Sant Kabir says that the result is that everyone dwindles away the priceless wealth of the human body given to them by Almighty God.

Sant Kabir is sharing His knowledge of Divinity with those people who are wasting their precious breath of life in the practice of wrong methods and outer rituals. He advises them, "You are making yourself as food for Kaal, because this is deceiving your own Goal of the precious human birth. The Treasure of the Holy Naam for which you are seeking, is not a worldly treasure." He says that the person who is sincerely after Truth, turns his attention away from the outer world.

He advises, "Keep away from the desires of this world and its Illusions, questions and suspicions!" He uses the example that if the devotee truly considers that his body, mind, and wealth all belong to the Master, then all his worldly possessions and family relations also belong to the Master! Outer things of the world will have no affect when the person has

God's Light and Sound embedded in him, and he continuously thinks about God.

There is a story from the life of the young boy Kabir which illustrates the futility of these outer rites and rituals. The boy Kabir would be about twelve or thirteen years old, and was about to be Initiated into the religion of Islam through the ritual of circumcision. It is an important ceremony. Many people were invited and a band was arranged. All the friends and relatives gathered together.

This is a big function, marking the passage from childhood into a full-fledged Muslim. However, the young Kabir child refused to let this ceremony happen. He said, "Wait! What will happen by this ceremony? How can this ritual help me to find God?" Of course, everyone was astounded that the child would even speak such questions.

The boy then informed everyone that He has been an Awakened Soul since His birth, and this ritual would not help Him in any Spiritual Way. The Qazi tried to explain that this function has been done for hundreds of years, and that this operation would make a man into a true Muslim. The elders tried their best to urge the young Kabir to comply, but to no avail. Nobody could ever force Him to do anything, and the young Kabir simply disappeared from that scene and made Himself available on the other side of the village.

Sant Kabir now poses the question to the reader as to who made up all these rituals and beliefs? He then goes on to explain how a person becomes narrow-minded and congealed in his own Faith, thinking that he is the higher status person and all others are lower.

"Who has made these different religions, and who has made all the different ways of saying that this is heaven and this is hell?" He tries to make people aware that God did not make up any of these so-called 'rules' of religion. These were made up by ordinary mortals, in order to fulfill their passion for power and money!

Sant Kabir has all along described in His verses that He never agrees with any outer ritual. "In these ways and rites, one cannot obtain God. Almighty God can only be recognized when one leaves off all these petty things. To be honest with oneself, means not to follow any blind dogmas."

During the time of Sant Kabir, there was a man named *Gorakhanath*. He was the founder of the Nath-Sampradaya Sect, an influential Sect in those days. He was a great exponent of *Hatha Yoga*, and had attained many Supernatural Powers by its practice. He considered himself to be a great Yogi, but somehow he was not quite convinced of the greatness of Sant Kabir. Oftentimes a person's doubt and suspicion, combined with pride, create barriers for him to come and surrender at the Lotus Feet of the Guru.

One day, it came in the mind of Gorakhanath to make some mischief on Sant Kabir. With his Yogic Powers, he recited a special Mantra that guided two poisonous snakes to go all the way to Sant Kabir's hut, with the intent to bite Him with their fierce fangs, and then return to the place of Gorakhanath.

Gorakhanath waited for several hours, but when the snakes did not return, he decided to go to Sant Kabir's house, and see for himself what had happened. He knocked on the door and called for Kabir Sahib to come outside.

Sant Kabir replied that Gorakhanath himself should enter instead, since He was too busy serving His two newly-arrived guests! Just see how Sant Kabir was teaching Gorakhanath that snakes also have the Essence of God in them, and that they had recognized the Holy Presence of the Lord in Sant Kabir!

Kabir Sahib then spoke to Gorakhanath, advising him that he would lose his Yogic Powers if they were misused in this foolish way. Lord Kabir suggested that Gorakhanath should use his wonderful Powers to help himself to rise above the body consciousness, and merge his soul with Almighty God.

By now, several other Yogis had gathered at this scene. Sant Kabir addressed Gorakhanath, as well as all the other Yogis who were misusing their Special Powers. He asked them if there was any Yogi amongst them who could keep apart from all the five vices. He advised everyone not to let these vices have their way. "Don't get use out of them, and don't ever allow the mind to come under their influence!"

He continued, "I will tell you what these vices want. *Lust* wishes for woman; *anger* wants to fight; *greed* craves money and possessions; *attachment* hankers for worldly love; and *ego* is desiring for pride. The passions want these particular things. Don't let them be together and don't fulfill their desires. Don't let *lust* go towards woman; *anger* should not fight with anyone; don't become *attached* to anybody other than God; don't let *greed* meet with anybody else; and don't join hands with *pride*. Try to stay in the Holy Company of the Master. Is there any Yogi amongst you who can stay away from these things?"

Taking the opportunity, Gorakhanath asked Kabir Sahib, "Please tell us what kind of Yogi we should be!" And Sant Kabir replied, "O Gorakhanath! Is there any Yogi in your following, or have you ever seen one who has made all the five passions burn into ashes to put in his shoulder bag, or who is aware of the Master's Shabd? Whoever has an Experience of the Divine Sound Current is the true Yogi!"

Then Gorakhanath asked another question. "If someone has the Discrimination of Spiritual knowledge, is he considered to be a true Yogi?"

Sant Kabir answered, "I will tell you how Discrimination works. The whole world is involved in the three *Gunns* (Qualities): the Gunn of *Satva* (Purity), of *Rajas* (Activity), and of *Tamas* (Inertia). Discrimination, however, is higher than this intellect, and therefore one should not become mixed up in the affairs of the world. You have to keep above all these things, because they come from and only relate to the Regions of Brahma, Vishnu, and Shiva."

Sant Kabir advised all the Yogis, "Don't have desires of any kind, except the desire for Grace and *Seva* (Selfless Service) of the True Master. If you leave aside all worldly affairs, then the real knowledge will come. This Spiritual Way is the true awakening within the person. Do you know anyone in this world who is fully Awake, and knows himself? Is there anyone amongst you who uses his Power of Discrimination to know the Real from the unreal? You have to keep the Power of Discrimination close, all the time, just like you wear those earrings close to you. Listen to the Holy Sound Current, and then whenever you need the assistance of Discernment, it will be there."

One of the Yogis was named *Bhartheri Gopi Chand*. Not understanding the full import of Sant Kabir's words, this Yogi spoke up, indignantly remarking, "Kabir Sahib! You will not find such a great Guru Yogi anywhere like *Gorakhanath, Machundernath,* or *Charpatnath!*"

Sant Kabir, however, patiently smiled and replied, "O Brother Bhartheri! Do you think that just wearing coloured clothes and big earrings will make one into a *true Yogi?*"

Bhartheri then defended the great efforts of the Yogis. He said, "We put on earrings and saffron-coloured clothes. We forsake our families and leave our homes. We take our stick and put it underneath our legs, and then we sit down under a tree in meditation. We try to leave off all worldly thoughts. We do so much effort, keeping all the prescribed rituals. When we burn wood, we even put the ashes into our shoulder bags!"

Kabir Sahib listened with great patience and then said, "But *I already have* that kind of 'clothes' and all those other things!" The Yogis were amazed. They squinted their eyes as they protested, "But we don't see them; neither the bag nor the begging bowl!"

Then Sant Kabir explained, "O listen brothers! I have Love and devotion for God. The 'earrings' that I wear are made of

Love. With my *Surat* (Attention), the Holy Sound Current became manifested in me. The five vices (lust, anger, etc.) don't even come near to me. This is the type of 'clothes' that I wear. The true Yogi wears *Inner*, not outer, clothes!"

Of course, by now all the Yogis showed interest, and almost in one voice they pleaded, "Please tell us more!" Sant Kabir continued, "The true Spiritual Regions don't perish. I have direct access to them. This is 'the bag of ashes' that I carry, whereas the world carries only the worldly ashes. Everything in this world will perish one day, because everything in the material world is subject to dissolution, just like our life. My attention, however, never wanders to any type of worldly desire. I am all the time in the sweet memory of my Master. The Holy Naam is not in the outer, worldly sounds that go on throughout all four stages of one's life (childhood, youth, middle, and old age). The true Yogi listens instead to the Inner Sound Current, which is vibrating continuously day and night." Greatly impressed with these words of Truth, the Yogis reverently bowed down to Sant Kabir.

Sometimes the Saint has to use strong measures to make the other person realize that in spite of attaining some Supernatural Powers, he cannot realize Almighty God in these outwardly, worldly ways. These extra Powers can fulfill worldly desires because these Powers are of this world, but they are of no avail on the Spiritual Path. The seeker must come to the Master in all humility, casting out his ambition to possess any world-worldly gains.

#5-3 The Mind and Its Desires

*K*abir Sahib explains that there are three minds attached to the soul when it descends from the Higher Spiritual Realms:
1. The *Brahmandi* or *Nij* (Causal) Mind, the true inner mind, functions in *Trikuti* (the Causal Region). It is also known as the Universal Mind.
2. The *Andhi* (Astral) Mind functions in the Astral Region.
3. The *Pindi* (Physical) Mind functions in the Physical world, manifesting itself in everyday life.

In addition, Almighty God has given the mind four 'tools' with which to work. These 'tools' all relate to intellect and comprehension, with knowledge and attachment as the result. With their usage, the heart has a connection with the intellect so that one can determine what is right and wrong. Knowledge is also one of the qualities of the mind.

These 'tools' are:
1. *Chit*, which gives the mind the ability to think. It is also memory; the Inner Attention.
2. *Mun*, which is the mind, the instrument of meditation.

3. *Buddhi*, which is the Discriminating Power of the intellect.
4. *Ahankar*, which is pride and ego.

The soul, however, has a 'tool' all its own, which is known *as* '*Surat*' or the *Attention*, and its quality is *stillness*.

Sant Kabir fully and very beautifully expounds on the nature and characteristics of the mind. All through life, the mind has been used to taste only the transient pleasures of this outer, material world. Desires of the mind always go ahead of the person, as one believes himself to be worthy of more and more.

It is very useful and important for a seeker after Truth to understand the tendencies of the mind, so that these can be used to befriend and cajole it into tasting the Inebriating Pleasures of the Divine. Man gets himself caught in the web of his desires and then wanders about within them. The Sat Guru rescues the person from the crushing effects of this Deception and Illusion. That person is so lucky that the Master comes to his rescue. Sant Kabir gives the example of being crushed with worldly desires and attractions, just like the person was caught in an oil press.

Man praises all his dreams and desires in many forms. But the worst part is that if the desires are not fulfilled, man is not satisfied. If they are met, again he is not content. All complain, the successful and the unsuccessful, the rich and the poor, the healthy and the sick. All desires of man can only end in regret, except the desire to meet God. Man wagers his very life for paltry gains. All 'wants' and desires represent a quest of the ego, and whatever is born out of the ego, is false and Illusionary.

At the first glimpse of God, the person suddenly realizes that it was because of his very self (the ego) that he missed Him all this time. The person now understands that all the efforts that had seemed so very intense and exhausting, are worth absolutely nothing.

There can be no comparison between man's effort and God's Grace. One realizes how insignificant and petty his own efforts are; all the going to the Temples; all that worship and penance; all the *Japa* (intense repetition of a Mantra), all the bending into different postures; all the shouting and beating of oneself; how much are they all worth? The Priceless cannot be had at any price in the marketplace of the world. Any labour or effort on the part of man is insignificant. At the moment of realization, man stands with his hands cupped, and the whole Ocean pours into them.

People haven't really made true efforts. For example, if one's house is on fire, that person would really run towards it. If his child was lost, he would run here and there, frantically searching everywhere, just like a mad person. One must ask himself if his search for God is really this intense. Has he really cried for God in intense grief and separation? Just like a fish suddenly out of its beloved water, every hair on the person would fill with thirst for the Holy Name of God! Everything else but *'I must attain Him!'* should be meaningless in his life. When God alone is the only purpose, it produces the needed concentration to attain the true Goal.

Truth is not far away, even closer than one's own heartbeat, his very breath! Unfortunately, when one takes upon himself the task of finding God, limits are set for what he wishes to attain. He imagines that it must be smaller than himself in order to grasp it tightly. Then how can one possibly attain Almighty God, the Supreme Lord, the Infinite Power? It is quite the opposite: only he who is ready to lose himself attains Him. When one puts himself in His palm, He can be attained. A Vast Expanse cannot be packaged and carried home to show off to others! As long as the 'I' is working, or fasting, or worshipping, or doing penance, or going on pilgrimage, the subtle but determined ego keeps repeating: "I am doing this!" The only condition to attain God is that the 'I' and 'Me' and 'Mine' must drop. There is room for only one--either the self or God!

The mind's predominant work is that it is the Agent of Kaal. Sant Kabir tells us that because the mind comes from the

Third Spiritual Region, its main job is to distract the soul by sending various thoughts whenever the person wants to sit in meditation. The mind won't let the person concentrate even for a second, because the total record of all the five senses stays with the mind. The mind keeps a record of all thoughts, words, and deeds from aeons of years, since the soul took its first birth.

That is why it is said that *'the mind is made of total Karma'*. And that explains why, when the person tries to sit down in meditation, the mind sends a bombardment of thoughts, distracting him very badly, taking his attention ever outward and downward, which is the usual direction of the mind. One cannot comprehend God by thinking, nor can he quiet the mind, however long he sits.

Nothing can be achieved by effort. By bending the body into certain postures, one cannot force the mind to follow suit. The cacophony of the mind will continue with even greater intensity. When the body is engaged in some physical activity, all its energy is divided, but when the body sits absolutely inactive, all this energy flows to the mind, producing thoughts at an even greater speed. All thoughts of the outside world are related to the desires of the mind. That is why one can do worldly work with such peace. However, just try to enter within, and the mind creates confusion, as it is not appeased. By forcing stillness, nothing is gained.

Sant Kabir reminds us that since the mind hails from the Third Region, it is naturally very powerful. He explains that if one should want to control anything in this world, it is only the mind. "Whosoever can control the mind, he has literally won the whole universe."

Until one doesn't have any control or restraint over the mind, he cannot be out of the reach of the Lord of Death, and have ultimate salvation. To have control over the mind, means that when the mind is ordered what to do and when to do it, then such things should happen without any distracting thoughts from the mind.

Fortunately, there is another Force at work, which is called *Grace*. It is an invisible Force that pulls one upwards, towards Him. As the pull of the mind diminishes, the pull of Grace increases proportionally, until the time comes when the mind can have no effect whatsoever on the soul.

Kabir Sahib explains that this constant controlling and restraining of the mind is very necessary. One's job is not to obey the mind but to become desireless, which then forces the mind to obey the person. One has to learn to harness the mind, and bring it constantly inwards. This is not an easy task, because the whole world dances to its tune. There is no need to fall into the mind's trap. The mind cannot give knowledge; it can only give untruth. He who listens to the mind falls into falsity. The mind is made of only lies and Illusion, and can produce nothing.

Sant Kabir, therefore, offers some very valuable advice, explaining how one can effectively exercise control over the mind. He says that the mind has to be kept busy by giving it more enticing, more sweet, more attractive things than what it is used to getting outwardly. Once the mind has the taste of that, it gradually permits the attention to go inwards, and from there one starts to rise above the body consciousness.

But, of course, all of this only happens when the person is really hankering to meet Almighty God, which in turn, invokes God's compassion and Grace to be showered upon the person.

"The true person is one who is in full peace, who leaves all the desires of the world. God Himself is searching out such a one. That person has no worries or fears, no greed nor attachment towards this world. He will want only God and His Holy Name on his lips forever."

Sant Kabir says that only in this way can the mind be conquered. "One can restrain the mind and obtain salvation only by knowing God, realizing the self and the Overself, and His Creation. Unless there is a thirst for Him, with zeal and passion, and a burning desire in the heart, one cannot obtain God.

God doesn't come of Himself. One has to ask Him for Himself."

In His own life, Sant Kabir was earning His livelihood by the profession of weaving, and from this He fed not only His own family, but also the hungry and the needy. In many verses, He gives His own example to those Sadhus who are really hankering to obtain God and salvation. He says that the Godman always becomes the true example for others. He shows the world how simple His life is, and how He honestly earns His own livelihood.

"By being simple, the full attention will be towards God. One won't be worried about possessions, attachments, and there won't be desires."

Man's hopes and dreams are endless. He possesses so many things. There is no way to fulfill these longings. Even if one obtains all that he desires, one is still not satisfied. The more one attains, the more he wanders in the multifarious objects of the world, and the further he goes away from the thoughts of returning unto God.

There is another story about Gorakhanath. Gorakhanath came across Sant Kabir on the latter's travels through the state of Gujarat. Gorakhanath, of course, wanted to show off his newly-acquired Yogic Powers. There were several of his

Yogi followers amongst the gathering which had come to hear the Discourse of Sant Kabir.

Puffed up with pride and feeling that he had vast knowledge of just about everything, Gorakhanath thrust his three-pronged spear (trident) upside down into the ground. He then quickly climbed up and sat (with his Yogic Power, of course) on the sharp tip of one of its extended prongs. He was overcome with pride of this achievement, and bursting with excitement, he called out to Kabir Sahib, inviting Him to come up and sit on another tip.

Sant Kabir just smiled and quietly took out a ball of thread. Holding one end of the thread, He threw the ball up into the air and the whole ball of thread soon unravelled. The end of the thread hung downwards, but did not touch the ground. It was just like a long, thin thread suspended in the air without any support. Sant Kabir then climbed up this thread and took His seat on the uppermost tip, inviting Gorakhanath to *come up there and join Him!*

When Gorakhanath saw that Sant Kabir was actually sitting on the very tip of this thread which had no visible means of support, and which was suspended above the ground, he was incredulous. His ego, naturally, became a fair bit deflated.

Sant Kabir then informed Gorakhanath that the Path of Sant Mat that He teaches, is not assisted nor aided by anything worldly, or by any other matter of this world. He said, "*I hail from where there is no support of this physical world!*"

Kabir Sahib says that the mind can be a tremendous hurdle on the Spiritual Path. The whole world has always succumbed at some stage or the other to its powerful impact. The mind cannot be controlled by outer pursuits, such as learning or studying the Scriptures. Even if it comes under check for a little while, it again goes out of control because it is always after sensual pleasures.

Ego, especially, is the subtlest of all the intoxicants. One tries to practice humility, but ego is still there, stirring inside. Sant Kabir says that one should bring a critic and keep him nearby. "Make a hut for him in your courtyard, for he can see your ego, which you cannot! He will remain as a 'watchdog' to constantly remind you of your ego!" Man is blind to his own ego, but others can see it clearly! He says that ego can only be dissolved when the realization of death becomes an absolute fact. Therefore, the wise person constantly remembers death.

Sant Kabir also says that wherever there is lust of one kind or the other (lust is another name for *desire*, born out of greed), one cannot expect to find the Holy Naam. The two are never together. He uses the example that if someone says that the two states of day and night can be together, that is not possible. Similarly, if the mind is not pure, concentration cannot be developed.

People so anxiously guard the body so that nothing defiles it, and yet the mind remains unchecked and unbridled. Until the mind is curbed, the Way Godward does not become opened. The mind has to be restrained at all costs. One becomes tied to the world because of his desires. Desires are the chains that hold the person, because each desire forms a fresh link in the chain. One's desires are only experienced through the senses, but the senses, in turn, do not experience anything without the mind. Their experiences rely entirely on the attention. If one's awareness is flowing towards God, the world will be lost to him; it fades from perception. Existence, therefore, fades when the attention is withdrawn.

Sant Kabir goes on to explain that there are mainly two types of attractions for the mind--beautiful things to see, and sweet melodies to hear. He advises that the only way to keep the mind under control is to connect it with the Holy Naam, which has both of these attractions. When the mind has more fascinating Experiences within than it does without, then it will automatically be subdued and restrained.

"Once the mind becomes attached to worldly things, it can be said that it is 'sleeping'. How possibly can that person earn the true Treasure? He is only after false, worldly treasure, in his greed." This vice of desire and wanting is a great sin. Sant Kabir says, "Don't become attached to greed. It is most undesirable and once you have acquired it, it grows and it won't let you take the Path towards Reality."

Most people don't rise above the tendency of asking for and receiving worldly things. Life just passes them by, wasted in the gathering of pebbles and shells. Man agonizes in his desires; yet does not awaken to the fact that he suffers because of these desires. Most ills are the result of desire and longing, but the one is never realized to be the result of the other. The person's prayers become coloured with these hues of longing.

The breath of countless prayers are offered to the service of desires. People become so much weighed down by misfortune that they gradually believe that this is what life is all about. They are unaware of the fact that life can be of supreme bliss.

He continues, "The mind is under the control of the outgoing faculties, but these five foes are not under the control of the mind, because whatever the mind sees, there it runs and becomes attached to that. The mind, however, is only one mind and it can do only one worship at a time. Either the person can do the worship of God, or he can put the mind towards the world. The mind has the ability to become attached to whatever the person directs it."

Sant Kabir compares the mind that runs about in all directions, to the waves of the sea. If one can control those waves, then he can restrain the mind from the attractions of the world. The many desires of the mind have different colours, and Kabir Sahib says, "It is a rare person who can keep the mind in just one colour."

Although the mind is so small, it can still become like a huge mountain in front of the person. However, with one Magic Touch of the Godman and His Blessed Sound Current, the mind can become small again and under restraint.

Sant Kabir is telling us that, unfortunately, the mind can also put doubt and suspicion (regarding the Master) into the person. If one looks upon the Master as an ordinary human being, he can become stuck fast in superstition and he eventually drowns in these doubts. The Master is none other than God Himself personified in a human form, and if one sees the Master only on the human level, then the person himself cannot rise above that same level. Until one's mind realizes the Divinity of the Master, he cannot do true Bhakti of the Master.

Continuing on the subject of the mind, Sant Kabir says, "If you are defeated by the mind, you become totally defeated. If you conquer the mind, you are the real conqueror. You have to be determined and win it over, because the mind has hundreds of thousands of doors, opening unto the numerous attractions and desires."

He says that the mind can be very ferocious, and whoever has tackled with the mind, is the one who knows just how fierce it is! It is very difficult to restrain the *Nij Mun* (the Brahmandi or Causal Mind). The devotee has to learn how he can make the mind turn its attention towards the Master and become contented in this.

Sant Kabir affirms that even if one gives all his possessions, including his mind and body to the Sat Guru, even that still is not enough. "What good is it, if one has not given up his mind? The mind has also eaten up all the Rishis and Munis! Everyone has fallen under its dominance!"

Sant Kabir points out that the mind is attracted to things such as praying to Kaal's lower agents, the Avatars and Lower Powers, the gods and goddesses, worshipping idols, wandering about on pilgrimages, or singing praises to those deities who lived in the past. If the heart really wants to think about, or pray to, Almighty God (Who is Highest above all), or to the Sat Guru (Who is God manifested), the stubborn mind just won't let it rest.

Kabir Sahib tells us that the mind is never satisfied, no matter how many pleasures it tastes. Everyone speaks through the mind. "The mind is the same, no matter where you apply it, whether in the Master's devotion or in the worldly earnings. Yogis have spent their entire lives in Yoga practices, but they could not subdue the stubborn mind. Even the Avatars as well as the gods and goddesses come under the clutches of the realms of the mind. They desire the boons of worldly enjoyments and as a result, they are unable to see the Creator within them. What to think of an ordinary mortal like man!"

Things are easily obtained in the world merely by not asking. The child, for example, who makes no demands on the parents, receives everything unasked for. Desires and demands separate one from God. When one stands as a beggar at God's door, one is implying that God should only serve his needs.

People pray, "Give me! Give me!" If God is the Master and the seeker is the slave, then what remains of the demands? A desire can never become a prayer. The essence of prayer is thanksgiving. God has already given more than one deserves. If one is constantly begging, when will his prayers begin? When will his true worship commence? If one's desire is fulfilled, ten more take its place. One can never be satisfied, because it is not the mind's nature to be content. When one is rid of the mind and its desires, then contentment and satisfaction appear.

Sant Kabir is telling us about the condition of the mind, that since all the thoughts which the Negative Power sends are coming through the mind, then without stilling the mind, there is no hope of making Spiritual progress or obtaining any salvation in this physical body. He compares the restless mind to an untamable ocean in which endless tides spring up. Unless it is stilled, the Goal cannot be reached. The waves which originate in the mind come from the Physical Plane of the senses, and these oscillations have to be subdued. The rebellious mind feels pleasure in roaming at large and does not like to give up its liberty, until it has attained higher pleasures in exchange for its present enjoyment, but only constant practice can compel it to give up these former habits.

The mind is made of desire, so when the mind is focused on something higher, such as the Holy Names of God, then another state of being is born. Then that person becomes filled with gratitude.

Sant Kabir says that the mind is like a magician who acts in the body, taking the attention away from the soul and from the All-Consciousness, out into the materialistic world, into the relations, the day-to-day basic work, and into all the myriad attachments of the mind. The mind, in its turn, takes the attention into building its own little world day and night not knowing, however, that this world will perish. This is the dutiful work of the mind.

Kabir Sahib advises, "Find a way to still the mind. Give something to the mind which is far more better and attractive than these worldly attachments. The mind is happy to do whatever it likes to do, to listen, to talk, as long as it is always doing something. These are all Illusions and consist of what is the untruth. Until one doesn't leave them off and learn how to rise above the body consciousness, or to be detached from these things, he cannot hope to obtain God."

He is saying that people foolishly believe they will obtain the knowledge of Almighty God by leaving their home, and going into the jungle. The mind, however, and all its actions, deeds, and thoughts, will go along with the person even into the jungle! Until and unless one doesn't remove worldly thoughts from the mind and the heart, there can be no solution or salvation acquired.

Even one's dreams stop when there is nothing left to be attained, for dreams follow in the steps of desires. If there are no desires, there are no dreams. When all efforts cease, the ego falls, and then Godly Grace descends.

Sant Kabir offers the solution to this problem by saying that one should not run away from his home, but rather he must try to control all of his thoughts, words, and deeds. These are all connected to the senses, which remain attached to the mind regardless of whether the person is in the forest or his own home. Good deeds and service to humanity cleanse the person's mind and heart. By having remembrance of Almighty God with all Love, the true happiness which people so earnestly seek outwardly, will be found as the 'All-Consciousness' right within the body.

Sant Kabir explains that if one can withdraw the attention inward and have control over the outgoing faculties, he will literally become desireless. By doing so, and with the help of the Holy Sound Current, he will be able to conquer the mind. By conquering the mind, which is made of thoughts and various Illusions, that lucky person will actually then be able to conquer the first three Spiritual Regions.

Kabir Sahib says very clearly that *"By conquering the mind, man conquers the world!"* He tells us that the true *Maulana* (Sage) is he who controls the mind.

He says that compassion and contentment are very valuable. One's whole life is contained within them. Contentment within, and compassion without, must be balanced in one's life. Dissatisfaction produces unrest and turbulence, when the person feels that things are not happening as he would wish them to happen, or that there is some lacking in one's life. Then restlessness begins. The mind will concentrate on all that the person does not have, and will see only insufficiency and misery.

When, however, there is satisfaction and contentment in all that one has, that person is filled with gratefulness towards He Who has given so much. The true devotee must always have compassion towards others, not for himself. Kindness, sympathy, and compassion develop into a sense of service to others that fills one with prayer and worship, because it then becomes the Path that leads to God.

The ideal devotee has contentment within, and compassion without. This goes hand-in-hand with meditation within, and kindness without. However, only being compassionate towards others will not take one anywhere. If one does not observe contemplation within, awaken Sweet Remembrance and meditate on the Lord's Holy Name, he can reach nowhere.

"If somebody takes the knowledge of the Master and truly practices on it, he will be able to do what is described. The person who obtains this condition in himself to contest and control the Universal Mind, is worthy to be saluted." It should also be pointed out that if someone can restrain the Universal

Mind (whose origin is in the Third Spiritual Region), that person is finally freed from the control of Kaal, because the Universal Mind belongs to Kaal!

With respect to those people who preach to others that God is far away, Sant Kabir tells them that when one is in control of the mind, he will realize that God pervades in each and every atom. By having full restraint and control over the mind, one makes his life fully disciplined in every aspect, and then he becomes aware of the Sat Guru's Presence watching over him. The mind, of course, remains under control by uttering the Simran of the Master's Holy Naam. "There is no release from this world, except through the Holy Naam."

This, then, is the predicament of the soul, which is now tossing about aimlessly on the waves of the stormy Ocean of physical existence, in the ship of the mind and the five senses. This ship has no captain to guide it, and the soul has become its prisoner. The worldly mind wanders ceaselessly. It is only the True Master, with His Enchanting *Shabd Current*, that can still and control this mind, which can never be satisfied with these worldly pleasures and luxuries.

The mind is a great mystery because sometimes it has elevated thoughts of a higher and more Spiritual life, and yet at other times, it lusts for wealth and other objects of this world. It wanders continuously here, there, everywhere. "The mind is the monarch in each and every person. It has totally forgotten its Source and the only way to subdue it, is through the Holy Naam."

#5-4 Fear and Fearless

Everyone, except the Master, has some kind of fear. Sant Kabir explains very clearly about the different fears that most people in this world have, such as a fear of dying, a different fear of worldly affairs, another kind of fear of the police, and the fears of thousands of little things which slowly, but steadily reduce the life, just like termites are eating away at the body. Fear very cleverly works like this, because along with fear comes worry and anxiety.

Sant Kabir is talking to a seeker. He says, "O brother! You have not had the true Spiritual Experience within your own self. Nobody has seen God outwardly. God can only be seen by the person who realizes the Light of God, and sees His Presence. Almighty God is only known and realized when one has the fear of God born in him." This point is very subtle. The devotee has to develop a fear of the Creator, that He is the One Who is watching his every thought, deed, and word.

Once the person hears or sees even the faintest proof of God's Hand behind this vast Creation, he cannot remain the same. Fear creeps into his heart and soul. One cannot continue to do what he has been doing; it all appears to be wrong. When man realizes that God does exist, he begins to think twice about his words and actions. Man begins to understand that now God can 'see' him and He is present everywhere. Whatever is being done to anyone, is being done to Him.

When the person accepts God's Hand behind the workings of the Universe, he is intimidated, and resorts to the Temple and Mosques for prayer, to beg for protection and the shelter of the worldly wealth and health. Fear forces him to beg, always asking for something or the other in his mundane world. The person, however, remains oblivious to the Munificence of God; otherwise he would not beg.

He who sees God's Presence everywhere, His Divine Grace in life itself and the unbounded Blessings He bestows with each and every breath, desires nothing but to express gratitude to Him. That person has nothing to ask for, because he has been showered with gifts. If he were to ask for anything, it would imply a complaint that God hasn't given enough. What remains to be given when one has obtained God's Love?

When someone gets sick, then he remembers God because he has fear of what might happen to him. He has a fear of dying, and of where he will go after death. This certainly grows in his heart, and he earnestly wants to have the help of a Godman to become 'fearless' of death. Sant Kabir explains that without having this particular fear of death, one cannot realize God. This type of fear develops as a growing restlessness to know the Truth, and to solve the mystery of death. This fear creates the desire and the further restlessness needed to know the Creator. Only with this anxiety of not knowing the Creator, can one obtain Him.

The fear always dwells in the devotee's heart that one day his body will perish, and if he has not obtained his salvation before the end, his human life will be totally wasted. Sant Kabir says that he who has this fear in his heart, tries to attain the Goal while living. However, a person not knowing himself, indulges in all kinds of sins and he has none of this fear of God. He will be doomed in this life, but those who put forth efforts in the search, get spared from the fear of the Agent of Death.

Nobody can cross the terrible Ocean of this world without this type of fear, which becomes a great Blessing from the Lord. One thinks constantly of the Supreme Power of Almighty God. Eventually, the question will arise in his mind about the mystery of death and how to solve it.

Where there is fear, there can be no connection with God. All prayers and worships are because man is afraid. They are not offered out of Love for God. All religious practices and rituals come into being out of fear--not out of a celebration of spontaneous joy. Fear creates separateness, whereas Love brings closeness. Fear and Love never meet. When fear is completely gone, only then does Love arise. How can one Love the One Whom he fears? One fights when he fears; he cannot surrender unto Him. One must attain His pleasure by being completely absorbed in Him, when the sense of being the 'doer' is completely annihilated.

Lord Kabir explains that it is definitely Grace from God if somebody develops a fear of dying. Each and every one of the person's hairs stands up when he remembers that his death is coming. That fear actually works in his favour, and he starts to look for the aim of his life--why he is born and where he will go after death. The true seeker will think in his heart and soul about the mystery of death. An uneasiness of not knowing where he will go, or what will happen to him after death grips him. Being helpless, he prays from the core of his heart and this type of sincere prayer is heard by God, Who then makes a Way for that soul to come to where the Lord Himself is manifested, as the Living Godman.

Sant Kabir says, "In the beginning of the discipleship, the devotee tries to hide a few things from the Master, but as his faith grows stronger, he comes to realize that the Master is all-knowing, that He is aware of each and every thing about the devotee. Fear, mingled with feelings of awe and respect awaken within, as he understands that the Creator Himself is manifested in the Master, and the devotee realizes that he cannot, therefore, conceal anything from the Master. The Master, of course, is aware of all the shortcomings and weaknesses of the devotee, as well as the amount of his Spiritual strength (or Will Power)."

Sant Kabir indicates that the devotee is aware of the Master seeing him while he is awake or asleep, and that He is all the time looking after him. The Master also knows all these thoughts which come into the devotee's mind. The devotee feels remorse and guilt when he thinks that he has fallen in sin on account of his own weaknesses, and wonders how can he ever be acceptable to the Master. He feels ashamed when he thinks about his bad Karmas.

When he sees the Master, he fears Him on account of these weaknesses combined with a feeling of remorse. He cannot raise his eyes in front of the Master in shame, but the Master has altogether different feelings of Love and forgiveness for the devotee. When the devotee comes to understand this, then he tries to recognize the Master's Commandments and respects them with full faith.

With fear, the devotee has more faith and devotion, Love and respect, and his honour increases day by day. Ultimately, with the Grace of the Master, and through the disciple's devotion, Love and faith, the devotee sees what Truth really is. That type of fear gradually develops into devotional respect for the Beloved Sat Guru. This only comes in the devotee's heart when he has no doubt of this world's Inner Realms. That *Gurumukh* (true devotee) never crosses the line of respect of that rule. This is a very subtle and high stage.

Sant Kabir continues, "Having a Master and His attention, the devotee fully develops a fear of Almighty God. Combined with remorse about his bad Karmas, his soul then becomes 'fit' for the unbounded Grace of Almighty God." That person recognizes his Master's orders and wishes, and respects them with full devotion.

Sant Kabir says, "He who fears heaven and hell doesn't know better, but once he recognizes God, then these things are not for him. This fear, of which everybody is afraid, doesn't come near to that person."

People who have this type of fear try to know themselves, and to learn this Spiritual Science from a Master. They try to 'attain' death while living. They work and practice on the Commandments of the Master. Whoever puts forth this kind of effort is spared the fear of the Agent of Death, but whoever isn't lucky enough to have this, always remains under the forces of life and death. This fear remains as a subtle fear which stays in the mind whenever one thinks about it, or whenever one sees someone who is dying or is very sick.

However, when the devotee has full faith in the Master and knows the Reality, that the Master is the Creator, with God Power manifested in Him, then he can overcome and conquer this fear. "Where there is realization of the Lord, there is no fear. Where there is fear, there is no Lord. The more fear one has, the more his attention will go towards the Truth, which is permeating and is forever. This is the only Truth which remains constant, and does not change."

When the devotee has this fear combined with remembrance of the Lord, he becomes purified very quickly. He develops more faith and devotion, Love and respect, which increases day by day. With the Grace of the Master and through the devotee's own efforts to worship, to have Love and faith, he sees what Truth is. This is Love intermingled with faith and full respect. This kind of Love, is true Love.

Sant Kabir says that a person will drink of this Sweet Nectar of the Divinity of God when he first has this fear of God. Slowly but surely, after rising above the body consciousness, this fear turns into a 'wanting' accompanied with great passion and zeal to know Almighty God.

When the Godman accepts the devotee in His refuge, the disciple's fear readily diminishes, becoming a totally different type of fear. It grows into respect combined with feelings of awe for his Master, born out of confidence that now he has the Divine Love of his Master, and has been accepted in His Shelter. Due to this, faith continues to develop in the devotee. As he progresses Spiritually, this faith and respect grows more and more. The devotee sees the Master with his own eyes, and gradually becomes more and more aware of the Master's unique Super-Powers.

When the devotee has this 'respectful fear', he readily absorbs the Teachings of the Master. With the Master's Grace, the devotee eventually develops true Love in him, and becomes fearless of any worldly affairs. "There can be no fear where there is Love, for perfect Love casts out fear."

Sant Kabir says, "When one does the Spiritual practices, he begins to feel the Divine Presence of God everywhere. Having this fear is a Boon to the devotee, helping him to know himself and the Overself. When he continues the practice given by the Master, he becomes fearless, because then he fully knows that the Master and God are One. Fear and Inner Spiritual Awakening cannot stay together. When the devotee finds that God is near to himself, then all his fears turn into Love."

Sant Kabir uses an example of keeping the Love of God in the eyes, just like a type of black eyeliner, known as *Kajal*. Usually the bride decorates her eyes in preparation for the ceremony of marriage. Similarly, Sant Kabir has used this image in comparison of the soul readying itself for union with the Beloved. He says, "If the collyrium of fear is put into the eyes which already contain devotion and faith, then those eyes will become more beautiful to the Beloved."

"If one truly Loves the Beloved, that person will become forever married. One who can never be widowed is known as *Sada Sohagun* (forever married)." The soul, which is considered to be the bride, is eternally married to the Lord.

Sant Kabir advises, "After partaking of the Nectar of Love, surrender your *Dhan-Mun-Pind* (service with wealth, mind, and body) to the Master." Thus, the soul enjoys the bliss of being One with the Lord. That devotee recognizes the sublimity of the Master and he tries never to cross that line of respect. Due to the great respect and honour that he gives to his Master, Love pours out from every atom of his body.

Sant Kabir explains another condition, called *'fearlessness'*, that is born in the disciple. He says that when, with the Grace of the True Master, the devotee sees God working everywhere, then he becomes aware of and knows that everything that is happening in the whole of Creation, is according to the Will of God (*Hukam*). When he becomes aware of this Will, he begins to say, "Sweet is Thy Will!" At this stage, he becomes fearless from death and Illusion. He says, "My wish is of no consequence. *What is, is from Thee!"*

The further one penetrates into fear, the more fearless he becomes. A devotee of God transforms his fear into devotion. Now he fears only God, so that through the fear, he can maintain restraint and balance in his life. With the help of this fear, he can regulate his life, and in this way, he is kept from going on the wrong Path. This is not an ordinary fear. The more that person fears God, the more he falls in Love with Him. He becomes anxious not to 'miss' Him for even a fraction of a moment. He prays, "O Lord! May Your Sweet Remembrance never leave me. Only Your Love can keep my remembrance constant."

Fear converts into prayer and whenever fear takes hold of him, he utilizes it as an occasion for prayer. Fear opens up awareness, as the intellect of the mind is left behind. In fear, the whole body trembles. Each hair of the body stands on end, and the Conscious becomes stable and concentrated.

Sant Kabir says, "O brother, whoever becomes fearless and understands true devotion, will obtain *Hari Ras* (Divine Elixir). Whoever can bestow this Amrit is the rare, True Master." The true devotee says, "I have finished with the intellect. I have made my attention into the Surat, and merged it into the Sound Current. Now I am fearless, and unaffected by the Illusions of this world. My mind is now my obedient servant."

"Where there is *Gian* (Truth, true knowledge), there is no fear. Where there is no fear or Love, there is no faith or respect. Where there is faith, respect, and Love, there is God, but where there is fear, there can be no true knowledge of God." In other words, when the fear of God is awakened, then the worldly type of fear (of death, taxes, etc.) diminishes. "In the Company of the Fearless One (the Saint, the Master), the devotee becomes fearless and goes confidently on the Journey to God."

He continues, "To do *Gurbhakti* (Devotion to the Guru) is not the work of a coward. Be fearless and *take your head off* with your own hand (discard the ego). That person is the only one who is worthy to take the Name of *Sat Naam* (God's Name of 'All Truth')."

Kabir Sahib describes to humanity at large that whoever has the Name of the Creator on his lips, the Creator looks after him like His very own. Almighty God saves that devotee from the Illusions of the world, and He makes him realize that He is his Supreme Father. The devotee then becomes truly fearless from the affairs of this world.

Sant Kabir gives us the story of *King Harnakash*, and his young son *Prahlad*, which took place thousands of years ago, in the time just before *Avatar Krishna* was born. Prince Prahlad's father was the King, but he was so fanatical that he wanted all his subjects to pray to him as God, and not to pray to anyone else.

Having done lots of penance, he had received a Boon from one of the Avatars. This Boon was that he will not die during the day nor the night, neither inside nor out, killed neither by man nor animal. In thinking of this Boon that he will never expire, he became very cruel and unjust to his subjects, even to his own son.

King Harnakash sent his son Prahlad to school. When the Pundit began to teach about the Mantras, Prahlad spoke up. Being an evolved soul, he requested the Pundit not to teach these Mantras, but instead he should teach about the Creator Who has made all this Creation. He wanted the teacher to write the Holy Name of *Gopal* (another Name for Almighty God) on his slate. Of course, the teacher told everything to the boy's father, that this boy accepts only his own Lord as the True God.

The King asked for the boy to be brought in front of him. The father told the son that he should leave off this habit of praying to *Gopal* (God). His meaning was that he (the King) was the Lord, and the son should pray to him, not to God.

After he repeatedly talked to Prahlad in many different ways to persuade him of this, the boy still replied that his Lord is Almighty God. The boy was adamant that he would not stop his Simran of God. "He is the One Who has made all the hills and valleys and oceans," the boy said, "and I am not going to leave his Name from my tongue, even if you put me to death!" He was determined to never give up his Bhakti.

It has been told in various stories that his father actually tried several methods to kill him, including death by drowning, throwing him from the cliff, etc., but each time the boy was miraculously saved. The father then attempted something different. He made various pillars, each one burning with a ferocious fire. He wanted to frighten the little boy. He ordered his son to wrap his arms around a red-hot iron column, in order to test the boy's faith in what he believed. Even the large crowd present at the time murmured "O God!" as the child bravely approached the column.

At first the boy became a little bit frightened by the fire. But what did God do to preserve the faith of the young Prince Prahlad? Suddenly the boy saw a small ant running up the fiery column, and with joy in his heart, he leaned forward and clasped his arms around it!

Seeing this, the father became very angry. Unsheathing his sword, he fumed, "Tell me now, who will save you? I want to see the God of your faith, and how He will save you now!"

Sant Kabir tells us that the very same pillar immediately split wide open, and out burst a creature (Avatar Narsing) which tore the King apart with his claws! This had all happened at the time of dusk, so *it was neither day nor night*. Also, the King had erected these pillars at the threshold of the palace, so *they were neither inside nor outside the palace*. The creature that had emerged from the pillar was *neither man nor beast*, so all the conditions of the King's Boon had been observed!

Kabir Sahib says, "No one knows the limit of God. He is vibrating in each and every atom." The Saints have Their own examples. Kabir Sahib gives this story for the benefit of other people, because many fanatics had persecuted Sant Kabir, trying to kill Him by putting His house to fire, throwing Him in the river, and trying to trample Him under a raging elephant. God has many, many subtle ways to look after His devoted followers. He has saved devotees like Prahlad many times.

Sant Kabir reiterates, "When one has utmost faith in the Fearless One, he also becomes fearless. He then sees with open eyes that he is being looked after and protected, both within and without. The devotee remains always in the Lap of his Master!"

#5-5 The Effects of Association With Worldly People

The person of sin and degrading deeds is repelled by the sermons of the Saint. If you tell this type of person long and juicy stories of murders and wars, of robberies and swindling, or of mysteries, he will listen attentively. However, just change the subject to the joys of meditation and the lovely Inner Sights, and he will move quickly away without interest!

Sant Kabir warns us never to have the company of these worldly people, with their physical and sensual attachments. These people don't have a Guru. "Run away from them; otherwise you might be affected by their company. All of them are consumed by the desire for useless, worldly things. Everyone is running a mad race for worldly possessions, and every house in every social group, every city in every country is afflicted with this malady. A man is known by the company he keeps. If you associate with someone completely engrossed in the worldly affairs, invariably you will find that person speaking only in terms of the world, and that affects the people around him. Everyone is haunted by unfulfilled desires for money and power, and this is a secret fire engulfing the entire world!"

He says that we should beware of those people in whom God has not manifested Himself, because they fill us with suspicion. According to Sant Kabir, having their company is just like being covered with a black blanket, which shrouds everything in the darkness of Illusion, doubt, and suspicion. No matter what one does by way of washing that blanket, it will not turn white. "Enlightenment will not come from that type of person. Stay away from them!"

He gives another example that if there is a black sooty pot, and someone touches it, he cannot help but have black hands, too. "If someone is seeing Light inside and others are not, the association of those people will create some doubt in the mind of the person who is seeing. Those people only have the Simran of the world with all its myriad attachments and sense allurements. Beware of the people in whom God has not manifested Himself, lest you become affected by them!"

He says that people become congealed in their own little communities, and thoughts of doubt and suspicion come in their mind. They wonder what will other people think if they are seen going to a person who is poor, or someone of a different caste. Others will see that he is low in status, and pass judgement. The shame of the community gets accorded priority, rather than the person's own salvation. When one wants to come to a Living Master, he should not be influenced by the community around him. This will keep him away from the Truth.

This hesitation actually inhibits him from coming to the Living Master. Pride of position and wealth swells up within the person, literally killing him by preventing him from going to the Master. The world deceives people with all its glitter and temporary attractions. There is nothing more important than to know the Creator, and Sant Kabir emphasizes again and again that this is the only purpose of being born in the human form.

He also tells us that the more pure the heart is, the quicker are the results of Spiritual practices. Hence, it is necessary to avoid people who are activated by lust and anger. Their company will have an effect of defiling the mind, in the same way that the Holy Company of the Saint will purify and cleanse the soul.

"Spirituality and salvation are a matter of the Inner Soul. If the Master is True, He can give an Experience of Light and Sound, and can show the Upper Spiritual Realms. The Company of One Who has controlled His attention, will bring peace and stillness to the wandering mind." The Saint's Godly qualities of Love, chastity, and humility radiate to those around Him. Even having the company of those who talk about the Master and the God-Path, gives forth its own Blessed Radiation.

"The best Company is that of the Sadhu. In His Holy Assembly, evergreen remains the sweet memory of God. Only the precious time spent with Him is of any real account. Since the purpose of life is to find God, every priceless moment spent in God's Holy remembrance is therefore of immense value."

#5-6 Untrue Masters

"Those who have not seen Almighty God themselves, cannot make others see!" emphasizes Sant Kabir. "When their own Inner Eye has not been opened, how can they open the eyes of others and make manifest the Light of God? They are not only deceiving themselves, but also deceiving all those who come to them. Had they kept to themselves it would have been much better, for then they would have lost this opportunity only for themselves, and not made others to lose it too."

Sant Kabir notes, "The Priests and Ministers become like the contractors of guardianship, selling God's Name. These false leaders who have not themselves solved the mystery of life, cannot give anything to their followers."

Sant Kabir tells us that for every one True Master (Godman), where God manifests to take souls back to their Eternal Home, the Negative Power creates millions of these false teachers, untrue prophets, so that Kaal can keep the souls under his control, and not let them finish their coming and going in this world.

Sant Kabir points out, "The eye of the intellect (the Power of Discrimination) is not working properly when one cannot differentiate between the *Sant* (True One) and the *Asant* (untrue one)." He says, for example, that some people just observe a few others in a group following somebody and then they also join that gathering, without determining if that following is true or not. They don't make use of their Power of Discrimination.

There are usually crowds of people around a pseudo-Master, for a crowd is usually made of deluded people, those with desires of health, wealth, or fame. One person wants children, another has an ailment, another has a court case to be won, and so on. In the field of religion can be found the greatest amount of hypocrisy and untruth, because the subject is so vast, so splendid, and so mysteriously appealing, that anyone can say anything about it.

However, there is no greater sin than having an ignorant teacher. The poor seeker flounders from 'Master' to 'Master', finding them worthless. His faith becomes shaken and all hope is lost. He begins to feel that there is nothing but hoax and hypocrisy practiced in the name of religion. Such a person, even if he meets a genuine Master, will invariably be very wary of Him, naturally suspecting Him to be like the others.

This prevalence of false gurus is the major reason behind much of the atheism in the world. People lose faith because of the impostors who masquerade as True Masters. When the gurus are fakes, how can God be true? People even refuse to believe that there is a Power that is God! However, God is an Experience, *the Ultimate Experience!*

Sant Kabir emphasizes that nobody in the Churches and Temples can help in this Journey of life, or teach how to cross over the Ocean of Existence. "One is able to only read about how he can go on the Ship to cross the Ocean of this world, but merely reading those words won't take the person to that Ship."

There is no ocean greater than the Ocean of Existence. The religious leaders don't know how to cross this Ocean, because they have nothing themselves in the way of Practical Experience to offer. They have no idea how to control the ship.

They don't even know anything about the terrible storms on this Ocean. They can only talk about the Experiences of other Godmen, which are written about in the Scriptures. None of the Ministers and Preachers can instruct how to get out from the bondage of this body.

Instead, they can teach only to pray to those Saints or Godmen Who lived several hundred, or even thousands, of years ago. They teach how to do the outer worship of those Saints, but they don't tell how these Godmen actually reached to their Ultimate Goal, how They became Godmen, and how They can take others in the same way.

Sant Kabir says, "The Brahmin of bookish knowledge pretends that he is the True Master for the whole world, but he is not the Guru of the true Devotee. These Brahmins are themselves entangled to death in the bookish knowledge of the Vedas!" The religious leaders put emphasis on the various religious Books, to have belief in them, and to have faith in the religion of these Ministers. However, these Ministers themselves don't reveal how to have the Experiences given in those Books, and how these Experiences can become a Reality in one's own life.

Kabir Sahib points out that what is the benefit of even meeting those who have not withdrawn from outside and entered within? The poor seekers very soon discover to their dismay that they have been duped, and then they begin to condemn the Gurus in general. Unfortunately, the very word 'Master' or 'Guru' then becomes an aversion to them, and they won't easily come near another, however genuine that Teacher might be. This is the root cause of disbelief in God and in the Godmen Themselves.

Sant Kabir says, "Those false prophets teach only theory, not practice. They are drowning in all of this and they are also taking along their followers as well. Shame on those Gurus who don't dispel the questions and suspicions of their followers! They use only bookish knowledge, but cannot demonstrate any Practical Experience of what they are talking. Without having any Practical Experience of his own, the person who only talks day and night about these Experiences is considered to be an illiterate, stupid person. Only talking about what one has heard, but not Experienced himself, is just like a dog barking!"

He says that the Ministers can only guide the seekers to wear beads, put holy marks on their body or shave their heads, but these efforts cannot lead one to Spirituality. The devotees are advised to give in charity, but the fact is that usually behind the gifts of charity is hidden some desire, whether it be a hope of return in heaven, or at the very least, some praise, or gain in status from the onlookers. Even going to the Temple or the Mosque has become a social obligation. There is actually no difference between charity and a business: both expect some kind of return. The giver has truly only invested for his future gain.

The Priests are also business-minded, telling the people that what they give in charity will be returned manifold. These exploiters know for certain that people cannot truly give selflessly in charity. No one would ever donate to a Temple if he were told that he would receive nothing in return.

The true meaning of charity is when one gives without any motive or expectation for return. Actually, only God and the Master can give in true charity, because their giving is pure and unconditional. When one becomes aware of all the gifts received from Almighty God and the Master, the devotee begins to dance in jubilation, singing praises not out of fear, but out of gratitude. People are given life, health, Love, beauty, and Truth, but never even dream of how they might repay the Lord!

Sant Kabir gives another example, saying that those false Preachers who just read the Guru's words and then tell other people about it, will make those people like themselves. "All will become ghosts and fall into hell!" In particular, He strongly warns, "Without understanding the Secret of Almighty God, whoever presents himself as a Master *will take on the form of a dog in his next lifetime!*"

He who preaches false sermons will realize his foolishness when fate slaps him in the face. When death confronts him and life ebbs away, he will realize the utterly useless nonsense he spoke about, when in fact he knew nothing. Under a garb of 'Truth', the false preacher speaks about falsities, actually hypnotizing the gullible public.

Thousands of these untruths prevail, that have no bearing whatsoever on Truth. With a topic such as religion, it is very easy to propagate untruth, because there is no way to test what these preachers say, and no criterion by which to judge.

Sant Kabir makes us aware that in all the Isms, there are many obstacles on the way to deter and to hinder the seeker. "All humanity, including the Saints and the Mahatmas, one day must leave the body. After the passing of the Saint, unfortunately His Message and Teachings become distorted. Thus, many false stories and delusions come about, with the result that people cannot take the advantage from the same Teachings that now have been changed and twisted."

Kabir Sahib opens our eyes by demanding, "Who distorts these Teachings? Those who are narrow-minded and who have never understood the Teachings, not just intellectually, but also practically, who have great pride and ego in themselves! They want to become models for others! They think that they will be made superior, but they are only after name and fame. They desire more of the outer knowledge than the Inner Truth, and these kinds of people bring about the terrible distortion and the eventual dissolution of the Master's True Teachings!"

He tells us that although we may say that we belong to a particular community, religion, or country, in truth none of these belong to us. Spirituality has been totally reduced to a business and a profession.

In some of the Temples, if one makes a large donation, he can go to the front of the line to view the stone deity located there; otherwise he might wait in the queue for hours, and then still not be able to see inside the Temple at all! This implies that God is the monopoly of the rich, but what about the poor? True Masters and Saints bestow the Gift of Spirituality free of charge. Out of sheer Grace, the Godman calls us to His Lotus Feet and presents us with the Boon of the Holy Naam.

Sant Kabir is expounding these Truths to some wandering Sadhus (people who are really hankering after God, but unfortunately they have no idea where to go or how to go about it). They have denounced their hearth and home in the pious hope of leaving behind all their worldly tribulations. Many of them don't have any money, food, or even clothes. Without work, their only aim should be to obtain God realization. They call themselves as 'Sadhu', but in fact the true meaning of the word 'Sadhu' implies a high degree in Spirituality. These people are not the true Sadhus. For example, if someone says, "I am God!" it doesn't mean that he has *become* God. One can give himself any name he wants, but not necessarily will he become that which is described by the name.

Sant Kabir says that when these so-called 'Sadhus' are starving, they beg for charity. They eat other people's share of food by going from house to house, accepting whatever they can get. They don't realize that by the law of Karma (the Law of Action and Reaction), they have to pay for those items they take without buying. This actually becomes a debit on their account, putting even more weight on their head. Then these 'Sadhus' go back to where they have their *Dera* (temporary living quarters).

He says that after that, again they wander around the country like gypsies. Some keep long hair, and some take their hair off. Some wear saffron-coloured clothes and others wear earrings, long necklaces, and beads, but they all keep a bag around their neck for begging. They do nothing for their own self-improvement, but allow their ego to expand when people come and bow their heads on the ground before them. They read the Vedas and other Books, but in their everyday life, they do not hesitate to tell lies.

In other words, they totally forget their aim of why they have denounced their homes, and they get caught up in this web of the Negative Power. They have all these outer signs and rituals of being a Sadhu, but unfortunately they end up depending upon other peoples' mercy. They call themselves as Spiritual people, but if somebody only knows a few quotations from the Scriptures or some Mantras, and makes a fool of himself and of others, this does not bring him nearer to Almighty God.

Sant Kabir says that there are very few Sadhus who really are hankering with full passion to find God. They look from city to city for the True Godman Who can bestow salvation, Who has the Power to show them the Light of God, or Who can make them get in touch with Divinity. They are looking for Him, but whether they find Him or not, is all due to their previous Karmas.

Sant Kabir then addresses the Ministers and Priests, saying "O Brahmins! Why are you forgetting about the true nature of your soul? Why are you reciting only a few lines out of the Vedas, but not knowing the true meaning of them nor even trying to understand them. These Vedas fall under the domain of the Negative Power, because they were given by Brahma. You are totally forgetting the Supreme God Who lives in you. You are not putting your attention on Him in order to attain Him."

Sant Kabir also remarks that it is ironic that people say that Kabir is only a lowly weaver, and yet the Brahmins have such pride that they are born in the 'high' Brahmin house, and are very 'learned' and 'respected' people. He asks them, "Have you ever realized that you are going to the houses of the poor and the low caste to beg for food, and you eat of their feasts during the change of the moon's phase? How possibly can you call yourselves 'great', after eating other people's hard-earned money? In which way are you great? You are lower than the low, if you don't earn your own livelihood and share with others who are less fortunate. In one way you preach to other people about Almighty God. You become the self-appointed torch-bearers who purportedly show the 'Light' to others, but you yourselves fall badly without having any Light in yourself. In your mind, you are the 'great' ones, and I am the 'low' one."

In all humility Sant Kabir says, "O Brahmins! I cannot be equal to you! I am dyed in the Colour of God. The Holy Naam is in each and every pore of my body. But you are the ones, O mighty Brahmins, who are going to drown in the faith you have placed in these Vedas!"

Sant Kabir explains that people easily get caught in the web of the Negative Power. They worship religious Books and do many different kinds of rites and rituals, remaining in various stages of 'drowning' in their idol worship, totally away from the Creator. He says that the Ministers and Priests are literally robbing the masses, taking advantage of the illiterate ones, not doing anything good for them, cheating them Spiritually by not enlightening them as to the Reality of Creation, nor are they trying to find Enlightenment for themselves. The religious leaders have no Experience of what they are talking about. They don't teach the people that they must come to the Living Master.

Kabir Sahib says, "Doing only empty rites and rituals will not lead anywhere. It is all wasted time and effort. Those people who talk so fluently, with rosary beads around their necks and with polished jugs as begging bowls in their hands, are nothing more than *robbers!*" He has labeled them as *"Benarasi thugs!"* (Thieves of Benaras)

Sant Kabir cannot help but use the strongest possible terms in condemning these so-called 'teachers' who profess to teach Spirituality without any first-hand knowledge of Spirituality themselves. They misguide the innocent masses, and live off their ignorance and their money. They profess to be holy, but they actually desire worldly possessions. "They claim to be detached but they sell the name of God and religion, filling their bellies with the spoils of their fraud!"

Kabir Sahib says to these false Sadhus, "You buy idols of stone in the form of gods and goddesses, and worship them.

You also go on pilgrimages, and there you worship more idols and take baths in the rivers. Other people see you doing this, and they also start thinking that they will obtain God in this manner. They copy you and in this way, the whole world is going astray in idol worship, but no one is receiving anything in return. Outwardly, you appear to be a Sadhu wearing coloured clothes, earrings, and carrying a bag, but you wander all over, begging for your meals. What a pitiful sight!"

Sahib Kabir comments on the many beliefs and Illusions of these so-called learned leaders, especially the belief concerning impurity. The Pundits, for example, are stuck fast in their man-made superstitions, shunning others who happen to be from the lower classes.

Kabir Sahib says, "O Learned Person! Everything in Creation is impure. The water is impure, even the earth which grows the food for your life--everything in birth and death belongs to the Creation of God. You shun whoever you think is not pious, but actually you are making a fool of yourself, with the result that all humanity follows your example. How impure this very act is!"

He continues, "The pure ones as well as the whole idea of the state of purity only reside where God Himself resides. O think, my dear learned friend, with the Power of Discrimination that God has given to you. This is all an Illusion. How you perceive this, how your thoughts affect you, and whatever you become out of it, all falls under the heading of 'Delusion'. If your thoughts are impure and you have anger, or even if your eyes see impurity in your very own skin, in your food, even in the air you breath in and out, this is all a trickery of the mind, and it is an Illusion."

Sant Kabir remarks that mankind is ruined by this superstition of impurity. He says that everyone knows how to make more bondage but it is a rare soul who, with his Power of Discrimination, makes an aim of realizing what is right and wrong. When the person contemplates the Name of God in his heart, these ideas of impurity have no effect on him.

In another verse Kabir Sahib is talking to a religious leader, saying, "O Intellectual Person! You have been given the Power of Discrimination from God. You should, therefore, be thinking about God, but you are thinking quite the reverse. You are using this Power and attention to acquire perishable things. As you are the elder, and head of the family of seekers under your care, you are also the one to teach and lead. You are going down into the Illusion of these worldly practices yourself, and you will also drag your family of devotees along with you. You will all drown in the Ocean of the world, thereby losing this priceless, Life-Giving chance."

He continues, "You read the Vedas and the Puranas, but only for the sake of reading, thinking that this will be enough to attain God. Unfortunately, you do not bring these Teachings into your own life. You don't know the value of the Lord's Name. You are just like a donkey carrying a load of such a precious commodity like sandalwood, but enjoying neither the fragrance nor the value of it."

"In the name of your religion," He adds, "you sacrifice living creatures for your own tongue taste. What right do you have to take the lives of others when you do not have the Power to give life? This action is a heinous crime that you commit!" Sant Kabir issues a stern warning. *"There is no forgiveness in the Court of God for this act!* You cannot say that it is not a sin! You may call yourself to be Spiritual, but in fact you are a very professional butcher, taking the lives of the creatures that God has made!"

Kabir Sahib asks, "By these actions and deeds how can your mind be cleansed? You are blinded by your own mind and outgoing faculties, being so much involved in bad deeds and actions. There is no such thing that you can guide other people about the Dharma and knowledge of God. You are doing all these things for the sake of gathering perishable wealth. You sell the Name of God, and you sell Godly knowledge."

Sant Kabir warns mankind against these so-called teachers and preachers, who black-market religion and make money as a result. Religion, like other commodities, has become very marketable. "Instead of the religious places being run by awakened souls, they are being presided over by paid preachers who work for the sake of their own bellies. They do not feed God's hungry sheep!"

"The noble buildings which were raised for virtuous motives, are being used to collect donations in one way or the other. In exchange for their hard-earned money, people are being offered some 'blessed' eatable, believed to have been sanctified by a stone deity, or even by the preacher himself. All this is taken in good faith, in exchange for the promise that sins and evil deeds have been forgiven!" The commerce of money-making is uncontrolled in the world, but in Spirituality, it is much more so. Spirituality has virtually become a business! Sant Kabir is very much against people collecting money in this manner by acting and posing.

Very clearly, He states that with all their best efforts, based on whatever Spiritual knowledge they have only been able to read about, these Preachers and Priests cannot give any Practical Experience of the Light and Sound of God. They are themselves groping in the dark, and they cannot take anyone else out of this darkness. They quarrel amongst themselves, and arouse others to unimaginable feelings of hatred and jealousy with their fellow beings.

During the time of Sant Kabir, it was a period of great religious prejudice and strife. The leaders of the religions of Hinduism (the *Pundits*), and Islam (the *Maulvis* and the *Mullahs*) were preaching to their followers the message of hatred and bigotry. The belief that someone is an enemy simply because he belongs to a different faith is nothing less than fanaticism. This is total madness. "There can be no room in such a mind for God or His Holy Naam!"

Sant Kabir is describing the Truth, that how pitiful and sad it is that people are following these untrue prophets. What can those leaders hope to give to their followers, when they themselves are in the bondage of rituals and their own Karmas? He says that to whomever one turns for liberation, they are themselves bound hand and foot! They are the 'shaved heads' and they call themselves as 'Yogis'. Still others have long, matted hair. They call themselves as 'Masters', and people follow them stupidly. What possibly can they offer anyone?

Sant Kabir explains again and again how to take away all doubts that have covered the peoples' eyes and hearts. "People are generally very simple-minded. They don't commonly use their own intellect, but would rather listen to other people. Whatever the mind likes, they accept that. Instead of listening to their conscience, they listen to the mind. They don't seem to understand that the mind is the agent of the Negative Power, and naturally it will make the person interested in listening to various tricks."

Sant Kabir talks about the Pundits who call themselves as Gurus, or Sadhus. He says, "They themselves are living under the influence of desire. How possibly can they tell anyone the Truth about God, because they know nothing about it themselves. They have made up a commerce just for their livelihood, selling the Holy Name of God."

He then addresses the Priests. "Without seeing God's Power, you have only bookish knowledge with no Practical Experience. This can have no effect on your talk and you are wasting your time preaching." He tells them that they should first practice what they preach! He illustrates that these untrue masters appear to save other peoples' lives, but in fact they are themselves drowning. "If the blind lead the blind," He points out, "both cannot help but fall into the ditch!" He also says that if outwardly someone appears to be a holy man, but inwardly he has the habit of a thief or an evil person, then he is liable for *double* the punishment!

Kabir Sahib is saying to the Brahmins and the other false prophets that they are carrying the weight of other people's heavy Karmas by 'blessing' them, eating up their food, and then taking their money and other wealth. He asks, "Do you think that you can walk straight with all this load on your head? You should think about your own Karmas, the actions and deeds which you are doing daily. You should be frightened with your own sins and deeds because the Way Godward is very difficult and narrow. You must think about that!"

Kabir Sahib paints the picture that "Dust is falling on the faces of those preachers who tell other people about God, but who don't practice what they preach." He says to them, "What you preach to others, you don't even see or know anything yourselves, and you eat only dust (i.e. your own form is being eaten up by lust, anger, etc.). With your eye on the wealth of others, you are being looted by the five thieves within you, and you don't have anything left for yourself. You have not realized anything Practically in the way of Spirituality."

"A true *Sanyasi* (a renouncer of the world) is one who has freed himself from craving and desire, and its resulting attachments," says Sant Kabir. "He does not look for food or care anything about clothes: he only looks to God. If he is a true Sanyasi, God will be his provider. He should not care if he has to go hungry for a few days. He should be content and thankful, whenever and whatever is offered."

The difference between a Sanyasi and a worldly person is that the Sanyasi understands that all life ends with death. He is aware of death and has begun to remember death. Man alone in all Creation has the Consciousness or attention needed to foresee death. The birds and animals do not have this. When the knowledge of death dawns, a transformation takes place. As one becomes aware of the end of life, the things that one holds valuable seem to change. What was meaningful up to now, becomes meaningless, as soon as the awareness of death occurs. When death knocks at the door, all dreams and hopes fall away.

Sant Kabir illustrates that in days gone by, those who renounced the world for the Spiritual life never collected any money for their efforts. However, this type of life started to become a vocation and these people began to collect not only money, but goods too. It is now something far different from the original purpose, and the ignorant end up leading the ignorant. The entire world is groping in this darkness.

People listen to the long-winded talks of the Priests and Ministers that are empty and devoid of Experience. Those types of people are ruining the lives of others, making them miserable. Sant Kabir prays that we should always be away from those misleading fanatics. He explains that those people cannot give us any Truth about God or the Creator, but the person who does have this Power is the True Saint, Who is often criticized and judged.

Lord Kabir says that when He sees the condition of the general public, He feels pity and concern about how these untrue people laugh at the others and then praise themselves in foolishness. "They have set their own houses on fire and they are sound asleep inside!" He says that this type of person may be considered very intelligent and scholarly, and seem to enjoy great powers of intellect, but he is unconscious of his true nature and his goal. He has no idea about the Chief Support of his life, and his life's highest Aim.

Sant Kabir says, "Dear friends, why are you still asleep? The night has passed; must you also waste your day?" The glorious day of human life has dawned. Why should man spend his precious time sleeping, instead of making use of the opportunity to break the bonds of the senses and rise up to meet God? Why be lost in forgetful slumber? "Wake up!" He implores, "Wake up! You have no time to lose!"

Sant Kabir describes how the Pundits wear a very thin cloth made of cotton around the hips and legs, and also a long thread of cotton, which goes around the neck up to the waist. This is called the *'sacred thread'*, and it usually consists of six to nine pieces of threads woven together. Those people truly believe that this will save them from evil. Some of them have a long, saffron coloured mark on their foreheads, lots of stringed beads around their necks, and they carry shiny metal pitchers with handles.

"They call themselves to be most pious and saintly, but they are the biggest swindlers who betray and deceive both themselves and the public!"

He says clearly and frankly that these fake Saints and Sadhus do nothing but eat of the most delicious sweets. "Look at their condition! They do not eat of their own hard-earned money. They eat from the offerings of sweets and other edibles given to the statues in the Temples, or from charity given to them. They clean their utensils so carefully, and even wash the wood that they want to burn. They show themselves so clean that they dig a small hole into the ground for cooking, but what are they eating? They are preparing dead flesh as meat!"

CHAPTER 6

THE SOUL'S RELATIONSHIP WITH ALMIGHTY GOD

Who is the Creator? Sant Kabir says that in the entire Creation, there is only one Power, All-Pervading, and everything is created from this one Light. We have a relation with the Lord, because we are made of the Essence of God.

Sant Kabir says, "The soul is a part of Almighty God." God's Essence is vibrating and shining in each and every one, and Sant Kabir tells us to Love those who have God as their Master and Lord. He says that between the Creator and His Creation there is no difference, because the Creation is born from the same Ocean of Love.

"I have come to the realization that there is only One God, and to Love all His Creation is like having Love for Almighty God. This is the true Religion, and the real Aim and Goal of life."

Taking an image from village life, He draws a beautiful illustration that "The Divine Potter has shaped the clay and made all the different pots (which are the physical bodies). He has made all Creation, and He is the Lord of all. Therefore, how can one person be considered as good or another as bad, as high-born or even low-born, because everyone comes from this same Light?"

Kabir Sahib asks, "Where does God not reside? He is down, He is up, He is in the sea, in every atom, All-in-all Pervading, and He is the One Who draws the souls back to Himself, with His own unbounded Grace and Loving compassion." The Beloved first Loves the lover, and then the lover in return begins to Love the Beloved.

Kabir Sahib says that God lives everywhere in the entire Creation that He has formed. Science has recently discovered that there is just one Force, one Energy, that is holding together the entire Universe. God is everywhere but the devotee, unfortunately, cannot see Him with these physical eyes. The devotee must realize Him within his own self. God is in every atom of every single thing and His mighty Power sustains every soul, every tiny particle in all Creation.

Kabir Sahib continues, "If God should withdraw His Power (the soul) from anyone or anything, it would immediately perish. God's Power is the Life of the entire Creation. There is only God and God alone. He remembers His devotees constantly, and also makes His devotees remember Him."

Sant Kabir describes Almighty God as being that Power which is beyond the effects and Illusions of desire. "Almighty God is above all. No one can even attempt to comprehend His limits, because He is Limitless and beyond the constrictions of the human intellect. There is no other like Him, as He is Unique and Knowing of all the knowing."

He continues, "Almighty God cannot be known by human reasoning, reading books, or even by discussion and intellectual wrangling. God is totally beyond the realm of thought. True information about the Creator can only be had from

Those Who have realized Him, *for They have seen Him with Their own eyes!"*

There is a story that once two learned Brahmins (Preachers) were engaged in a philosophical discussion. One asserted the Oneness of God; the other denied it. They could not come to any mutual agreement, so they decided to approach Kabir Sahib for His valuable opinion.

After listening to both of them with great patience, Sant Kabir asked them in what particular colour did they perceive God, as green, yellow, black, or red? Both of them were amazed at this question and said that, of course, God is truly colourless!

Then Kabir Sahib questioned if Almighty God was fair or dark complexioned. They both answered, "Neither!"

Next Sant Kabir inquired about the form and size of God, and both readily replied that God is beyond such limitations and conformity.

Sant Kabir then gently explained to them, that if God has neither colour, nor form, nor size, how could they consider Him to be countable? How could He possibly be expressed in numbers? He is neither One nor Two! He is One and All!

Sant Kabir states that in this 'Oneness', all sins and good deeds are actually being created by Almighty God! The Doer is only One and it is all His play, both the good as well as the bad deeds! "Everyone is so busy in this drama of events in the world, but nobody wants to even recognize the One Who has made this play," says Kabir Sahib.

He continues, "There is only one Power, the Creator and Sustainer of all life, referred to by various names according to the different religions and beliefs." Sant Kabir tells us that these diverse names are only meant to focus our scattered attention on God. The names, however, denote God's Mighty Power made manifest in this world to create and govern it, but that aspect of God which has not come into expression, cannot be known by the limited human intellect. "God is the Microcosm in the Macrocosm, and it is a rare Sadhu who will be able to recognize Him for what He really is, and thus see God working everywhere in His Creation."

Lord Kabir tells another story. Ram Das was a wealthy Brahmin landholder who lived on the banks of the Narmada River. As the years passed, he became aware of the emptiness of mundane life, and thus he was filled with Spiritual longing. He had searched for Truth, meeting many learned men, and reading countless Holy Books, but still he remained without a first-hand Experience of the Divine.

One day he went to the river to bathe and to his great joy, he was met by Sant Kabir. Ram Das humbly requested Sant Kabir to fulfill his desire that he should see Almighty God. The Saint assured him that he would certainly see God, as God would visit his house the very next day!

Ram Das quickly went home and made many elaborate arrangements to welcome the Lord. The house was thoroughly cleaned and purified according to different rites, and many delicious delicacies were prepared. A throne was set up and beautifully decorated. No details were spared. He worked tirelessly throughout the whole day and finally all was ready.

The next day, he sat down to wait for God and as he was waiting, a muddy buffalo slowly ambled up and wandered into the house. The beast plopped itself down near the man, right in the middle of the floor!

A furious Ram Das jumped up and grabbed a stick. He shouted and began to beat the buffalo. The huge animal eventually got up and started to move away. Ram Das then cleaned up the mess and sat down again, albeit somewhat ruffled, to wait for God. He anxiously waited all that day and far into the night, but God did not appear.

The following day, Ram Das went to the river and again met with Sant Kabir. In bitter disappointment he complained, "I cleaned my house, made all the preparations, and waited all day but God did not appear. He didn't come as You said He would!"

Sant Kabir smiled and replied, "God certainly did arrive at your house, but you gave Him a proper welcome! You beat Him with a stick and chased Him away!"

Ram Das was speechless when he realized what had happened, and he immediately felt greatly ashamed. Sant Kabir was telling him that God is everywhere in His entire Creation. God is in each and every atom! There is nowhere that He is not!

Sant Kabir has written a verse in which He quotes Almighty God as saying that when there will be nobody left, He (God) will still be there, because all Creation was made by Him. The existence of God has always and will always be there. In humbleness Sant Kabir says, "O God! What Seva can I possibly do to please You?"

The Man of God (the Saint) sees God with His own eyes. Not only does he see God, but He also reveals the Lord to others. The devotee must develop the *Third Eye*, that Single Eye, which is concealed within him, because God can only be seen with this special Inner Eye.

#6-1 First Separation From God

In the beginning of time, during the period when souls first incarnated in the human body, then at the time of the physical death of the body, those souls went straight back and merged into Almighty God. Sant Kabir says that the time of separation had just begun, and the span of alienation from Eternal Bliss in the Lap of the Lord was very short. Kaal had only a short interim to try and deceive the souls from knowing the Truth. He began to entrap them in the enticing words of the various Scriptures, such as the Vedas, Shastras and Puranas, as well as making them fully engrossed in the numerous religious rituals.

Thus, the souls became more and more engaged in the outer part of religion, neglecting the Inner study of man. The souls, without exception, developed attention solely in outer devotion, and thus in the worship of Kaal. When the soul began its descent from the highest Spiritual Region, it slowly turned its back towards God. As it descended throughout the Spiritual Realms, it fully turned away. Now, in order for it to return unto God, the soul must face in His direction. The angle of vision must change.

In addition to this, man's dilemma became even more heartfelt, as the period of separation from the Supreme Creator became longer. Sant Kabir poignantly says, "O Almighty God! You are the Ocean of the Water of Life and I am a fish of Your Water. I can live only in the Water. Without Your Water, I will die!"

In another verse, He gives a comparison by saying, "Just as water goes into the Water and becomes as one, and then it cannot be separated again, so also Kabir, the weaver, has merged into the Lord."

During the time of the formation of Creation, Kaal had done a lot of penance and worship of Almighty God. As a reward, he was able to ask God to grant him these three Boons:

1. When the soul leaves the body, it should not go straight back and merge into God directly.

2. The soul should forget all about its Origin, the Home of Almighty God, and it should be totally oblivious to its past lives. Thus, it should not remember any of the deeds it has done in those past lives.

3. If God wants a soul to merge into Him again, God Himself should assume the human form, come into the world in flesh and blood, and then take that soul back, but only through the medium of Discourses and Satsang, not by showing miracles.

As a result of this third Boon, Almighty God created the Positive Power that He sends from time to time into the physical world as a Saint, the True Master. Therefore, it is Almighty God Himself Who manifests in that physical body as the Master.

#6-2 Sweet Is Thy Will

*K*abir Sahib says that with the Sweet Will of God, the whole Creation came into being. *"Whatever happens, is with Thy Will, O Lord!"* Whoever recognizes and understands the Truth of this statement, surely will merge back into God. When one puts all faith in himself, he turns his back on God, but when one obeys His Will, he faces God again. Whoever knows God's Divine Will, is in total bliss in every way. Divine Will is also known as Fate, or Destiny. "Almighty God is the One Who is knowing of all, and it is all His own Will if He wishes to Enlighten some souls to realize Him. When God is pleased, He bestows His own Grace on that devotee."

'Contentment' is a significant word that has become distorted. When a person finds himself helpless, he becomes contented, but this kind of contentment serves only as a consolation to him. Contentment should be a state of power, not an outcome of weakness. It should not be a state of helplessness, but a state of supreme *helpfulness*. It implies that one has much more than he requires. He has both what he has asked for, and what he has not asked for.

Contentment naturally includes gratitude. In contentment, all anxieties fall away. Anxiety is born out of discontent, worry and restlessness. Contentment implies acceptance of God's Sweet Will. Behind all the apparent sorrow, is a hidden joy. The contented person conceals all his true possessions within. One should remain tranquil no matter what happens, for it is a part of destiny. Things have to happen in this way, and so they happen. Since it only happens which has to happen, there should be no discontent. One should accept whatever fate ordains.

In God's Will, all suddenly becomes tranquil. Where there is absolutely no cause for worry or concern, what was not Experienced through a thousand meditations, begins only by leaving all to His Sweet Will. Worry arises when things do not go according to one's wishes. Man has great anxiety and restlessness when he tries to force his own will on Creation. There can be only one Spiritual Practice: *His Divine Wish.* All that happens is by His Command alone. When this realization occurs, a gentle shower of peace washes away all tension and worry.

Sant Kabir continues, "Almighty God can turn the oceans into dry lands, and the dry lands into wells. The physical and mental states of suffering, joy, honour, health, wealth, meeting God, name and fame, life and death--all these things are under the Will of God. The pen of God flows according to one's Karma, and one cannot himself wipe out these Karmas."

Sant Kabir advises, "O brother! Don't think about the future, heaven, or hell. It is all God's Will what will happen to you. What the Lord proposes, must happen no matter what, so it would be better for you not to waste your precious time and breath worrying about it." Sometimes in everyday life it happens that howsoever one might try, success or failure is just not in his hands. It is one's duty to make an honest effort, however, but then the outcome of all endeavors should be left to God.

The words Sant Kabir uses in prayer are priceless. "What pleases Thee, O Lord, is best for me! Whatever You Will, is always best for me. You are the Formless, the Almighty, the Birthless One!"

What can a drop of water ask from the Ocean? If one does not accept what is happening, it proves that his faith is not complete. It would appear that the devotee is actually keeping an eye on God: is He doing his bidding? If not, the person complains. No matter how tender the words he uses, a complaint is a complaint. The perfect devotee has no complaints. The drop of water's desire cannot be different from that of the Ocean. If one accepts an outcome with complaint, it means that the acceptance is incomplete. Faith must be wholehearted: *Whatever He wishes!*

Sant Kabir says that even to be able to worship Almighty God, is all the unbounded Grace of God Himself. Whoever has been granted this Grace, that person becomes God's true devotee and will have the great good fortune to meet Him.

Furthermore, Sant Kabir says that whoever remains within God's Will, is His true devotee. In the heart and mind of that person forever abides the Order *"Sweet is Thy Will!"* If somebody has received even some small portion of Love from the Master, it is enough to enable that lucky soul to meet God. It is all His Grace.

Kabir Sahib says that it is also God's Will that the soul can obey God's Order. Using the imagery of a ship crossing the Ocean of Life with its terrible storms and tribulations He says, "Almighty God will take that lucky person's ship (the soul) across the Ocean of Life to the other Shore (to meet God). Then that person's questions and suspicions will vanish, to be replaced by everlasting Love, hope and faith."

Whatever is most significant in life cannot be put into words. Divine Will is most significant. There exists nothing beyond it. There is no way to express the extraordinary in mere words, because knowledge of the Beyond can occur only in stillness. Stillness cannot be expressed in speech. How can one express in words what he has Experienced in silence? Stillness is beyond the measure of time and space. Words, however, have form and are capable only of expressing one's day-to-day life.

#6-3 The True Temple of God

In the time of Sant Kabir, it was the custom for many people to go on a *Hajj* (pilgrimage) to some sacred place as an act of religious devotion. The Muslims would travel to *Mecca*, because it is the birthplace of Mohammed, the founder of Islam. The Hindus, on the other hand, travelled to the river banks of such Holy places as *Hardwar* and *Gomati*. There are about 68 places of Hindu pilgrimage. The people think that God lives only in those places of pilgrimage, in the buildings made by the hand of man.

When one returns from this Hajj, if he had truly gone on pilgrimage, he would have returned a more humble person. Actually, the reverse happens--he expects great applause and praise for his actions. Actions, of course, make the ego stronger. Since effort, labour and hard work are necessary to achieve anything in this temporal world, it is only natural to conclude that even more effort is needed to reach the Supreme Existence!

The rules of the Divine Realms, however, are exactly opposite to the rules of this world. To attain God-head, one needs to turn his back to this world. One needs no action to achieve God--no worship, no prayer, no austerities, no Yoga. God can be obtained only through Love! The system of Divine Love and the system of deeds are very different from each other. Love is not work, and Love never tires. Love keeps expanding. Love is a Divine Gift, not a result of labours. Even in physical love, the lover feels refreshed, joyous, what to think of Divine Love!

Sant Kabir says to come to the True Master with one's head on his palm! If ego also comes along, one cannot listen to the Master, because the ego concerns the head, but listening concerns the heart. Weighing what the Master says as right or wrong, judging from one's own limited angle what suits oneself, cannot be called faith or surrender. Only when the 'self' is left behind can one benefit from the physical presence of the Master, and learn from His Teachings.

The Master's Teachings can only be understood by the heart, not by the mind with its load of ego. When the intellect is pushed away, what remains is a purity that is crystal clear. It is this cleansing effect that is referred to as 'bathing in the Ganges'. When Sant Kabir speaks about bathing in the sacred rivers, it is an internal bath where understanding becomes clear, and the mind is put aside.

Kabir Sahib points out that the Hajj to river banks should not consist of wearing yellow clothes or of putting beads around the neck. He says that taking ritual baths might wash away the outer dirt from the body, but that is all that happens. One cannot enter the Lane of the Beloved until he starts cleansing the 'inner chamber of the heart'.

"O Friend! Listen carefully and consider this. If you think that by bathing in this so-called holy water that you will obtain God, don't you realize that in the same water the frogs also live and bathe? Don't you understand that fish exist in the same water, but they never reach God and they never become clean and sweet-smelling?"

Kabir Sahib gives the example that if one takes a certain vegetable called *Tumbi* (a type of bitter fruit) to all 68 places of pilgrimage, and also gives it a bath at the same time that one takes his own bath, at the end of all this effort, that vegetable will taste just as bitter as before. And the same condition will be the person's! The taint of evil tendencies cannot be removed by water.

He points out that the fruit, at least, will keep its own level of bitterness, but the person's level of ego will skyrocket for having been to these places, because now he can proudly say, "I have gone to all 68 places of holy pilgrimage!" Thus ego, attachment, and greed become even furthermore developed. "O Friend! By doing these outer rituals your life and death, your coming and going in this world will not end; rather you will become even more entangled in these outer practices!"

These are all nothing, but a waste of precious time. Sant Kabir implores everyone, "O People! Listen! These places of pilgrimage are naturally places of importance because some great Saint had been there. After He left, people started worshipping those places because He had placed His Godly Feet on that land. Wherever the Godmen lived, or visited, those very same cities became places of pilgrimage."

Sant Kabir explains in one of His verses how Almighty God appeared to some people who, with much effort and difficulty, went a great distance on pilgrimage. God asked them, "Who told you that I reside there? I reside in the heart of my devotee!" God does not live in any building, such as a Temple or Mosque. "The human body is the true Temple of God. This is a great secret, that the whole Creation of God is contained within this body." Sant Kabir advises people to "Look carefully for the Eternal Spouse, Who is not far away."

How possibly can any person understand God's Creation if he thinks that God is far away and beyond his reach? Kabir Sahib says, "I tell you that He is right within your own body. That person who obtains the Supreme Father, does so right in this body! This human birth that we accept so casually comes only with great good fortune."

One's very life is a gift given by Almighty God. It is very precious. Sometimes, however, people feel that wealth is more valuable because life has been given freely, but wealth has been acquired with great difficulty. The human birth is given because of some special Grace bestowed by God. The day one realizes this, the prayer will arise on his lips, "Whatever can I do to express my gratitude? However can I repay Thee for the Blessings Thou hast bestowed on me? I am not worthy of these gifts!"

Sant Kabir emphasizes that in the human form alone can God be realized. The soul cannot reach God through any type of outer actions; these only cause one's attention to become more dispersed. He gives the example that a letter can be written to the Beloved if the Beloved is living in another place but God, the Eternal Beloved, is right within one's own body and is its very Life-Breath. "How, therefore, can a letter be sent to One Who is already within? God asks the devotee, *Where are you looking for me? I am within you. I am the very Soul of your body!"*

Sant Kabir says that each and every person has the Light of God within. In this same body, there are the sun, the moon, and the *Unhad Shabd* (the limitless Sound Current). Sant Kabir pleads, "O dear friend! Why are you looking outside at the stones? Why do you waste time going on pilgrimages and worshipping idols, looking for God outside of your body. Due to the mind constantly being diverted by these spectacles of the outer world, you cannot hear or benefit from the Inner Harmony."

The person, however, does not pay any heed to the unbounded praise for Almighty God and the Divine Sound Current, which is referred to at great length in the Holy Books. Nor does he realize that he must turn within to find the Spiritual Treasures. Sant Kabir advises people to focus the attention inwards. "Put the mind and full attention towards God, Who is Nameless. The soul has to be united with the Holy Shabd to achieve everlasting peace and happiness."

He goes on to compare the person to a bubble of water which has air in it. "Almighty God has put His own Light (which is the soul) in this bubble." Lord Kabir is describing that the human body is the Temple of God, and that God Himself resides in it. "The human body that does the Simran of God's Holy Names, is so precious that even the gods and angels reverently bow down to it."

Kabir Sahib earned his livelihood through the trade of weaving, and using expressions of patterns familiar to weavers, He describes how God made the human body. The terms of 'woof' and 'warp' represent the *Ida* (Left) and the *Pingala* (Right) Currents in the finer body (the Astral body), which criss-cross like the pattern of threads on a weaver's loom. He also mentions that the *Sukhmana* (the Central Current) is used to reinforce the other two, making the body strong and tightly woven, just like the weaver's finished cloth.

He cautions, "The person who is looking and praying for worldly things, is actually praying to the Lord of this world, which is Kaal, the Negative Power. The Lord of the material world (the Physical Region) alone can grant material objects." On the other hand, "When one prays to Almighty God, then God Himself arranges for that person to meet the Living Master, Who provides the Path into the Beyond, to eventually merge and become One with God."

Sant Kabir advises, "O brother! I tell you a secret of the Creator and His great Love for the Creation. Almighty God and His Power are in each living being, and every living being is in Him. Once you realize this, with the Grace of the True

Master and without effort, you will see the God Power working in each and every atom. This is the true realization of the God Power, of His Creation, His Grace and His Divinity."

#6-4 Sweet Praises of God

It is a great Blessing to sit with Lovers of God and to hear sweet praises of the Lord. When like-minded people meet, they naturally talk only about what is of common interest-- God and the Love of God.

Kabir Sahib offers supreme praises of Almighty God. "When the ego vanishes, one receives bliss, ecstasy, and Divine Love. Now God has become the True Companion of that lucky devotee. Whoever has sweet remembrance of the Creator will be with God, and become One with Him."

Kabir Sahib says that we must Love the One Who will not leave nor forsake us till the end. That Divine Personage will stand by us in all our trials of life on this earth Plane, and also lead us not only into the Beyond, but all the way up to God.

People hear and see the Master, but they draw their own individual conclusions about God, which they follow accordingly, never putting into practice what they actually hear or see.

Whatever one sees, passes through the windows of the eyes, which impose their own colour on everything. Some people sing of God's Power and others of His benefaction or munificence, His attributes, His beauty, His Truth, but however one sees the Divine, reflects his own insight. Almighty God is everything, and yet none of these. Unless one's sense of outer sight drops, one cannot know God. For whatever one will know, he will ultimately only know through his own seeing, his own point of view.

When one becomes like Almighty God, how will he speak? The person will no longer be separate, but rather he will be one with the Absolute. Unless the soul becomes one with God, no such point of view can be correct, because Illusions begin when the 'part' is proclaimed to be complete and perfect. However, only praising God does not bring about awareness of God. No matter how much one sings His praises, the 'distance' persists.

Sant Kabir says, "When the soul reaches to that condition which is attained in the Higher Spiritual Realms, then he sees God everywhere, in every atom, up and down, here and there. He sees God permeating everywhere."

He continues, "God dwells in all of the ten directions. Almighty God can be seen in and out, in every atom of the body." It is He Who breathes the person's breath. It is He Who gives Life!

Kabir Sahib explains that the Names of God are many, but God Himself is only One. "The Muslims call Him as *Allah* (One Who is Great). The Sufis say that *Khuda* (One Who comes of His own accord) is Great. The Hindu Brahmins say that *Ram* (God) is All in All. The Yogis say that *Gorak* is the Great One. But I, Kabir, say that my Creator, the Lord Almighty, is the One Who permeates all and resides in each and every atom. There is only the One!"

Kabir Sahib is explaining that when the soul realizes Almighty God, the two merge into each other and then with God's Grace, that person begins to see the Light of God in every atom and in every person. God not only vibrates in, but also lives in, the whole of Creation.

Sant Kabir says that when the devotee 'realizes' God, then he sees His existence everywhere, and can say only "You, You, You! Everywhere!" When the devotee loses his own self, he also loses the difference between himself and others. When he sees that the Power of God is everywhere, then his ego begins to vanish. When one sees God in all of Creation, then that person suddenly realizes that nobody is in a 'low' or 'high' position in life. That person discerns that everybody God has created is just like his own, because he beholds the Light of

God (as the soul) in them. He does not see just the physical body.

The devotee now understands that the Oneness of God is permeating amongst all creatures. In every atom, the Power of God vibrates. That person's condition is such that he can see the Truth with his attention and contentment. The Enlightened ones who have Experienced this state of Truth, see that God's Will is at work in everything.

Kabir Sahib proceeds to tell us an incident from His own life to substantiate this reality. As a weaver by profession, He would first weave the cloth on His loom, and then take it to the marketplace to sell. From this vocation, He was able to provide for His family, seeing to their every need.

There is a story that one day it happened to be very cold. Sant Kabir was on His way to the market to sell some cloth He had woven, when He was approached by a poorly-dressed and shivering Sadhu who humbly requested Him for assistance.

Kabir Sahib generously offered him a few yards of the cloth to protect him from the cold, but the mendicant would settle for nothing less than the entire bolt of material.

Sant Kabir, therefore, gave away all of it. The Sadhu thanked Kabir Sahib, and then left. Of course this meant that there was no money at the end of the day with which to feed His family, but Kabir Sahib as usual had left everything to the Almighty. But then a wondrous thing happened!

On the other side, at His house, a merchant brought food and other household necessities, the very same ones that Kabir Sahib was supposed to have purchased with the selling of that cloth. That person told Kabir Sahib's wife that Kabir Sahib had sent these items for His household, and that He was coming back soon. That man delivered the merchandise and then left.

When Kabir Sahib arrived home and saw that everybody in His household was very happy and praising that He had bought so many articles with that small amount of money, He immediately understood how the merciful Father works, never letting Him down for a single moment. He felt so thankful to the Lord for His unbounded Love. Who else but Almighty God could have helped Him thus in His need? Kabir Sahib kept what was needed for His household, and as usual, distributed the rest of the goods amongst the needy.

Another attribute of the Lord about which Sant Kabir speaks most eloquently is Divine Radiance and Beauty. He asks, "How can this paragon Beauty be explained? There are no

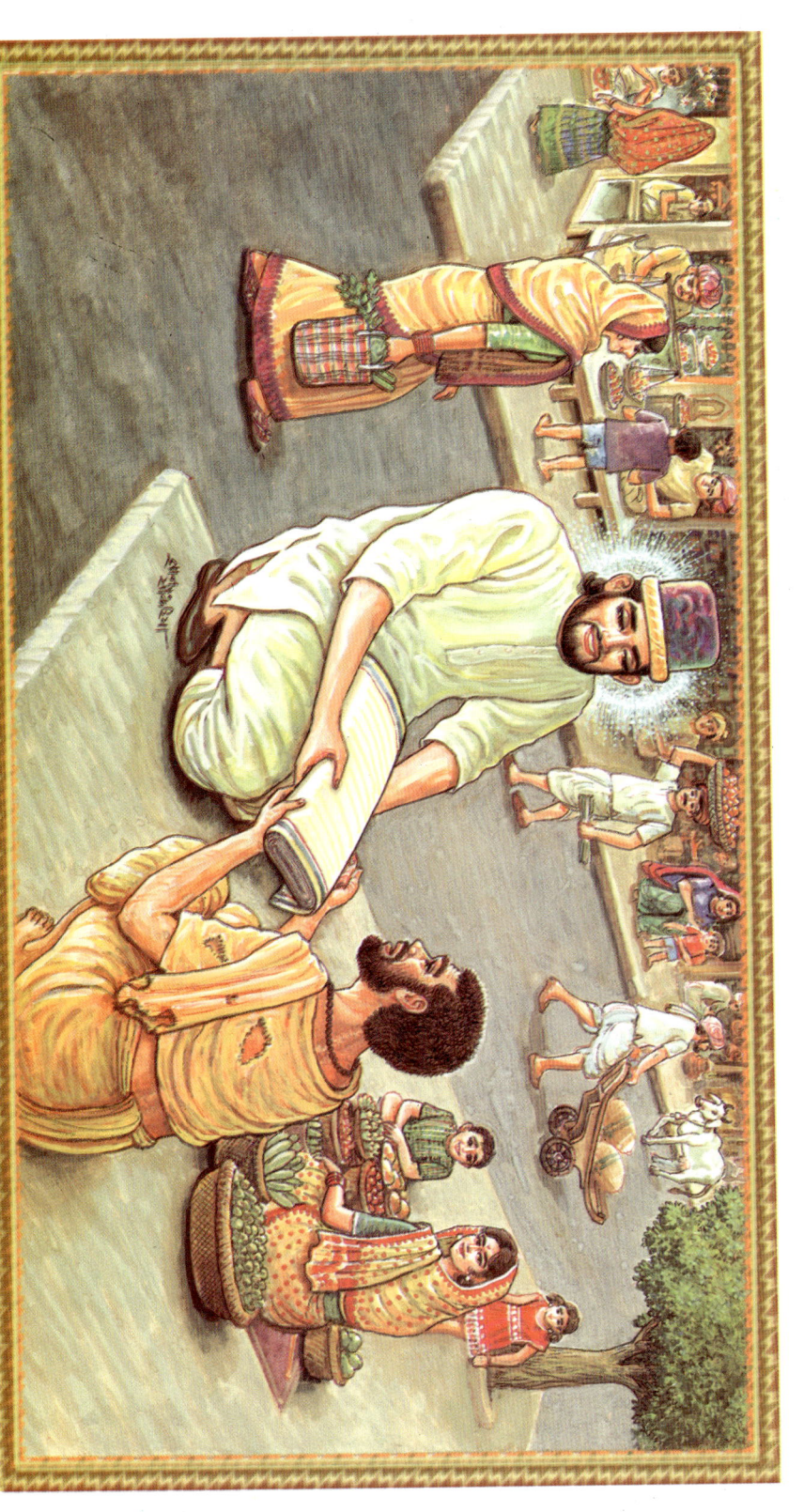

Sant Kabir was approached by a poorly-dressed and shivering Sadhu who humbly requested Him for assistance. Kabir Sahib generously offered him a few yards of the cloth to protect him from the cold, but the mendicant would settle for nothing less than the entire bolt of material. Sant Kabir, therefore, gave away all of it.

words to describe it! Millions of cupids cannot compete with the Beauty of the Lord, the stealer of men's hearts. There is no place in one's mind or heart for any doubt about this. All questions vanish because God Himself takes that place in every pore of the body. When one gathers with his fellow beings to listen about the Truth of God, everyone listens attentively. They enjoy the time spent in the Holy Presence of the Godman, and they delight in His Radiation and Grace. The Creator is unique, and is like a never-ending book."

There is no end to God's praises. When explaining the Ocean, one can speak only of the drop, but discussing the drop cannot even begin to hint at the vastness of the Ocean. The Mighty Ocean can hardly be compared to the insignificant drop.

Sant Kabir has provided a very interesting description of the Abode of Almighty God, especially of the wonderful 'throne', where God Himself sits. "Trillions of suns provide Light in this Region, but this Light cannot compare even to one hair of the Supreme Father. Such a mighty Countenance! When the soul goes there, this is what it sees! Such Radiance in this Region, and it is far above and away from Sach Khand." (i.e. It is in the Region of Anami, the Eighth Spiritual Region).

Kabir Sahib also illustrates that when the devotee has single-pointed attention, he and the Godman become alone. How Lovingly He mentions this in His verses. "The Holy Naam pours out from God's mouth like Flowers of Ecstasy. That time and that moment is calm and peaceful. It is totally inexplicable in the worldly words just how enticing and enjoyable it is. The Love of God is so immense, that day and night the devotee dances and bathes in the Colour of His Light."

Sant Kabir says that Almighty God, the Oversoul, is the Beloved Creator of all Creation. The Sufis, for example, look upon God as the Beloved, so the seeker becomes the lover. The Hindus speak of God as the Father, so the seeker, according to them, becomes the child. However, Sant Kabir sees God as the Lord, the Master, the Owner, so the seeker becomes the servant, the devotee. Thus, in His writings, the relationship between the Lord and the devotee is only of Divine Love.

Sant Kabir melts our hearts with His sweet words that speak in such Loving praise of Almighty God. "O God! You are in every atom and You are vibrating everywhere. There is no place without You. You are the Breath of the breath of this whole Creation. All the material and immaterial worlds are made by You. You are the very Air that gives Life to all!"

He goes on to say, in His own humility and with sweet remembrance of God, that if the whole world should burn to ashes, He has no worry or concern because Kabir Himself is

One with God, and Almighty God resides in every pore of His body.

He eloquently sings the praises of the Lord, describing that "O my friends! God is in each and every atom. He vibrates in the Divine Light and Sound. There is no place without Him-- in the sky, upon the earth, in the lower and upper Regions of this Universe. He is everywhere! He is the Source of all Ecstasy and Power, the Energy, the Powerhouse sustaining everything in this Creation."

Again, He praises, "O my Supreme Creator! My Lord! O Supreme Being! My Master! I pay obeisance to You, and thank You a million times for everything that You have provided to me. You have quenched my Thirst with the Sweet Nectar of Your *Holy Naam*."

"O Almighty God, Who contains the Divine Nectar! Kabir is the only One Who knows You, that You are the Creator of all Creation. This is all Thy great compassion and Grace. Whoever has received Thy Grace, this Holy Food, has no need of anything more than that. He becomes fully satisfied, and there is no more 'wanting' of anything." Sant Kabir Lovingly gives His own example, explaining that now He has obtained God, the Creator. "I Drink God's Divine Nectar and I realize His sweet ecstasy all the time, with His unbounded Grace."

Sant Kabir explains in His verses of praise that the Lord, the Creator, Almighty God, is limitless. It is not possible to establish in any sense just how great and magnanimous He is. Although the Saints say that God is immeasurable, His Divine Countenance, His Expression-Into-Being, on the other hand, is so minute, so small, so subtle, that He is the Microcosm of the human body. His very Existence vibrates in each and every atom, in all Creation and in all the Universes. There is no place where He is not.

Kabir Sahib praises the Lord. "O my Father! O my Creator! You have given me hope with Your Graciousness and compassion. You gave me the Nectar of Holy Naam, the Divine Sound Current. You are my True Father. You are all the time vibrating in me. I can never forget Thee, ever. My Lord, my True Master, my Guide will go along with me to the other world, and I will never be defeated by the lower Negative Powers."

He continues, "My Illusions have now been left behind for good. I used to feel the burden and the web of the unreal, but now I am out of its bondage. I no longer fear the five thieves, because my Father has vanished them from my mind, from my life. They were congealed with me, but now I am free. I have no relation whatsoever with them. I have, day and night, the sweet Simran of only You! I take Thy Beloved

Name on my tongue, and my whole body is drenched in the pool of the Sweet Nectar of Thy Holy Naam!"

Further He says, "My Father is the Creator of the Universes and of all the Creation. *The only way to reach the Creator is to come to the True Master.* With His compassion and Grace, He shows the Path, and with His Guidance the Journey starts upward toward the Creator. The devotee can reach the Goal, where he can say that he is a part of You and You are his Father, O Lord. Now the devotee can merge in You. There is no other than You or him. This revelation one receives due to the Grace of the True Master."

Sant Kabir says that He has come to know everything. "From the beginning of time until the end of time, there has been only Love between Almighty God and Kabir. How can such Love be extinguished? As the river plunges into the ocean, so does my heart in Thee!"

#6-5 *The Four Categories of 'Ram'*

In order to clarify the Illusion that most people have about the meaning of the word 'Ram' (one of the Names for Almighty God), Sant Kabir has devoted a few verses to say that the name of 'Ram' has always existed, having been in use aeons and aeons before this Age of the Kali Yuga. He outlines the main applications as follows:

1. One use of the word 'Ram' is when people are referring to the son of King Dasarath of Ayodhya. He is known as *Ram Chandra*, the prince-hero of the great epic poem *Ramayana* (the Wanderings of Ram), which took place in the Treta Yuga (the Silver Age). *Ramayana* is an epic poem written in Sanskrit, and it tells the story of the dramatic fight of good over evil. Both Ram Chandra and his wife, *Sita*, had to spend fourteen years in exile before finally being able to return to their kingdom. Many people worship Ram Chandra as an incarnation of Avtar Vishnu.

2. The name of 'Ram' is also used to imply the ever restless, Universal Mind of Brahm, which abides in every heart and has complete control over the person. Sant Kabir says that this 'Ram' is all powerful at many different levels.

3. A third use of the word 'Ram' is the referral to Kaal, the Negative Power, who has created the three lower Regions of the Physical, the Astral, and the Causal. Kaal is the one who brought these worlds into manifestation, and now he sustains and maintains them. His different activities as Creator, Sustainer, and Destroyer are symbolized as Brahma, Vishnu, and Mahesh, respectively.

4. Sant Kabir, however, says, "The fourth and Greatest 'Ram' pertains to the glorification of Almighty God, Sat Purush, the Supreme Lord, Who eternally abides in Sach Khand, the Fifth Spiritual Region, and is far away beyond all these other lower manifestations having the name of 'Ram'. This 'Ram' is free from conception and comprehension. He is Eternal and Supreme. He pervades everywhere, and is inherent in every living being and form in all Creation."

This is the 'Ram' of the True Masters, and is the 'Ram' to which Sant Kabir refers when He speaks of the Supreme Lord as 'Ram'. Sant Kabir has carefully pointed this out in His verses, so that there will be no misunderstanding.

He says that men of the world seek this fourth 'Ram' (Almighty God) by worshipping the stone idols, by bathing in so-called 'sacred' rivers, by wandering in the forests, in the deserts, on the mountain tops, everywhere outside, but alas! He is not to be found without. He dwells within the heart of the devotee, and this heart is not the physical one, but rather the point between the two eyes, called the Third Eye. One must look within, at that point, under the direction and guidance of the True Master.

The Heart and the Seat of the Soul is between the two eyebrows, at the back of the eyes, the point from where the Consciousness spreads throughout the body. This is called the

Single Eye, the Third Eye, the Seat of the Soul, or the Tenth Door. This is the point from which the soul must start on its Homeward Journey.

Referring back to King Ram Chandra, Sant Kabir says that even King Ram Chandra had to receive Spiritual Initiation from his Guru, *Vaasishth*, and that Ram Chandra recited the Holy Simran in order to have Divine knowledge of Almighty God.

CHAPTER 7

TRUE WORSHIP

All religions have the same Goal of One Truth. They all teach that a person should serve others, he should have Love for all Creation, know himself, and know God. Human beings are social, but at the base of this sociality is the development of the soul. If the soul is sleeping and dormant, how possibly can one develop into a social being?

Sant Kabir reveals that the body has value only as long as the soul lives within it, and the body gets its power and development from the soul. Exactly in the same way, the evolution of the soul cannot take place if there is fanaticism, bigotry, fighting, and animosity. Obviously, there is no need of more social groups. "If there is a shortage of anything, it is only of Spiritual faith, the true faith of the soul."

All religions have Spirituality as their base Teaching but, as Sant Kabir tells us, this is all disappearing and becoming almost secret, because so much attention is put to the outside materialistic world, not the Inner one. Only the outer rituals of Spiritual education are left to practice.

There are two types of religion, namely, social and Spiritual. Social religions are communities which have members who sit together to do such things as make rules, remember the ancient festivals and stories, and engage in worship. This is the outer religion, which helps people to remember their forefathers and fore-Gurus.

But the soul's religion is only Spiritual. The main aim of the soul is its own development and its reunion with the Creator, so that it will have freedom from the outer world, with all of its Illusion, intolerance, selfishness, and narrow-mindedness. Then the soul can have true, practical knowledge of the Creator, and eventually become One with Him.

All religious places and all Scriptures are worthy of respect. The original intent was that people would gather together in order to have the real meanings explained to them. These priceless Teachings need to be gone through carefully in order to put them into practice. Unfortunately, with the passing of time as well as the passing away of the Spiritual Teachers, people began to only bow their heads and make offerings such as flowers or money at these places, thinking that this is the only way of worshipping.

Sant Kabir tells us again and again that those whose Third Eye is not opened, offer prayers to those things that have no life in them, such as stones, books, paper, or statues. These kinds of objects cannot speak to the devotees, nor can they offer any solution to the problem of knowing oneself.

He says that all such practice and worship go in vain. "In front of the Lord stands all Truth, and only Truth is accepted and liked by Him. There is no worship equal to this. Truth is the highest, and untruth is equal to sin. Whoever has Truth in his heart, has the Lord in his heart. No harm can come to such a person; neither can Kaal come near him. One has to become a True Person in order to merge with God."

Spiritual knowledge is given out by the Saints from time to time. There is no difference in the Way of Spirituality that They teach, and They do not come to found any particular type of religion. Saints can come in any 'Ism', and all religions belong to Them.

Sant Kabir says that the Saint comes to this world to make all humankind as One, because for the Saint, all are the children of God. The Creator, Almighty God, is the One God of everyone, whether theist or atheist. He continues, "O worldly people! Your soul is asleep in the Illusion and Deception of forgetfulness. This body will die one of these days. You must come to the Feet of the True Master and remember Almighty God. The Sat Guru is the only One Who is fully awake and knowing of everything. The true ritual bath is to do Seva and service of the Master."

Still further on this subject He says, "You have lived a life of 'four days', and you have seen and done all the worldly things. You have gathered a lot of possessions, but nothing will you take along with you. The Holy Naam is the Power of God and is the true Internal Diamond, vibrating in each and every atom. Only the Master can manifest this Secret Jewel within the devotee."

The human body is the most unique 'Mosque-Temple-Church' which was made by God in the womb of the mother. The soul, however, is wandering around in the outer structures and artificial buildings of worship made by man. Thus, it cannot obtain any peace or happiness. To honour these outer Temples and Mosques is a sign of respect, but the true Temple is the Saint Himself. God has manifested Himself in the Saint, and God lives in Him. Kabir Sahib says, "That is the only place where a person should bow his head."

"With the Grace of the Master and through His Spiritual Initiation, the mind which is always moving like the wind, now becomes stilled with the Power of the Master's Holy Naam. The soul becomes absorbed in the Master's Divine Light, which has pierced through the darkness of this world. Those who are lucky enough to come into contact with a Spiritual Adept are granted Holy Initiation into the Mysteries of the Spiritual Regions. They live happily in the world and even more happily return to their true Home."

Sant Kabir explains, "That lucky soul leaves behind heaven and hell, and goes up into the Lap of God. But those who do not have this great good fortune first come into the world, and then leave it empty-handed. They just waste away their lives."

All the precious time of this life is spent on the body, to decorate it, to look after it, and nourish it. Sant Kabir says that truly, this is not less than idol worship, but to *decorate the soul* within the body and then to develop it, and ultimately attach it to God, is called the *true Worship*. He says that people are, on this point, absolutely ignorant, because they don't put any attention there. They don't even know how to decorate the soul, or to develop the Inner Self.

There are many ways to worship, but the purpose is the same. In the different religious Books, due to different times and different climes, it has been written down how and in which way one can pray to God, but all of these methods desire for the same purpose: to create Love for Almighty God and to meet Him. Many ways of worshipping God have been created, and many are the places to worship. It is exactly like thousands of archers, but the target is one.

In the beginning of one's Spiritual search, he goes into the Mosque, Temple, Church, or Gurdwara, but then after that he has to go into the *Hari Mandir* (the true Temple of God, which is the human body). If the heart is pious, then the devotee will ask only for God. The sincere seeker who is hankering for God is always in the process of trying to clean his heart of all vices, because he knows that place is the only true Temple, where one can see the Master's Inner Beautiful Luminous Form. For the Saints, there is no other true Temple. Nature has made the Temple of God within the person, where he can leave his sorrows and pains outside.

Kabir Sahib asks, "Why does the person go outside, when he has all the Godly Colours in his own house? With the Grace of the Master, the Sat Guru, he can find this Temple of the

Creator." He points out that the true worship is to go inwards, which one must do from his whole heart and mind with full Love and devotion.

"When the attention is on the Sukhmana, with the Grace of the Master, the soul rises up and drinks the Elixir of Holy Naam. The Master's Arrow of Illumination opens wide the Tenth Door (the Third Eye) and the Effulgent Light suddenly dawns. This Arrow opens the Way to *Charan Kamal* (the Radiant Form of the Master) at the Tenth Door. This Nectar of knowledge can only be drunk by the person who puts his attention at the Third Eye."

Sant Kabir says that when one offers the flowers of the heart and mind as devotion, then that worship is accepted by God. True worship is the worship of the Holy Naam and the Shabd.

#7-1 All Humanity is One

Every person has the same rights and privileges from God, so these should be examined. What is the outer worldly condition? Kabir Sahib says, "Whether king or subject, rich or poor, from one sect or the other, all are born the same way. Everyone takes birth after ten months, due to the mother and father."

At the time of Kabir Sahib, the Brahmins were supposedly the most 'learned' people, being the 'highest' in knowledge and caste. Kabir Sahib points out, however, that when the person is in the womb of the mother, his body being formed by Almighty God, he has no caste. He is blissfully unaware whether he is a Brahmin or a Muslim. His face is totally without blemish, because he has no ego.

In light of this fact Sant Kabir questions, "Where did people get the idea that they are Brahmin or Muslim, because inside the womb one doesn't know about, neither does he have, a caste!" He reasons "Why, then, would a person waste his life in repeating that he is a Brahmin?"

If he is a child of a Brahmin woman and of so 'high' a class, then why is he not born in a different way? Why are others of the 'high' caste of Brahmin, and He, Kabir, of a 'low' caste? Both were born in the same way!

"The Brahmins don't have milk in their veins, and the low caste have only blood in theirs. Only that person can be called a true Brahmin who thinks day and night about *Brahm* (another name for Almighty God), and actually goes up to *Brahmand* (the Third Spiritual Region)."

In those days, the Brahmins declared that they had come to the world by direct orders from the mouth of Brahma, but

Kabir Sahib points out that if they came directly from God, why were they not born differently than others?

"The caste of all humanity is one. These numerous religions and sects are only a result of the Creation of man! Until one enters into himself, he cannot hope to achieve salvation!"

All people have the same features, eyes, ears, parts of the body, and they all have the same life in them. Not only that, their very bodies are made of the same Essence (Earth, Air, Fire, Water, and Ether). They live on one earth with one sky overhead. Sant Kabir says that first humanity came into being and then all the religions came afterwards. Religion was made for mankind, for the upliftment of his soul. Humanity was not made for religion. Man's true aim in life always has been, and still is, to obtain the ultimate tranquillity and to meet Almighty God, the Creator.

The Message of the Master is for the whole human race. "Although man seems to be awake from without, he is Spiritually asleep within. His soul's attention is divided and scattered in diverse ways. The heart should be pledged to God, but instead man makes it the seat of the world. However, all that is of this world will remain here at the time of death, because in the end, everything will be taken away or left behind."

Man dissipates himself in fruitless disputes and in worthless worldly tasks. He makes little or no effort to know himself. Realization only dawns when his life comes to an end. When he dreams at night, even the dreams seem to be real, but on waking he realizes they were not. In the same way, man says that he is wide awake but actually he is not. When death draws near, he says that *this life was only a dream!* Now is the time to awaken from that dream and do whatever he can for his Spiritual progress.

#7-2 Human Body is the Golden Opportunity to Meet God

When one is young in years, he is in sound body, mind, and intellect. Sant Kabir says that this is the ideal time that he should try to meet God and to solve this mystery of life, but instead of doing that He is engaged in all trifling worldly matters which are not so important as knowing his own self. Whenever one is asked if he is doing something in the way of knowing himself, the answer always is that there is no time! There is so much work to be done! We will see when we get old!

There was once a man who liked to pass his days sitting in a garden. Sant Kabir urged him many times to spend some time in Spiritual practices, but he always replied that his children were still young. He said that when they would be grown up, he would have time to put his attention towards Higher Studies.

Many years passed and then Kabir Sahib met him again, saying "Well, dear friend, you must be enjoying meditation now." The man shook his head and replied, "You see, I am waiting for all my children to be married, and then I will have time to devote myself to this."

Again many more years passed before Sant Kabir appeared again to him. "Well, friend, your children must all be married now. Have you begun your Spiritual practices yet?" But the reply came, "No, not yet. I am waiting for my grandchildren to grow up and get settled."

Again, after a few more years, when Sant Kabir went to see this man, He learned that the man had died. Kabir Sahib went to the man's children and told them that while that man was living, he had lost the golden opportunity to solve the mystery of death, and fulfill the purpose of taking the human birth. His life had been wasted.

People always have some excuse or another to put off these Supreme practices. As the responsibilities of life increase, one tends to relegate meditation to the back burner. Even if it is on one's list of things to do, it generally has the last place in priority. But who knows for certain that the person will reach old age? *"Who knows, the world may end tonight!"* Life is fickle and can leave at any moment. This Spiritual Work can only be done as long as there is breath in the body.

"We have been born in this world, created by God for the most important objective of solving the mystery of life. This has been given to us by Almighty God." Sant Kabir says that He has solved this enigma of life and death, but others have forgotten and totally abandoned this Treasure, which is lying within their own body.

Sant Kabir doesn't advise to leave off worldly duties and responsibilities, and devote one's whole time to these practices, but He points out that the Godly pursuits end up being restricted to only reading some Scripture or attending some place of worship. This, however, is only a beginning. The main aim of life is to know oneself, at which point the person will then be in a position to know, to see, and to come into contact with that Great Reality, the Almighty Lord.

"The human is at the highest point of the 8.4 million species of life forms. If someone doesn't obtain God and remember Him while in this body, then one can ask, *what is the difference that he even took birth?"*

Sant Kabir says that the material world of matter is continuously changing, but God's Divine Presence will always be and will never change. It permeates everywhere. The human body is made of five Elements. The body is bound by these Elements, and God gives Life to them. This very body has been God-given for the purpose of knowing God, due to good Karmas in previous lives.

Kabir Sahib explains that God can only be seen with the soul, not with the physical body. However, all man's objectives so far have been concerned with the physical body, and not with the soul. Man's worldly accomplishments only concern the outer comforts, such as wealth, health and happiness. All outer rituals, therefore, are only concerned with outer worship, but the soul's reverence is Inner.

Therefore He advises, "Leave off all outer, temporary pleasures to do the worship of the Sat Guru with full devotion. This precious human birth is not going to happen again and again. This life is an invaluable treasure. The person who has wasted his nights in sleeping, and has frittered away his days by eating and talking, has sold his life in the market for a price similar to that of a little seashell!"

He emphasizes that people must learn the value of the human birth. They have sold out the valuable opportunity to know their higher self, in exchange for trifling matters of this world. Life will pass and death will stand on one's head. The person will regret and wonder why he wasted himself in all these dreams and Illusions.

Kabir Sahib outlines the person's life by saying, "The good days came and went, wasted by the chores of fulfilling worldly desires. The person neither looked for, nor loved, the Master. Now when the man is about to leave, nothing will be achieved by repenting." Kabir Sahib gives the example that when the small sparrows have eaten up all the grain from the fields, and nothing remains of value, it is just like the desires and attractions of this world have eaten up the man's precious life with trifling things, making him totally forget the real Goal.

However, whatever is gathered in this world holds significance and value as long as understanding has not awakened. When the flame of understanding is lit, one comes to know that all that has been held as precious, is merely clutter. What was attained by collecting this? Suddenly, it all becomes meaningless and worthless in a vast transformation. A complete revolution takes place within that person.

"When one takes abode with the Master (at the time of Spiritual Initiation), that soul escapes from hell and heaven. That person experiences utmost joy and ecstasy in the Company of Whom he was with from the beginning of the world until the end. Sant Kabir Himself very clearly says that heaven and hell should not be the ultimate destinations, because both objectives are binding. The soul, after spending time in these Regions, eventually must go back to the Physical Plane and again take birth in another form.

Sant Kabir reveals that the Saint is the One Who will put the person on the Way back to God. To be in His Holy Company, one receives so much unbounded Grace and compassion, that he cannot think of leaving that Godly Association. By seeing the Master, one becomes purified. Being One with the Master, the Master makes the devotee also to become One with God. As soon as one sees the Beloved, that person becomes pious and purified. The Master Blesses the devotee with His Magic Touch, and just like when iron touches the *Paras Stone* (Philosopher's Stone) and turns into gold, the Master will make that person into a Saint!

Sant Kabir is explaining that when one obtains the *Saccha* (Perfect) Master, also known as the *Puran Guru*, the *Sat Guru*, or the True Saint, that Godman bestows on the devotee the Supreme Treasure of Holy Naam, the Light and Sound of God at the time of Spiritual Initiation. The Master's Divine Teachings 'pierce' him deep in his heart of hearts. That Holy Naam forever has made a place there, because the Master is the only One Who can reveal the knowledge of this Truth.

Sant Kabir emphasizes that it is only in the human body that one can attain Godhood. "Every day, the person wastes 22,000 breaths on this world doing worldly work, but accomplishing nothing in the way of Spirituality."

He warns, "You are wasting each moment while sleeping. You should wake up to the Reality! Every breath you have is like a priceless ruby or diamond. You should Love God with each breath and surrender it to the Master."

Kabir Sahib keeps saying it, even with the beating of a drum for emphasis, that each and every breath that goes wasted is worth the price of the three *Lokhs* (the three lower Spiritual Regions). The human body is an extremely precious possession. "Each second that comes and goes is so valuable that the wealth of the entire world cannot buy it. Whoever exchanges his life in the human body for the pleasures of the senses and other worldly objects, is most unwise."

That person looks after his family, his children, his friends and relatives, the amassing of wealth and his physical comforts but very little time, if any, does he focus on Spiritual aspirations. He does nothing to really fulfill the purpose of his taking the human birth. In total forgetfulness, he is literally gambling away precious moments, dissipating his life's capital. The body becomes very frail, and time slips by so quickly.

Sant Kabir says that it is necessary for people to turn aside from wordly pursuits, so that they might be Blessed with the heavenly gifts. He advises us to carry on with the worldly work, but to keep the attention ever on Almighty God, and to have constant Simran of the Lord. "It is a very easy thing to do, and the reward is that ages of darkness give way to Radiant, Godly Light inside."

This human birth is a gift which is intended to be used for devotion to the Supreme Father and for self-realization. "Everything else is just Illusion and a dream. Showers of Divine Ambrosia are continually falling within, and these are the cure for all the pains and myriad worries of this world."

He advises, "Before this body comes near death and into the clutches of disease, remember God and do His Simran. If you don't perform devotion now, when will you do so? When death comes, how possibly can you do any *Bhajan* (Spiritual discipline)? Only in the human body can one do the Repetition of God's Holy Names, and thereby obtain salvation. Now is the best time for this."

Furthermore He says, "Remember the Lord breath for breath. Turn inwards and practice on the *Sadhan* (Spiritual discipline) of the Sound Current. Don't miss this golden opportunity, for it might not come again!"

"This body will die one of these days. You must come to the True Master and remember God; otherwise you will be looted half-way. The bones will burn like wood and the hair like grass. To see the world on fire has made Kabir sad. The human birth is so priceless, but the person dies without fulfilling his true Aim and thereby wastes this precious opportunity."

In yet another verse He says, "How sad it is that when the body dies, it will be burned to ashes. It is the same body on which perfumed sandalwood paste was rubbed, but the body will end up being burned along with the ordinary wood."

He continues, "This same body will be literally eaten up by ants and worms from head to foot when that body is buried. It will be taken apart bit by bit." He is trying to make the person aware that the same head which thinks it is very knowledgeable and beautiful, will become food for the crows and the insects.

"After man leaves this Temple (by dying), it is empty, and the crows gather to sit on the bones." The same eyes that used to see this transitory world, will also perish. Where will be the pride and ego, when one willingly or unwillingly leaves behind his possessions, the same ones he spent day and night gathering? There will be absolutely no arrogance at that time. Sant Kabir stresses that one should heed these words, because this will be the condition of all.

"O man! You cannot come back and see your children, your wealth and your house. Why not do the Simran of the Lord's Name now? Your life is passing without any purpose. Put your attention towards God. It is only in the human body that one gets an opportunity to understand the mystery of death. God gives the human form and brings the person to the Sat Guru. On meeting the Master, that person begins to commune with the Holy Name of God. He gets an Inner Awakening, and testifies as to the Light of God within. Who knows when such an opportunity may come again?"

Sant Kabir advises, "O Child of God! You should praise the Lord all the time, because in order to have this precious human life, you have suffered through 8.4 million species of life forms, which took many aeons of births in different forms. Each and every life span of these forms is different. Some are only a few hours (insects), some are a few months (plants), some are a few years (birds and animals), some are several hundred years (trees), and some are thousands of years (rocks). If you have not availed yourself of this valuable lifetime to come to the Perfect Master by praying for guidance, you may slip back again into this Circle of millions of species. You might die suddenly and none of the precious attachments, relatives, or possessions will accompany you, the same ones for which you have forsaken all the promises you made to God when you were in the womb of the mother. As you grow older, you indulge even more and more in perishable things, and are carried away just like all other people."

He says, "Pray to the Creator day and night, not forgetting Him even for a moment. Make each breath you take as an offering to the Master. It is so valuable, and people fritter away a fortune! Time lost is gone forever!"

People are dissipating their energy in worthless worldly attachments. They are letting go of this marvelous chance for the sake of things which are of no value, things of a transient nature and which will soon pass away. Everyone is taken up by his family, his relatives, his empty pursuit of pelf and power. He is lost in all these things, even though he knows in his heart of hearts that none of them are here to stay; neither will they accompany him after his physical departure from this world.

How soon are wealth, power, beauty, and health lost! "One delights in acquiring them, and even sees them in dreams. They occupy the whole waking hours all through life. And yet a sudden change in fortune or luck and they slip away just like a dream, or they depart of themselves as the years go by. If there is anyone Who can befriend another even beyond the grave, it is the True Master, the Sat Guru. If there is any Gift which can remain even after death, it is His Blessed Gift of the Holy Naam."

Sant Kabir says that if we do not take the prescribed medicine, who can blame the doctor? The only Medicine which can control the mind is the Holy Naam. If one does mistakes, they can be corrected, but if one does nothing, what can he expect?

"What can the Sat Guru do if the person does not make an effort to Experience the Lord? The blind see not, just like the wind howls vacantly through a hollow reed. The Truth cannot make any impact on a person, if his heart won't accept it." That person who does not endeavour to come to the Master is just as a 'hollow reed', void of Spirituality. The person must be sincerely seeking Almighty God, the Supreme Father, to have the good fortune to come to the Master.

The remedy for this state of sleep is to seek the counsel of an Enlightened Soul, One Who is wide-awake Himself and can shake another out of slumber. Kabir Sahib says that the person has been given a golden opportunity to awaken the soul, to know and to see the Truth.

"Whoever has not done Simran or any remembrance of God, won't be able to meditate. Putting attention constantly to the worldly affairs has become his bad habit." He compares that person's fragile body to a pot made of wood. If it is put on the fire to use for cooking, it can go only once into the fire. In other words, the golden opportunity of the human body will be forever lost. Sant Kabir explains that if one doesn't remember the Creator and come soon to the True Master while he is young, how possibly can this be done in old age?

The Temple of God is within the body but people have not recognized this. What good will it be when the person dies, when the body is put to the fire and everything is lost? The golden chance will have been wasted. If one does not remember God when there is time to do this, there will be no time after leaving the body.

"Don't wait for tomorrow. What has to be done tomorrow, do that now, and what has to be done today, do that immediately!" In other words, there should be no delay in starting the Spiritual discipline. If the person wastes that time, and leaves everything for tomorrow and tomorrow, nothing will be done.

When the Agent of Death stands on one's head to take the soul away, there is no time left to do anything. "Don't waste even one minute. Pray from the core of your heart, and look for a Saint, a True Godman. The person takes the human birth with the sole purpose that he can become One with God."

Kabir Sahib is advising people to realize how precious is every single moment, that one should have remembrance of God and his attention always turned towards Him. "Do Simran with Loving devotion, as much as the fish does regarding water. When the fish is separated from its beloved water, it will do the Simran of the water very intensely."

He says, "What good is it to sleep? You should rise up and wake up. From Whom you are separated, you should become attached. The whole world is sleeping. You came into this world to become One with the Creator. That is why you have taken the human birth. You are separated from God. You have to go and be One with Him again."

Who knows if the opportunity of the human body might come again? "How frightening and horrible is the Truth! O friend! I give you examples of the type of punishment inflicted upon the soul by Dharam Rai. The same soul today is in the human body but due to his deeds, tomorrow he might become a bull, with four feet and two horns. How terrifying is that stage when you cannot even speak words! Now you will work for perhaps a farmer who will beat you with a stick. In this condition, how can you possibly sing of the praises of God?"

"When you had the opportunity, you wasted it! Without being in touch with Divinity while in the human body and making some effort to recognize yourself, you came into this animal body. Look at you! They have put a ring through your nose, tearing your nostrils by pulling you wherever they want you to be. They beat you on the shoulders and give you only the leftover cover of the grain to eat. All day you run here and there, and in old age they just leave you to wander, but your belly never gets filled."

Sant Kabir says that this condition happens to people who are stubborn, and don't accept the Truth of the Godman. They have to reap the Karma of their bad deeds to take birth in the animal body, or other species of animals. In each and every form, they have to suffer immensely. Who is going to listen to their cries at that time? Life is full of misery in the animal body. Those animals will become the tools of a farmer who will make them work day and night for his various tasks.

Sant Kabir advises, "O foolish person! There is still time. While you are in this human body, you must recognize yourself and the Oversoul, the Creator. Without doing the Simran of the Holy Naam, you will be full of regrets. You must listen to the Godman and not lose this priceless, invaluable human body in which God has given you a chance to recognize Him."

Sant Kabir is giving these worldly examples to show the value of the human birth. The person has come to this world after aeons and aeons of paying off Karmas. He has taken the human body only to know God. With his own eyes, he can see everyday that breath by breath, life is passing. The life of a person goes by from minutes to hours, from hours to days, from days to months to years.

Sant Kabir pleads, "O man! You know all about this transient world, and you see this Truth with your own eyes as you take other dead bodies on your shoulders to the cremation ground, not realizing that one day you have to depart the same way."

Sant Kabir is describing that He feels great pity when He sees the wasteful status of the precious human body. He wonders that why should a mother even give birth to a child, if that child will waste his life, not knowing himself or God. It would have been much better if she had not carried the child. He asks, "Why did the mother have to suffer, carrying the child in the fire of her womb for 10 long months. If he is not going to know the Truth of Divinity, it would be better if he had not been born!"

He says that without coming to the True Master, there is no difference between a person who has no knowledge of himself and one who is dead. He may be beautiful and handsome, but without having Spiritual Initiation, and without knowing himself and the Overself, he is exactly carrying a dead body around and making himself more actions and reactions, to be reaped in future lives.

Sant Kabir points out that the ideal aim of every person who is born into a human body is to find the Creator; otherwise the human life is wasted. He says that the person should be ashamed if he doesn't put thoughts for even a moment towards his True Father, the Creator.

Sant Kabir instructs that for the man whose Master is the Most High, it is not becoming for him to entertain worldly thoughts in his heart and mind. The Master is with the devotee until the end of the world, but the person is running after trifling things.

He gives examples that people pray to Lakshmi, not knowing in their foolishness that millions of Lakshmis themselves are hankering and pining to see the Lord, and yearning for His Grace. Even Maya seeks shelter at the Lotus Feet of the Lord. "The pity is that until man doesn't invert and go inwards, he cannot realize this. His life becomes wasted without being in the Company of Truth and never having praised the Lord. That man can only die in sorrow and turbulence."

In this world one gives such great deliberation to form intelligent decisions in matters of worldly pursuits. What a pity it is that one has so foolishly forgotten that his own number of breaths is finishing, and he has to leave the body. In this matter, the total wisdom and cleverness of even knowing all the world will not help. Day and night man thinks only of how to run the world, his household and his life. He does not sacrifice even one moment of attention for the Creator. Every moment he forgets that his friends and relatives die. He does not really think about why he has taken this important birth.

Sant Kabir is talking to one of the learned Priests and advising him, "Turn your face towards Mecca, and call the people together in your Mosque with the Holy Name of God. I tell you the Truth! In this very physical body, the True Speaker of God lives. Your very own self, your soul, is the true Temple. Make this as your holy, true Mecca. Rise up from the Nine Doors (apertures) in the body and come to the Tenth. Say your prayers at this Tenth Gate."

He Graciously continues, "I tell you the Truth. Become 'mad' in the Divine Love of thy God, Who is the Creator of all. The more you receive His Divinity and peace with sweet remembrance, the more your mind will turn inward and will be stilled. Ultimately, it will merge in the ecstasy of God."

He then refers to the Muslim ritual of slowly slaughtering animals. "O Mullah! Don't sacrifice those who cannot talk. Those animals also have God in them. Don't sacrifice them in the Holy Name of God. Instead of sacrificing these helpless creatures of God, you should give up your own evil tendencies!"

#7-3 Helping Factors For Spiritual Progress

There are several requirements to make progress on the Spiritual Path, but as Sant Kabir points out, to obtain these qualities and attributes, one has to pray from the core of his heart, to Almighty God, the Supreme Father.

One needs:
1. The **Sat Guru** (a True, Living Master).
2. The **Satsang** (which means to be in the Company of the Master and to listen to His Spiritual Discourses).
3. The **Sat Naam** (the *Holy Naam*, and *Shabd*, which is the Divine Sound Current). This Sat Naam is obtained only from the True Master.

One needs a Sat Guru, but that Guru must be a Perfect Master, One in Whom the Truth vibrates and resides. Sant Kabir always refers to Him as the Puran Guru (True Master). The Master should have merged in Truth, and there should be no difference between Him and the Creator. In His Holy Company (the Satsang), the devotee will have the 'Colour' of Truth (known as the Holy Naam) drenched on his soul. As long as one has not met such a Master, one cannot hope to come out of worldly Illusion.

Until the soul has this Company of the True Master, it cannot have His attachment, and the Inner Spirituality will not be awakened. As long as the person does not withdraw his attention from the nine apertures (the eyes, ears, etc.) and meet the Master within at the Tenth Gate, he can make no Spiritual progress.

"In this human body, one has a priceless Jewel, and because of its energy, the body is working. The Master takes this Gem and with His unbounded Grace and attention, He infuses His own Life-Impulse through Spiritual Initiation, and makes this Jewel as a great Powerhouse within each person. However, only when the devotee focuses his attention behind the eyes, at the Third, or Single Eye, can he be aware of it." Sant Kabir refers to this Jewel as the soul (or the attention, also known as *Surat*). He says that the attention is the outward expression of the soul.

When the person's attention is connected to that Ultimate, Eternal Truth, gradually his condition changes as his angle of vision changes, until he begins to find that everything else is worthless in comparison to his search for self and God-realization. The devotee has to practice on the Sound Current to stay free from the evil effects of this world. The five deadly sins furthermore won't have any affect on him. They will have been reduced to dust. The person will be like a lotus flower which flourishes on top of the dirty water, forever dry and unaffected by the ripples below it. He will have severed all connections with the body, uprooted the mind completely, and swept away all attachments with this world.

There are several qualities which should be inculcated in the devotee for success in the Spiritual arena. Sant Kabir outlines these in numerous verses, stressing that the cultivation of these attributes can make the human into the Divine.

1. When one has **compassion** in his heart, then he has mercy for all Creation. For example, when one sees somebody else in pain, he will try to reduce that pain. He cannot bring himself to hurt anyone's heart; rather he will think only goodness for all. In the heart of that true follower, true faith (Dharma) develops.

2. Whoever has the quality of compassion, has obtained the Blessed quality of **forgiveness**. Due to the devotee cultivating forgiveness, he becomes also Blessed with the Boons of **peacefulness** and **happiness**.

3. The devotee should pray for the quality of **patience**. When he has total contentment and peace, then worldly desires and worries leave him.

4. One then becomes Blessed with the **Truth** in him, and when he lives in this Truth, he becomes the very Form of

Truth. Whoever has his attention in Truth, then all his work in life will be also Truth. He eventually becomes **Fearless**, going boldly on the Path of Truth, guiding other people to also go on the true Path.

5. The devotee must have **gentleness** and a **honey-tongue**, and meet all with full radiance and **humbleness**. This is the true human honour in him. He should have a Loving relationship towards everybody.

6. The devotee must practice **charity**. However, if somebody has compassion, only then can he give in charity. To give in charity is the quality of a human. However, charity should be given to the truly needy and destitute, such as widows and orphans. Whoever distributes his hard-earned money, receives the unbounded Blessings of Almighty God.

7. The devotee must have **purity** and **piety** in his mind, his body, his house. Also, his thoughts and outward sense tendencies should be restrained. To worship God and to obtain the Grace of God, one needs honestly-earned money with which to purchase clean (vegetarian) food.

Sant Kabir describes the true devotee, in constant absorption in the Absolute. He says, "Whether sitting, standing, or walking about, he ever remains in a state of **eternal equipoise**."

Kabir Sahib then reveals how one can get this work from the mind. He says that the soul has to become detached from the mind in order to go beyond Brahmand, but up to Brahmand the mind goes along with the soul. Now, the question remains, how can one detach himself from the worldly desires, rise on the mind and go into the Upper Spiritual Regions?

"With the Power of the intellect and the Discrimination, one can get work from the mind. Without any hesitation, one can ride on this horse-like mind to go beyond Par Brahmand. Catch hold of this horse (the mind) with the Sound Current! Put your foot in the stirrup, and hold the horse with both sides of the saddle (Simran), restraining it, regardless of its tricky ways. One can then surely go there. Just leave behind the *Mun Roop* (form of the mind) at Brahmand."

The devotee's mind will always be filled with **gratitude**, because he should feel unworthy of all that he has been given. His prayer is always of thanksgiving and gratitude, with never a complaint. The Door opens only for those who have annihilated themselves totally. The Guest arrives in the house of one who is 'empty'. No sooner does one become empty, than the Guest appears. When one empties himself, He fills him.

Kabir Sahib explains that the mind should work for the devotee, not that the devotee works for the mind. He has

Graciously given us a Secret Way of travelling, illustrating that if a family person wants to become a perfect horse rider, he must ride on the horse with both feet planted firmly in the stirrups, one foot for the worldly life and the other for the Spiritual. When they are both tightly held, that person will have the best of both the worlds in this human form. One cannot rise up on the Spiritual Path without having both feet firmly in place. If one loses on just one side, he will fall badly. In other words, he must fulfill all duties and responsibilities in this world; otherwise he cannot progress Spiritually.

Sant Kabir also explains that **chastity** and **forgiveness** are two of the main prerequisites for Spirituality. "Chastity is life and self-indulgence is death. Chastity is easier to practice than forgiveness. Outwardly, the person seems to be humble, but inwardly he does not hesitate to harm others, especially by thoughts. In the absence of forgiveness, back-biting, anger, jealousy, and hatred emerge. The mind and heart are filled with this, but one cannot realize God unless the mind has total equipoise."

The worldly desires attack from the level of the body and the Plane of the senses, pulling us to pieces. Sant Kabir says that only by transcending the body consciousness, is one able to contact the Light of Life. As long as one has a thought of this body, he cannot rise up above the body consciousness.

His desire to have this body results in further entanglement and desires.

"One can easily give up gold, possessions, and even all comforts in life, but pride and jealousy are very difficult to cast out. It is a rare person who is truly humble. Anger, jealousy, malice, and ill-will fan the flames of an unseen, but smouldering fire all around. Forgiveness washes away all inner defilements and leads to peace of mind. One whose mind is pure and his intellect at rest, will surely reflect the Light of God."

Sant Kabir says that a person will be called a True Person only if he has the quality of **'humanity'**. "That man should see the other fellow being as his brother, and share others' sorrow and pain. He should have the utmost Love for all of God's Creation, and have Love for God Himself."

The more one Loves God and His Creation, the closer God comes near. If a person really thinks that every heart contains God, then without any hindrance he will have Love and respect for every human being. "When somebody goes around the heart of another, and respects him as his own, that is real Love for God. This is much better than going around thousands of outer *Ka'abas* (most sacred place of worship in Mecca for the Muslims)."

"As soul we are all formed of God's Essence. All souls are the children of God, the One Father, and that is why we are all brothers." He says that we should share with others. "As long as you have the human body, give, give, and give! The main factor of having this body is that you keep giving."

He points out that the fruit of the tree is not eaten by the tree. The river does not keep all the water to itself. Both the river and the tree live for others, and in the same way, man should be of use to his fellow-beings. "It is not good if water comes into your boat, because the boat will sink."

In other words, there are only so many material items that one can use in his daily life, and excess of anything will be the cause of his 'sinking'. It is a wise person who gives away in charity, with both hands. That person will never be out of funds. "If you take water from the river, the river doesn't have less water. You can see this with your own eyes."

Sant Kabir devotes many verses to the subject of one's food. A Spiritually-inclined person both eats and sleeps very little. The correct way of taking food is half the lesson of Spirituality. From His verses, we find that Sant Kabir ate food mainly made of a combination of rice and lentils cooked together (*Khichri*). He advises that food should be purchased out of the hard-earned income acquired by honest means. Food should be light, and thus easily digested.

He prays, "O God! Please give me simple food to eat, like grains, fruits, nuts, and vegetables." Then He explains that He doesn't want to ask God for lavish food for fear that God might also take away the simple food. For example, if someone is looking for richer and exorbitant items in life, and puts down the lower and simple things, sometimes even the modest articles get taken away.

Sant Kabir gives out the maxim that for simple food, one needs simple living. Lavish food has much more involvement and implication, because there is a tendency for desire and greed to develop. Man then does wrong things in order to obtain and sustain this excessive life style. Kabir Sahib always taught that simple living combined with simple food taken in small quantities, is more than enough to satisfy one's needs.

He says that the whole world is following the dictates of the mind, but it is a rare soul who follows the Master. "Don't go after the wayward tendencies of the mind, and the wanting of things of the world. It is a rare person who can even recognize that he is actually following the dictates of the mind, and can also exercise restraint. Put the desires of the mind down, and break them into pieces. What good is it if a farmer sows the seeds of poison, and then repents why he did so? It would be better now to do the right thing in the first place!"

"People who eat all kinds of fish and meat to make their body grow are mad and insane! Don't cut the throats of others for the sake of your tongue taste, but instead eat simple food like *Khichri*, or even bread. The birds and animals are just like us, going around in the various incarnations. In previous births, they might have been kings or emperors, rich and famous persons, but due to their wicked deeds and other sins they have had to undergo these wretched rebirths. We should have pity on ourselves. God resides in everything, in all Creation and everywhere. If we want to meet God, we should not kill others!"

To those who sacrifice animals in the name of their religion He warns, "You are killing animals who have life in them! Do you think that you have only killed dust, or dirt? You have killed a living being with the *Allah-e-Noor*, the Divine Light, the Essence of God, in it. The body that you have slaughtered was made with the Light of God in it. What you have killed, O Learned One, had the Light of God as its soul. These birds and animals are a part of God's Creation, and He is enlivening everybody because He resides everywhere. There is no place where He is not. If you want to Love God, you have to Love all His Creation."

Kabir Sahib is advising the Spiritual aspirant to eat vegetarian food, not animal flesh that is sacrificed. "Don't butcher those without a tongue (who cannot speak for themselves), or torment them. Bring 'clean' food which is purchased with hard-earned and honestly-earned money."

Kabir Sahib explains that for every action, there is a reaction. If one kills others for food, such as animals, birds or fish, that reaction will take place in a future life. "The cows, goats, chickens, pigs, and buffaloes are crying for help but no one listens to their shrieks, and they are being continuously slaughtered daily."

He warns that meat, eggs, and alcohol are poisons, and he who uses them will suffer the consequences. There is no escape from this. He cautions, "Go inside and see with your own eyes what tortures that the eaters of these things have to suffer, *whether initiated or not!*"

"O brother! How will you belong to God? God comes to those who are hankering for Him, who ask for Him, who want Him with passion and zeal. God listens to those prayers of the true hearts."

Then He explains further, "What basic things do you need for living in this world? You are running around and begging from house to house. Actually, you need a small amount of food and very little cloth, a simple bed with a pillow and a blanket. All of them can be obtained with only a little labour. Don't desire anything further, except the privilege of being devoted to

Almighty God, with all humility. This is the only way of learning to be simple, and you should not have any more desire than of God's Holy Name. You have to work for only the basic necessities, but don't have any more desires. You need only essential things; otherwise you end up guarding numerous possessions. These desires grow more and more, and create unnecessary problems."

Kabir Sahib gives the example, "I don't want my own throat to be cut, because if I cut somebody else's throat, he is going to cut my throat in a future life! I can eat simple bread. Why make the body full of filth, with dead flesh? This simple food is as Amrit. It is vegetarian, clean and pious, because one is not hurting anything in the higher life forms."

#7-4 Discrimination (The Fifth Element)

The human body is made of five Elements, and out of the five, four of them consist of matter. Only the fifth one, Discrimination, is the All-Consciousness, the soul, the spirit. From this fifth Element comes the *Buddhi*, the intellect to know what is right and what is wrong. It is only with this Buddhi that one can recognize the Creator.

This power of the intellect is the only one that can distinguish and understand the workings of worldly Illusion, and rescue the person from it. Man has a unique position: he has the freedom to go right or wrong. However, with the Grace of Almighty God, he also has the ability to determine what is right and what is wrong. He can make a conscious choice to go whichever way he pleases.

With the Grace of the Sat Guru, the devotee's soul rises to the *Dhaswan Dwar* (Tenth Gate), quite beyond the worldly Illusions. Sant Kabir says that due to the devotee's attention no longer functioning in outward tendencies, it appears that Illusion for him is now sleeping. Now that his attention is turning inward, he sees God and His Light in every atom. Illusion doesn't bother him, because that connection with the five senses has been broken.

"That lucky person can now state that previously, he could not taste the delicious flavour of the Divine Inner Nectar, which is provided by the Master. In those unlucky times, that person was under great Delusion, but now that has changed. Now he knows what is the Reality, and what is right for him to Spiritually progress."

Millions and millions of years have already gone by, and lifetime after lifetime has been wasted in this world. The boat has been ever adrift on the fierce and terrible sea of life, subject to the chance winds and waters. Seeing such pathetic conditions, the Master takes pity on mankind. "The Eternal Elixir is given by the Living, True Master, and only he receives It, who has good fortune recorded on his forehead. That person blissfully remains in the Lap of God."

Sant Kabir describes a condition, where the effect of attachment is so great, that even as people grow older, they have such hopes that they will live forever. "What a pity! You are now old and you are going to die. Yam Raj is counting your breaths, and as soon as they finish, he will come to pull your soul forcefully out of the body."

It is known in all the Scriptures that when a person is born, he is allotted a certain number of breaths, and when they are finished, he cannot have even a single one more. According to the Pralabdha Karma, the circumstances of death is fixed before the person takes birth. Kabir Sahib says to the dying person, "Why do you cry now? What good is it to cry at this late stage? There is no benefit in crying for lost time!"

Sant Kabir says again and again that life is like a play of the Negative Power. "God has given you the intellect, the power of Discrimination (the Fifth Element), with which you can see what is right and wrong. Unfortunately, at the same time, the Negative Power ties you up with all these outer attractions and desires. You have to judge all your own deeds, and come out of this Deception. You must find out who you are, and Who your Creator is. When these questions come, and you pray from the core of your heart to the Lord, such prayer will always be heard, and benefit will be given. You will realize that Illusion is playing with you. And then you will certainly win the game of life, and become One with God, with the Grace of your Master."

Sant Kabir says that in order to be able to see God in all His Pristine Glory as a shining Diamond, God Himself makes that person into a diamond. He explains that one must be subtle and become a 'part', in order to see the 'Whole'. This state is quite beyond the limitations and the comprehension of the human intellect.

When the Master comes into this world, He directs the person's attention to the most important Reality--the inevitability of death. With all the person's intellectual attainments, however, he acts as if he never would have to leave the world or the body.

"From whence came the soul, there it must go back. In order to rise in Spirituality, one has to think clearly and deliberately, and for this he needs the Power of Discrimination. He should know that what is true is really the Truth, and what is untrue is the untruth. To know the difference between the two is called *Discrimination*, and to even know about this, one needs very higher thoughts."

Whoever comes under the clutches of tradition and bigotry all through life, that person stays engrossed in the outer world, without obtaining any assistance from his ability to think. His Power of Discrimination does not work, and he cannot understand the true value of that. "When one has Discernment, he can separate water from milk. He can accept what is right, and then can leave the water aside."

Sant Kabir advises, "Catch hold of the True Naam, and the True Master. All *Jap* (repetition of a Mantra), *Tap* (austerities), fasts, pilgrimages, charity, ritual baths, silence, *Karam* (action), *Dharam* (religion; mode of life), all come under Discrimination. Without awakening and keeping vigilance from inside, we are living a life as though we are dead. We do the day-to-day basic worldly things, but we are just passing time. We think that this is all there is, and we don't try to find out about the Creator."

He says that one should use his intellect to know the higher self, where there exists the Truth. If one thinks about the Creator, then the Creator starts thinking about that person. Even if he has not seen the Creator, if he starts praying sincerely to Him, then God will send Somebody (the Master) to help that person to meet with Him.

Sant Kabir repeats that "It is a very rare soul who uses his Discriminating thoughts to know the Truth and the Creator.

That type of person will have no conceit left in him, because he will be fully engulfed in God's Love. Without Discrimination, one cannot obtain God, and he can only have this Discernment in the Holy Company of the Saint."

"If only the person would become innocent and pure like a child, without any preconceived ideas or prejudices, God would surely meet him!"

#7-5 Prayer

Prayer, according to Sant Kabir, is the focusing of the mind into a one-pointed stillness at the Third Eye, the Seat of the Soul. It is the call unto Almighty God for supplication, the soul's cry for His mercy and Grace. When one prays from the core of his heart, he is speaking directly to God. Prayers of the restless soul naturally grow in the person as he searches for Truth. The very act of searching for Truth is due to the Grace of God. In response to this sincere request coming from the depths of a yearning heart, God brings that lucky soul to the Living Godman, where the Lord Himself is manifested.

Prayer is an expression of gratitude for Blessings that have been already received. Prayer must never be a complaint. One should be so filled with gratitude that he sees God all around. Everywhere is His Divine Hand, guiding, protecting, giving.

Sant Kabir gives many examples of the different types of prayers, not only from the perspective of a devotee, but also as a True Master, concerned with the welfare of all God's children. In one of the prayers, He is appealing to the Lord to remove the misery of burning, both in the womb and on the pyre. He advises that the only remedy for this, is that one should hasten to come to where God Himself has manifested (as the Master), and surrender to Him.

This prayer, when it comes from a true seeker, invokes mercy from God and then God, working through the Sat Guru, winds up the coming and going (Transmigration) of that person in this world. The person's fear of physically dying is ultimately finished when he rises above the body consciousness, and sees first-hand that he is something much greater than the physical body.

Sant Kabir speaks to a Priest saying, "O Mullah! Almighty God, the Creator, is not deaf! God can hear even the footsteps of an ant in the forest! Why are you shouting so loudly, screaming your prayer-call from the upper floors of the Mosque? Will this voice reach Him sooner? The Temple of God is within you. You should pray inwardly, in your heart, because God dwells there. The call to prayer should be in the unspoken language of the heart. Address thy call to the mind, so that it will turn within."

What can one say to God? All words are useless. All actions are trivial. Only certain things can be attained by actions, things which are, however, petty and meaningless. The Vast Absolute cannot be obtained through any kind of worldly actions. Sant Kabir says that everything in Spirituality happens by 'non-doing'.

The need to beg for worldly things hides all gratitude. When one is beyond the needs and various demands of the world, then the correct form of prayer bursts forth. Whatever a person wishes for, he attains sooner or later, but it should be carefully noted that all desires are eventually fulfilled.

One should be very aware of what he asks for, so that he won't regret it later. One first wastes much time in asking, and then later wastes more time in regretting what was received. People even try to establish a bargaining situation with God. "O Lord! If You help me in this matter, I will go to the Temple every day!" Even then, they try to get off as cheaply as possible. When their desires are fulfilled, they conveniently 'forget' that they had even asked for them!

Sant Kabir explains that when one has a problem such as health, family, or other worldly difficulty, he always remembers and puts his prayers towards Almighty God. What would be the Grace of God if that person would continue praying in the same way to God also in times of joy and happiness? "If we would pray in time of pleasure, then pain would not come up. When we pray only in pain, such prayers go all in vain."

He points out that people remember God only when they are hard-pressed from every side. "It is affliction that turns the devotee Godward, but hard times come as a result of sins committed when one is in good times and totally forgetful of the Lord. God does not listen to such selfish prayers which are muttered in distress over illness or troubles. *Prayer should be ceaseless!*"

He uses a very colourful image of the village maids who move about, talking with their attention always fixed on pitchers overhead. These women go to fetch water, carrying their pitchers of water one above the other on their heads. All the time they keep talking and jesting amongst themselves, while the pitchers remain steady.

"Similarly, one should not forget their prayers even in the midst of all the hustle and bustle of everyday life and worldly obligations. One's true focal point should never waver." When one remembers God, God hears that prayer. The

Creator dwells in the heart of the devotee, and He makes the Way for that person, through the Master, to be One with Him.

Sant Kabir says that prayer is a natural instinct in a human, and is very necessary for Spirituality. Prayer is a call for help to a Living, True Master, Who is complete and Perfect. Prayer is very important in order to have Grace.

Sant Kabir says that people also pray to have their worldly desires fulfilled. However, when the person sees that none of his worldly ways of doing prayer and ritual efforts have brought forth fruit, then he gets discouraged by these outer methods.

"To know the Truth," suggests Sant Kabir, "the person prays for his Ultimate Goal, to know himself from his heart and soul, believing that the Creator is the Doer of all. He fully surrenders himself, body, mind, and heart, and then when he has complete faith that God knows what is best for him, he accepts it without question." That kind of person prays to God, "Whatever You do, whatever is right for me, I will accept and You please give it to me." He prays from his heart that who could know better than the Creator what is best for him. He gives thanks for the Divine Will of God, and he accepts its outcome gladly. Sant Kabir says, "At every step, that person receives the help of the Master."

The devotee prays to the Master to have His Grace. God is an unlimited Ocean of all Powers, and when one puts his attention towards Him, that person receives patience, peacefulness, and stillness. When these Powers are received, one is able to face all worldly problems with strength. People who are Spiritually wise, go inward and pray to God for His mercy. The true Aim of life is to have the Grace of Almighty God, and for that, one always has this kind of prayer on his lips.

"To obtain Spirituality, one has to pray to a Living Master, to help him to know himself. Prayer is the only true, straightforward and natural Way to meet with God." With prayer, one gets help to save himself from all the ills of the world, and to have control over all the outgoing senses.

All Powers run with the Power of God. Kabir Sahib says, "Whatever one wants, he should ask Almighty God for it. There is no shortage in God's supply of any kind. Even the gods, goddesses, and angels get their Power from the Creator. They are all under Him. If one wants something, he should get it from Him."

To ask the lower Powers for salvation from this world is not successful, because the lower Powers cannot give something higher than what they have themselves. Sant Kabir tells us, "They cannot grant salvation, because they don't have salvation themselves. In truth, these lower Powers salvation themselves. In truth, these lower Powers constantly pray for the human body, so that they can come to the Godman, and thereby obtain final liberation from Him."

Sant Kabir raises the crucial point that we have not yet seen the Creator. "Without seeing for oneself, one cannot have full faith. Where full faith is not, there prayer cannot be accepted. God speaks through the Sat Guru, and when one prays to Him, it is just like one is praying to God, because God Himself works through Him. He has all the Power. He is complete. Whatever one wants to ask, he should ask it from Him. He should ask from the Sat Guru Who represents God; otherwise, he should never put his hand out to request anything from anybody."

Sant Kabir says that prayer can be done in three ways:
1. One can pray with the tongue, loudly. Many prayers are meant to be read aloud, but until the prayers do not come out from the heart and also from the eyes (in the form of tears), they are not beneficial. Prayer, however, is the voice of one's own heart and different hearts have different prayers.
2. One can pray through the tongue of the thought, mentally.
3. One can pray with the *Rooh* (silent attention). Sant Kabir says that this is the best type of prayer.

He also says in many verses that one does not have to go to any outer religious place to say prayers, because prayers chaste life in order to gain God's acceptance, because God's faith and Grace is needed. The whole earth can be a place of prayer. God does not live in outer buildings, in books, or in photographs.

"One should just bow the head and turn into the mirror of the heart. He should turn inward and do prayer in the human body, where God is living. There is no other peaceful place for prayer." To Whom one has to pray is already in this body. Then why do people have to run around outside? For prayer, one has to forget about the outer body and its attachments.

"That kind of prayer should come out from the heart. No special language or words are needed. It has to be what is in the heart that comes out. If prayers from the outside have beautiful words, but from inside the life has all kinds of vices, than those prayers will be all lies! Almighty God hears that sincere prayer that comes from the core of the heart, with humbleness, zeal and great Love."

He gives the example of a prayer for salvation from this world of Illusion and endless attraction. "O God! How can I swim across this Ocean of Illusion? O my God! Help me! Save and protect me. I have sought Thy shelter. The Ocean of Illusion is so deep and vast that it seems endless. O my gracious Lord! You are the One to have Grace on me and only then can I cross over. I am full of bad qualities, and without even one good attribute. From my heart and mind, I am full of ego and pride. If I meet the True Master, the True Sat Guru, then only will I be taken across to the Other Side!"

In another very heartfelt prayer He says, "O Lord! Don't forget me even if thousands of people come to You. Like me, You have many but for me, *You are the only One!*"

It is a rare soul who searches for the Creator. When the Lord hears the true prayer of the devotee who wants to know the Creator, He makes the devotee to be in touch with that Human Pole where He has manifested. Sant Kabir is explaining that only a rare soul hankers to know the Truth and also God.

"Among high and low, among rich and poor, great is he who prays, and greater still he that motivelessly does so!" When one prays from his heart of hearts for God and God alone, that is the greatest prayer of all! That prayer will surely be heard!

Kabir Sahib gives an example of the prayer of a devotee to his Beloved Master. He is humbly saying, "O my Lord! Open the door of Your Divinity and Your Grace! You are the humblest of the humble. My Sat Guru! Kindly forgive my sins, the bad deeds that I have incurred. You are the Emperor of emperors, and I am standing at Your doorstep. Kindly grant me Thy Godly Darshan and make me Your own. There is no other place for me except at Your Lotus Feet. O my Lord! I bow down to You and pray to You to kindly grant me the Boon of being in Your Holy Assembly. Kindly grant me the knowledge of humbleness. From whom should I beg? Everyone I see is a pauper! Thou alone art the richest of the rich!"

He continues, "My salvation, my success of coming to this world will be only fulfilled when I see You inwardly and recognize myself. Almighty Lord! You have many true devotees who pay obeisance at Your doorstep. They have obtained the true knowledge that You have bestowed on them. O all Powerful and Gracious One! Take me from the desires and Illusions of this world, above the four Regions of Maya, and on to Sach Khand!"

He adds, "All the three Lower Spiritual Regions, and even the fourth Region where Maha Kaal resides will also one day have Grand Delusion. Sach Khand alone is the imperishable House of Almighty God!"

The person who is hankering to know the Creator, the True Father of all Creation, prays from the core of his heart, "O God! O Almighty Creator! Resolve my question: how can I meet You? You are the Creator of all Creation. Please reveal Yourself! You are the Lord! Please catch hold of my hand very tightly and take me to the Ultimate Goal. Please don't leave me in the way!"

Sant Kabir gives several examples of the prayers of a devotee seeking the Creator. "O Lord! You are the support for my fragile body. Your prop is a protection just like a mountain for me, and steady as a rock. I realize Your Holy Presence everywhere. You look after me just like I am Your own, and You do not let me fall into any worldly pit. When You grasp me tightly by the hand, I have all peace and ecstasy in me."

Kabir Sahib speaks as a grateful disciple, saying, "I am One with God. Now there is no difference between Kabir and God. We are as One. Nobody can recognize the God Power bestowed on me. I would not have reached to this stage if the Master had not granted me Spiritual Initiation. All of this Blessed Divinity is showered on me by my Beloved Sat Guru. Kindly keep me with You. The true Way is the Way of the Saint. The Sat Guru has made me to see the Reality."

He is describing the cry of the soul who wants salvation while living in this body. The devotee prays, "Almighty Master! Save me from the worldly Illusion. There is no way out without ridding this delusion from my mind. I feel ashamed that I know not how to pray to You, O Lord! I do all the wrong things while in Your Holy Presence. How will You ever make me Your own?"

Again, He presents the prayer of the soul to the Master that how can he spend the precious life which is given to him to find the Truth? Sant Kabir says that He searched up to the heavens, but nothing He saw could equal the sweet Contemplation of the Divine Lord!

"O Mighty Sat Guru! Until You don't bestow Your Sweet Holy Naam and without having Your Grace and Your mercy, I cannot cross this terrible Ocean of the Life of Illusion and Deception. These desires of the world won't leave me and without Your Holy Naam, there is no hope!"

Sant Kabir gives another example of prayer. "Please look after me! I am surrounded by Illusion, and I will drown if You don't catch hold of my hand. When I hear even one word of the Guru's Holy Naam, that clears up all my doubts. You are the Great One, O Giver of Life! You are the Gracious Lord, full of all humility. Please catch hold of me and take me to the Other Side. You are knowing of all the knowledge of God and You are everywhere. If You let me go from Your hand, Who will take me across the Ocean of Life?"

Sant Kabir gives the example of a prayer to the Creator for humility. "Almighty God, Who is permeating every atom and every soul. O Lord! Your Command, Your Order, is my true prayer. There is nothing above Your Direction. I don't have any outward thoughts. I only think of You day and night. You are the Creator of the whole Creation and you are the only Power which vibrates in every atom, and You are my own

Saviour. You are the very Life of my life. You must accept me as I am. I am Thy slave of Thy slaves. You may Love me (give me life), or You may turn away (give me death)."

The Master always represents 99.99% humility in this world. Giving an example of this unbounded humility, Sant Kabir continues, "I don't even have one quality. O Master! Only due to Your Holy Name, people respect me. Of my own, I don't have any attributes. You have all the attributes and qualities, but when I went into my own heart, I saw only bad deeds. *O Lord, forgive me, forgive me, forgive me!* You are my Father and You look after me. I am Your disobedient son, but still You look after me. I want only Your Love. I don't know how to obtain it, so kindly show me the Way. I am false and untrue. I have all heat in me, the fires of ego, pride, and anger. I am a sinner, who is coming to Your Lotus Feet, to Your *Sharan* (protection), that You will lift me unto Yourself. From many births, I am full of sins and bad deeds. You are the Great One Who can take away my sorrows. You are the Only One Who can catch my hand and lift me up! I am full of ills and bad deeds. You have all the good qualities. You are the only One Who has any good qualities. If I forget You and do wrong things, please have Grace on me. My Supreme Lord is all Grace. Forgive me for doing these wrong things. I forget and defile myself. I am under Your protection and You are my Saviour. If You should forget me, to whom can I turn? You shelter everyone! I have done all kinds of sins and I feel ashamed of this. I come to surrender myself to You. Either You take away the sins, or You take away my life!"

#7-6 Bhairag (Detachment)

"On the Path of Spirituality," Sant Kabir advises, "one should not become a hermit, leaving behind a weeping and lamenting spouse, and children. One should live in the world, meditate on the Holy Naam, and offer worship and devotion to God. The Master's guidance is received while one lives in the world, earns his own livelihood and fulfills all obligations and responsibilities toward family, parents, and society. Wherever one happens to be, whether it be on the mountain, in the forest, or on the ocean, the Master is always with His disciple. He is also with the disciple at the time of the disciple's physical departure from this world."

Sant Kabir urges the devotee to work in this world, but to always keep his true aim in front of him. He says that one should remain in the world, but be as if he is not there, as if he is in the forest. Keep doing worldly duties, but maintain the remembrance of God's Holy Name ever throbbing within. If a person's Goal is not constantly before him, any step he takes in the wrong direction is a total waste of time. If the Aim is right and one does a little work on it, that will not go to waste.

"Therefore one should have only one objective and work hard to achieve it, but to attain the Goal one should know what he is aiming for. If you have lost yourself and your true Aim for the world, this world will not go along with you."

Through God's hands alone, does both joy and sorrow come. Therefore, how can one still look upon them as happiness or pain? When one becomes aware of His Hand behind everything, then both states of being lose their impact. Happiness will no longer raise one up, nor sorrow produce pain. The duality of both cease, as one becomes aware that God is the Owner of all responsibility. When everything is left to God, then only peace and contentment remains.

A person who has begun to see the reflection of God within himself has no tension or worry. He will be simultaneously concerned and unconcerned. He will share in the sorrows and the joys of the world; yet remain indifferent to both. That person cannot be made anxious or worried.

Sant Kabir says to remain a Sanyasi, but to stay within the world. Outwardly, one should do everything required and expected, as a son or a daughter, a husband or a wife, a father or a mother, but nothing should attack the person from inside. Unless one becomes a Sanyasi within his own household, he cannot reach God. Sant Kabir practiced the art of remaining outside of everything, while remaining within everything.

That alone is the Way of God, and that alone should be the Way of the seeker.

Sant Kabir points out that to be very knowledgeable in the way of the world makes one restless and without peace, because that person does not have the right Aim in front of him. That person is concentrating only on the affairs of this world, which never end, and which focus on materialistic items. The person should, instead, be thinking about where he will be going after his physical death. Sant Kabir advises, "Read the book of the body and go inward, because revelations of Spiritual knowledge are only found within the body."

Kabir Sahib was a family man. His wife's name was Loi, His son was called Kamal and the daughter, Kamali. He recommends that people should lead a family life, rather than one of forced celibacy or worldly renunciation. He teaches that the Spiritual life goes hand in hand with a restrained worldly life, and contentment with what God has given to the person. It is only natural that continence should be a result of the bliss of Inner Spiritual Experience, rather than simply the suppression of lustful desires.

Throughout His whole life, Lord Kabir happily served whoever came to His door. He was always accommodating and looking after them. He was a weaver by trade and sold cloth in the market. All through life, He lived on His own honest earnings from the practice of weaving. He never accepted things of this world from anyone.

In many verses, He talks about the condition of *Bhairag* (detachment from the objects of this world). He says that one must obtain the True Sat Guru, Who will take the soul to the Pure Spiritual Realms above the three Regions of the Physical, the Astral, and the Causal, all the way to the fourth Stage, the Super Causal Region.

When one knows the Sat Guru and Loves Him with great zeal, the Sat Guru in turn shows the Way to God by granting Spiritual Initiation. The Master takes the devotee above the body consciousness upwards to Higher Spiritual Realms. Then the state of *Bhairag* is born in that person. 'Bhairag' means the condition of being detached from the worldly pleasures, with the attention now attached to the Master.

Sant Kabir says that the true Yogi is one who has full control of his mind and his breath (and leading a disciplined life), so that he can progress on the Spiritual Path towards God. The mind goes along with the soul only up as far as Brahmand. The breath leaves the body even before, when one departs from the physical body at the time of death.

"When the true Yogi practices this discipline of meditation, all questions and Illusions are cast out. When he comes into this stage of detachment from the world, he becomes known as a *Bairagi* (one who is detached from the world). That person has fulfilled his aim of coming into this world in the human body."

Sant Kabir points out that man has spent his entire life toiling to care for his family and friends, none of whom remain with him to help him pass out of the body at the time of his physical death. No one can accompany him into the Beyond.

Sant Kabir says, "Due to the person not developing Bhairag, he has not put himself or his attention towards meditation. That person's life is just wasted because none of these activities constitute his real work in this lifetime. Only the repetition of the Holy Names of God, as revealed by the Master, and listening to the Holy Sound Current are of lasting value. This forms man's Real Wealth, which he can carry away with him into the Beyond."

Once there was a King called *Hazrat Ibrahim Adham*. He was the King of Balkh-Bokhara, but upon receiving Spiritual Initiation from Kabir Sahib, he renounced his kingdom and devoted himself to God. One day, he was on his way to make a return visit to his homeland, when he met the ministers who had been sent to accompany and welcome him again into the kingdom.

They sat down together to rest for a while beside a river. The ministers began to entreat him to once again reign over the kingdom, and to take back the throne with all its responsibilities.

The king just kept silent, and taking a small sewing needle from his pocket, he threw it into the river. He then said to the astonished ministers, "I command you to bring that needle back to me!"

Of course, the ministers exclaimed that this order was quite an impossibility. Such a deep, fast-flowing river and such a tiny needle! They protested, "We can bring you all kinds of new needles, but there is no way to bring that same one back! How on earth can we do such a thing!"

The king just kept quiet and focused his attention on the river. Suddenly a small fish rose up out of the water with the needle in its mouth. It presented the needle to the king, *dropping it at his feet!*

The king then smiled at the stunned ministers and told them, "Just see how they serve me! I am the king now of that Region *which is still unknown to you!* I am a servant of the One Who is the Ruler of all the Creation. Whoever is unattached to this world, is no longer concerned with worldly things."

*The King just kept quiet and focused his attention on the river.
Suddenly a small fish rose up out of the water with the needle in its mouth.
It presented the needle to the king, dropping it at his feet!*

The first step that leads us towards our true Home is a state of Detachment from the world and its material attractions. Sant Kabir says that the enjoyment from these transient objects must be firmly rejected, and then the mind will begin to cease its restless activity. As one develops Love for the Master and listens to His Holy Discourses, he will become more and more surrendered to His Will. One begins to rise above the mundane temptations.

Sant Kabir says, "It is a rare soul who drinks the Nectar of the Holy Naam. That soul knows only God and Simran, which bring about the necessary passion and zeal needed to find God." This is called the true state of Bhairag.

Sant Kabir has mentioned in many verses that Discrimination is the factor which helps to develop the state of Bhairag. "Discrimination helps one to realize the difference between the True and the untrue. When the person distinguishes between Truth (representing the Eternal and the Permanent), and the untruth (as the changeable and temporary), then the outcome can only be Detachment."

He reveals, "I developed this state of detachment only by thinking where my soul came from, and where it is going to go. When the person with Discernment is away from the Creator, he cries out for Him. He cannot live a second without God's Love. When this Divine Love wakes up, very intense and full of passion, then all worldly desires vanish and that lucky person realizes their little value and transient qualities."

No desire can remain anymore for any worldly object, and no attraction for them is left in that person. His mind and heart only want to get away from the world and its so-called 'charms'! That person now says, "I have finished with my intellect. I have merged my attention into the Sound Current. Now I am a true Bhairagi and quite fearless. I am unaffected by any worldly Deceptions, as my mind is now an obedient servant."

Sant Kabir says that once the mind finds itself free from all these desires, it longs to be constantly in the Holy Company of the Master and other lovers of God. The true devotee, in his heart of hearts, really wants this condition to remain perpetually in his life. That person realizes that it is not necessary to leave this world in order to rise above it, for he can have the best of both the worlds, the here and the hereafter!

One should Love all Creation, but he should remain simple in his living and thinking. *A devotee's Love for God increases as much as his love for the world decreases.* Whoever has full determination to have this kind of true Detachment will finish his coming and going in this world.

Sant Kabir says, "Without this Detachment, Illusion will not go away. This state of Detachment is a gift from the True Master, and is bestowed on whoever lives by His Commandments. Whoever practices on the True Master's gifts of the Holy Naam and Shabd Sound Current can Drink the sweet Nectar of God through this Detachment." He tells us that the person obtains control over his mind and has peace in his heart by staying desireless. He is always thinking only of the Truth, and not of things of this world.

Sant Kabir advises that people should stay in their families and have Dharma, practice righteousness, do right deeds, and not hurt anyone. If one uses his Power of Discrimination, he can find out what is right or wrong. It is most unfortunate if someone is able to bring Detachment in his heart, but then slips and falls under the spell of the world's charms. That person was going on the right Path, but due to forgetfulness and carelessness, he came under the distractions of the world.

#7-7 Humility

"Nothing is mine!" says Kabir Sahib. "*Whatever there is, is all Yours! I lose nothing in surrendering to You what is already Yours, O Lord.*" He says in all humbleness to God,

"Whatever is in me, is Yours, O Creator. My soul, my mind, and my heart, are all Yours. Nothing is mine!"

Sant Kabir says that this human body does not belong to us; it is to be left behind. "If, O people, you would go inwards and see the Father, you would know that He is the One doing everything. He is the Creator. If you give your heart, mind, and soul to Him, He becomes Yours. He will show you the Way, and then you can merge in Him. If everything belongs to God and He takes it away, it doesn't affect you at all, because it is all His."

Sant Kabir gives the example that water never stays on the hill. It always comes to flood the lowest levels of ground. Likewise, the person who is humble and gracious, can Drink of the Divine Nectar as much as he wants. Whoever is proud, however, and up on the crest of the hill, cannot receive any Amrit, and thus remains ever thirsty.

Kabir Sahib is explaining that when ego leaves the person, humbleness comes in his heart. When the person leaves off pride, he does not boast that he is better than another; rather he states that everyone is better than himself.

Sant Kabir says, "I don't proclaim myself to be great." He gives the example of how a true devotee should behave, and show respect. A truly humble heart never says that he is the most perfect person, for whoever considers himself to be the least, he is the greatest amongst all men.

Sant Kabir has written in all humility that He is the worst of all, and everyone else is good. And then He says, "When this angle of vision becomes embedded, and the person realizes that he is full of faults himself, his ego vanishes. Whoever has solved that mystery, he is the one who is the true Friend of all. He is the One Who becomes the Knower of all knowing."

In all humbleness, Sant Kabir explains that He is like a dog who is known for its faithfulness to its owner. No matter how much one kicks the dog or beats him, the dog won't leave his post at the door. The dog is so faithful that even if he is beaten, he can only talk back to the master-owner for his grace by way of barking to him.

Sant Kabir is all humbleness for the Lord. He says, "I am like a dog at Your doorstep, barking to receive Your compassion and Grace. In all my previous births, I have obeyed Your command like a true servant. I am a part of You and I only do what You command me to do. Night and day I rub Your Holy Feet. You have made me Your own, and given me this task to come into this world. Your Unstruck Melody, the Celestial Music, and Your Presence are in each and every pore of my body. Whosoever has Your Grace stamped on his forehead as a sign of mercy from You is the greatest soul and the bravest warrior. He is the one chosen by You to fight with the outward desires of the mind."

Kabir Sahib uses the worldly example of the precious sandalwood tree, which is very porous, to describe a humble person who can 'absorb' the Teachings of the True Master. A simple tree like the bamboo can be growing next to the fragrant sandalwood, but the bamboo never becomes a fragrant tree. The bamboo bark is not porous; rather it has some kind of oil on its covering.

As a result of this, it doesn't absorb any of the charms of the sandalwood tree. The air passing the sandalwood touches the bamboo but just goes away, and the bamboo does not keep any of the sweet fragrance of the sandalwood. "In the same way, ego and pride close up all the pores of the heart, and results in narrow-mindedness."

There are several stories of Gorakhanath, a Yogi well-known for his many Supernatural Powers gained through the long, hard toil of Yoga. Inflated with pride, Gorakhanath one day challenged Sant Kabir, saying "I am going to change my form and disappear into this water. You have to find me!" He quickly changed into the likeness of a small frog and dived into the water but Sant Kabir, Knowing of all, immediately grabbed him.

Sant Kabir then invited Gorakhanath to find *Him* and He dived in, *merging Himself with the very water itself!* How possibly could Gorakhanath find Him? How could an egoistic person like Gorakhanath, who had attained Supernatural Powers in order to gain only worldly desires, possibly know about the Higher Spiritual Realms? He had no ability to know where Sant Kabir was, and he quickly gave up. He called out, and then Sant Kabir came out of the water in His regular Form.

Gorakhanath thought that he had obtained everything there was to know about Spirituality, but Sant Kabir explained to him that Almighty God is within each and every atom throughout all Creation. By becoming the subtle form of the water, Sant Kabir was showing that He Himself is an Ocean of God, so how could a worldly person, interested only in outer worldly attainments, possibly even hope to find Him?

Sant Kabir says, "God's House is the House of all Love. It is not an ordinary house. It is the Way that one can go beyond Sach Khand. To enter this House, you must take your head off and put it on the ground. Not only that, but then you must put your foot on top of it. Then you are truly 'dead' (detached from the world). Only then are you able to sit in this House, and have a taste of Divine Love, as your Consciousness is raised up to the Highest Spiritual Realms." In other words, Sant Kabir is saying that one must cast out ego, have full control over the tendencies of the mind, and then the resulting humility will readily grant entrance to God's House.

Sant Kabir emphasizes that whoever drowns in their own praises, believing that they have great intellect, can never bring himself to come to the Master. "I hope that nobody drowns in this way. Whoever is humble can see everyone, but he who is not humble, cannot be seen by anyone." A humble person can see all others, but no one notices him.

Kabir Sahib continues, "Whoever can solve the mystery of becoming humble, can meet God. Whoever thinks himself to be less than others, has achieved humbleness and this is his greatness. Everyone bows down in respect to the full moon, due to its greatness."

The Path to find Almighty God consists of becoming humble and meek, because one cannot obtain Divine Grace until he gives up pride and serves the Master with full heart and soul. Kabir is telling the people that one has to become meek to search out and know the Creator. One also has to have a Spiritual hunger. Whoever is drowning in his own praise, will never receive Grace from the Master, because that person is fully and completely in his own praise.

There is a legend that once Sant Kabir and *Guru Nanak* met together with the eighty-four *Nath Siddhas*. Old Yogic traditions claim that these men were the eighty-four 'accomplished' Yogis or Siddhas, who had attained 'perfection' through their Yogic practices. They were well-known for these attainments and were considered by all to be 'holy' people.

At the same time, a devotee of Guru Nanak also arrived. Thinking that it would be improper to greet his Master without having something to offer, this devotee reached into his pocket. Unfortunately, he found only a single sesame seed which was duly presented to his Master.

According to the customs of hospitality, it could not be eaten by just one person, but must be shared with everyone present, so Guru Nanak consulted with Sant Kabir as to how They could divide this tiny seed among so many ascetics. Sant Kabir suggested that the seed be crushed in some water and then distributed.

It was observed, however, that there was no water anywhere nearby, so Sant Kabir made water to flow in a nearby dry river bed. The drink was prepared and everyone drank the sesame seed crushed in that water.

The Nath Siddhas were grateful for this show of respect and in return, they offered to give Sant Kabir anything He might ask for. Sant Kabir just smiled and looking at them all, He asked for a "full five paisas' worth of poverty". A paisa was a coin of currency in India at that time. Sant Kabir's meaning thereby, meant "a great amount of humbleness".

The Siddhas knew that they themselves did not possess this amount of humbleness, so Sant Kabir politely said to them, "Why don't you ask your own Master's Guru about this, and then come back to me?"

Therefore one of them, as a representative of them all, decided to go first to Brahma, in charge of Creation. Unfortunately because of his great pride as Creator of all, Brahma told him that he could not supply it.

The Siddha then went on to Shiva, but due to his vanity as Destroyer of the worlds, he also could not grant this gift.

Then that Siddha went all the way to Vishnu, the god of Sustenance. He listened to the story and accepted the request, but he claimed to have only *three* paisas' worth. In all wisdom, Vishnu informed the Siddha that it was only Sant Kabir Himself who possessed this full five paisas' worth of humility!

Then all the Nath Siddhas realized how great Sant Kabir is! They understood that it is only the Saint Himself who is all humbleness, all Grace, all Love. The True Saint hails from the Region of Sach Khand, where there is not the slightest tendencies of pride or ego. The eighty-four Siddhas were suddenly overcome with shame. Humbled by this experience, they returned to Sant Kabir and begged His forgiveness.

Sant Kabir is explaining that whoever has obtained Divine knowledge from a Godman, that is the true knowledge of knowing oneself and the Overself. That is called the true Dharma, and salvation is thus obtained. He says that whoever tells lies has sin, and whoever has malice of lying and deceit to obtain wealth and other possessions, that is also sin. Wherever there is greed and desires of wanting things of this world, there is the Negative Power.

All through life the person keeps gathering possessions any way he can, and in any manner. The more he gathers, the more his greed grows. He wants more and more, and this never finishes. His pride grows with their acquisition and then malice and ill-will fester in his heart, as he finds that now he has to guard these numerous things. He becomes afraid that someone will steal them. His whole attitude towards others changes, as he becomes suspicious of others and selfish.

In this regard Sant Kabir says, "The devotee must keep mercy, humbleness and forgiveness in his heart, not to hurt another. Everything and everyone, from the small ant to the towering elephant, all belong to God. All are His children." He gives the choice, "You can either have pride or Love, but not both together. I have never seen two swords existing together in the same sheath!" Similarly, pride and Love cannot exist together.

He says "What a beautiful plan it is, that whoever has forgiveness in his heart, there God the Creator, resides!" Having mercy and forgiveness in the heart for any human, plant, or anything of God's Creation, brings forth the sweetness of humility. "A person who is not humble, cannot have forgiveness. Forgiveness is a Godly quality."

Sant Kabir gives the example that some people distribute their wealth to others in charity. "What good is it, if in their hearts, they have pride of doing that?" They should give selflessly, in the Name of Almighty God. Ego comes into the heart when the person says, "I have given!" or "I have done this!" Sant Kabir reminds us that giving in charity cleanses the mind and reduces sorrow, but to believe that charity itself will unite one with God is a false hope. He points out that great acts of piety can sometimes lead to an increase in pride. Therefore, it is important not to let others know about these acts. Only in this way can the heart be made pure and the soul cleansed; otherwise the ego swells with the thought that one is a great benefactor of mankind.

Kabir Sahib says, "Wherever there is 'I', there is ego." Not only the common person has ego, but also the Munis and

Rishis. Some have done a great number of years of penance as well as other rites and rituals (like Yoga for example), but all have fallen badly through ego.

He continues, "Ego is one of the strongest enemies because wherever ego comes, there is no Oneness. Whenever there is Oneness (dwelling in God), there is no ego." Sant Kabir is disclosing a very simple, fundamental law of Spirituality, that wherever is the existence of ego, or 'I-ness', there is no manifestation of the Truth. There comes a veil or a curtain of ego between the person and God. This ego is created from all the worldly possessions that one gathers, and all these attachments keep him far away from realizing God.

Sant Kabir says that the humility of the Saint is of the utmost. He says that the Saint has reached the highest Stage of God, and is literally a walking and talking God even though He is in the human form, because God has to come in the human form in order to teach the people. He gives a worldly example of a tree with fruit on the branches, and how those branches bow down to the earth with the heaviness of this fruit.

In the same way, the Master has almost all of the humility in this world, humility being the 'fruit' of Divine Love. The worldly mind is boggled, and wonders that all Creation honours such a Power as the Master. With the Master, there is no question of ego, no thought of passion, or any kind of Power. The Master is made of Love from head to foot. There is nothing but Love, and this Love of God radiates through Him and goes into all the Creation of God. Why? Because Almighty God Himself has manifested in that body.

The Master doesn't break the law of the Negative Power to show miracles, to demonstrate His tremendous Powers, or even to convince people that He has these immense Powers. This is all about humbleness and humility, but He does use His Powers in a subtle way. He stops the destruction of this world, and even of the other worlds of which ordinary human beings don't even know about. He listens to the voice of the lowly ant first, rather than the elephant's blatant trumpeting. When the devotees of the Godman practice according to the way He says, they go inwards and realize what He is, and see His immense Power.

Sant Kabir expounds the genuine picture of this world, and in a few words He has explained the whole knowledge of Truth which has its basis in humility. He says to God, "I am Thy servant of servants, O Lord, my Master, my Creator." This is Sant Kabir's humbleness: *"Sweet is Thy Will!"*

In great meekness and demonstrating the greatness of His humility, Sant Kabir refers to Himself as just 'a dog of God'. He says, "My name is *Motiah* (a very common dog's name). I have a chain around my neck and wherever Almighty God pulls me, there I go."

He says that with this collar of Love, He has no choice but to go to the place where God bids Him. When a dog has a collar, it means that the dog belongs to somebody, because a dog without a collar doesn't belong to anyone. When God put the collar of Love around His neck, it means that He now belongs to God! "Almighty God, the Supreme Father, has accepted me as His own! I am now His! I am so fortunate and I have a great good Karma. Now I realize the greatness of God's Divine Love."

"The Lord is like sugar, scattered amidst the sands of the world. Only the humble ant can go into the sand and find that sweet sugar of God." Anything large cannot separate the sugar from the sand, because it is not possible for the huge elephant-like ego to find these Teachings in the sand of the world. Only the soft-hearted, humble person can benefit from the Master's Teachings.

When the ego and the sense of the separate identity is destroyed, the coming and going in this world (the Cycle of births and deaths) ceases. However hard a person may try, and however pure a life he may lead, still the thought that he *wills his actions* does not depart from him, until he is able to see that he is being controlled from within by another Power.

Despite every precaution, man is easily lured away by the attractions of the senses. When his heart gets filled with the joy of Holy Naam, these same worldly pleasures cannot claim his attention.

#7-8 Divine Love

*L*ove is another name for Almighty God. This Love is God's Divine Love. It is very difficult to accurately describe the nature of this Love, because Love itself is beyond the limitations of words. In the presence of Love, the intellect cannot function, and thus the mind does not disturb the sanctity of this peace and bliss. All the evil tendencies of the mind are removed in the name of Love. This kind of Love is not to be found in the temporal satisfaction of either the senses, or the worldly sensual pleasures.

Divine Love grants true happiness, and lends sweetness to all other gifts of God. True Love demands nothing in return: it knows only how to give. This kind of Love comes from the heart, with no motive of selfishness. Divine Love is the Treasure of the Holy Naam, and the essence of the Supreme Amrit. This Love cannot be had from other than the Master. The Master possesses the unique magnetic power of Divine Love, which automatically draws the devotee towards Him.

Sant Kabir says, "If you wish to know about Love, go to the Master and ask Him." Divine Love is the real meditation, the true prayer to God. Love cannot develop from reading Scriptures. These Books can only provide the motivation to know about God, but one cannot Love somebody whom he has not seen.

Sant Kabir says that the Lord is beyond human perception. However, God assumes the Form of the Sat Guru, and in this Holy Form, one can see and Love Him. When one looks at the Master, that person becomes inspired with devotion, because the Master is the Source of all Love and in a like manner, He inspires Love in others.

Almighty God is a constant Existence, an eternal Manifestation. He is like a flower that is eternally blooming. It has been blooming before, it is blooming now, and will keep on blooming always. Constant remembrance increases Love. The heart keeps repeating the Simran, while immersed in the Nectar of His Holy Name. If tears flow in such moments of happiness, they will have the sweet tinkling of music in them. One's very breath will then become music and the heart-beat will lend rhythm to the song.

"Dry-as-dust prayers and simple fasting without the tears of Love, cannot bring any fruit or benefit to the soul. However, with a sea of water the true devotee soon receives the unbounded Love of God. Without this kind of Love the devotee cannot have the Secret, nor the true Worship, of God. Whoever doesn't have a Drink of Divine Love cannot know and understand the Secrets of God and cannot have Spiritual development."

Sant Kabir points out, "Everyone says *Love, Love, Love!* but no one has any inkling of the true knowledge of Love." One who is absorbed in it day and night, alone knows about Love.

He says, "Love has come, but where has it gone? I have seen it! If somebody cries or laughs, there is not Love at all. This is only temporary, which comes and goes. True Love, however, is permanent and does not change." He illustrates that the person did once Love, but where is his Love now? That same person now laughs and cries! Everyone sees him in this ever-changing condition. This cannot be called as true Love!

Without true Love, and without going on this Path of Love, nobody has found nor obtained God. "Without Divine Love, one cannot reach to the Supreme Lord. This Love is very rare. All kinds of different practices are done in order to develop Love, but without Love, all worships are dry and in vain."

Sant Kabir has written many verses about the conditions of true Love. "With Love one has to sacrifice his body, life, and faith to the Beloved. In this way, the devotee even gives his head if needed (meaning that he has to surrender himself completely to the Master). Divine Love knows no bounds, and one should prepare to ultimately and totally surrender, wholly and solely to the Beloved Master. One should travel on this Path only if he is prepared to surrender himself completely, and then claim nothing!" Only under this condition, can one drink from the goblet of Divine Nectar. The person who is greedy cannot make this sacrifice.

"From the large vat of Love, there is an abundance of delicious and enticing Nectar, but it is very difficult to drink because the price of it is an offering of one's head. Only those can drink who do this surrender. No one else can drink from there. Others can only talk about the name of Love, but they cannot have it. The world is lost in reading Scriptures; yet never comes to have knowledge, but one who knows a jot of Love, to him all is revealed."

Sant Kabir writes verse after verse on the subject of Divine Love. "Love is the theme of life. It works as Nectar to keep one going in this world. Love neither grows in the fields, nor is it sold in the market. Love cannot be found in any shop, and one cannot bargain for it. It is so valuable that whether king or beggar, one must give his all. He must sacrifice his body and his faith to his Beloved, if needed. The true lover, however, doesn't even mention or give a tiny hint of this sacrifice.

One must carry his head upon his palm as an offering, if he would step into the Lane of Love!"

He adds, "Everyone is equal in the Lane of Love. On this Path, the poor and the rich are on the same level. Whosoever surrenders himself to the Master, gains thereby. In Love, there is no desire of any kind. Until the intellect and its cleverness, as well as the worldly skills are stilled, one cannot know the Reality."

He continues, "Go into the heart of the Beloved, lose yourself in Him, and have ecstasy and tranquillity from His thoughts. Intellect, knowledge and skill become a hindrance in this kind of Love. The lover can only see through his own rose-coloured glasses. The Path of Love is not one of arguments and debates. Where there is Love, there is no duty. Love doesn't care about the world. There is no clever intellect or scheming. When one is enticed in Love, he doesn't count the days or the numbers."

"Love makes two hearts unite into one, and makes the devotee into a true Lover." This condition of Love is the goal of all practices of worship and austerities. The lover himself becomes Love. The devotee enters a state where the lover becomes the Beloved. "Where there is 'I', there is no 'Thou'. When one sees only 'Thou', then 'I' cannot exist. The lane of Love is so narrow that two cannot pass. The devotee merges into the Master and they both become as One. This true Oneness of Love develops through being in the Company of the true Lover of God, which is the Master."

He says, "Love cannot be concealed once it has entered a person's heart. He does not speak of it, but his eyes reveal all. Once Love enters a person's heart, it keeps him eternally happy, for then he becomes free from worries. Wave after wave of Love flow out from him automatically."

This stage of Love, which may not be reached even after years of practicing alone, can be quickly obtained just by gazing into the eyes of the Lover. It comes through the eyes, and one gets benefit in a very subtle way. Love has such a bliss and intoxication which takes the person above the body consciousness, making him One with the Beloved.

Kabir Sahib says that day and night He is dipped in Love. This is called true Love. "The person who has respect and humbleness knows true worship. He has true Love in him, because he has respect for everybody. He is the one you can call as great, whose habit is full of good qualities, and his manner is calm and quiet."

He says, "My Beloved is continuously staying in my eyes, like a collyrium. There is no place for anything else, other than the Love of my Beloved, to stay there. There is no place even for sleep in my eyes!"

"The eyes of the lover, full of the tears of Sweet Remembrance and Love, bring forth Spiritual blossoms of untold bliss and ecstasy." This stage of Love is the highest of all, because God Himself is contained in this Love. The meeting with God can only take place through Love. All Scriptures highly praise this true Love. "When Love comes, all the Blessings of the Lord come together, and when that Love is not present, they fly away."

In another verse He says, "The condition of being a true spouse is when the eyes see only the Beloved, nobody else. The spouse is drenched constantly in the memory of the Beloved, speaking sweet words all the time."

Sant Kabir tells us that one may attain this stage after practicing alone for a long period of time, or it may be obtained in a moment, just by gazing into the eyes of the Beloved. "It comes through those Godly eyes. The benefit from that is very subtle." Whoever is hankering for the Divine Darshan of the Beloved should, with the Water of Love, wash away all the internal dirt of bad deeds, and replace it with Love.

He says that Divine Love is hidden in every soul, but it is there. This Treasure of Love is revealed in the seeker through the compassion of a Living Master Who is the manifestation of God. With His Grace, this Love is born in the devotee. With devotion and Love for the Master, this Love increases and the devotee's ecstasy and tranquillity is likewise increased. When the soul is in touch with the Holy Naam, a constant stream of Divine Love flows to the devotee.

Sant Kabir says that Love for the Master can be developed in many ways:
1. Through the Grace and compassion of the Master Himself. The Master reveals Love in the devotee, who thus becomes intoxicated by the flow of Divine Love from the Master.
2. By listening to the Master's Holy Satsang (Discourse).
3. By the practice of Simran (Repetition) and Dhyan (Contemplation), Love and devotion for the Master is manifested within the devotee. By following the Path of Spirituality, this Divine Love is awakened.

Sant Kabir explains that if one Loves the Creator from the depths of his heart and soul, all doubts and questions will dissipate. In other words, the devotee should put all faith on the Master Who can truly show him God. Love takes hold of the devotee when he encounters the Master, and God can be realized through the fullness of this resulting Love for, and devotion to, the Master.

CHAPTER 8

THE TRUE MASTER

People ask, "Why do we need a Master?" Sant Kabir replies that the Master works as a representative of God coming from the highest Spiritual Region to take souls back unto God. The Master is 'God-sent', and therefore He belongs to all mankind. "The Creator ordered me to work in this world for the benefit of all humanity."

When Saints like Kabir Sahib come, They give out the knowledge of the Way back to God. Sant Kabir tells us that this method of inverting the attention has been handed down from aeons and aeons. It is not a man-made system, but it has been made by God Himself.

The Saint's aim and Teachings are to free the soul from the bondage of the body, and to give it a Divine Connection with the Creator. The Saint is able to grant this Divine Contact because He has Himself Experienced and realized God. Only talking and hearing will not take anyone far.

"Man tries to gain Spiritual knowledge in the outer world, but the Treasure he is seeking lies within. If he would but seek the Company of an Adept of the Divine Sound Current, he would secure the long-sought-after Jewel. The Master removes the darkness of this Illusionary world of ignorance and doubt." The Company of the Saint is elevating. His Energy and Power is active and infectious. In His Divine Presence, the person becomes changed. The very atmosphere about the Saint is Charged with sublimity.

"One's attention is mostly spent on the outer body, but not much is directed to the development and knowledge of the inner soul." Everyone ignores the fact that the body will be left behind one day. In this condition, people have forgotten about God, and have strayed far away from the Reality of life.

"O worldly people! Your soul is asleep in forgetfulness, in Illusion and Deception. The Sat Guru is the One Who is fully awake and knowing of everything. He is the One Who has all the Boons of bliss and Inner happiness. When He speaks, it is God speaking through Him!"

The True Master has the Special Key that unlocks the Tenth Gate. People have so many other keys, gathered with so much information. All other keys, however, are useless. Carrying the burden of so many keys, it is necessary to consider whether any of them actually work to open the Gate of Life. Does any Light come in? Does one Experience any Internal peace and bliss? Complaints are many, thankfulness is non-existent. People carry this load of useless keys, and because these keys do not require any transformation, one can remain exactly as he is. One even feels pleasure in the loud noise and clanging of these keys. People are satisfied to have these keys and avoid the difficult process of reformation. The ego will not easily accept the Master's Golden Key. A lot is at stake: if the person changes, his whole life will change. Whatever he has invested in, up to now, he will find to be totally wasted. Whatever he had dreamed about or wished for, will all prove false.

These things have been written about at great length in the various Scriptures, but without anybody to expound and give a practical Experience of them, the seeker cannot proceed on the Spiritual Path. Until this Method of inverting one's attention away from the Illusionary world is clearly explained, the whole idea of Spirituality remains just like a closed book. If the Master says something that is not in the Scriptures, one should readily accept it, because the True Master is the Living Scripture.

When any book is read, the reader interprets the words in his own way, according to his level of understanding. Those who have seen God within their own eyes cannot describe Him completely. He cannot be expressed through words. Thus, explanations and words cannot take the place of a Living Master. Only the Master's Holy Presence will make one understand what the Master really *is*, His very Being. He is the One Creator of all. The Maker is hidden behind all. It is He Who is Life!

The Saint Himself has had many Spiritual Experiences of God, and He is competent to help others to have those Experiences, too. "By meeting the True Master, the Spiritual Eye (the Third, or Single Eye) 'Sees'. He Whose Eye is open, can open the Eyes of others and He Whose Lamp is burning, can light the Lamps of others."

Sant Kabir says that whoever comes to the Master will never again return to this world. That person's coming and going in the *Wheel of Transmigration* (his birth and rebirth), is forevermore finished.

The door to salvation and liberation is very narrow. Sant Kabir describes that it is the size of one-tenth of a mustard seed.

"Due to all the attachments of this world, ego makes the person blown up as big as an elephant. Now, how possibly can one pass through this narrow door? The vices of ego and lust are the attachments pulling back the soul, hindering it from going forward and reaching to the Realms of Almighty God. If one meets such a True Sat Guru, with His Grace and with His Holy Naam, the Door of Liberation is thrown open wide." This means that the Master helps the devotee to cast off these vices, so that he will be small and subtle enough to go through this narrow passage opening.

The Master alone is the sincere Friend and Saviour. He is true to the devotee from beginning to end, and never leaves him. In this world, friends and relatives leave when the person is in adverse circumstances such as poverty, illness, ignominy, or any other bad situation, or when he is unable to serve their needs.

If one is lucky, a few loyal souls may remain until the end but even they, too, can do nothing when the Agent of Death comes and wrenches the soul out of the body. The True Master alone stands in His Radiant Form ready to receive the devotee when he quits the body. This, then, is the unbounded Blessing from the Sat Guru.

Sant Kabir says that when one hears about a Saint or a Master, he should just go to Him and sit near, in deep humility and reverence. If the devotee looks into His eyes and forehead with deep receptivity, he will feel an upward pull of the soul, and Divine Radiation coming from His Godly eyes and forehead. Any questions left rankling in his mind are automatically answered by the Master's Spiritual Discourses, without any effort on the part of the devotee.

"To be in the Holy Company of the Saint and to have His Blessed Darshan, will invoke remembrance of the Lord. That moment is the only one that is counted as a true moment of life; the rest are all wasted." Kabir Sahib says that one should go to a True Master with full devotion, leaving behind all worldly ideas. There should then be only one thought--the thought of the Master. If one sits near Him and listens with full attention, that person will have Inner Experiences of the Divine, through His Grace. "When you come near to a Godman, you come near to God. One feels Love for the Master because of the God Power that shines forth from Him, and this helps in the Spiritual Experiences."

Sant Kabir says that when a person comes into Divine Company, true faith blossoms forth. All fear and desires fly away. In the Master's Company, the True and the false are analyzed. In His August Assembly, Inner Vision and Right Understanding are bestowed upon the audience, but all this is only possible from One Who is fully 'Awakened'!

When the Master Graces the world, He does not come for the salvation of only a single community, or even of a particular nation. He is the manifestation of Divine Truth in the world. There are many wonderful phrases that Sant Kabir uses to describe the Manifested Incarnation of the Lord. For example, "The Sacred Body of the Master is a mirror of God. His Message of Hope is a message for all mankind, indeed, all Creation!"

The devotee is at first attracted to the Divine Effulgence coming from the Master's Godly eyes, and the soothing radiance He emits from His Holy body. Sant Kabir describes that the devotee feels an overwhelming sense of bliss and peace in this Company.

To a new seeker on the Path, the Master may appear to be rather like a dignified gentleman, but this gradually changes into the realization of the 'Other Worldliness' when the devotee begins to see the God Power working through the Master. Then the seeker comprehends that the Master is 'God-In-Action', a God-Personified Being, the Divine Beloved.

Sant Kabir describes the Master's perfection at great length. "The Master has full Powers of Discrimination. He is not subject to Illusion or Deception. He can distinguish between right and wrong, true and false. He is the fountainhead of all beauty and perfection, and there is none to compare with Him." In actuality, the Master is beauty personified, but as one progresses Spiritually, he grows in receptivity and sees for himself that the Master is more and more perfect and resplendent.

Kabir Sahib continues, "The Saint always bestows true happiness and bliss. His Holy Company is an Ocean of bliss and happiness." Remaining in the Master's Holy Presence, one feels Love and peace pour forth, like a current of ecstasy. The True Master has pure and pious words coming from His mouth. Being all the time in the sweet intoxication of God, the Master smiles and says sublime words. He is an Ocean of all the knowledge and bliss of God. He calls people again and again to come to Him. He knows the pain in other peoples' hearts, because His own heart is full of humbleness. He lives in this world like the lotus flower, with its blossom floating high above the muddy waters. This world has myriad attractions, but the Saint teaches the devotee to live above these false desires.

The true value of the Master's words is not less than the greatest treasures on earth. Their worth is much more for those people who are searching for it. The Scriptures say to invert and go inward, and know oneself, but the printed words themselves cannot take the person inside. Neither can they make the attention attach to and merge with the Creator. They give out purely bookish knowledge, which further entangles one in this world!

"There is no way out unless one meets with a True Master!" The Books mention about many internal Secrets, but the Secrets themselves are not there. A person can read these religious Books again and again, but he cannot have the Practical Experiences contained therein, nor can he act upon them. He can only read about them, but he won't know the actual meaning of what he is reading.

Sant Kabir reminds us again and again, that without a True Master, one cannot obtain the real Way, the Real Truth. Even after reading everything contained in those Books, the seeker still will not be aware of the Mysteries of the Beyond. He will remain absolutely in this bookish knowledge, and live in Spiritual ignorance. The real knowledge is only to know the Reality for oneself. When one goes to a Godman and has His Grace and Blessing, he can then go inwards and have firsthand Experiences of them himself.

The body and its wealth, possessions, and attachments are all reflections of the mind's focus. When one truly surrenders himself at the Lotus Feet of the Sat Guru, one becomes 'blanked out' and all shadows vanish from the mind. When one is in this condition, he becomes a fit receptacle to imbibe the Life-Impulse from the Master. It does not matter what words the Master is speaking, or even in what language.

One becomes free from the preoccupation of the mind, and is automatically influenced only by the Charged atmosphere in which he is sitting. The powerful Spiritual Rays emanating from the Master, cannot but affect the devotee. The Master grants this 'out-of-mind' Experience and the 'vacant' mind easily takes in and quickly grasps the unbounded showers of Grace from the Master. The influence from the Higher Source is received in this state of 'all-attention'.

One should try to understand the essence of the Master's Discourse, and his whole being will be flooded with Love and Light. The Master emits Loving Impulses which take hold and fill the devotee with Love. As a result, his mind grows quiet and still. In this condition, the devotee can make his way into the Master's Godly heart, forgetting all about himself. This one-pointed attention wells up great Love for the Master as His Life-Currents begin to flow into the devotee. The Master takes the wandering attention directly to the eye-focus within, and the devotee enjoys an Experience of the Inner Quietude. It is from this point that the Path leading to the Kingdom of God starts.

Sant Kabir says that the Living Master encourages every faltering step towards the Infinite, Graciously extending His own hand when the devotee stumbles. He showers His Eternal and never-fading Love. He even goes to the utmost extremes to conceal the greatness of Himself, but occasionally it cannot help but come to the surface. There are times when inevitably something happens which proclaims His hidden greatness.

In all humility, the Master says, "Do not look upon me as God; look upon me as His humble servant only." Sant Kabir emphasizes that these Masters are not made or trained: *They are 'born'.* In the Master resides the Power of God, and through the Master, one can reach and contact that Power.

Masters of all ages have always preached the same Truth. The Master emphasizes the Oneness of God and the brotherhood of mankind. Sant Kabir says that the Master's Message is one of Love, Grace, humility and compassion for all Creation. He comes to unite people, not to found new religions and beliefs. His Mission is to take the souls, longing and pining to be once again with their Creator, back to their true Home. He comes to lift mankind out of the web of Delusion. He labours out of Love, and sacrifices Himself out of sheer compassion. The True Master is very rare in this world, and one comes upon Him with great good fortune.

The task of the Master is always a demanding one. If the disciple is to progress upwards, he has to be detached gradually from the entanglements of this ever-beckoning and appealing world. Life, however, must go on and not be interfered with. It is an arduous task that the Masters take upon Themselves out of sheer mercy and Grace.

Before coming to the Lotus Feet of the True Master, one's life is clouded with grief and sorrow. The mind leads the person down the worldly path of darkness and confusion, with all of its doubts and suspicions. The Spiritual Path, however, is not one of intellect and reasoning, but rather one of Divine Love.

It begins with a yearning deep inside one's heart and gradually, as one progresses, it turns into a kind of 'madness' where everything else is forgotten, where the Beloved and Divine union with this Beloved become one's very life. This so-called 'madness' burns away all attachments with this world and its five Deadly foes. It is surely the Grace of the True Master which carries one upwards and on to Divine Oneness.

Millions and millions of years have already gone by, and lifetime after lifetime has been wasted in this world. The boat has been ever adrift on the fierce and terrible sea of life, subject to the chance winds and waters. Seeing such pathetic conditions, the Master takes pity on mankind. Only a Soul Who is free Himself, and is One with the Supreme Being, can come to the aid and show people the Way out. His Holy Naam ferries the devotees across. Without His compassion and guidance, no one can safely pass over. Sant Kabir says, "The Eternal Elixir is given by the Living, True Master, and only he receives It, who has good fortune recorded on his forehead. That person blissfully remains in the Lap of God."

The Master looks at the soul, a child of God, who is yearning to once again be united with his Father. His soothing words bring solace and peace to the heart, filling it with continuous waves of strength and courage. At the same time, He is an extreme example of infinite Love, compassion, power and humility.

The Master's Holy Discourse acts like a soap that cleanses the soul, which is besmeared with the filth of ages of lives. The Master comes to release humanity from eternal bondage. He brings with Him the gift of the Higher Worlds and elevated states of Consciousness which are, as yet, hidden and unknown to the world. The Master asserts that anyone, young, old, even the infirm, can rise above the body consciousness and discover the hidden mysteries of the Spiritual Life.

Sant Kabir describes how the Master gives out pearls of profound wisdom. The Master is the Awakened One. He has laboured hard and long, and has merged in the Supreme Father. He reveals the Way to the Tenth Gate that leads inwards, but most of the people pay Him no heed and remain instead in the filth of the Nine Doors that continually take the soul outwards.

Most of the world is misled in worshipping the lower Powers, the gods and goddesses, stones, fires, and photographs, all of which really are a worship of Kaal because all these things fall within the realm of the Negative Power. Without the Living Master it is utter darkness both within and without.

The humility of the Perfect Saint is extraordinary. Even after reaching the ultimate stage in Spirituality, He does not forget gratitude to His own Master. The Saint is too modest and humble to call Himself a Master, so the Master and the Holy Shabd alone teach the Way of true Worship. If one should ask the Master *'Who is the Master?'* He will answer that it is *Shabd*. "Thus Kabir became merged in God, and became God Himself!"

Sant Kabir says that listening to the Master is indeed a great Boon. In His elevated, Holy Assembly, one leaves off bad habits. God moves amongst His children seemingly disguised as a human, weaning them from the path of sin and directing their steps to righteousness. The Master is all Grace, all Love, all compassion. His Teaching is universal and for all mankind. His Satsang is open to one and all, regardless sinner or virtuous. He is always forgiving.

In serving humanity, the Master sets an example of absolute and genuine humility. He has no ego, nor does He talk about what He does to help mankind. He welcomes sinners, liars, cheaters, all the worthless ones into His Godly Lap and transforms them into shining jewels. With unbounded Grace, He bestows upon the seeker the Priceless Gift, the Practicing of which makes the soul pure and takes it to the ultimate destination, Sach Khand.

Sant Kabir tells us not to look upon the Master as an ordinary human being, however, for He is God Personified. When Kabir Sahib talks about Truth, he denotes Sat Purush, the True One, Almighty God. This is the Name of the Creator Himself. Sant Kabir says, "*Hari* (the Lord) and *Sat Guru* (the True Master) are One. This Truth is All-Pervading and sustains all."

In another verse He tells us, "There is only One Power, All-Pervading, and everything is created from this same Light." He says that this Truth is obtained when one meets a Master and carefully follows His directions. Truth, however, can dwell within the devotee only through the Grace of the Master. The Truth manifests itself in the Higher Spiritual Regions, beyond the clutches of the various worldly Illusions.

"When the Master's *Parshad* (the Holy Sound Current) makes the mind into a state of stillness, then one Awakens and comes into touch with Reality, singing unending praises of Almighty God!"

Sant Kabir explains the Love and compassion of Almighty God, by the way of how the worldly love of the mother has such an importance. The mother forgives and forgets any misbehaving on the part of the child, because she has the quality of being the mother of that child. What to think of God, the Creator, Who is the mother and the father of billions and trillions of souls! He is all forgiveness, all mercy, all compassion, all Grace. Nothing but Love pours through Him regardless thief or devotee. He has only Love and Grace for all His Creation.

Sant Kabir is explaining that in this world, many times due to the child's ignorance, he does make mistakes but the mother doesn't keep anything in her heart. She just simply forgives and forgets. Even if the same child to whom she has given birth does a heinous crime, perhaps it could happen that he might even run away, but still then she has the same merciful heart and forgiving nature.

Sant Kabir says that the Master has such a loving heart and forgives the lapses of His devotee. The devotee says, "While I have all the faults in me, You are all goodness. If I may forget You, I pray that You may not forget me! O my Master! Please forgive my sins! I am Your child! My mind is full of attachments and sorrows. How can I possibly reach the Other Side (of this worldly Ocean) without Your help! O my Creator! Grant that I should do Your Simran. I should praise Thee every moment of my life. Kindly bring Your Divine attributes into my heart!"

He stresses that one should realize God and know that He is in the human, and that the human is in Him. The human being is a Treasure House of all the Secrets of God. He is like a mirror from where God's rays of Illumination emanate and shine. Almighty God is the Life Impulse of the human being, and what would be the value of a person without Him?

Mankind should have one Aim: to become Perfect. One should become a Perfect human being and be an example of Spirituality. In all religions, whoever's Goal is good becomes a true human being, and then his worship becomes pleasing to God.

The Godman is not an ordinary man. He is the very Theme of Shabd. The person without the Inner knowledge sees the body of the Master, and nothing else. It is not his fault if he doesn't have the knowledge of the Inner Sound Current, because he lacks the understanding of it. When he progresses on the Spiritual Path, only then does he begin to understand the fullness and greatness of the Master.

Almighty God has hung a curtain behind the eyes and has left one's attention outside. Then God comes in the garb of man, and instructs the devotees how to open the Door that He Himself has closed. Sant Kabir emphasizes the fact that within man are the five Melodies. "Do not look for Them outside, but go within and draw the veil aside."

It is only the True Master Who can administer to the Spiritual malady. When one leaves the body and passes out of this world no one, neither mother, father, wife, husband, children, nor any possession, not even this body, will accompany that person to the other world. One must awaken to the fact that only the True Master and the Holy Naam are his unfailing friends. All else are, in reality, his enemies because they remain with him only out of the bonds of selfishness. Only a True Friend can remain with one even beyond death. Even on the day of ultimate reckoning, the Master is at the side of the devotee.

In reference to worldly circumstances, Sant Kabir says that one might have become a king, an emperor, or even a recluse. But in all conditions, without coming to the True Master and having His Grace, these efforts are wasted! All this comes under the category of Illusion, with its myriad desires and attractions, and everyone caught up in this, will pass out of the body without achieving anything for his higher self.

In order to liberate himself from the bondage of the body, one needs a Godman to impart the Internal knowledge. "This true knowledge is only given out by the Master. When He gives you the Holy Nectar, you are able to rise further and further into the Spiritual Realms. In His Company of Truth, He makes you One with the Lord."

Sant Kabir praises, "God is so great, so supreme, so unique! He is the One Who comes in the form of a Saint to take the souls back to Him. With the Master's Parshad of Spiritual Initiation, all thoughts of heaven and hell are left behind, as one goes up into the Lap of God. When the Master bestows His Amrit, then one can see God first-hand. All questions and doubts vanish. The devotee can obtain access to God, with the Grace of the Sat Guru."

One who is devoted to the Master need not fear the so-called 'last reckoning' with Dharam Rai. For sure at the time of his physical death, he will not be visited by the Agent of Death, but by his own Master.

Sant Kabir says that whoever does not have a True Master, must go to Dharam Rai after the death of the physical body for reconciliation of his deeds, but whoever is lucky enough to have come to the True Master, has the account of his deeds torn up. The Yamas (Messengers of Death) cannot come near. The devotees of the Lord are spared this fear of death, of which everybody else is terrified. Even the devotee's last moments in the physical body are attended to by the Master, Who leads his soul directly up to the Spiritual Regions. In addition, many devotees who have accumulated some Spiritual wealth, learn about their impending demise many days, weeks, or even months ahead of the time!

The Master does not advocate any change in one's outer form, nor of the religion into which he was born. He only advises the people to live up to the ideals which these religions preach. In other words, one should become a good Sikh, a good Hindu, a good Christian, a good Jew, a good Muslim. Sant Kabir says that the Master enjoins the devotees to do their duty, and fulfill all worldly responsibilities toward family, parents, and community.

Sant Kabir stresses that one must accept the True, Living Master, where God has manifested Himself. Whoever left this earth Region thousands of years ago, or even a hundred years ago, cannot help anyone now on the Physical Plane, simply because that person no longer has the physical body. There is no way that someone living years ago can answer any questions. The Master of the current time is the only Saviour of humanity at the same particular time. When that Godman leaves this physical world, then some other Godman appointed by God alone, brings the souls back to God.

Sant Kabir has given some guidelines to indicate if a Master is True. He says that the Master always earns His own living and does not live as a mendicant, begging food from door to door. The Master entails that one should stand on his own feet, earn his livelihood honestly, and share with the poor and the oppressed. The Saint never accepts any possession for His own use. He is always the Giver, pouring out cup upon cup of His Divine Elixir. He does not ask any recompense for any service including Holy Discourses, interviews, or even Spiritual Initiation. He may eat and drink like us, look like us, but He is different, for He is constantly in touch with the Supreme Lord. He lives in the world; yet is not of the world.

Sant Kabir tells us that the True Master stops the outward and downward trend of the mind and turns the attention inward and upward. After coming into contact with the True Master, the attention completely turns around, becoming asleep to the world and Spiritually awake towards God. The Holy Satsang of the Living Master, combined with being in His Divine Presence, reorientates the mind and turns it Godward.

Kabir Sahib says that liberation from the Cycle of birth and death can only be achieved by the Grace of a True Master, for it is He Who rends the veil, or curtain, so that one can see the Light of God and can hear the Divine Melodies streaming forth from the Supreme Father.

"The call of the Master ever resounds. Some heed it, while others pay it no attention. Blessed is that lucky soul who succeeds in finding a genuine, True Master, and who obtains from Him the Boon of Spiritual Initiation. Whoever seeks the Divine Names from the Saint and follows His instructions, is the most fortunate of all."

At the Lotus Feet of the Beloved Master, all are on a common level and worldly distinctions are forgotten. There, learned and illiterate people from all walks of life sit together, eat together, and talk together in His Holy Assembly. The Master does not establish any new religion, nor does He interfere with the existing ones. He earnestly advises the disciples to devote time to the Spiritual practices in order to attain liberation.

Sant Kabir reveals some of the duties of the Sat Guru, the Saviour of the World. "With God's order I give Spiritual Initiation to liberate people from the bondage of the Negative Power and Illusion."

Kabir Sahib describes the Master as being like a 'sheriff' of the Lord, honouring the Saints, and bringing sinners to the Spiritual Path. He says that He knows all the Secrets of God, and He brings His Message to all mankind. He is the knower of the true Home of the Father, and He has come to give the Message of God to all. "I come from the Kingdom of God, and hold a Direct Commission from Him."

In this world, the Master has always come to put Reality and Truth in front of the people. All Godmen have stressed the meaning of being a true Human Being, and of having Love and selfless service for all. The Godman colours everyone in the many hues of Almighty God. He makes the human thoughts turn upwards, and He vanishes bad deeds.

Sant Kabir says that the Master Himself comes from the pure Spiritual Regions. He is the mouthpiece of God, without narrow-mindedness and bigotry. He is free from all of this. All Saints and Mahatmas, Whoever reached the pure Spiritual Regions, have put Their own examples in front of humanity at large.

Sant Kabir warns, however, that one should not accept all Saints unconditionally, insisting that the devotee should find out those sincere, true-of-heart and Perfect Saints Who have Themselves tasted something of the Blessings of fellowship with God.

Recitation of the Names of God naturally implies the gathering of Saints, and Their Discourses on Spiritual subjects drive away the confusion and ignorance of the listeners.

The Sacred Company of the Saint always helps to direct one's Attention towards God, because the very atmosphere about Him is Charged with Divine Radiation. He who has recognized the Guru, has discovered the Hand of God. He has found the Gate, and once the Gate is revealed, everything is attained.

When one looks into the eyes of the Master, no words are needed, because the Master speaks the language of the heart. The devotee becomes lost in this wonder of the Master. The personality of the Sat Guru is instrumental in perfecting the devotee as a true worshipper of Almighty God. Throughout his whole life, the devotee should never for a moment become forgetful of the Blessings of the Master.

When one meets such a Beloved, his eyes sparkle with tears of joy, his face radiant with Love and gladness. This is no theological belief or blind faith. This is the Living Lord, bestowing Eternal Life on one and all. One's heart takes flight while hope springs forth. "In the Master's Holy Presence it is all Light, illuminating the Truth and Reality. All that is required of the devotee is *Love*, for it is this Love that takes the soul upwards."

It is most necessary for the seeker to sit in the Holy Company of such a great Soul, to see for himself the true greatness of God. The Saint is a God-personified Soul sent by God on a Mission to bring the devotees back Home. Only the Person Who knows Almighty God Himself, is the One Who can grant an Experience of God and can make others to see Him.

Kabir Sahib emphasizes that the devotee should only go to that True Master Who is able to put him on the Spiritual Way, and *grant him an Experience of the Holy Sound Current.* He states that there are many kinds of Masters in this world, but only He is the true Sadhu Who knows the Sound Current.

He points out, "The Master is the One Who will take care of the disciple, now and in the hereafter. It is a very rare Blessing from God. He wears the Crown on His Godly head. He is the One Who inspires the devotee to sit on meditation."

In this connection, Sant Kabir gives a comparison to the jungle, where there are only one or two tigers at any one time. "Likewise, there are never hundreds of bags of jewels. There are maybe one or two True Saints in the world at any given time. Whoever can bestow the Divine Amrit is the rare, True Master. The Master is a Treasure House of the Sound Current. He bestows the Godly Nectar free of charge; yet it is a rare customer who takes it. The Sat Guru is the only One Who can make the devotee realize the Shabd. This Shabd is above and away from all the worldly Shabds. The person who recognizes it and understands the Truth of that, begins to sing the praises of God, as he becomes separate from the material world."

He continues, "Whoever knows Almighty God is the only One Who can give the Experience of God and make the devotee to see God. If you want to find something, and you are looking for it somewhere else, there is no way that you can find it. However, if a guide is taken along, surely you will find it!"

He compares the Power of God to be the true internal Diamond, vibrating in each and every atom. Only the True Master can make manifest this Secret Jewel; otherwise it just remains as a Secret. Millions of births and deaths can be finished in a very short time, by coming to the genuine Master. Sant Kabir says that whenever one is in the Company of a Saint, he cannot help but remember his own Master, and these are the moments that count towards his Spiritual credit.

The Master puts the devotee on the Inward Path and Enlightens him as to what God is, where He is, and how to worship Him. The Master is the only constant and never-failing Guide on this Path. He takes the disciple by the hand, and guides him through the Inner Spiritual Regions. Sant Kabir says that it is impossible to progress inside without a Living Teacher, because there are so many temptations and pitfalls which become obstacles in the way.

People go to schools and colleges where they get some practical training, before they can say that they have acquired some knowledge in their line of study. One needs a teacher at every step of life. If man cannot achieve worldly ambitions by his own efforts, how can he possibly achieve God-realization by himself? Why should one hesitate, when he realizes that he needs help in the matter of Spirituality? If a teacher is needed for the outer matters, why would a teacher not be needed for the Inner matters? One has to develop in all ways.

Sant Kabir advises that one should seek shelter with a Godman, a Spiritual Person, and keep His Holy Company. He should seek His assistance, for the Godman not only has all Spiritual knowledge but He also knows about Almighty God, Who created all of Creation.

All sciences come under worldly knowledge, intellect, and philosophy, but what is needed in the Science of the Beyond is a Practical Experience, a first-hand Demonstration of the Light and Sound of God. What is definitely and unquestionably needed is the Guidance of a Living Master. Sant Kabir repeats over and over again, "The seeker needs a True, Living Master *to even begin* on the Spiritual Path!"

The Master is not concerned with nationality, sect, religious, or political groups. He speaks to the person, to his soul, and explains to him what his Essence truly is. "In His Holy Company, one can develop *the Eye* with which God can be seen. Only through an Awakened Soul can ignorance be dispelled. The Master can grant the knowledge that God is the Soul of the soul, and the Mainstay of life."

The Master says, "My friend, listen to the Five Melodies that are proceeding from within, and link your soul up with them. God is in you. If you long to meet the Lord, come with me and I shall take you to Him." Whoever is the True Master will make you to be in touch with Almighty God all the time.

As the devotee begins to have Inner Experience, the outer, worldly enjoyments lose their charms. Naturally, this Conscious Contact is only granted when the person goes to a Master and obtains Inner knowledge, in the Form of Divine Light and the Holy Sound Current. Without the True Master, this Great Wealth cannot be found and man stays outside, begging for trifles. He neither discovers his own self, nor does he merge in God.

First-hand Experience is given by the Master to the devotee at the time of Spiritual Initiation, and is the testing criterion that the Master is True. The Sat Guru is the only One Who is competent to guide the devotee in the Higher Spiritual Regions. The Master also grants a Boon to the disciple that He will receive and protect the devotee's soul, at the time of his physical death.

This knowledge of the Saints has been written about in the Scriptures and other religious Books, but just to read about these Truths, cannot grant the person the true Experience that the Godmen have attained. Spirituality is not obtained by merely reading and writing. A real, practical Experience is necessary to secure one's own salvation. Theory without actual practice is worthless. "Without Spiritual Experience, life is empty!"

Sant Kabir says that the soul rises up because of this Application, and whoever has knowledge of this Experience but does not do any further exercise on it, cannot rise up. This is why Sant Kabir always places such great emphasis on self-Experience, in practice as well as theory.

It is this viable and verifiable Life Current which distinguishes the Path of the Masters from all other methods of study. The Master gives an immediate and first-hand Experience, a Contact with this Sound Current, which is the one sign by which a True Master may be distinguished from so-called pseudo-masters. Only the True Masters of the highest Order are able to bestow this Living Contact with the Spiritual Power of the Almighty. The True Masters say, "Sit down and have it! First *see*, and then follow this Way! You must *see* for yourself."

Without this Conscious Contact with the Divine Light and Sound of God, there can be no real Spiritual progress. Furthermore, the Holy Sound Current cannot be contacted until one comes to the True Master Who is capable of giving the devotee that direct Connection. And without this direct

Experience, there can be no salvation from the Ocean of worldly existence.

Sant Kabir says that the person who is a *Sadhak* (a Disciple, or a true human being) is He Who rises above the body consciousness, and enters the first Spiritual Region. And the one who traverses the Second Inner Region, is known as a *Sadh* (a Disciplined Soul). When He eventually gains access to the third Spiritual Plane, He is known as a *Hansa* (a Purified Soul). He who goes yet further up is called a *Param-Hansa* (an Immaculate Soul).

But whoever goes beyond the Super Causal (Par Brahm) and enters into Sach Khand, is the One Who is called a *Sant* (a Saint). And a Sant Who is commissioned by the Supreme Father to teach and to demonstrate Truth, is called a *Sant Satguru* (a Perfect Master).

#8-1 The Master Makes People Into True Human Beings

The Master makes people into true human beings. He makes this world pure and pious with selfless service and Love for all, where there is no fanaticism, jealousy, bigotry, mischief or anger. He makes one's thoughts turn away from outer differences, and guides the devotee to realize his inherent Oneness. He directs the attention, which is constantly flowing outwards into this world of sensual pleasures, to turn inwards to the pure Spiritual Regions. He is a Mouthpiece of God, and He is a living example of a Perfect Person.

Sant Kabir gives us the story of Dharam Das, who was a very rich and prosperous businessman. He would meticulously attend to all religious ceremonies and pomp, spending much of his time in the ritual worship of idols and the study of the Bhagavadgita and other Scriptures. In his house, he had installed a large stone image of Avatar Krishna and other smaller stone images for adoration.

One day when Dharam Das was absorbed in his devotions, Kabir Sahib suddenly appeared and stood beside him. The Great Saint asked, "Well, Dharam Das, the large stone appears to weigh about two pounds, but how much do the smaller ones weigh?"

Before Dharam Das could answer, Kabir Sahib asked another question. "Have any of these stone images ever spoken to you? You ask them many questions, but have you ever received an answer to even one prayer?"

Dharam Das was astounded that someone would refer to his idols to mere stone but before he could respond, Kabir Sahib had disappeared. Just see the wonderful way that Kabir Sahib began to direct Dharam Das to the right Path! The Saint knows what is in the heart of the devotee, that he is searching for Almighty God.

Later, when Dharam Das had a chance to contemplate on what Sant Kabir had told him, he realized that what had been said was correct. He thought that *yes, it is true that the statues have never spoken to him!* Although he had fervently prayed to them throughout his life and offered them delicious food and drink, not a single word had come out of their mouths. They had never answered his questions, nor given him any guidance in his life.

His faith in idol worship began to waver as time went on. He kept remembering those words uttered by Sant Kabir. He wished to find Him, but that Godly Man had seemingly vanished.

After some time had passed, Kabir Sahib again came to that man's house, on the pretense of asking for charity. The wife, Amna, answered the door, and told Sant Kabir to wait, that Dharam Das was busy in worship.

After a little while, Kabir Sahib called "Dharam Das!" in a louder voice, but the wife became upset, angrily saying, "Wait! He will come out!"

After still more time, Sant Kabir again called out. This time the wife shouted with rage, "I told you to wait! He will come!"

Just then Dharam Das himself came out from the house and he heard these words, but before he could say anything, Kabir Sahib solemnly said, "O Dharam Das! You are going to commit a great sin!"

Dharam Das was startled and Amna, who was at his side, by now was full of anger, and confident because of her enormous wealth. She sharply retorted, "Anybody who calls my husband a sinner, is a sinner himself!"

Kabir Sahib just smiled and gently advised Dharam Das to split open the firewood before burning it. "It is full of ants and you are taking many innocent lives!" And then Sant Kabir suddenly disappeared, just as before.

It came in Dharam Das' mind to open the wood and sure enough, when he closely examined it, he found that indeed there were thousands of tiny insects hidden in the cracks and under the bark. His heart was heavy and full of remorse as now he had twice missed the opportunity to speak with a really Great Soul. Naturally he became angry and blamed his wife, saying that had she not become upset and rude, the Saint would not have disappeared.

Kabir Sahib just smiled and gently advised Dharam Das to split open the firewood before burning it. "It is full of ants and you are taking many innocent lives!"

She, however, in defence responded, "Don't worry. *Wherever there is a lump of sugar, the flies swarm around!* Don't be concerned about what has happened. You have lots of money. Just announce that you will host a great gathering of all the Saints, and everyone will be lavishly fed. After all, He is a poor wandering Sadhu, and He will also come. Like this type of person, many will come!"

So Dharam Das held many big gatherings, one after the other. Various Saints and holy men came from all over the country, and everyone was fed on a very lavish scale, but Sant Kabir did not come. As Dharam Das' money dwindled, his eagerness to meet Kabir Sahib increased. After the rich man had spent virtually all his money on these huge gatherings, he suddenly realized that the Great Saint that he so desperately wanted to meet, had never once appeared. Every other holy man had come and eaten his fill but the Great Kabir, for Whom his heart longed and cried, did not come. His money, which had brought him much honour and pride, was finally exhausted.

Sinking into a deep depression, he felt that life was meaningless and no longer worth living, so he decided to commit suicide. Admitting defeat, he thought in despair, "I am reduced to a pauper, and yet I have not met the Sadhu I so fervently seek. What good is it to go back to my home?" He went to the far side of the River Yamuna and slowly walked a long way down the river. He was about to plunge himself into the flowing torrent, when suddenly he found the Great Saint standing beside him.

He immediately fell at His Lotus Feet and wept bitterly. Tears streaming down his cheeks, he cried "You have come now when I have nothing to offer you. Had You come earlier, I could have offered You anything You liked. I could have done so much for You!"

But Kabir Sahib gently lifted him up and embraced him, replying, "Had I come earlier when you wished me to, you would have taken me just *for a fly who had come for the sugar!* But now that you don't have anything to give me, I have come to give you something--Something very Special."

Then Sant Kabir Spiritually Initiated him into the Mysteries of the Beyond. Since Dharam Das had become purified through his sufferings, he made very quick Inner progress. Kabir Sahib had many followers, but Dharam Das is regarded as one of His chief disciples, and one of His successors.

The Master is God personified, and His Word should become the law of the heart. The definition of Spirituality implies the knowledge of the Beyond, far away from discussion and arguments. Many scholars, very advanced in book-learning, remain void of Spirituality throughout their lives just because

Kabir Sahib gently lifted up Dharam Das and embraced him, replying, "Had I come earlier when you wished me to, you would have taken me for just a fly who had come for the sugar! But now that you don't have anything to give me, I have come to give you something–something very Special!"

they are unable to accept the fact that perhaps someone else just might know something that they do not.

As regarding the effect of the Master's Radiation, Sant Kabir explains it in the following way. If the person goes to a perfume vendor's shop, he may not give him any perfume, but that person will return home with some of the fragrance by radiation.

However, if the shopkeeper gives him a small bottle of that scent, then he will surely become saturated. With constant hearing, the Master's Godly Hue will begin to spread. The association and company of these Exalted Souls means that one is where Truth is discussed, where Almighty God is being praised.

Realized souls are the true Lovers of God but people, unfortunately, are the lovers of this world. A Gurumukh has forgotten Himself in the Sweet Remembrance of the Lord so much so, that He has also completely forgotten about the world. This, of course, is according to the various stages of Love through which the disciple passes.

Kabir Sahib explains that the person only becomes pure when he rises above the body consciousness with his Master's Grace and compassion, and beholds the Master's Ethereal Form, and then he can cross the first three Planes, the

Physical, the Astral, and the Causal. "O brother, whoever becomes fearless and understands devotion, will obtain this Har Ras, and Whoever can bestow this Amrit is the rare, True Master."

King Ibrahim Adham of Balkh-Bokhara left his total crown and kingdom to become a disciple of Kabir Sahib. In the olden days, a devotee had to stay with a Master for many years before he would be ready to receive something. During this time, he was expected to have stilled his mind and made efforts to cast out ego and wrath, becoming humble in a manner so as to benefit from the Spiritual Gift which the Master would Graciously bestow upon him. The Master would first make the vessel ready to receive the true Spiritual Wealth.

This king went to live in Kabir Sahib's humble home for a few years, in order to rid his heart and mind of the thoughts of kingship. During this time he appeared to have a calm and quiet manner, humbly performing any household task given to him.

One day, Mata Loi (Sant Kabir's wife) asked Kabir Sahib, "Well, he has been here for so many years. Can You not give him something now?" Kabir Sahib replied, "The vessel is not yet ready!"

THE TRUE MASTER • 437

Naturally, Mata Loi was surprised and asked Sant Kabir what more signs of readiness were there, as the king appeared to be in complete obeisance, quiet, humble, etc. Kabir Sahib, however, repeated, "No, he is not yet ready."

Kabir Sahib told her that the next morning, when the king would leave the house, just to throw from the roof a basket full of garbage on his head, and then to listen to what he says. He also told her to hide herself from the king's view.

Mata Loi did according to the way that Sant Kabir instructed and the king shouted in an angry tone, "Oh, had this happened in Balkh-Bokhara (his kingdom), we would see what would happen to the person who did this!" He could not let the kingdom leave his mind.

Mata Loi went and reported this to Kabir Sahib. She repeated the king's words, "I am a king! Had I been in my own kingdom, we would see what would happen to this person!" Sant Kabir said, "Just see! I told you that he is not yet ready!"

A few more years went by, and one day Kabir Sahib told Mata Loi that the king is now ready. Mata Loi was amazed and said that she found no change in the outer living of the king, as he showed the same humility and the same obedience. "I don't see any difference! He is the same!" she insisted.

Then Sant Kabir asked, "Do you want to see? I will show you the difference between then, and now! The 'vessel' is now clean and he is ready to have Initiation."

Kabir Sahib told her to take the night soil in a pitcher and go up to the roof, and as the king would leave the house in the morning, just to pour it on his head. She did this and was shocked when the king suddenly exclaimed, "O God, I am even worse than this!"

Mata Loi duly went back to Kabir Sahib and described what had happened. Since the king's heart had no longer any hold on his kingdom, Kabir Sahib knew the king was ready, and He gave him some Experience of God within. This is an illustration to show that outer actions mean nothing; it is a matter of the attitude of the heart. When the heart is empty of the worldly treasures and desires, then it can be filled with the Treasure of the Holy Naam.

Kabir Sahib teaches that to know about Spirituality, one has to lead a true, pious life. He has to be able to become Conscious, and keep away from the outer disturbances of the mind in order to have internal peace, without being affected by distracting desires. Exactly in the same way whenever

Mata Loi did according to the way that Sant Kabir instructed and the king shouted in an angry tone, "Oh, had this happened in Balkh-Bokhara (his kingdom), we would see what would happen to the person who did this!" He could not let the Kingdom leave his mind.

one wants to perform a scientific experiment, he has to have one-pointed attention.

Many people would come to Sant Kabir. He would arrange for their meals and see to their comfort. One night it happened that there was no food in the house with which to serve them. As He had no money at that time, He sent His devoted wife, Mata Loi, to the neighbourhood grocer, that she might ask him to give them some food on credit.

Mata Loi went to the grocer, and explained the situation, that she had no money to pay right now, but that she wanted to buy some groceries. When she asked for credit, he told her that he would give her whatever items she needed, but there was one condition: she must spend the night with him. Naturally, she was shocked at this request, and she told him that she would respond to him later.

In the meantime, she came home and whispered to her husband that this is the condition, that she must return to him in the night. Sant Kabir said, "Do not worry. It is alright. Tell the grocer that we agree. Bring the food, because we have to feed our guests."

Later that night, Kabir Sahib reminded her of the grocer's request, but He also told her not to be concerned, that everything was proceeding according to plan. It happened to be raining very hard, and the streets were full of mud, so Kabir Sahib accompanied her. When they reached the grocer's house, Mata Loi went inside while Kabir Sahib remained outside the door.

The grocer was rather startled that she had actually come to him, but his amazement grew even more when he discovered that her clothes were absolutely dry, despite the heavy rains outside! He became even more bothered when he also observed that her shoes were quite clean! He asked her how could that be, after walking through the muddy streets?

She replied that her husband, Kabir Sahib, had accompanied her and was now waiting outside the door to take her home again.

As soon as the grocer heard the Holy Name of the Divine Saint, he immediately was ashamed of his intended actions, and felt very badly in his heart. He went to the door, brought Sant Kabir inside and fell at His Lotus Feet, kissing them again and again, begging to be forgiven. Kabir Sahib pardoned him, and the grocer soon became one of His devoted disciples.

Kabir Sahib explains how a devotee, when he obtains the Light of God within himself, praises the Lord. He forgets all the bad deeds that he used to have and he begins to listen to the Celestial Music, the Holy Sound Current. Gradually, all

Mata Loi replied to the grocer that her husband, Kabir Sahib, had accompanied her and was now waiting outside the door to take her home again.

that is complicated and useless will fall away on its own, because the connection with it has been broken, and that which is meaningful will begin to take its place.

The devotee says, "My mind was always as restless as the wind, never still. I was in the clutches of Illusion and Deception. When I came to my Master, I surrendered myself and my heart, mind, and soul. Now I have seen the Light of God in me, with the Grace of my Beloved Master. Those thieves of my mind and my eyes (attachment and greed) were stealing my time and taking me further into their web. Now, with the Grace and compassion of my Master, I have closed all the doors of the outgoing faculties, and I listen to the Unstruck Melody which is vibrating throughout my body. All ego, greed, and Illusion have run away from me. I have cleansed myself inwardly of all the dirt, bad thoughts and jealousy that was in my heart. Now I am so grateful to my Master, my Sat Guru, Who has put me on the right Path, and has accepted me as His own."

#8-2 The Unbounded Grace of the Master

The Master is our only hope in this Ocean of worldly existence, and this hope can be summed up in one word: GRACE. Grace from the Master brings about unwavering faith deep within the devotee. Sant Kabir describes that when the showers of Grace come to a devotee, then God's Love and Power is bestowed on him. "This Grace of Divine knowledge comes as a strong wind which blows away the Illusions of various fears, hesitations, questions and superstitions, so that the devotee can progress day by day on his Spiritual Journey. This Divine Storm, shatters the devotee's ignorance and ideas of attachment with the body. There are no worldly desires left whatsoever, and his Spiritual forgetfulness gradually turns into Divine Enlightenment. Such is the unbounded Grace of the Master!"

Before coming to the True Master, one's life is clouded with grief and sorrow. The mind leads him down a path of darkness and confusion, with its doubts and suspicions. The Spiritual Path is not one of intellect and reasoning, but rather one of Divine Love. It begins with a yearning deep inside one's heart and gradually, as one progresses, it turns into a kind of 'madness' where everything else is forgotten, where the Beloved and Divine union with this Beloved become one's very life. This so-called 'madness' burns away all attachments with this world and its five Deadly foes. It is surely the Grace of the True Master which carries one upwards and on to Divine Oneness.

There is no difficulty in attaining God, because He is always present, everywhere. Wherever one goes or sees, there He is.

The difficulty is that the ego stands in between; hence, the need for the 'Master's Grace.' The seeker may labour, but the attainment will always be by the Guru's Grace. This Grace is a priceless alchemy to annihilate the ego. Whatever the result, is due to the Master's Grace.

Kabir Sahib gives examples from everyday life, saying that a storm brings all the problems and tribulations of dirt and dust, rain and winds to the human heart, smothering the person with coverings of Illusion and doubt, until Almighty God takes pity on his condition and brings him to the Master. Then the Grace of the Master shines on that devotee just like bright sunshine after the storm, and the devotee's body becomes filled with this Godly Light.

The methods of the Yogis are based on effort. All energy is devoted to this labour. Sant Kabir's Path, however, is one of surrender. The seeker realizes that nothing happens through his own effort--only through the Master's Grace can one achieve. This does not mean that one should make no effort. Try one must, but also he should remember that the outcome will happen only through His Grace. To rely on one's own efforts only serves to strengthen the ego. It is easy for the Yogi to be proud, because he begins to think that things go his way due to his own efforts. However, by the Master's Grace alone, can the happening occur.

Sant Kabir says, "Nothing is cold enough to cool down the raging fires of the mind's desires." He says that the coldness of the moon and even of ice are not enough to quench this searing heat. In true fact, it is only the Master Who can extinguish this fever.

Sant Kabir talks about the Master having unbounded compassion and Grace for His followers. The Master willingly and without complaint takes upon Himself all pain and sorrow, all of the burdens and suffering of humanity. Sant Kabir especially points out that no matter how undeserving the person might be, the Master Loves him and protects him more than His own. Rich or poor, high or low, the Master bestows the Gift of Life on one and all.

Sant Kabir says that once the person is granted Spiritual Initiation by a Master, that Divine Contact with the Holy Naam is never wasted. It will fructify sooner or later. The soul might have to be given another human birth, but eventually it will reach to Sach Khand.

Sant Kabir continues, "Don't ask what is the caste of the Sat Guru. Don't see to His outer form or colour. You should go by the knowledge of what He has. When you want to buy a sword, you must see the value of the sword alone, and not care about the cover."

He continues, "Dear friend, hold firmly to the hem of the One Who has Awareness of this world and the Beyond. The Master knows of the World that one is destined for, and He will impart this knowledge to the devotee." Sant Kabir warns, however, to accept only a True Master of the Highest Order. "This Enlightenment cannot be given by a person who has not risen above the senses. That kind of person cannot transport another to the Worlds Beyond. If someone follows a 'blind' man (Spiritually blind), that person will engage him in only the useless outer ritual practices of religion."

He advises, "O people! Bring the attention inwards, and when you do so, the mind will have the Saving Nectar of God, and then you will truly know God. God ordains the one He chooses to seek Him out." How possibly could a person otherwise set out on this tremendous quest all by himself? How can one even arrive at the idea of this quest, and acquire His remembrance, if He does not Will it? He has already chosen, the Search has begun, and He has entered that lucky devotee's life. It is He alone Who awakens the thirst for Him. It is His Grace alone that confers the quality of singing His praises and expressing gratitude for His bounteous gifts.

"Almighty God Himself will appear and talk to you. With the Grace of the Master, your Spiritual Thirst will be quenched. After this Experience, you yourself will announce to the other people how much Grace you have received from your Master, and how your stubborn mind was unwise not to turn inward earlier. Now it has become more discerning, and is under control."

He says, "The True Master's Arrow of Illumination opened the Way to Charan Kamal, and the Effulgent Light dawned. All bliss, Blessings, and Grace are coming from the Lotus Feet of the Lord. Until one actually sees this for himself, he cannot praise anything about this. Only he who sees it, can truly tell about it. One cannot obtain any part of this Blessing by way of the intellect. It is only bestowed upon one with the Grace of the True Master."

What is the meaning of *Charan Kamal*? When the person comes to the Living Master and puts his attention towards His Teachings, he will receive first-hand Experience of the Divine Light and Sound of Almighty God. When the devotee practices one-pointed attention, the Radiant, Effulgent Form of the Master will manifest at the devotee's Third, or Single Eye. The devotee will then see for himself the greatness of the Guru's shelter of unbounded mercy and Grace.

Sant Kabir advises that a Living Master is very necessary, and the devotee should bow only to Him. This means that the devotee should meet Him and take unconditional shelter with Him. Sant Kabir describes the Lotus Feet of the Master as being the true place of pilgrimage. "By serving the Living

Master, one is accepted in the Court of God. There are many benefits of meeting a Master. Have the Holy Company only of the Saint, Who will grant salvation."

The devotee begins to search for a Godman, a Saint, Who can help him solve the mystery of death, and with the Grace of God that person comes to the True Master. Sant Kabir says, "The very day that the Master Initiates someone, the God Power resides with him. From that very moment, the Master is watching and guiding the devotee. When one has the Grace of the True Master, the Master accepts the follower as His own, and grants him Divine Intoxication. With the Grace of the Almighty, the devotee begins to see the Light of God, and eventually he sees the Master as *Guru Dev* in His Radiant, Effulgent Form."

Kabir Sahib says that, "A person doesn't truly realize the existence of God until he comes under the Grace of the Master. When His existence is realized, then that person knows the Truth and the Reality, and can understand that God is the One Who works in every aspect throughout all Creation. God is the One Who permeates the whole universe. Then the devotee will realize that there is no difference between the soul and the Oversoul." He realizes that there is no 'I', 'me', or 'mine' left, as all ego has vanished. There is only HIM! Sant Kabir says that people are deeply under the influence of Illusion and Deception, forgetting the Lord and His Love, but on the other hand, Love and devotion cannot grow without the unbounded Love and Grace of the Master.

Sant Kabir also refers to *Guru Charan* in many of His verses. This means that the Master's Effulgent Form appears within, at the Third Eye. When the soul withdraws itself, then this Astral Form of the Master appears on the forehead. The true devotee then merges into that Effulgent Form. All through his life, the devotee keeps singing praises of the True Master, as the Master's qualities begin to reflect within him. "Whoever has God's Grace and Blessing, he is the one who will realize himself. That person's every thought is of his Beloved Master."

Sant Kabir gives many examples to show how the benevolent Master looks after His devotees. He says, "The Creator is the Giver of all Boons. Almighty God, the Creator, is the Source of all goodness and happiness. That follower who remembers Him is looked after by Him. All the worldly sorrows are washed away. God's Holy Name is imparted only through the Master."

He continues, "With the Light of Divine knowledge of the Master, my heart became full of Light. He is the One Who made me focus my attention at the Third Eye, and my attention went upwards in stages. My mind then reached its true Home, and became full of peace and bliss."

"When Almighty God gives the Grace to get out of this whirlpool of the world, then the soul gets dipped into the Colour and bliss of the Almighty. The Holy Assembly of the True Master grants all peace and bliss. It is a golden moment, indeed, when one meets such a Master. Only the Master can break all the Pralabdha Karma, and free the soul from the bondage of aeons of years!"

Sant Kabir says that both the soul and God are made of the same Essence. They have the same qualities and are of the same nature. One should seek shelter with a Master, and keep His Company. The Master not only knows about Spirituality, but He also knows about the Spiritual Life from where He has obtained God, the Supreme Creator.

Kabir Sahib explains the Grace of the Sat Guru, His compassion and His humility. He tells us something of the whole Ocean of Grace. "The Sat Guru is giving the Divinity of Spiritual Initiation, becoming embedded in the devotee in the form of Light and Sound, which is the Nectar of the Creator. This Light and Sound opens the devotee's Inner Eye and Inner Ear, so that his attachment with the world will vanish as he imbibes the Celestial Music, the Unstruck Melody of the Creator."

Sant Kabir also tells us about the immense work that the Master does. The Master grants peace of mind, He brings the devotee's attention from the outward attractions to the inward, and He is responsible for taking that soul to the Higher Stages in the Spiritual Realms of God. The Master doesn't charge any fee from the devotee for any of these Blessings. He freely gives, gives, and gives.

"The Master's Divine Nectar is embedded with the Charging of the Creator. One single Drop of that Nectar can make the person dance in ecstasy, and the radiation of that Charging then begins to flow from that person. The atmospheric effect cannot but be affected to a certain extent. This Divine Charging of Love is the special Connecting Link between the soul and the Oversoul."

#8-3 Sharan (Surrender to the Master's Will)

From the verses of Sant Kabir, we learn that there are two ways to accumulate Spiritual wealth. The first is known as the Way of *Karni,* the method of labouring hard at meditation. The result of this Path is the feeling that one's will is different from the Will of the Whole as the person's tension, restlessness, anxiety, and ego are strengthened.

The second is known as the Path of *Sharan,* unconditional surrender to the Master's Will. In the Path of Sharan, one feels that he is a part of the Whole. The result is peace, contentment, and joy, which ultimately destroy the ego.

The Path of *Karni* is the easier Way, for it is not difficult to devote time to one's Spiritual practices but the second method, that of *Sharan*, although more efficient in bringing about result, is much harder to practice.

Sant Kabir tells us that one can be in absolute surrender to the Master only if he can give his mind, with all its powers of thinking. He then becomes totally absorbed only in the Master, which results in the soul easily rising within. However, the mind is a great hurdle on the Path. Its nature is to continually wander downwards and outwards, while one is physically sitting in meditation. Entire movies begin within, the moment the devotee wishes to be absolutely still. As long as thoughts and desires keep chasing each other in the mind, this type of self-surrender is not possible.

With the benign Grace of Almighty God, the person finds a True Master Who guides him on the Spiritual Path. Using the analogy of a married person, Sant Kabir describes that the person throws out his old companion (the mind, with its tricks of Illusion), which Sant Kabir calls as the person's first wife, with the help of his new wife and companion (his Beloved Master), Who is so beautiful, so enchanting. The person then feels a great peace and happiness, bringing her home to his heart, to every pore of his body. She is wise and her ways are so enticing. He immediately surrenders his heart and mind to the Lotus Feet of the new wife, the Beloved Master. What more better thing could happen in his life that his first wife (Illusion) has died at last? He has now found salvation with the Creator. He becomes very happy that his life has been fulfilled and the desire of finding the Truth, at long last has been realized. He prays to Almighty God to never, ever, leave him. He was waiting for Him for aeons and aeons. He requests, "Please don't ever leave me. My first companion is now clinging to some other person because this is its commission, but I am free at last, with the Grace of my Beloved Master!"

Sant Kabir says, "In the Court of the Lord, there is no shortage of anything. There is only a lack of one's own efforts to sacrifice and surrender himself to the Master." Due to this reason, the person doesn't receive God's Grace. However, once the devotee of Spirituality has the Experience of that Divine Nectar of Truth, he cannot furthermore have love for worldly engagements and worldly attractions. They are all left behind, and one's heart wants at every moment only to see the Glorious, Radiant, Light of God.

"If you really Love the Saint, then do as He says. If you put full faith and Love towards your Master, then do as He tells you. Don't leave anything in the middle, but develop and fulfill it." Thus, hard work and perseverance are necessary for success on the Spiritual Path.

The Master's enticing Love then grows in the devotee's heart more and more, day by day, drawing him steadily towards his goal, his True Home. The Guru's Grace makes him so happy, and he becomes totally absorbed in the ravishing beauty of the Master, forever staying in His Holy Company.

Kabir Sahib describes the condition that comes when a person with devotion and Love surrenders himself and his mind (with all its possessions, desires, and attachments) to the Master. That lucky devotee is then able to say, "I am a sacrifice to the Sadhu, the Sant, my Beloved. I am totally engrossed in You! I am Yours! I have surrendered to You! *I am Your unbought slave!*"

Sant Kabir remarks, "When one casts out all ego, and sacrifices his own head in unbounded Love for the Master, only then can he become absorbed in the Master. Thereafter, he does not worry about anything of this world."

One day, Sant Kabir went out of the area to give Satsang. While giving this Holy Discourse to the followers, someone ran up to Him and blurted out the news that Kabir Sahib's house was on fire!

Sant Kabir told that man, "Sit down with the others, and listen carefully to the Message of God. Don't have any fear or worry, but leave everything to Almighty God!" He went on to tell the followers about the beauty of Almighty God and His presence everywhere.

After the Satsang had finished, Kabir Sahib started His journey back home. On the way, He heard from many more people about the news of His house burning. His answer to them was that everything is going to be alright, as the Lord is looking after all. Flocks of people followed Him right to His house!

When He finally reached home, everyone was amazed to find that His house was not only made new again, but that *it was in even better condition than before!* Everyone marvelled at this astonishing event! No one could provide an explanation. They had seen with their own eyes that the building was burning, and yet here it was untouched and looking brand-new just before them. With great reverence, they all bowed down to His feet, realizing that here was God's true Beloved.

Sant Kabir proceeds to give an interesting illustration. "From the goblet of Love, there is an abundance of delicious and enticing Nectar. However, it is very difficult to drink, because the price of it is *an offering of one's head!*" By this, Sant Kabir means that one must surrender to the Will of the Master.

The devotee must give up pride and vanity, at which time his mind will become humble, and he will enjoy untold inner bliss.

In many verses He advises, "Surrender your body, mind and even your own head to the Master, and then keep absolutely away from the world. This total surrender is the true Way of obtaining realization. When you are in Love, then you have to unconditionally surrender yourself. You don't expect any return for this kind of Love."

"If the devotee surrenders his mind and body to the Master, the Master will make that devotee like Himself. If you give everything to the Master, nothing remains with you, and then *you are automatically His!*"

#8-4 Satsang (The Master's Holy Discourse)

Sant Kabir says that if one wishes to hear the Supreme Father, it is through the lips of the Master that He will speak. "To find God, one must come to a Godman." In the Master's Company of Truth, one can have a Contact with the Holy Naam, and it is only through this Connection that he can have the sought-for salvation. This is the Power that links the devotee to the Named One.

Sant Kabir continues, "Man is entrapped in the City of Thieves (the five senses), which drag the attention constantly downwards and outwards into the materialistic world, while his life is athirst for the Satsang of the Master. Being in the Holy Company of the Saint, Love for God increases day by day. In His Association, one can change his habits, and rise up above the body consciousness. This can be compared with somebody who visits the perfume market. Even if that person does not buy any perfume, just by entering the shop, he becomes saturated with scent."

The Saints and Godmen, regardless of where They are born, always talk about God, bringing all mankind together as children of One God. The Saint could be Hindu, Muslim, Sikh, Christian, Jain, or any other. Sant Kabir tells us that the Master always gives out the Message of God to awaken the people who have been slumbering for aeons and aeons of lives, to all those who are wasting their precious human birth. The Master tells them to invert their attention and go inwards.

"By sitting near the Master, one can receive the *Water of Life*, which will not only satisfy their Thirst for Spiritual knowledge, but will also clean the heart from inside. This will become like a well. which will spring forth with the Nectar of Everlasting Life. The Divine Light will then do the work of soap, cleansing the soul, the heart, and the mind."

Sant Kabir has given an interesting example, saying that to have the Holy Company of the Master for a short period of time, 'even for eleven minutes', can be compared to doing Simran alone for fifty years. This is the Treasure of the Master's Grace, which drenches the devotee through and through with Love and peace. "Likewise, the amount of rain that falls in a downpour on the fields for only twenty minutes is equal to the amount of water that a well keeps pumping out continuously for a whole twelve months!"

Sant Kabir emphasizes the importance of the Master's Holy Presence, warning that as long as one cherishes even the remotest hope of attaining heaven, he cannot reach God, because God does not dwell in heaven. He explains that heaven is in the lower areas, not in the Higher Spiritual Realms. "It is very universal in this world to talk about heaven, but unfortunately people don't have any knowledge whatsoever of what they are talking about. They have in their heart that they want to go there, not knowing where it is, what it is like, or even how they can reach there. They don't even know about themselves, what to think of knowing where heaven is!"

He asks, "Is heaven in the ditch, or is it made of mud? Most people have only this kind of empty talk about heaven. What can be further said? Now I will tell you where heaven is. Just have the Holy Company of a Godman, and there *at His Lotus*

Feet you will find the True Heaven, in the Spiritual Realms of God, the Creator!"

In the Satsang of the Master lies untold benefit, for the Holy Discourse swiftly reveals the Master within the devotee, but the worldly do not understand its true significance. Sant Kabir says, "Being in the Holy Company of a True Saint and talking with Him for 20 minutes, 10 minutes or even for 5, grants the true benefit of a great Boon."

Sant Kabir reveals that the Master is Charged through and through with Divinity, and His Divine Infection pours from His Godly eyes to those who come in contact with Him. His words are highly Charged, and cannot help but profoundly affect those who are receptive. "Even if one is sitting physically near the Guru, but the mind is just going around, that is not devotion. One cannot derive the full benefit from the Holy Presence of the Master in this way."

Using terminology that is easily understood by everyone, He says "How can one put colour on a new piece of cloth, if it is so filled with starch that it cannot be dyed? No colouring can enter a starched cloth. If one just sits quietly and attentively in the Holy Presence of the Sat Guru, even if he cannot follow the Satsang fully, he will derive some benefit. If the mind is elsewhere, that person not only harms himself, but also spoils the atmosphere for others."

elsewhere, that person not only harms himself, but also spoils the atmosphere for others."

"People go to many places of worship, but without having the True Master and His Holy Satsang, they will leave those places empty-handed. One Love-laden Glance from a Master is enough to raise the spirit to immeasurable heights. And all this can be gained through the Holy Satsang of the Living Master."

He again advises, "One can only meet God through the Sat Guru and His Satsang. Stay in the Holy Company of the Saint even if you have to sacrifice all luxuries of this world. The person who does so, even though he might have to make his life very simple, will be a true Lover of God and will merge in Him. All worldly treasures have to be left behind, as their value is nothing compared to the benefits of the Master's Holy Discourse."

There is a great need for the Satsang of the Master, in order to have benefit from all the true practices of Spirituality. In whose company one stays and associates, the same effect that person will have, and then he gradually becomes like the first person. Sant Kabir says that if one has the company of worldly people, he will have the effect of their 'colour' on him. Conversely, in the Holy Assembly of Spirituality, one will have the effect of Spirituality. "Have the Holy Company of the Saint and attain liberation. In the Society of the Saint, one has no fear of dying."

Kabir Sahib gives the example that ordinary trees may exist near the sandalwood, but they quickly become sandalwood just by being in the company of the sandalwood trees and absorbing their sweet fragrance. Similarly, it is a great boon to have the Holy Company of the Master, and His Association of Truth. Regardless from where the person comes, when he is with the Saint, he begins to turn his attention inwards, and then becomes just like that Saint.

Sant Kabir reveals, "The Master is sent by the Lord to bring forth the Message of the Creator. The True Saint is One for all. He is the One Who makes people turn their attention towards the Lord. In His Company, one listens to the Sound Current and sees the Light of God. This is all the unbounded Grace of the Master, and due to His Assembly of Truth, people become One with God."

In the Master's Sangat, Divine Nectar comes to the people who are sitting around Him, and it has a great effect of Truth on them. People 'awake' in His Holy Discourse, which gives upliftment to their souls. The Godman bestows His own Life-Impulse, and gives the balm of Divine Inspiration to those lacerated and wilted hearts that have become injured by worldly sorrows. It is just like when someone keeps flowers in the house, the whole atmosphere takes on that fragrance. In the same way, whoever has the Company of the Godman, gets the effect of His compassion and mercy.

The ignorant ones indulge in the company and pleasures of the world, and stay dyed in the colour of Illusion. If one has the Company of the Saint, his soul will become of the very hue of Truth. The seeker should imbibe the peace and tranquillity of the Higher Company, and have its effect on himself. The company of the wise makes one also to become wise. Sant Kabir advises that one should keep away from the Company of the narrow-minded people, or he will develop a closed mind himself.

When one has the Holy Company of a Godman, he should sit with Him so that His Spiritual Rays may affect his soul, bringing much peace. Kabir Sahib emphasizes again and again that the Divine Radiation coming from a True Master cleanses the heart, and brings peace within. If one cannot have the Holy Satsang of the Master, then it is better to sit alone in the sweet memory of the Lord. That will bring about a definite Charging, and one will become fond of hearing about Spirituality, as the passion to know God grows in the heart.

One will have a prayer on his lips to always have the physical Company of the Godman. "There are great Blessings to be had from Holy Satsang. Whoever goes to the Satsang gets is full of the rays of Love, and everybody gets his share of this according to the purity of his heart. "Satsang is the fastest Way to meet with the Creator. With the Holy Satsang of the Saint, worldly effects and attractions vanish. In His Blessed Company, one gains salvation forever."

The Ganges River is known to be very pious. People worship it and take baths in it. However, there are also many small rivers and creeks that enter into the Ganges from upstream, but when their dirty waters mix with the Ganges, it will be found that they become as pure as the very Ganges itself. This is a worldly example given by Sant Kabir to show that people don't care to go to water which is dirty, but when that very water enters the pure flow, suddenly it takes on a new purity!

Likewise, whoever attends the discourses of the Sat Guru, has the Colour and the effects of those rays of Blessings and Grace on him. All kinds of people attend the discourses, and all of them will have Divine rays and the Power of God radiated to them. Sant Kabir has given great emphasis to this, saying that the thoughts of the Jiva who drinks that Nectar of Truth, henceforth become pious and clean in the Holy Satsang of the Master. In His Divine Company, thoughts of the Creator replace thoughts of the worldly life.

Sant Kabir says that there are two types of Satsang:

Sant Kabir says that there are two types of Satsang:

1. The *Outer Satsang* is the Holy Company of the Saint. By listening to His Discourses, one is able to know the Truth and all Spirituality. The mind becomes cleansed with the Master's Grace and attention when the devotee accepts the Teachings. The devotee then goes into the True Lane of the Creator, and rises up in Spirituality.

2. *Inner Satsang*, where the Surat becomes attached to the Lord and merges with Him. The Attention rises from the Inner Self into Higher Spiritual Realms, which comes about after the Master accepts him as His devotee, by bestowing on him His own Life-Impulse.

Being in the Master's Satsang is like entering into a Spiritual college where practical lessons of Love, as well as being attached with the Reality, are taught. It is a unique 'factory', where the Master turns out Perfect Human Beings. Greed, desire, and other worldly tendencies are crossed over, as the Master prepares to make the devotee's soul ready to be One with the Creator.

Satsang is the only true pilgrimage where the sins which have been developed over aeons of lifetimes get burned off, and the person becomes pure and pious. Sant Kabir says that to have the Holy Company of the Saint gives more beneficial results than sitting in penance for hundreds of years, because in the Satsang one sees first-hand the true life of Spirituality.

People become Spiritually awake in the Master's Holy Company, which gives upliftment to the soul. The Master bestows His own Life-Impulse, and makes the devotee to become One with God. Those hearts that are full of anguish and distress receive Divine inspiration. The Master's Life-Impulse is His Divine attention, and whoever goes to Him has the effect of this compassion and Love.

Kabir Sahib says that by having the Company of the Saint, the soul develops the faith of God. The unbounded peace and tranquillity of the Master's Higher Company has a great effect on the devotee. But in order to have the full benefit of His Grace, when one comes into the Holy Company of a Great Godman, he should sit quietly with Him and let His Spiritual rays cleanse his heart and affect his soul. There is great peace in the Godly Charging that radiates from the Master.

In the Holy Company of the Master and His Satsang, all worldly afflictions vanish. "Have the Holy Company only of the Saint, Who will grant you salvation. He is the One Who will take care of you, now and in the hereafter. Where God's devotees live, there God also lives. In the Holy Presence of the Saint, this Grace drenches the devotee in a tranquillity

Sant Kabir says that day by day, the soul becomes dyed in the Colour of the Master's Truth, which enables the devotee to cross over the Ocean of life. The Saint doesn't see the caste or creed of the soul. He sees only the soul inside the covering of the body. Even sinners and atheists attend His Holy Company, and all receive Divine Radiation of the Power of God. These Blessings of Grace affect the person, regardless of whether he knows it or not.

Due to the Master's benevolence, one can understand the true meaning of Spirituality. Kabir Sahib says, "Only from the True Master can one know the Truth. In His Holy Company, thoughts of the Creator take place. One understands more and more Spirituality, with the effects of His Divine and Spiritual Radiation. Wherever the Discourses of Oneness are given, where only the Creator and His Truth are spoken of, that is called the True Satsang."

"In the Holy Company of the Saint," He continues, "the mind becomes refreshed and revived. Evil thoughts, vain beliefs, wrong notions and superstitions run away, to be replaced by a peace that is no longer disturbed by lust, anger, and greed. The soul begins to imbibe the Master's qualities of compassion, detachment and Discrimination. Do not waste a single moment in the conduct of the search for a True Master. Make all haste. Life is uncertain, and one should lose no time in striving to make progress on the Spiritual Path."

moment in the conduct of the search for a True Master. Make all haste. Life is uncertain, and one should lose no time in striving to make progress on the Spiritual Path."

Some people have never taken work from the Fifth Element, the faculty of Discrimination. Their nights are spent in sleep, and the days in material gain. That kind of person has not, even for an instant, put any thought on the Name Divine. Sant Kabir is describing how almost the entire world is going in that direction.

On the other hand, those lucky people who have the Holy Company of the Saint and obtain His Grace, have the Master's Love and compassion. They have made use of their Power of Discernment, and know what is right and what is wrong. They can think and realize where they are going after their physical death.

Sant Kabir says that those who have been inspired to repeat God's Holy Name remain wrapped in the fragrance of His Loving devotion. He emphasizes again and again that one receives real benefit and a Living Impulse of Life only on meeting the Living Saint. Such an encounter is the greatest good fortune of the human birth, because devotion to the Master precedes devotion to the Holy Naam.

Being in the Master's Sacred Company, one begins to have the same thoughts that the Master has, and the devotee slowly imbibes the Master's Divine qualities. With continued devotion to the Beloved Sat Guru, the person begins to view all those around him as his loving friends. He sees the same Effulgent Light of Almighty God in them.

Sant Kabir says, "This Blessed condition only comes when the person knows himself. He feels sweet peace and tranquillity permeating every pore of his body. Before that, the person used to have so much malice in his heart, and many illnesses throughout his body. When he is lucky enough to receive God's Grace through the Master's Satsang, then he begins to see the Light of God everywhere, in every atom, in every flower. Eventually, he has absolutely no fear of physically dying. He becomes fearless, and joyfully merges in God's Nectar of Grace."

He continues, "By the Grace of God, the Word made flesh has entered my inner house. The Master has given me a Contact with the God within me. The result is that my heart is completely still, in bliss and peace, and my mind becomes calm and serene. So fortunate am I! I have escaped the *Wheel of Life*, the Cycle of birth and death, and I am at home with God. I am greatly fortunate that I have met with the Master. When I looked into His eyes, I received from Him an Impulse of Life, since life comes only from Life."

When the devotee meets a Person Who is an Embodiment of Spirituality, his soul becomes inspired. "One endowed with Spirituality can uplift the soul. That person sees the Truth for himself. Whomever looks intently into the Master's eyes gains Life, with which the Master is overflowing because His soul is fully developed. The Master has complete control over His whole being. In the Company of One Whose soul is strong, one's own soul will start seeing the Truth for himself."

Sant Kabir says, "The Sat Guru is He, meeting Whom the mind becomes still. We do not get this from books. This is what one can have from the Holy Presence of the Master Who is God-Intoxicated. Through His Godly eyes, whoever goes to Him becomes purified. The Master's Radiation has a cleansing effect, through and through. In due course of time, the devotee will be dyed in whatever Radiation the Master has in His soul. This can be developed only when nothing remains between the devotee and the Master, not even the body. The devotee forgets the body and all its environments."

The True Master has withdrawn Himself from all the entanglements of the mind and the outgoing faculties. Turning within His own Self, He has come in Contact with God. We should pray for the Holy Satsang of such a soul, because this Association is had only with the Grace of God. "When one comes near the Master, it is just like coming near to God!"

#8-5 Faith in the Master

When the devotee becomes eager, with all passion and earnestness to find God, then with the Grace of the Sat Guru he crosses the Ocean of this worldly attachment and Illusion. Kabir Sahib says, "That devotee should have full faith in the Master, where God Himself, in all glory, all-wisdom, here and hereafter, is manifested. However, whoever thinks of the Sat Guru as an ordinary human being is illiterate about Spirituality, and he is doomed to drown again and again in this Deception and Illusion."

Sant Kabir tells us that Almighty God and True religion are not the property of any one sect or creed: They belong to all humanity. In many verses, He points out that Almighty God is One for all. True religion is not any sect. Every person is made up of soul, mind, and body, and whoever directs his attention towards the soul can attain the Spiritual miracle of God.

Sant Kabir says that when a person sees God's beauty with his own eyes and listens to the Sweet Melodies with his own ears, he has full conviction in his heart that there is an Oversoul. After developing full faith, he will have complete tranquillity and he will start to see this world as his own. As man is the image of God, he begins to see the whole world as One.

That Godly Colour comes on him, which teaches him how to take birth into the Beyond.

Sant Kabir asks, "What good is it, after death? Where is the proof that one will obtain God after death? There can be no true faith based on worldly wrangling." He explains that one has to come to the house of the Beloved with full heart and all devotion, without any fear or doubt. "Doubt and Illusion have to be cast out. One has to be a brave warrior and not to worry about what society thinks." He gives the example that when a true soldier goes to the battlefield, at that time he doesn't think of himself or who he has left behind. He goes there only to conquer and be victorious. In the same way, when one goes to a True Master, he should not concern himself with petty things that might deter him on the Spiritual Path.

Kabir Sahib says, "One doesn't have to be concerned about the world's opinion when he comes to the Master. Once the resolution has been made to surrender oneself wholly and solely to God, he should not look back! He should jump into the Love of God, Who will give unbounded Love, peace, and tranquillity."

He encourages, "When one becomes a devotee of a True Master and His Charan Kamal manifests as the Radiant Effulgent Form of the Master, that person's faith becomes completely steadfast." With the person's total faith in God, all questions, suspicions and Illusions vanish!

As the many wonderful stories about Kabir Sahib's greatness spread to neighbouring communities, more and more people began to flock to His house, some sincere in their search but many were just curiosity seekers. The ever-increasing flow of visitors began to come in the way of His Communion with God. He decided that this steady stream must be curtailed, so He thought of a way out. This scheme also provided an opportunity for Him to test the level of faith of one of His disciples.

Sant Kabir took along with Him a highly evolved Soul by the name of Ravi Das and another close devotee, a woman by the name of Ganekha (who later became known as a great *Mahatma*). Wandering through the streets, Sant Kabir brandished a flask of coloured water, pretending it was wine. This naturally created a scandal throughout the town. People began to laugh and shake their heads, saying that Kabir Sahib could not live the difficult and rigorous life of a Saint! The Brahmins and Mullahs started pointing Him out, "See! He is such a low caste person calling himself as 'pious', but the real thing has now come out!" They could only see from their own angle of vision, such narrowmindedness they had!

Sant Kabir went to visit *Raja Bir Singh*, the local King who was also His disciple. This King had always shown great respect whenever Sant Kabir would visit him. In fact, the King was so devoted that he used to get up from his throne, and let Sant Kabir sit there whenever He would visit the Court. However, today the King was totally shocked about this strange behaviour of Kabir Sahib. The scene in the Court today became so disturbing, with Kabir Sahib brandishing a bottle of 'whiskey' in one hand, and a woman on the other arm! It appeared as though Kabir Sahib was drunk!

The King was wonderstruck! What had happened to Kabir Sahib! Filled with despair and convinced that his Master was deceiving him, he was immediately filled with doubt and suspicion. In a voice that was both alarmed and annoyed, he thundered, *"What is this?"*

Suddenly Kabir Sahib began to pour coloured water from the bottle on the ground. When asked why He did this, Ravi Das spoke up and explained that there was a fire in a certain Temple, called *Jagannath Mandir*, at some distance away in a city called *Puri*, and that Sant Kabir was at that Temple not only putting out the fire, but also saving the life of a certain Priest. The King, in total disbelief, secretly noted down the time of this occurrence, and right away dispatched some messengers on horseback to that very Temple to find out the truth of this matter.

Sant Kabir took along with Him a highly evolved Soul by the name of Ravi Das and another close devotee, a woman by the name of Ganekha (who later became known as a great Mahatma). Wandering through the streets, Sant Kabir brandished a flask of coloured water, pretending it was wine.

In the meantime, Sant Kabir quietly went home, and the King was left to think over what had happened. When the King's inquiry ultimately revealed that indeed there had been a fire at that particular time, and that Kabir Sahib was there to put out the fire, as well as save the life of that Priest, the King was suddenly overcome with shame. Realizing the rudeness he had shown to Sant Kabir, he decided there was nothing to do but to seek His forgiveness, as was the custom of the time. However, it was known that Kabir Sahib would accept no gift from anyone. Therefore, in humbleness and remorse, the King took his whole family and started out on foot for Sant Kabir's house. The King realized that a devotee must have absolute faith in his Master. By surrendering his ego in a thus manner, the King became an example for others to develop intense devotion.

On another day, a wise and learned prominent political minister paid a visit to Benaras. This man, unfortunately, had been suffering from a chronic fever for some time. All manner of remedies had been tried by the best physicians from all over the land, but to no avail. After hearing about the greatness of the Godly Sant Kabir, he went quickly to Benaras.

When the Qazis, Mullahs, Brahmins, and Priests heard that this important man had arrived in their city, they flocked to him. They wanted him to use his governmental influence to uphold their list of grievances against Sant Kabir. They told him that this simple weaver was guilty of heresy, as He had given up the ways of Islam. To make their case seem all the more dramatic, they complained that Kabir Sahib spoke ill of the Hindu religion, too.

They recounted that Sant Kabir condemned putting full faith in the Vedas, the places of pilgrimage, and all the gods and goddesses, like Shiva and Ganesh. They protested that Sant Kabir placed Himself outside the boundaries of both Islam and Hinduism, and that He claimed to be God Himself! They went on and on with their complaints, being careful to point out that as a result of Kabir Sahib's growing popularity, there were very few people left in the city who even cared for the Pundits or the Priests!

However, in spite of all their best efforts to convince him otherwise, this man had in his mind to see Kabir Sahib for yet another reason. Now, it is a well-established fact that ardent lovers of God are invariably tried, sometimes in most unusual circumstances, in order to test their faith. Therefore, this man paid no heed to the bickering Priests. He left them all behind and went straight to the house of Sant Kabir. As soon as his eyes met those of the Great Master, the ailment mysteriously left him! Without his saying anything to Kabir Sahib, he was cured! His unwavering faith in Sant Kabir as the True Master, a Mouthpiece of God, was richly rewarded!

Sant Kabir describes several different attempts made by the various rulers of the time to persecute Him. He is teaching a great lesson that no harm can come to those people who have complete faith in their Master and God. Those people develop the insatiable longing for the Master that arises in the hearts of all true seekers. They realize that the Godman is the Personified Form of God.

#8-6 Seva (Selfless Service to the Master)

In Spirituality, it is an honour for one to serve in the Master's Divine Mission. Sant Kabir says, "Selfless service and selfless attendance is the True Seva. Whoever does selfless service always receives honour." He says however, that if one does Seva for the purpose of obtaining a reward, he doesn't get the full benefit from doing that Seva. Seva must be a selfless service. Any service rendered should not be with the thought of attaining salvation. While serving others, the person should not manage to serve his own self-interests. "How possibly can a selfish person meet God?" He continues, "The true devotee requests his Master for the Boon of Bhakti, saying, *I don't want anything for myself! Only I ask for Your Seva, day and night!*"

"If one does not render service, he is worthless and cannot expect to receive any reward in the Kingdom of God. The house where there is no regard nor interest to know about God or the Saint, no Seva of God or the Godman, that house is considered to be just like a cremation ground. Ghosts and demons dwell therein." He says, "People have only lust, Illusion, greed, and jealousy in them. Not even in a dream do they practice compassion, piety and service of the Master."

"All other types of practices without service, have no value. The True Seva of a Sat Guru is to continuously merge in Him. This Seva will take one into the Lap of God, both here and in the hereafter." He continues, "True Seva is done through the Saint, Who is in my heart forever. I have learned from the Master that whomsoever has continuous remembrance of the Master is doing true Seva." Sant Kabir objects to the rituals of outer worship, saying that the true ritual bath is to do the Seva and service of the Living Master.

There are four kinds of service:
1. By way of the physical body.
2. By way of wealth.
3. By way of the mind, which is when the devotee has full faith in the Master. That person withdraws his attention from outside attractions, and eventually separates it from the body and the senses.

4. By way of the Surat, meaning that the devotee gathers the attention by the method of the True Master.

Sant Kabir says that by doing Seva of the True Master, one should not bring along himself, his wealth, his property, or any honours that he might have. These should all be left behind, because they only serve to foster ego in the person. The intellect and all its clever schemes of the mind should be left aside. True service, done from the heart and the mind, is the only successful service. In this way, the devotee will have progress in his devotion.

The highest and the purest Seva is done for the Master, because He is the One Who is detached from all the material objects. By doing His Seva, one can also become free from worldly attachments. In other words, if the devotee worships the Master, he becomes the Master. He can see his fellow beings in the brotherhood of mankind. Love for the Creator and His entire Creation readily comes into the heart of the devotee. If the Master is the 'everything', then Seva is the 'prayer'.

Service is worship. The more one gets involved in selfless service, the nearer he will come to God. If one serves in the Master's Holy Mission selflessly, he is serving God Himself. Service becomes worship when the one who is being served, is considered to be God. When one sees the 'God' in that person, then the server becomes the servant. That person being served has provided the server with an opportunity to serve.

There is an old Hindu custom of giving alms to the Brahmin, as well as an offering in love, a gift as a token of gratitude for his having accepted the alms, and that the person has accepted that service. Feeling indebted to the one being served converts the service into worship. Service, therefore, creates humbleness. Service sees God in the lowly.

Sant Kabir emphasizes that the human body is obtained with the Grace of Almighty God for the purpose of doing Seva of the Master. He says that there are many great benefits of performing such service. That human body that does the Simran of God's Holy Names is so precious that even the gods and angels bow down to it. Whoever God grants the Grace to worship Him, that person becomes the True Devotee of God and he will meet God.

What is wanted is true service done from the heart and the mind. One should give the self and the mind to the Master and in that way, whatever one thinks will be through Him. "The intellect and the clever schemes should be left aside permanently. This type of devotee will have success in his devotion to the Master. This manifests the Love of God, and then one starts to Love all His Creation because it is made by the same Creator." Sant Kabir says, "Both of these Seva are good: remembrance of God, and remembrance of the Saint. God and the Master are One, because God works through the Master."

Sat Guru Seva is when the True Master gives Spiritual Initiation to the devotee, and then the devotee abides by the Master's Commandments with great devotion and Love, with full zeal and passion. The more one thinks about the Master, the more Grace flows from the Master to that devotee, regardless of where the Master is sitting physically. "Whoever worships the Saint, in Whom God is vibrating, that Saint makes the Creation to worship Him."

#8-7 Bhakti (Devotion to the Master)

"*Bhakti* is the first and most important condition in Spirituality," says Sant Kabir. *Bhakti* means devotion or worship done through meditation. The most important condition of Bhakti is Divine Love (also known as *Ishq* or *Prem*). "Love has to be there. Love and devotion have two different names, but they have one form. Without Love, one cannot do devotion and without devotion, there cannot be Love."

Sant Kabir explains in His verses that there is only a very slight difference between Love and devotion. Devotion is a spontaneous attraction which draws the devotee towards the Beloved, to further merge with the Almighty. Love is the merging of the soul with God, and the ecstasy of that bliss. Love for the Beloved makes a stillness in the heart of the devotee, and this becomes his very aim in life. The devotee drinks the Nectar of that stillness, and then he becomes complete in himself. Love is the true worship and true *Namaz* (Prayer) of God.

Sant Kabir says that the devotee must fully understand true Love and devotion. He says that in order to do this, the devotee should do such deeds as are pleasing to the Lord. One can know the Will of the Lord through the Graciousness of the Master, because the Will of the Master is the Will of God. God speaks through Him, and is manifested in His human body. It is the duty of the devotee to always act according to the Will of the Master. The secret of this is that when the disciple repeats the Holy Names given to him by the Master, he begins to live in His Will. His doubts and fears vanish, and he experiences an all-engulfing peace in his heart. Sufferings and miseries are removed, and he becomes blissfully happy, knowing that his coming and going in this world is forevermore finished.

Sant Kabir gives the example of a soldier, whom He describes to be a brave warrior. When that man leaves his home for the battlefield, he doesn't look back to think of anything else, and neither does he think of leaving the battle in the middle of the fighting. He only believes himself to be a great fighter and a supreme conqueror. He wants to win the war. Kabir Sahib is explaining that when one unfortunately has petty desires of the world, then that man has to fight with his own senses, just like a warrior. The Upanishads say, "Awake, O Man! Arise and stop not until the Goal is reached!"

That person, therefore, is the true conqueror, the true soldier, who has overcome the desires of his mind. He has reached his ultimate Goal, and he is the most lucky person in this whole Creation of God. However, as Sant Kabir emphasizes, this cannot be done without the guidance of a True Master, a Master General, Who guides the devotee at every step of the Spiritual Journey. Thus, the devotees of the Lord remain always in touch with the Lord. They see Him face to face, and therefore live in a state of perpetual Divine Intoxication and untold happiness. Those lucky people are rich in Divine Love, and they would gladly give away everything for His sake.

The Master is our real companion and true friend, for a true devotee of the Lord takes great delight in hearing sweet stories about the Lord. The Master speaks of things which are so dear to the devotee.

Sant Kabir says, "If anyone even in his dream should mutter the Holy Name of God, I would give my flesh to make shoes for his feet! If one has such a Love for the Master, that even in his sleep he takes His Holy Name, for their shoes I would give my own skin!"

His meaning is that the person should be devoted wholly and solely to God, and should look to the Master with full devotion. Every little gesture, every word that He says, how He looks, in contemplation of this, that lucky devotee forgets everything else. The devotee may be living in the world, but he remains unattached to the world. This type of devotion bears fruit.

A person who has not contacted the Holy Naam, whatever his religion, cannot enter within. Usually at the last moment, at the time of death or even when going to sleep, people are thinking of the world, and of the undone things they have left. But the person who is imbued with the Love of the Master, when going to rest he always sleeps in sweet remembrance of the Master. He feels that he is just going into the Lap of the Father. That person sleeps in His Sweet Remembrance throughout the night!

So Kabir Sahib is saying that the true devotee of the Master never forgets the Beloved Master. All through the day and night, no matter what he might be doing, his attention is always engaged in remembering Him. All the while, the thought of the Beloved takes possession of his mind. This is the symbol of a true devotee. He alone can be called a disciple, who sees the Light of God within himself.

Sant Kabir says that He prays everyone should listen to these Divine Words with full attention of mind and heart. If the mind keeps wandering into the outside world, that person cannot listen. Hearing is done with the ears, but *listening is done with the heart!* Withdrawing the thoughts from the world and connecting them with God, is the true devotion of the Master, which is devotion of the highest order.

"The Master bestows the Five Holy Words of the Sound Current, and these can take one into the Lap of God. This is called the True Worship. These are Unwritten Words, which come from Almighty God Himself!"

Sant Kabir has told us that once true Simran enters the heart, then Love in the Form of the Beloved comes to the eyes and stays there. Every pore of the body calls out to the Beloved "O Come!" and every cell vibrates with His Divine Nectar. The true devotee humbly requests his Master for this Boon of Bhakti. That lucky devotee says, "I don't want anything for myself. Only I ask for Thy Seva, day and night."

When this Blessed stage comes, then the devotee is performing a higher form of Bhakti, known as *Gurbhakti*. The word *Gurbhakti* means to have devotion for the Master. Sant

Kabir says, "To do Gurbhakti is not the work of a coward. You must take your head off with your own hand! That brave person is the one who can then fearlessly take the Blessed Holy Name of Sat Naam."

Acting and posing is very easy and commonly found, but true devotion from the heart for the Master is very difficult and rare. Sant Kabir remarks that when one receives the unbounded Spiritual Treasures, then the Guru helps the devotee to have devotion full of Love. This requires great good fortune, and one must come to the True Master. "Leave off all these outer, temporary pleasures to do the worship of the Sat Guru with full devotion. This precious human birth is not going to happen again and again. This is the golden opportunity while one still has the human body."

"Everyone has remembrance of God during times of hardship. When the life goes smoothly, no one even cares to think about these things. However, if one has prayer during good times, then the pinching effects of sorrow won't affect him."

One must, however, do Gurbhakti only for the sake of serving the Guru. He should not have any other purpose in his heart. "People are fond of doing Gurbhakti, but they have in their mind that thereby they will obtain worldly desires. Until the devotee doesn't cleanse his mind of these thoughts, he cannot have the Blessed Nectar of Bhakti. Those people call themselves to be the Guru's slave, but they don't even attempt to curb their minds. They say that they have fully surrendered to the Master, but actually they have not done so in their heart of hearts!"

Sant Kabir says, "If God becomes displeased with you, then there could be a way out of this, but if the Sat Guru should become displeased, there is no way out! However, if the Guru is pleased, God will also be pleased, for God has manifested Himself in the Guru."

All Boons will be granted to that devotee who does as the Guru instructs. The disciple should try all the time to do his best, and to listen to the commandments of the Master, trying to put them into practice in his own life. He should be careful never to overstep the bounds of respect for the Guru. If the Sat Guru should give a command, the devotee should carry it out, believing in his heart of hearts that the Sat Guru knows what is truly best for him.

#8-8 Puja (Worship of the Master)

One worships the Master with his full heart when he listens to His Holy Discourse attentively, without letting any other thought come into the mind. Sant Kabir says, "As long as one desires for heaven, he cannot have the bliss of the Master's Sacred Company in his heart. It is True Worship when this Charan Kamal becomes manifest in the heart."

One does this Puja to a Power that is higher than himself, in order to have Spiritual attainment. However, external worship is most predominant all over the world, and throughout all religions. People are supposed to gather together in religious places in order to have the true meanings of the Scriptures explained and understood. These precious Teachings must be gone through carefully in order to put them into practice. However, almost everyone just bows their head and offers flowers at these places, thinking that this is the only way of worshipping.

The outer Temples are to be respected, but there is no truer Temple than the Master Himself. God has manifested Himself in the Saint, and God lives in Him. That is the only place that a person should bow his head. The True Puja is to go inwards, and when one offers the flowers of the heart and the mind for devotion, then that worship is accepted by Almighty God.

As the Master and the Supreme Lord are One, so also the worship of the Master is truly the worship of the Lord. Sant Kabir says that the Master is God's Holy Form. "The Master has merged in the Creator. Whoever worships the Master, is worshipping the Creator."

Saints believe in the Religion of Love, which comes from within. Their concern is the Love and devotion in the heart for God, and the sincerity and earnestness in one's desire to meet the Lord. Only real Love and devotion for God through the Saint can take the soul back to God. People want to meet God and to merge into Him, so they search for His Lover, the Godman. He is a God-Realized Soul Who is in constant tune with Him. It is through association with Him that one automatically comes in touch with God.

Sant Kabir tells us about the Master's method, full of Love and compassion. "O Soul! If you continuously remember the Lord with great Love, you will never be defeated in this worldly life. Sincerity is the basis of this Love."

He says that those who are devoted to the Master and follow His Commandments live carefree in all the three worlds. "If you put full faith and Love towards the Master, then do as He tells you. Don't leave anything in the middle, but develop and fulfill it." He gives the example that if unripe mustard is harvested, nothing can be done with it. No one can eat that seed, nor even give it to the animals. In other words, patience and perseverance are required for success on the Path towards

God. In the same way, if the Spiritual pursuit is left in the middle, nothing will be gained from only that beginning effort.

#8-9 Bireh

(The Longing and Pining of Separation)

Separation is when the devotee is away from his Master, and he cries for Him. Sant Kabir says, "A true devotee cannot live without the Master's Love. Every long second is just like misery for him. When these pangs of separation come into the heart of the disciple, all worldly desires vanish into the air." There are no attractions left for him in the world. His forlorn heart just wants to run away from them. The devotee longs only to be in the Holy Company of the True Master and other lovers of God. That person cannot, even for a moment, bear to be away from the Godman. "Without seeing the Master, the devotee burns in the agony of this cruel separation."

This is known as the condition of *'Bireh'*, and this is a very intense pain. The devotee has developed so much Love for his Master that he feels he will die in this absence. Sant Kabir compares this condition to a fish out of water, which cannot live for a moment without the water. The fish gasps for its very life-breath, because the water is the only Life-Impulse that the fish has.

In the same way, without the Master the breath of the devotee is just gasping and fading away. "This separation has made a very strong army which has covered me all over. Neither it will let me die, nor let me to live!"

In another verse, Sant Kabir speaks like a devotee smitten with Bireh. "This separation is like a cobra that has controlled me fully and has wounded my heart. There is no Mantra (magic words) that will wash away this pain of separation from the Lord. Whoever has felt this kind of pain cannot live, but even if he does survive, he lives like a madman in this world. The Beloved Spouse should not turn His beautiful face away." Sant Kabir prays to Almighty God to have mercy on such a devotee afflicted with this condition.

Another illustration that He uses is of the *Koonj*, a bird which flies all through the night trying to meet its mate. Both the male and the female Koonj fly here and there all night, each looking for the other, but unfortunately they are doomed to meet only in the morning. The person who is separated from God, however, neither meets Him at night nor in the morning!

In yet another comparison Sant Kabir says, "The sky is full of clouds and the rain has filled all the low and high places.

The poor *Chatrik* (rain bird) really wants the first rain-water, and will surely die without it. Its thirst is overpowering. Tell me, what could be his condition?" This bird will only partake of the first rain-water. There might be puddles of water all around, but unless the bird drinks at the beginning of the rain, he will die of thirst.

This same painful condition cannot come in the devotee without the Grace of the Sat Guru. Sant Kabir talks about the sweet Nectar, the ecstasy of tranquillity, of having the Sweet *Darshan* (Blessing) of the Master, and how the devotee is pining to have it. He is suffering badly in body, mind, and soul without having it.

"A million speak of these pangs; yet how few realize that *Divine Love is not to lose remembrance even for an instant!* It is by this kind of Love that one rises above the body into the Beyond, and becomes selfless. Love can only be imbibed from the Love-laden heart of a God-inspired soul."

There is one condition, however, for all this good fortune to happen. Sant Kabir reveals, "One has to have the stamp of good Karma on his forehead. These Karmas are the reactions of good deeds made in both previous births and the present life. It is the Grace of the Creator that God makes the Way for that Jiva to obtain the True Master Who will take him to his Eternal Home in Sach Khand."

Whoever is One with God cannot live even for a moment without His Divine Nectar, and without listening to His Unstruck Melody, the Celestial Music. The Saint will imbibe only that Godly Nectar, none other. "The natural Inner Melody is continuously flowing of itself, but only a rare soul knows of this communion. The true Simran consists of the perpetual attunement of the soul with the Inner Music, without any outer aid. He who is in contact with this hidden Crest Jewel is the true friend of humanity."

The highest honour that one could have in life, is to have God's Life-Impulse. The more that person Loves God and His Creation, the more God comes near to him. One single thought of the Beloved, and tears start flowing like rain-pearls from the eyes of this forlorn lover.

Sometimes, however, it happens that the devotee is away from the Beloved Master, and that time is very painful for the poor disciple. In this connection, Sant Kabir prays, "O my Master! It is better that instead of turning Your back to me, that You cut me so that I die! Without You, it is very hard to live! I am suffering greatly. When You come and embrace me, I am so very happy. O listen to my earnest prayer and kindly accept it. I can sacrifice myself for You. Why are You killing me by turning Your back to me?"

All True Devotees eventually go through the pain and fire of this separation. The Path of Spirituality is paved with the pearls of their countless tears. Sant Kabir offers their prayers, "Come at once and comfort me; otherwise I shall give up my life! Either bring death to my body if it is to be separated any longer from You, or give me Your Darshan, the Glory of Your Sight. I am unable to bear the pain of this separation any longer."

With Simran and Dhyan, a person is given the courage to endure this separation. He can go towards his Beloved by way of this 'wet rain' coming through the eyes. Sant Kabir says, "If you try to hide from the world the secret of your Love towards God, and even if you don't speak from the tongue, the eyes will reveal all. Whoever is in the body and has manifested true Love, cannot hide it. It cannot be spoken through the mouth, but the eyes reveal all!"

Sant Kabir has fully described the condition of one so drenched in the Love of the Beloved. He says, "The flame of Love is not so easy to disguise once it has entered a person's heart. He will not talk about his Love but if you look into his eyes, they will reveal the secret of his condition." That lucky person reaches the Ka'aba of his heart very soon in this way!

When one falls in Love, life thrills with the magic of Love. One's feet hardly seem to touch the ground. He seems to fly in the air, as if he has developed wings. His face lights up with an unknown charm, as his eyes begin to convey something not of this world. It is very difficult to hide Love. The eyes and everything about the person will give the news of it.

Every pore of the body will be saturated with Love, because Love is automatically a remembrance. The devotee is always thirsting for the Lord, as the lover is for the Beloved. Even a single drop satisfies. One drop becomes a pearl. When this afflicted person becomes so very thirsty, even ordinary water becomes like pearls. When the longing of the true devotee becomes so great, a single Teaching of the Master becomes like a Jewel. The Master fills the person with all His Godly attributes and stirs the Glory within. The Music inside, that lay dormant all this time awaiting His Magic Touch, bursts forth in glorious melodies.

Sant Kabir continues, "O God! My fervour to drink of this Divine Nectar will never vanish. Almighty God is an unending Ocean of all this Nectar!" The devotee cannot survive without Divine Ambrosia. Giving worldly examples to show that He is so much absorbed in Almighty God, Sant Kabir says that God has kept Him like a parrot in the cage of His Godly palm, safe from the Agent of Death which comes like a cat, ready to pounce upon the poor bird. He gives another example, that Almighty God is like a tree, and that the devotee is a little bird sitting peacefully high up on one of the branches.

He says, "The unfortunate ones cannot see God without His Grace. What would be the condition of those who do not even have a glimpse of God, who do not have even one Drop of that Divine Nectar? People who have bad Karma cannot have this Blessed Darshan of Almighty God." Sant Kabir says that the true devotee is all the time with God, in His Lap, and will continue to be so, even after the end of His physical existence. He affirms that He is God's determined follower, now and forever more!

Sant Kabir is describing the condition of a true lover of God, who has Drunk deeply of the Divine Nectar obtained through the Grace of the Master. That devotee has become dyed in the Colour of his Master's qualities and attributes. The Master is filled with the Love of God. He is all Truth, an Ocean of Love, Sweet Ecstasy and Nectar. If the Master gives even a little taste of these Blessed qualities, the devotee's body begins to burn with the fire of longing, of pining, of zeal, combined with passion for more and more! Ultimately, as these fires continue to rage, there are no words to describe the condition of that devotee!

With heart-breaking gasps, the devotee pleads, "O my Master! Come and meet me quickly; otherwise I will give up my life right away! Either give me death, or come and Bless me with Your Darshan! I cannot bear any more the burning of this cruel separation from You! With the pangs of separation, my body and limbs are becoming lifeless. My soul has left the body and has attached itself to Your Lotus Feet. In this condition, death comes looking for me. I cannot live; yet strangely enough, I cannot die!" The devotee says that he would welcome physical death, just to be free of these 'painful' symptoms of Divine Love!

He continues, "Each passing moment is giving me great pain and anguish. I have no peace of mind, day or night. My breath is finishing! This anguish is continuing, and is not leaving the cage of this body. The pain of separation is eating up my heart!"

Then Sant Kabir comments, "It is a strange thing that the fire which burns inside the heart has no smoke. Whoever has that fire, he is the only one who knows of its heat, as well as *the One Who has caused the fire!*"

There is no medicine to relieve these symptoms, nor to calm down the raging fires of anguish within the devotee. Sant Kabir compares this sweet pain of separation from the Beloved to an arrow that has become lodged halfway through the heart. This kind of Love is so intense, that it will bear all the pains of the world for just one sweet Glance of the Beloved Master, Who will quench this Thirst with His Blessed Darshan. No matter how much the lover Loves the Beloved, however, the Master's Love is much more for that devotee who has this condition of true longing in his heart. Sant Kabir is describing the true anguish of the soul for its Master, with great longing and pining to see Him.

Sant Kabir uses the theme of the soul as the *'bride'* or the *'lover'*, and Almighty God as the *'Eternal Spouse'* or the *'Beloved'*. He says, "The bride is crying from the core of her heart to have the sight of the Beloved. At the Seat of the Soul behind and between the two eyebrows, the soul is eagerly watching and waiting to catch a glimpse of the Beloved Spouse. She knows only the overwhelming hunger and thirst to have the Darshan of her Beloved, and she will not move until she has received this Blessing."

Kabir Sahib uses another example from everyday village life as an example of this Bireh. He poetically says that in the East when a crow sits on somebody's house and sings, it means that a very special guest will soon arrive. No doubt this is a myth, but still people believe it. He compares the person seeing this crow to the soul, who is crying and yearning with all her heart to have the Darshan of her Beloved, and doesn't want the crow to move from her sight.

This signifies such a great anticipation that the Beloved Eternal Spouse is the special guest, and is bound to come! He *must* come; otherwise all life will drain out of the body. This kind of Love can be known only by those souls who have experienced such deep devotion and zeal. It has come to the stage where the soul says that the Holy Naam is the only thing at her side, and the Holy Name of the Beloved has kissed her lips. She doesn't forget her Beloved, even for a moment.

Sant Kabir is giving another example of this pain of separation. He says that in the worldly love affair between a man and a woman, once they know each other well, nobody can make them apart in their love, faith, and compassion for each other. They have an affinity so much so, that they feel like they are two souls in one body. There comes a time in most relationships between the spouses that the two souls cannot be separated from each other. They feel very restless if they do not see each other even for a moment. They wait only for the times when they can be together. Sant Kabir describes this painful separation that worldly lovers, as well as Divine Lovers, experience.

Giving many different illustrations of painful separation, He tells us about the bird called the *Chakkor*, who has such a love for the moon that as soon as the moon rises, the bird looks at it without blinking or moving. The moon slowly moves across the sky, but this bird does not move even one inch. It just keeps turning its head so that it does not leave off seeing its beloved moon even for a fraction of a moment. As the moon rises further, its head turns even more until finally its head is resting totally backwards. Even though the bird's neck might be aching, it does not leave off seeing the moon!

This is the 'pull' of Love that comes between the lover and the Beloved, and when that condition comes, they are inseparable. They become as one. "Where is the Master, and where does the spirit dwell? How can the two unite? For without union, the spirit has no rest."

"Come to my eyes and I will close them. I won't let anyone see You; neither You to see anyone. Whenever I sleep, You are always with me, and when I wake up, You will be always there with me. My desire is to be with You, not to forget You for a moment!"

He continues, "Without You, my eyes are becoming full of anguish and zeal. I search for You every moment, but You have not come. Without meeting You, how can I be happy? My condition is quickly deteriorating."

Sant Kabir explains that the devotee spends all his days in waiting for the Beloved. His eyes keep waiting and longing for Him. The night has gone, but the Divine Spouse has not come. He is waiting very anxiously and impatiently to meet Him. Sometimes the Beloved plays and teases the lover. The lover says, "O Lord! I am waiting, but You have turned Your face away from me. I cannot bear this. Why kill me by turning away? It would be better for me if my body was cut into pieces, rather than You turn away from me!"

This type of prayer happens when the soul is pining in separation from the Lord. The soul can only pray for union with Him. "O my Lord! O my Saviour! Accept my humble prayer! I will sacrifice everything I have, even my own self. I am so much hankering to see Your Blessed face. O my Beloved! Please have mercy on my condition, and turn Thy face towards me. I can't bear any more this condition. You will realize why, when You see me! Don't even think of turning Your back towards me. Look at me! I am dying! I will turn my face towards You, even if my body becomes into pieces!"

"O Lord, my body will have no life left in it without Your Love. You have put me in this condition. I am Yours! O have mercy upon me! There should be no gap of separation between You and me! You are playing hide-and-seek with me. You are the Lord of Lords, and You have all the patience, but I have none. I am Your spouse and You are my Beloved. There is no world without You, O Lord! Have Grace and compassion on me. The radiation of Love that You have given to me, I want more! I cannot live without that!"

Although the times of Love are the most happy ones for the lover, there are times of seeming 'indifference' of the Beloved.

There are basically two times that are the hardest for the lover. One is in waiting for the Beloved, when time is so cruel that it doesn't even move. The second is when the Beloved has just left. These times, however pathetic and painful, are actually beneficial for the lover, because these Blessed moments bring tears of pearls which wash the Path (clean the heart) for the Beloved to come. In this type of pain, all the attachments with the worldly relations leave, one by one. In other words, the devotee doesn't put his attention towards the world to the extent he was involved in it before. Actually, now he doesn't have any interest in it at all. Now he recognizes what the true form of Illusion is, and exactly what the worldly attachments are, and why they become as hindrances on the Spiritual Path.

It seems to be beyond expression to properly describe the pitiful condition of Bireh. Actually, it has to be Experienced, because this is also a great Boon given by the Sat Guru to make His devotee become more patient, while at the same time makes him burn more and more with passion. This pain of separation is exactly what is needed to produce a zealous 'wanting' to be with the Master. One can reach all the way up to Almighty God Himself, with one truly heart-felt sigh!

Sant Kabir is explaining the condition of a true devotee who has these Experiences, and tries to tell about them in worldly words. "It was a great good fortune that I have come into the

Company of a Perfect Master, and with His Grace and His compassion, I quaffed of the sweet Nectar of God's Love. I readily surrender my mind, body, and soul to Him. To be in His Holy Company, and to have His Divine radiation fills me with Inner knowledge and righteousness. I only desire to drink deeply of the Godly Nectar streaming forth from His eyes."

He continues, "My condition can be counted in minutes, hours, every moment, for He takes me and my attention inwards. I have totally lost my *Buddhi* (the thinking and reasoning ability). Due to this Divine Intoxication, the world thinks that I am not in my right senses."

Then Kabir Sahib explains this condition even further. It is called '*Pahgul*' in the East, and in the true sense of this word, Pahgul means Love. But when there is a little pause between '*pah*' and '*gul*', it means something different. '*Pah*' means the person who has obtained something he wanted, and '*Gul*' means the Treasure, the Reality, that he wanted to obtain. So, somebody who is '*Pah-gul*' is actually somebody who has obtained something for which he passionately desired. He not only has listened to the Master, but he has also absorbed His Teachings. He became that Truth, that Reality. They are the fortunate ones who attain their objective in life, especially in this way, rather than being lost in the pursuits of the world and its affairs.

In another sense, this word *Pahgul* is also commonly used to mean someone who has become crazy, or mad. To the worldly people, it seems that the God-realized person has gone 'mad' to the world. That devotee says, "People say that I have lost my senses, and I do not recognize even myself now. What can the world know of my condition?"

He says that those people are truly 'mad' who have not realized their own selves. They have not seen the True God and have not Experienced the ecstasy, the Inebriating Power of the Sat Guru. "I am so much Intoxicated in my Master and in His Love, that this Intoxication is now my very Life. It is the Life of my life. It is my Wealth. Now I know my True Self, through the Grace of my Master."

Sant Kabir gives yet another example of Bireh. He says that ocean divers bring the conch up from the sea floor, and it is this same conch that is blown at sunrise in each and every Temple. It is said that when the conch is blown, it actually cries out in separation from the sea, that it wants to go back to its home. Like a small child separated from the mother, the conch screams in the pain of this separation right there in the Temple. Sant Kabir compares this conch to a person who is given a human birth, but has totally forgotten his Source, the Creator. The person does not cry out in separation but this lowly shell does, right in the Temple, hankering to once again merge in its beloved ocean.

The devotee cries out to the Master, "In this separation, I have made my eyes as two begging bowls, which are beseeching for Your Beloved Darshan and Grace, day and night. I have made my body into a lamp and my tongue into a wick. Instead of oil, my blood burns as fuel. O God! It would be so wonderful if I could see and have Your Darshan!" He has very graphically portrayed this painful separation.

He continues, "I have only bones left in my body. All my flesh is gone. Now the crows are waiting to eat these bones. My misfortune is that until now my Beloved has not returned. This separation has eaten up my flesh, and has made a living cremation ground of my life."

Continuing on this painful topic, He says, "When the 'hit' of this separation strikes the devotee, then the whole body breaks into pieces. This pain can only be known by the One who is giving it, or by that person who has that same pain within him. In separation from the Beloved, the soul is most anxious and restless. Day by day, the face becomes pale, like the dry *paan* leaf."

He says, "One should remember the Master until his body turns into dust! He should never leave off this sweet memory."

In heartfelt separation from the Master, the devotee says, "Even this place doesn't appeal to me. My beloved Inner City is so enticing, so beautiful, that nobody wants to leave once he has arrived. Here, there is no moon, sun, nor water. Is there somebody who can take this message to my Beloved, and tell Him of my great pain and anguish? What a wonderful day it would be when the Master catches hold of my hand, directs me to sit in the shadow of His Lotus Feet, and makes me His own!"

These are the only words that can be used, because what the devotee gets from the radiation and the Love-laden Glances of the Master has no worldly equivalent. When the devotee anxiously waits for these Glances and very eagerly wants to see the Master and have His Darshan, then each and every moment for that devotee is like the passing of hundreds of years. He feels that way without seeing the Master, but then that burning desire of pining, that smouldering fire of anguish, which is called Bireh, develops deep in the heart of that lucky person.

#8-10 Sweet Praises of the Master

Kabir Sahib writes passionately about the Master, "I wish and long for the Dust of His Feet--the Holy Naam that has created the Universe. His Lotus Feet are the True Wealth and a Haven of Peace. They grant ineffable wisdom and lead one on the Path Godward."

He continues, "In all the three Regions (the Physical, the Astral, and the Causal), there is nothing to compare with the greatness of the Sat Guru. God may not be doing anything for the follower in these Regions, but the Sat Guru does *everything!*"

He says that there is no one compared to the Sat Guru, not even in the seven *Deeps* (the Worlds), in the nine *Khands* (Regions), neither in the three *Lokhs* (Regions) of the Physical, the Astral, and the Causal, nor in *Brahmand* (the Super Causal) with its twenty-one Stages.

He emphasizes, "Even if one searches all throughout these Regions, he cannot find an equal to the Sat Guru. He is the only One Who truly cares about and remembers the devotee."

"The Sat Guru resides in the *Gagan* (the Great Spiritual Realm above), and the disciple in the *Ghat* (the place between the two eyebrows). When the two, the *Surat* (the attention) and the *Shabd* (the Holy Sound Current) meet, they are united forevermore." Kabir Sahib is saying that one should come to the Perfect Master, a Godman, Who is commissioned by the Creator to bring back the souls from this world of Maya and Illusion.

Sant Kabir gives thanks to the Master for all His unbounded Love and Grace. "This sigh will ever leave my heart; that *I can do nothing in return for all that the Sat Guru has done for me!* Without a True Master, there is no right understanding, and therefore no real progress. Without the right understanding, each one sits in his own pride, saying, 'My way is the only right one!' and attempts to force everyone else to accept it."

He says, "The more the Beloved gives me of His compassion and Grace, through the Glances of Love from His eyes, the more it seems to me that the whole world is saturated with His Love. Godly Light pours forth through His body and His Blessings of Light and Life stream unending from His Love-laden eyes. I have no interest of any kind in the world. I don't want to cling to this perishable world now that I know the Reality and the Truth that Almighty God resides in my Master. I know that I cannot live without His Darshan, and the more He showers His Grace on me, the more I crave for it. His Divine Love makes me more and more Thirsty. In His Blessed Company, I receive peace of mind and untold bliss."

The person who does exercise of the body can become a great athlete, and thousands of people will respect him. When one does exercise of the heart and intellect, he becomes a wise person. In thousands of people, he is one of a kind. However, one who does exercise of the soul in meditation, becomes revered and powerful. That person is Loved and adored *by millions!*

The Masters are Those Who have seen the Truth, and therefore, Their statements are correct. The Scriptures contain the words of Those Who had this right understanding. Meeting the Sat Guru opens the Path of right perception, and by Experiencing the Inner knowledge, the devotee becomes the one who sees. When the attention withdraws from the outside world, and the body becomes numb, then that devotee can say, *"Yes, I have Experienced It!"*

The Master does not impart anything of Himself to the devotee, but rather He awakens the disciple's latent faculties. The Master is Truth Personified, and is beyond the intellect and the senses. There is no difference between the Master and Almighty God. Devotion to the Master is the same as devotion to the Lord!

In the normal waking state, it is not easy to gather the concentration at the eye focus. However, when the disciple's heart becomes pure and devoted with constant practice, the mind gradually becomes motionless. It is this one-pointed attention which reveals the Reality. The world within is stable and permanent. The soul becomes virtually bathed in Celestial Light. Once the Radiant, Resplendent Form of the Master manifests itself, it will always be there to protect and take the soul to the Upper Spiritual Realms. The Master is like a sheet anchor, the sustenance and the only constant companion in this world and also the next. His Radiant, Effulgent Form urges the devotee to ascend to even Higher Regions.

Kabir Sahib had a very advanced devotee by the name of Queen Indra Mati. She has praised Sant Kabir, saying that "You are the One Who bestowed such Grace and the Godly Blessing of Spiritual Initiation on this Path, and granted me great peace." She was an especially devoted soul, who dedicated herself with great passion and zeal to her meditations. Making quick Spiritual progress, the doors to the Upper Realms were opened and she soon reached the abode of the Lord.

Such a spectacular scene she had never seen! Myriads of Lights dazzled the drops of air, making the whole atmosphere into millions of tiny light bulbs. The warmth and fragrance and brilliance of so many lights blended all together showered her in a very fine drizzle of great Love and untold peace. She glided through the air almost as if on wings, floating ever onwards and upwards. As she approached the Holy Throne in the Region of the Highest Spiritual Bliss (*Sach Khand*), she was astounded by the sparkle of inlaid precious diamonds, emeralds and rubies. She drew ever closer to observe that there were many other jewels and shining pearls, all bursting with Light, each new one looking more splendid than the last! She had never seen so many precious stones together in one place! The throne itself was spectacular, with a very high back, and large arm rests flowing in graceful curves. As she came even more near this amazing sight, she was flabbergasted to find Lord Kabir sitting there in all His Godly splendour! He smiled, beaming such Loving happiness from His Godly eyes. She was enveloped in so much joy and peace that she was dazzled.

Wonderstruck and with great astonishment, she gasped, "O Master, O my Great Lord! Why didn't You tell me earlier that you were the King (*Sat Purush*) of Sach Khand? Why did you hide this great secret from me?" She marvelled how was it possible for such beauty, such radiance and supreme glory to be concealed in the physical world! However, in truth, the physical world does not have the power to reflect even *one millionth part* of the radiance and brilliance of that place where resides the Supreme Being!

Sant Kabir smiled His Godly smile, and gently replied that if He had revealed His True Identity earlier, she would not possibly have believed Him! This is the True Spirituality, that until one does not see with his own eyes, he truly cannot have faith! ***Spirituality is a matter of personal Experience!***

In all humility, Queen Indra Mati was so thankful to Sant Kabir to have Graciously awakened her from the worldly slumber to behold the beautiful Vistas within. "Blessed is my True Master, by Whose Grace, I have achieved union with Almighty God!" She also had great love and respect for her husband, and related to her Great Master that her husband had never interferred in her worship. She realized that if he had not allowed her to serve the saints, she would be nowhere Spiritually. Sant Kabir was touched by this utmost devotion, and in His great mercy He granted her heartfelt prayers to bring her husband also back to Sach Khand. Thus, Lord Kabir Himself graciously went down to the Earth-Plane to rescue her husband from the clutches of Maya.

Those who meet the Sat Guru are granted a Connection with Almighty God. The Master does this through His own Life-Impulse, uniting the devotee directly with God. The Master merges the devotee with Himself, and then with God. Kabir Sahib says, "He lifts the veil before my eyes, and I gaze on Him day and night. O Sadhus, such is the Sat Guru I cherish!"

Almighty God resides in the human body. Where He has manifested Himself, He is called a *Saint* (because the Saint is the highest level of attainment). He is also called a *Sat Guru*. There is a huge difference, however, between a *Guru* and a *Sat Guru*. A *Guru* is like a teacher, just like a doctor or a carpenter can also be a teacher, but a *Sat Guru* is One Who is chosen by God to take certain souls back to their Eternal Home. The Guru can also be illustrated to be a Saint, but only the Sat Guru is met inside, in His Luminous Astral Form at the Seat of the Soul. He is competent to take the souls under His care beyond the third Spiritual Region.

Only these special Souls, where the Creator manifests Himself, are commissioned by God to take the souls back to their True Home. They are called as *Sat Guru, Puran Guru*, or *True Master*. There is always one or sometimes two in the world, out of millions of so-called *Saints* or *Sadhus*.

Sant Kabir says that the devotee must have determination and perseverance on the Path, as well as follow the Master's instructions with implicit faith. The Master is an embodiment of the Lord Himself. He descends from the Higher Spiritual Realms to bestow upon the seeker the Blessed Gift of Spiritual Initiation, and to guide him back to his True Home in Sach Khand. The Master showers immense Grace on mankind willingly, without complaint, and without any form or recompense. The Master might also have a family, a caste and a creed into which He was born, but nevertheless His

Real Form is very different. He is God-manifested on earth, as a "Godman".

The True Master is like an Advanced Teacher who can help and train his students (devotees) in the Science of the Soul. One cannot go into the Higher Spiritual Realms without a Living Adept of this stature. When the devotee puts one-pointed devotion towards the Master, he achieves communion with the Lord. The Key to the Tenth Door is in the possession of the Master. Without true devotion and service to Him, the Pathway remains closed.

Kabir Sahib asks, "What do you really need? Come to the True Saint, and He will bestow on you the rare Treasure of Holy Naam. By having this, you don't have to beg for anything else. You won't owe anything to anybody when you come to the Master. He wipes out all previous actions and reactions with His Grace and compassion, and He takes upon Himself the heavy burden of these past Karmas. Only a True Godman can do this!"

He points out that one cannot get the Spiritual Initiation without the Master, and liberation is not possible without this Gift of the Holy Naam. These two Boons lead one to salvation, and the devotee prays to the Supreme Father that He might be Gracious enough to grant them. He says, "My God is so great, so supreme, so unique! He is the One Who comes in the Blessed Form of the Saint to take the souls back to Him."

Such praise Sant Kabir lavishes on the Guru! He says, "*Gobind* (God) and the Guru are both standing in front of me. To Whom should I bow down first?" Then He says, "Let me bow my heart and soul to the Guru first, because *He is the One Who so Graciously brought me unto God!*"

He continues, "It is easier to obtain a throne in the earthly regions, than to find a True Master. The Master Who can grant Spiritual Initiation, and take the soul to Sach Khand is that rare Drop that has merged with the Ocean and become One with it."

"The Creator and Kabir have become as One. Now nobody can differentiate between the two. The True Saint has merged in God, and none can distinguish between them."

"The True Master is free from the unreal and Illusion, and also from the Cycle of birth and death. O worldly people! Your soul is asleep in forgetfulness and in Illusion. The Sat Guru is the One Who is fully awake and Knowing of everything. He can take the seeker on the Journey to the Inner Spiritual Realms. He is the epitome of humbleness, calling Himself the 'Servant' of the Sangat. He comes only to preach Love for the Supreme Lord. His benevolence and Grace are like a refreshing Shower raining down from the Heavens on the parched earth, which soothe the devotee's burning pain and fires of worldly desires. The Master represents the Creator. If you contemplate inwards and do the Simran of the Sat Guru, you will easily cross over the terrible Ocean of this earthly life."

One receives very precious Gifts in the Company of the Master. True yearning for the Lord is created in His Sacred Assembly. Sant Kabir describes the Master to be an overflowing Cup of God's Unlimited Love. Just by enjoying His Holy Presence, the necessary pining and yearning for God is born within one's innermost being. When the Master speaks, the very air becomes Charged. If one is even a little receptive, he feels great rest, perfect peace, and untold joy. It is a great privilege to come to the True Master. Through Him, the access to Spiritual Realms are unlocked and the doors are flung open. The Master holds the Precious Key to these Secret, Inner Regions. That lucky devotee says, "I am very Blessed by my Sat Guru, by Whose unbounded Grace I have obtained unlimited access with God. Blessed and very wise is my True Master, by Whose Grace, I have thus realized."

To have the general knowledge of Spirituality is fine, but to have Practical, first-hand Experience of the Beyond is the True Spirituality. First-hand practice is everything. Without having a True Master, one cannot have this Practical Demonstration, and thus absolutely nothing can be achieved. The full development of first-hand knowledge can only be had in the Practical Experiment that the Godman gives.

The Spiritual Experiences described in the Scriptures cannot be had from only reading about them. Spiritual life is empty and desolate without this Direct Experience. One can comprehend all the theory of Spirituality from books, but only when he practices on it, will he gain actual personal knowledge of it. *He will see for himself!*

What is the difference between the Master and other people? Physically he looks just like others, but He is specialized in self-knowledge and God-knowledge. Just like there are doctors and patients, the doctor has put in dedicated study and has accomplished his goal. The Master is a human being just like any other, but He is the Mouthpiece of God. As the flow comes from God, so the Master expresses those words. The Master is the very Form of Truth.

Sant Kabir warns, "Don't talk ill of the Saint. He and the Creator are as One." There is no one except the Beloved Master, Who can be the Guide for this world and into the Beyond. "The rest of the relatives, mother, father, children, spouse, all are temporary and will perish. They are total Illusion, but people think them to be real."

The devotee is able to hear the Divine Radiant Melody only when God manifests His great mercy, and brings him to the Lotus Feet of the Godman. Release from bondage is in the Master's Holy Word, *the Voice of Heaven*, which is already contained within man, but is in a latent form. When one listens attentively to it, the senses will cease to cause trouble and the mind will desist from being rebellious.

Sant Kabir talks about the abode of Almighty God. "I wished to see God, so I went to the Heavens. When I travelled to the Spiritual Regions, I wanted to take the souls back to God, but I found those Regions to be empty. Then I realized that God resides with the Saint."

He continues, "Consider this carefully. Devotion to God keeps a person entangled in this life, but *devotion to the Sat Guru carries one back unto God!* The Holy Assembly of the True Master grants peace and bliss. All sorrows and sins vanish. It is a golden moment indeed when one meets such a Saint!"

If one wishes to know God, he should approach a True Master, a Perfect Saint, Who regularly travels into the Higher Spiritual Domains and meets Almighty God daily. That True Master will take him unto the Lord. The Master is like anyone else, but He is very exalted Spiritually. He has devoted Himself to the practice of virtue, whereas generally people keep thinking of the worldly ways. His speech is sweet and true in every part because He goes within.

About this Sant Kabir writes, "In anger, people say wrong things and that nullifies many other good qualities they might have. The Saint is the reverse of this, because He has no anger. His actions and words are only sweet and Loving. Whoever is able to control himself in this way, can be called a True Saint. He is filled with the intoxication of Inner Bliss."

The True Master is not motivated by even the slightest consideration of greed. He does nothing for selfish gain, freely offering His services for the good of mankind. He is an Ocean of All-Goodness. Ever engaged in the practice of virtue, He teaches others to be good. The Master bestows the Holy Gift of Shabd and when the devotee dutifully concentrates, it will exercise such a powerful attraction that his soul will be irresistibly pulled upward.

The Sat Guru is the One Who can help the devotee to become disentangled from the attachments of the world, and to find contentment in the Will of the Lord. He not only helps in this world, but also in the next. He is the One Who vouches for the soul and takes it away at the time of death, because He has freed His own soul from the prison house of the mind and body. He can transcend His body at will, and become absorbed in the bliss of God. He can take one to God, and give others a taste of that same happiness.

When one encounters the Master of the Age, the poisonous effect of ego begins to wear off and vanish. When one gazes on the Master's Holy Countenance, the worldly passions are cooled and sins vanish. That person awakens into Reality. He detaches himself from the body and its identification with the mind and senses. The lower tendencies to cheat or to dupe others are overcome, and sensual desires are allayed. One becomes free of attachment, and then he can say, "I have come to the True Master, Who has enlightened me to the Truth, the Internal knowledge of God. This is the difference between a person who has a Sat Guru and one who has none."

The True Master gives out the Path of the Sound Current. Outwardly, He is like any other earthly teacher, but He teaches the theory of the Mystic Science, Sant Mat. Inwardly, His Radiant Form guides the soul from one Spiritual Region to the next, and He does not rest until He has taken that soul back to the Home of the Father. None, but One competent in the Inner Science, can do this work.

Sant Kabir says that wherever you find such a True Master, take a firm hold of Him! "When one takes refuge in the Master, He will tell of the Straight Path which brings an end to the

Cycle of birth and rebirth. He is not the monopoly of any one religion. He is the Beloved of the whole world. His Mission is to free people from the web of Kaal and his Illusionary world. The Master is One with God and when the devotee learns the Inner Way from Him, the Veil will be torn away and he will find peace."

When one enters within, listens to the Shabd and drinks the Divine Nectar, the five mortal enemies run away. One's heart is now at peace. Such is the Master's kindness! When one begins to take joy in the Shabd, he becomes free from the bondage of birth and rebirth. "The Holy Shabd is supreme. All the worlds and the Spiritual domains are its Creation. This Treasure, however, can only be found with the Master's assistance. One cannot enter within unless the Master has unlocked the Door of the Spiritual Realms for the devotee."

He says, "When one comes to the Master and surrenders himself, with His unbounded Grace the devotee becomes His own. The Gracious Master makes him to become One with Him. Masters come to develop a Love of God in the devotee." Although one cannot see God, Sant Kabir says that one may see God's reflection when he looks at the Master. *God's Love will radiate from the Master to the devotee.*

To whomever God is merciful, that person begins to desire the wealth of Love. God Himself brings that lucky soul to the

Master. God creates in that person a desire to see Him, and then makes Himself visible. Only he gets it to whom God is Gracious. That kind of Love is the True Wealth.

Kabir Sahib says, "With His Graciousness, the devotee's Love, devotion, and zeal are always towards the Master. With the Master's Grace, he remembers Him with every breath. He used to have the burning fires and desires of this world, which were put out by cooling showers of the Holy Naam. He has now only contentment within him. The Master's Power is so Great that His Countenance reaches to Sach Khand. Wherever the devotee sees, he beholds the Master's Illustrious Form and Drinks the Nectar of that."

With Loving devotion to the Master, one can meet the Power of God. The Master gives out first the theory of the Divine Path, and then grants a Conscious Contact with the Divine Link within. "Such a One as the True Master is rare. He cannot be found by the thousands." Such a One can give Practical Experience of withdrawal from the body, and a Direct Contact with the Heavenly Light and the Celestial Sound within.

Sant Kabir says that with the Love and compassion of the Sat Guru, He abides in him and fulfills forever his Thirst from aeons and aeons of lives. He quenches this with the Life-Giving Holy Naam and unlimited Love. He has made the devotee His own. Sant Kabir is describing that it is the greatest Blessing in the human birth to come to the True Master.

Kabir Sahib reveals the condition of that devotee when He says to the Master, "You are my mother. You are my father. You are my God! There is no One except You! My soul is a part of You, and I worship Thee from my whole heart and soul. I have reached to Dhaswan Dwar. There I see the Light of God in me. My attention has become focused, and the stillness of my mind has increased. All my sins, bad deeds, and the fear of this worldly Illusion has run away from me. Now I am in tranquillity and bliss. My soul has been perfumed with the fragrance of Divine devotion. I only want to know Thee, O Creator, Who resides in my heart, and is in each pore of my body. My ego has totally vanished. The fragrance of God is permeating through me, with the Grace of my Master."

He continues, "I wish to have the Lord's Simran and I praise to God that every moment He should reside in me. Now I am in Him, and He is in me. This is my good fortune to be in this condition. The Illusion of this world can't come near me and I have taken abode in the Lap of the Lord, Who is all Effulgent Light, my Eternal Spouse, my Beloved Master."

CHAPTER 9

THE HOLY NAAM

A study of the Scriptures will not reveal the Holy Naam, just as if one examines the ledgers of a wealthy man's account, he will not find any money therein, only the account of it. Similarly, a study of all the Holy Books will not avail anything, except to read about other's Experiences into the Beyond. They can only provide the noble inspiration to proceed further on the Path. Just like one can read a cookbook, but the practical experience of actually doing the cooking is needed in order to become a perfect cook!

Sant Kabir says, "I will tell you the total theme of Spirituality in one line. You might have gone through hundreds of thousands of Holy Books, but *the Holy Naam is the One and only Truth!* Put your attention to the Divine Shabd, and recognize that this world is false and made of Illusion."

He says that everyone suffers from the diseases of pride and vanity. All are trapped in this Illusionary world, congealed in their families, creeds, castes, and nations, blinded by the mind, as well as the resulting Karmas that are created by the mind's desires. The only cure lies in attaching the mind to the Holy Naam which resounds within.

"The Master gives the Gift of Liberation by merging the devotee in the Holy Naam. When the curtains of Illusion are pulled asunder, the soul will soar to the heavens within and this disease will vanish. When one obtains this priceless Gift of the Holy Naam from a True Sat Guru, even Dharam Rai bows his head in reverence."

The vibrations of Holy Naam can be heard as Heavenly Harmonies by those lucky enough to have been Blessed with Spiritual Initiation by a Master. For this reason, Holy Naam is sometimes termed as the *Audible Life Stream*, and it continuously resounds within. It is also known as *Gurbani* (the Inner Teachings of the Saints). It is the very Life of the life of all the universes. Sant Kabir tells us that this Bani (Divine

Sound) has existed since the beginning of time, and will continue to exist forever. Its very powerful attraction pulls the soul up and beyond the dangerous Ocean of the material world. It can be contacted only by the soul, not by the mind or the senses, because it becomes visible only to the Inner Eye and Ear of the soul.

This is the Divine Sound of the Stream of Life that flows within. It is already there. If one closes his eyes, ears, and mouth, he can hear it resounding deep within. It is the Holy Naam alone that brings tidings of Almighty God. Through the Power of the Holy Naam, one can be drawn gradually towards God.

Sant Kabir says that the Holy Naam is continually ringing within as Five Melodies, five different Spiritual Sounds, one for each of the five Spiritual Regions above the Physical Plane, up to and including Sach Khand. This Shabd is the All-Pervading Energy, or Power, of the Supreme God Almighty. From this same Shabd, emanates the entire Creation. Through the Holy Shabd the Creation ends in dissolution, and through Shabd again it comes into being.

Holy Naam, then, is the Creative Power of the Supreme Lord. Sant Kabir explains that it is not a combination of the letters of the alphabet in any language, nor can it be found in any religious Scripture. The Scriptures, however, do contain praises of the Holy Naam, and describe the glories that the Saints Experienced on Their upward Journeys.

Sant Kabir says that there are fifty-two letters and sounds in the Sanskrit alphabet, and the whole Creation of the lower three Spiritual Regions is contained within them, but these letters will one day perish. "However, the Eternal Word (the Holy Naam), is not to be found in these fifty-two sounds."

Sant Kabir points out that the Pundit lectures on the Vedas and the Puranas. Similarly, the Qazi discusses the Qur'an Shariff, but not one letter of the Holy Naam, the Holy Name of God, can be found in any of these Books.

This Holy Naam has also been called by Sant Kabir as the *'Unstruck Melody'*, because its harmonies resound endlessly within the human body. This is God's method of continuously contacting each individual soul. Almighty God is calling His children back Home, but most people remain totally ignorant of the existence of this Heavenly Melody, and what it really is. "Mankind is busy in searching for happiness in the gratification of the senses, which do not permit it to contact the Holy Naam. That person is truly poor who has not come to the True Master, and received the Holy Naam."

Kabir Sahib teaches that there are two stages that lead to the realization of the Sound Current within--*Simran* and

Dhyan. Simran means the repetition of the Five Holy Names of God as revealed by the True Master to the devotee at the time of Spiritual Initiation. These Special Words are Charged by the Master's attention, and help the soul to rise until it reaches the Master's Radiant Form.

The next course is Dhyan, which is contemplation on the Effulgent Form of the Master. At first, the Inner Light seems to oscillate, but in reality it is the attention of the disciple that wavers. Gradually, as the mind becomes steadier and the attention is focused longer, the Light becomes constant. Ultimately, it will burst to give a way to pass through. The Inner sky with its own stars, moon, and sun, will appear.

When the devotee gazes constantly, eventually the soul sees the Radiant Form of the Master, and then merges into this Form. This Form will start talking to the soul, and it will thereafter become his constant Companion, and faithful Guide to the Inner Spiritual Realms.

As soon as the Dhyan is complete, the real Sound Current appears. Sant Kabir praises this as being the Heaven-sent Music that breaks all worldly attachments at the time of physical death. He tells us that this Divine Music pulls the soul upwards into the Higher Spiritual Regions. Kabir Sahib says that to contact this Divine Sound Current is called the True Worship, for it can purify the mind and rid it of the various coverings that keep the person's attention away from the Spiritual Path.

Millions of acts of penance, performances of rites, pilgrimages, acts of charity and other such-like deeds that are traditionally regarded as meritorious, are of no value on this Spiritual Path. Sant Kabir makes it clear that salvation is only obtained by devotion to the Holy Naam. All good and pious acts have their own reward of richness and fame, but after enjoying the fruits of these actions, the soul is once again sent back into the Cycle of the 8.4 Million Species of life forms. It is only by accumulating the Special Wealth of God, that one can be free from his coming and going in this material world.

Sant Kabir stresses that in this world and into the Beyond, the Holy Naam is the most valuable possession of all. There is no treasure that can equal it, because it can unite one with the Lord. "The Holy Naam has the power to restrain the mind and stop its oscillations. The Secret to this Naam lies with the True Master, for He alone has the Golden Key that unlocks the mystery of the Creation. This is important because without this Naam, the soul can never find escape from the web of the mind and the attractions of this material world. The soul is so deeply involved in this world that it has, unfortunately, forgotten its Origin and True Home."

All religions begin with a means of reunion between the child humanity and the Heavenly Father, Almighty God. The two basic principles of every religion originated as the Living Master and the 'Word'. By means of this Holy Word, the devotee can Experience the Love, Power, Life and Grace of the Lord.

In the Hindu and Sikh Scriptures, 'Word' is called the *Holy Naam* (the Holy Name of God), *Shabd* (Spiritual Sound, Sound Current), *Bani* (Word), and *Naad* (Inner Music). In the Qur'an Shariff, it is known as *Kalaam-i-Ilahi* (the Voice of God), and *Baang-i-Aasmani* (the Sound from the Sky). The Zoroastrians call it *Sraosha* (Something that can be Heard). The Greek philosophers refer to it as *Logos* (Word). Plato calls it the *Music of the Spheres*. In Chinese, it is known as *Tao* (Word).

Sant Kabir is teaching that the Way Godward can be found within, but He carefully points out that no Priest or Minister can reveal the Secret of this Mystery. The Holy Naam is the Kingdom of God itself, and it emancipates the soul with its great bliss and peace. Without Holy Naam, the soul is a captive of the mind, ever following its dictates and aspirations, never at rest or peace. The same thoughts of fulfilling these ambitions bring the person back again and again into the world. The person is tied, bound hand and foot, to the Wheel of Transmigration, moving helplessly from one species to another.

With the Grace of God, and devotion to the Holy Naam, the devotee can come in communion with the Shabd, the Divine Sound Current, and be Connected with the Power of God. Once he has tasted this Divine Blessing, a profound peace and contentment overwhelms him. Love transforms, and Love purifies. This is the Love of the Beloved, the Supreme Lord, and when it is bestowed, the veils of worldly Illusion are lifted.

Without the Holy Naam, the soul is living in a hell, for the mind is like an uncontrolled beast that leads him into a life of sin, wasting the precious gift of the human birth. "Holy Naam is not just a word or combination of words. If it were, there would be no need of searching for a True Master, for the Scriptures are already full of words. It is a Divine Power that lies within each and every person. However, a thick veil of Deception and Illusion covers everyone, making them oblivious to this Divine heritage that is the right of every individual soul. The Treasure of the Holy Naam is within the human body, but people search for it without."

Sant Kabir also refers to the Gift of the Holy Naam as *'Guru Parshad'*. He says that it is Charged with the attention and the Life-Impulse of the Sat Guru. Once obtained, the person has to practice on it, and develop it further. This is the 'Gateway Pass' to the Higher Spiritual Regions, and it means that the Sat Guru has accepted that lucky soul as His own.

These very special words of *'Guru Parshad'* are used at the end of almost every verse of Sant Kabir!

Many Sanyasis and other holy men used to visit Sant Kabir's humble home. He would discuss Spirituality with them at great length, and then serve them food. On such an occasion, one Sanyasi stayed behind after the others had left. This man had observed the simple circumstances of Sant Kabir's house and His frugal living conditions. Out of the goodness of his heart, he could not help but feel pity for Sant Kabir.

Extremely impressed with the Master's Discourses, he understood that Sant Kabir didn't seem to have any money and was living in a very simple, but rather poor condition. The Sanyasi was very respectful as he requested, "Kabir Sahib, many people come to You, and You always serve them food and other amenities. This is a continuous expense for Your household to feed so many. Please bring me some metal and I will turn it into gold, which You can then exchange in the market for money. Almighty God has a lot of Grace on You, and You have obtained such a vast knowledge of Spirituality, but You need money to make Your Mission grow."

The Sanyasi apparently had a Philosopher's Stone that would turn ordinary base metal into gold. Kabir Sahib just smiled and quietly answered, "Yes, yes, I will see to this."

Sant Kabir called out to the Sanyasi, "Look back here!" and when the man turned around, all he saw was gold! Everywhere! Then Kabir Sahib said, "Look front also!" And when the Sanyasi saw there, everything all around the house was shining with gold!

When at last the Sanyasi was ready to leave, he again turned to Sant Kabir and sadly shaking his head remarked, "Had You brought me the metal, I would have turned it into gold." Sant Kabir replied, "O, I have *lots* of money!"

With a surprised look on his face, the Sanyasi asked, "But I don't understand. It doesn't seem so! Where is it? I don't see it!"

Kabir Sahib answers him in a verse, which says, "The 'money' that I have with me is the True *Dhan* (true wealth) of God. This is the real Treasure of existence. I am very happy with the Grace that I have received from God Almighty. I am so happy that even a king doesn't have that much peace and bliss that I have found in the service of the Lord. This is such a Treasure that whoever has it in his heart, will not go along with the Agent of Death. Such is the wonderful Treasure that I have. It cannot be consumed in the fire, it cannot be stolen, and neither can the windstorm blow it away. This Treasure is the *Holy Naam of God!* Whoever recites the Name of God becomes fearless."

Sant Kabir gives the example of a king's palace which is filled with all kinds of beautiful treasures, servants ready at every beck and call, beautiful horses and the like, but without Holy Naam the king is restless, and in deep sorrow with all kinds of worldly storms in his mind. He can experience no peace of heart, for true joy and everlasting bliss can only be found in the Name Divine.

Again and again, Kabir Sahib praises the Power of Holy Naam, and says that whoever has that Treasure in him, has found the Truth. He uses many different expressions to say that Holy Naam is imperishable, using examples from everyday life such as saying that fire cannot burn it, no person can steal it, or if any kind of storm comes in the life of the devotee, that Treasure cannot be blown away with the fierce winds of chance.

This Seed-Treasure of Naam, which is the Life-Impulse of the True Master, becomes deeply embedded in the heart and soul of the devotee. It grows, and never vanishes. Nobody or anything in these three worlds can hurt that person, or take that Seed away when the person has joyfully surrendered his heart, mind, and soul to the Perfect Godman.

Sant Kabir explains that this Jewel is so precious that Shiva, has been hankering and pining for it for aeons. "The worldly treasures consist of money and other possessions, but in my home (body) I have Almighty God, the true Spiritual Treasure!"

Whoever has this Treasure will not be taken away by the Agent of Death at the time of his physical departure.

Instead, he will be met by his own Master, Who will then take care of his soul. This Treasure of Holy Naam cools down the worldly fires which have been burning in the mind for aeons upon aeons.

Sant Kabir wanted to show to the Sanyasi that worldly money cannot bring permanent happiness and internal peace of heart. More money only brings more material thoughts. How humbly Kabir Sahib describes this Treasure of Holy Naam! He says, "He who has It, has no need of any perishable worldly treasures because those do not bring true bliss. Instead, they only bring sorrow and unhappiness."

In great excitement, the Sanyasi asked, "From where can I obtain this *Dhan* (Treasure)?" And the answer from Lord Kabir was, "O listen, dear brother! This Guru Parshad of the Holy Naam can only be obtained through the Grace of a Living, Perfect Master and His Spiritual Initiation. Upon receiving this Treasure, the mind becomes stilled and all troubles, delusions, and worries fly away." The Sanyasi thought for a moment and then said, "It is good to have this Treasure, but You still need money in order to make Your life run smoothly."

Seeing the goodness in the Sanyasi's heart and knowing that he was ready for Spiritual knowledge, Sant Kabir said, "O brother, could you please bring me a stone from the courtyard?" The Sanyasi went out to get it, but as soon as he picked up the stone, it turned into gold! He was so astonished that he could not speak a word! He just stood there looking at the stone in his hand.

Sant Kabir called out to him, "Look back here!" and when the man turned around, all he saw was *gold!* Everywhere! Then Kabir Sahib said, "Look front also!" And when the Sanyasi saw there, *everything all around the house was shining with gold!*

Fully convinced of the Truth of Sant Kabir's words, he fell at His Lotus Feet and humbly requested Spiritual Initiation into the Divine Light and Sound of God.

Sant Kabir explains, "If one wants a Treasure forever, he should leave off the so-called worldly treasures and have the salvation of the Holy Name of God. Come quickly to the Master and grab that Eternal Holy Naam. Worldly treasures must be left behind. This is the only opportunity that one has in the human body; otherwise he will regret when he leaves, when the breath will finish. As long as one is still in the body, there is time. This is the Golden Chance given to snatch that True Treasure, the Holy Word, the Name of God, from the Godman."

"That person who obtains this Nectar and listens to the Celestial Music of the Unstruck Melody is the only one truly Alive in this world," says Kabir Sahib. He compares those who are without the Naam to being dead, just like walking corpses.

Sant Kabir praises that this Holy Naam belongs to the Creator. "This is not a worldly commodity that can be eaten or sold, or grown in the fields. This Naam, this Spiritual Initiation, is given by the Creator, the Sat Guru, when one comes to surrender himself at His Lotus Feet. It is given by the Divine, and this Divinity is the Truth, which goes along with the person when he departs from the body."

In all humility Sant Kabir says, "I am that person's slave whom the Creator keeps far away from all the human vices and attractions, and who has made only the Lord's Word, the Holy Naam, as his prime Aim in life."

He says that there are some people in this world who keep Sweet Remembrance of the Creator with great passion and zeal. They come in contact with the Master, Who kindly bestows the Gift of Holy Naam upon them. They then practice on His Method earnestly and turn inwards, eventually becoming One with the Lord.

"But there are others who have done thousands of years in penance in many, many different ways, such as reciting Mantras, doing Yoga practices, reading books, going on pilgrimages, but they could not achieve the Blessed Sight of Almighty God. When, however, they suddenly realized that they could not reach anywhere with their own efforts, then God Almighty listened to the sincere cry of their soul, and made the Way for them to meet the Living Godman of that time and *with His Grace*, they crossed over the terrible Ocean of this World."

One can gain very little peace from other practices, because after a while the mind starts its racing again. This is why meditation upon the Holy Naam is very necessary to calm the mind and keep it stilled.

He says that to have the Naam given by a True Master, Who is One with the Creator, and to be able to recite the Charged Words of His Holy Naam, is the greatest Boon from God. That lucky devotee has an Experience of Divine Nectar, and learns to rise above the body consciousness to reach God. Without this Naam, the soul cannot see its Goal. It wanders from place to place, from birth to birth. The mind is fond of worldly pleasures, but all the glitter and rapture of the world cannot give it any form of everlasting peace. When once the mind partakes of the sweetness of Holy Naam, it gladly leaves off everything else. When the soul soars into the Higher Spiritual Realms, it gains Eternal Life!

Kabir Sahib describes this bliss as *a Drop of the Secret of the Inside,* in which He Himself is absorbed all the time. He has revealed these Experiences in a worldly manner, so that anyone can understand them somewhat in their own limited way. "Into every pore of my body, the Form of God and His Divine Nectar are streaming. All the senses are fully under my control, and all worldly ambitions have burned themselves up, just like wood burns into ashes. That Nectar of which I am partaking and which is pouring into my body, brings the Master's Grace, and the lucky soul who receives and drinks of that Ram Ras, has Divinity permeating throughout his entire body."

#9-1 Dying While Living
(First-Hand Experience of the Light and Sound of God)

The experience of true peace is obtained through a careful analysis of the soul. With the help of the Holy Naam, one rises above the body consciousness, and the soul becomes separated from the body. Sant Kabir says that rising above the body consciousness, or *'Dying While Living'*, makes it possible for the devotee to 'die' to the material world while still living in the physical body, before the time comes for him to physically die. This term refers to a process of ascension each day into the Higher Spiritual Realms during the time of meditation.

When one rises above the five outgoing senses, he can see that the body is but a piece of clay. Separated and freed from the pull of the outgoing faculties, the mind begins to taste the sweetness of the Inner Nectar. Kabir Sahib says that when one withdraws from the outside, he will 'awaken' from Inside.

Genuine knowledge is that which the person has attained by his own Experience. The intellect (the mind) is normally filled with borrowed knowledge, such as memories and all the information and rubbish of this Illusionary world. On the other hand, real knowledge is born out of life's experiences. The mind is deeply involved in worldly actions and keeps dragging the soul back into the world, but when the Master bestows the Contact with the Holy Naam, then the mind has something more enticing and enrapturing to hold its attention.

He continues, "When one inverts and rises above the body consciousness, this body can be seen as the true Temple of God. Thereafter, one can see the Light of God, and all darkness vanishes. One sees the Creator and all His Creation, and he knows that God is the One permeating each and every atom in full Effulgent Form, throughout all Creation. All the person's doubts and fears vanish, and he becomes the true devotee of God."

"Just withdraw the Consciousness from the Nine Doors below the eye focus and direct all attention to the Third, or Single, Eye." This Tenth Door is the Gateway to the House of God, which is opened at the time of Spiritual Initiation by the Master. At this point, the oscillations of the mind cease. The mind becomes motionless, and the soul is then free to ascend to the Higher Spiritual Planes.

Those who have the guidance of the Master and practice according to His instructions, 'die' this type of death daily. They go through the practice of coming and going, in and out of the body, at will. The person leaves the body behind in exactly the same way that a person leaves the body at the time of physical death. The only difference is that at the actual time of physical death the *Pran* (also known as the Silver Cord, the Life Force, the Vital Air of the body) leaves as well. In meditation, however, the Silver Cord is not broken, and the devotee can return to the body at his will and pleasure.

Sant Kabir explains that the devotee should rise up from the body consciousness, and come to the Seat of the Soul, at the Third Eye. The person tries to focus his attention into one place, bringing it from all over the body into that one point.

Slowly, the attention rises from the feet and then passes through the six Chakras. Each and every part of the body 'dies' as it is 'cut' from the attention, and of course, wherever there is no attention, that limb doesn't work.

Sant Kabir says that the Master teaches the devotee how to slowly rise up to see the Light of God. Normally, the total Consciousness is all over the body, but when one fully practices regularly day by day in the Spiritual arena with full faith, he can rise up quickly. All his doubts and questions vanish as he progresses upwards into Higher Spiritual Realms. He beholds the Creator wherever he looks. That devotee says to God, "Calling on You constantly, I have changed into You, losing my awareness of myself. When the thought of 'mine' and 'Thine' vanished, then wherever I looked, I found only You!"

Sant Kabir says that there are three ways to rise above the body consciousness:
1. By practicing *Simran* (Repetition of the Holy Names of God).
2. By the technique of *Dhyan* (Contemplation).
3. By listening to the *Dhun* (the manifestation of the Shabd, the Holy Sound Current).

In this process of Dying While Alive, the whole body will become numb, just like it is dead, as the attention gathers at one focus. One sees the Light of God at this point. This means that the devotee has conquered his death, and this is the last enemy that has to be overcome while alive.

Sant Kabir says that it is a very rare soul who remains dead in life (Dies While Living). "It is a rare soul, maybe one person, who Dies While Living." That person then becomes fearless and sees God's Holy Presence everywhere.

"Everyone has to die in his turn, but everyone dies in delusion. No one knows the proper way to Die While Living, which is the purpose of taking the human birth. Once a person goes above the body consciousness, with the Grace of the True Master, that person's coming and going in the Cycle of birth and rebirth, is finished forever!"

Sant Kabir advises, "Die that type of death that you don't have to come again into this world to die again. Die such a death that your coming and going in this world will be finished forever, and you will not have to take another birth!"

When one rises to the eye-focus, he becomes inattentive to the sensations of this material world. Behind the eyes is a Door, and on one side of the Door is the Material World, while on the other, the Astral. When one crosses through this Door, one 'dies' to this world of matter, and comes into Life on the other side.

Sant Kabir says, "The death which terrifies the world is a source of great joy for me, for it is only by 'dying' that I can attain union with the Lord and become Blessed with Perfect, Supreme Bliss."

He advises that people who are afraid of dying should become attached to the Truth. Even a physical death in one's family can become an experience of Truth for the other person, by which he can attain knowledge. When someone dies, the other person uses his 'gathered knowledge' to absorb the shock, because the whole world is afraid of death. It is only the borrowed knowledge of others which buffers the shock of a death, and makes one to feel comforted and 'safe'. Unfortunately, however, that person is lacking in any kind of firsthand Experience of death himself.

There are two reasons for the fear of physical death. One is that the person does not know how to leave the body, and the other is that he does not know where he is going when he does leave. Usually, those who have not solved the mystery of life and have not learned how to die, suffer difficulties at the time of death, but with the mercy and help of the Master, he can learn about the self, and how to rise above the body consciousness. Death is life's greatest mystery, and this can only be solved while living in the human form.

Kabir Sahib says, "My mind has now gone to its original place, in the Third Spiritual Region. I gained the understanding about the nature of the mind when I practiced 'Dying While Living'. I am totally engrossed in the Ocean of Eternal Bliss. That person becomes fearless and seeing God's Presence everywhere, he praises the Lord in great intoxication and bliss."

When one is Blessed with Spiritual Initiation and rises upwards, he meets the Creator Who is Holy Naam and Shabd together in the Secret Bani. That Blessed devotee now says, "After Spiritual Initiation, I have seen God! God cannot be known by the outer senses. When the True Master bestows His Amrit, then God can be seen first-hand and all doubts vanish."

The Master has already achieved emancipation and can help others in this matter. Sant Kabir says that when Almighty God sees people suffering so intensely, He is moved with Love and Grace. He descends to this earth Plane, and in all mercy dons the human form, and then reveals the Way back Home. The Message of the Master has always been the same for all mankind, and will be in future. Sant Kabir says that this world is not the soul's True Home. The soul is only visiting here. It has descended from Sach Khand, that Heavenly Region far away from this Physical One. There, birth and death are unknown.

"True and lasting contentment," Sant Kabir points out again and again, "does not lie in this transitory, material world. Happiness can only be achieved if one obtains liberation from the Cycle of birth and death. Without the guidance of a True Master, however, it is not possible because the duty of the Negative Power is to keep the souls here in his domain."

Sant Kabir reveals the reason why He came to this world. He tells us, "Kabir gives the Eternal Amrit to the world. This Nectar is given by a Living, True Master. Only he can receive this Blessing of Divine Elixir, who has good fortune recorded on his forehead. That person becomes forever married to God."

The Master comes to take those souls who are hankering to be once again with their Father, back to their True Home. He so Graciously grants a Connection with the Almighty, through Spiritual Initiation into the Mysteries of the Beyond.

To describe the Experience of tasting God's Sweet Nectar is very difficult. Sant Kabir compares this situation to a person who is without the faculty of speech, and who tries to describe the taste of sugar, as he is in the ecstasy of its nectar. The taste can only remain indescribable. When a person comes to this Blessed condition with the Grace of his Master, the ecstasy and bliss which he is enjoying can only be described by using worldly examples that might be similar.

Lord Kabir reveals, "Saying is easy, but doing is difficult. Describing and discussing about the Spiritual Path is like eating sugar, but the true practice of the Discipline requires great patience and perseverance. It becomes like a Nectar for the devotee and once the mind gets a drop of that, forevermore it is the devotee's friend."

When one rises above the body consciousness and soars into the Beyond, new vistas of indescribable joy and beatitude open up. Sant Kabir uses wonderful imagery, saying that "New horizons loom into view, giving greater and greater awareness of the Higher Spiritual Regions. The liberated soul enjoys perpetual bliss in the life of the Spirit, with the outlook on life entirely changed. The vast Creation of God now becomes the manifestation of the One Life-Principle pulsating everywhere in and around the person, and in all things. The world that he now sees is quite different from the one known to him before. He looks upon it as the veritable abode of God, and sees God truly dwelling in it. With repetitive Experience of the death process, he triumphantly conquers death in victory."

Sant Kabir describes how the devotee's attention should become focused, as he goes into the Hari Mandir. "The person who has cleaned his body from outside, but not from the Inside (meaning that if his heart is not clean), will be wasting time both in this world and in the hereafter. Ever engaged in the sadness of the five Evils, he has no true Aim, or Focus, in his life. He becomes empty, dissipating his energy and concentration through the senses, and he suffers badly because these impressions take away all his good qualities."

Sant Kabir advises that restraint over the mind and its outgoing faculties, including the senses, is necessary to make progress in the Spiritual Realms. He gives a very interesting illustration from his own life as a weaver. "With the thread of Shabd, one should put the needle of his attention at the Third Eye." In other words, the attention should be focused at the Single Eye.

He continues, "Whoever Experiences the Holy Naam, is drenched with unfathomable, limitless and sweet bliss beyond description. That person has everlasting Divine Intoxication and Blessedness. In its invisible rays of bliss and joy, he forgets all worldly pleasures. Communion with the Holy Naam opens a Grand Vista of Divine Light and Sound of God within."

Sant Kabir says that this tremendous bliss and untold Blessings of Grace are coming from the Lotus Feet of the Lord, but until one sees this and Experiences it for himself, he cannot even begin to praise it. He says very emphatically, *"He who sees the Grace of the Master, is the only one who can tell about it!* It cannot be obtained by the way of the intellect, because it does not include any kind of discussions or arguments. It is only bestowed upon one with the Grace of the Master. The secret of Spirituality is in *Practical Experience!*"

Sant Kabir explains that the Path of Spirituality can be realized only with first-hand Experience. "It is not blind belief or hearsay. The intellect cannot even think about, nor realize the happiness and bliss that one enjoys from being in the Holy Company of the Master. Without seeing, no benefit is gained, and that person is accepting blind faith. First-hand Experience is needed!"

With great enthusiasm He says, "This is the real thing--how happy I am at His Lotus Feet! This is why I am happy: I SEE!"

"Outwardly," explains Kabir Sahib, "a city or a town cannot be made without land, but when one goes inwards, rises above the two eyes and sees all the Vistas of God's Creation right inside the body, he will see how many towns and huge cities there are. There is no need of any land, or anything of this material world. The devotee sees this for himself, and then he can say 'I have seen for myself the Truth!' He receives a first-hand Experience!"

Sant Kabir says that with the Grace of the Master and His Spiritual Initiation of the Holy Naam, one can get out from the clutches of Kaal, and achieve the state of *Mukti*

(Salvation). The Master, Himself, is salvation personified. True *Mukti* is a state of true liberation, being free of bondage. The soul has been in bondage for aeons and aeons, under the power of the Negative tricks of Illusion and Deception.

Sant Kabir asks, "How can I swim across this Ocean of worldly Illusion? O my God! Help me! Save and protect me from this! I have sought Thy shelter!"

Then He explains, "If the devotee lives up to the Spiritual Teachings, he can easily receive the Kingdom of God. In worshipping the Saint Who is already liberated, the follower also becomes liberated. Once the person has the Parshad of Spiritual Initiation, he leaves behind the heavens and hells, and goes up into the Lap of God. All worldly attachments are released from the clutches of the heart. When one has this Treasure of Divine Love in him, and lives in the Celestial Music, then the condition of true Mukti develops in him."

#9-2 Simran (Repetition of the Names of God)

The word *'Simran'* is Sanskrit, and it means a constant remembrance of some one, some place, or some thing of one's liking. Sant Kabir has talked about *Simran* all along in His verses, because this is the most important beginning of

Spirituality. He has defined Simran as being "Every breath that continuously remembers God."

He continues, "One's Spiritual Awareness wakes up in the sweet memory of God. The mind, senses, or intellect cannot know God; only the soul can know God, when it detaches itself from outer worldly attractions and gathers at the eye centre, known as the Third Eye."

All the world is engaged in Simran of some thing or the other. For example, the farmer thinks of his fields, which ones need to be ploughed and what seeds are to be sown in which field, the lawyer thinks of his cases and how to prepare them for the court, the student thinks of his lessons and examinations, the housewife thinks of the supplies of salt, flour, and sugar needed for the household, the businessman thinks of the prices and commodities to run his business.

The object of the Simran becomes the essential factor of the attention. Sant Kabir says, "After one dies, he is reborn in the environment wherein his attention has been fixed. If he has dwelt constantly on the affairs of the world, then his attention becomes firmly rooted in the world. On the verge of his death, all the thoughts of the world become his ruling passion, and thus are the effective cause of the next life. However, if one ardently practices Simran of the Holy Naam to the exclusion of remembrance of the world, the mind will slowly begin to see inward and come to rest at the Third Eye between the two eyebrows."

There are three types of Simran:
1. One remembers someone by uttering words by the mouth, like singing or speaking.
2. One has the remembrance of someone done with the flow of the breath. In other words, as one breathes, the attention is towards that person who is being remembered. This is a better type of remembrance.
3. One thinks slowly but continuously about a person, by the silent tongue of his thought. He remembers the person by deep contemplation. This is the best way of practicing Simran and is the most fruitful, accomplishing the true aim of the Simran.

What does one gain by doing Simran, the incessant Sweet Remembrance of God? Sant Kabir explains that a longing to see the Heavenly Father takes root in the heart of the devotee, and he then becomes so drawn to God that he feels he will die if he is not able to meet Him.

Kabir Sahib says that one should keep that Personality whom he wishes to meet in the forefront of his thoughts and prayers. This will help to build up an irrepressible yearning to see that person. One should dedicate all actions to Almighty

God. When one begins to see God all around, in whatever is said or done, a rich harvest of joy and peace will be reaped.

Sant Kabir says that in truth people are actually *swimming in God!* Every pore and atom of the body contains the Essence of God, and yet they ask, "Where is God?"

Just like the rivers and the streams fall into the ocean, but they have no Consciousness. Therefore they fall, but they are not aware of it. Man also falls into God, but he is not aware of it. In every death, one falls into Him, and with every birth, he arises from Him, but His Sweet Remembrance fails the heart. One goes in and out of Him every moment, all day long, with each and every breath. When the breath goes in, God flows in. When the breath goes out, even then the person goes out into God. Again and again, Kabir Sahib says that there is only one kind of true wealth: to remember God.

However far away the person is from God, he cannot step outside His Orders. God is always present within. If God is not, the person cannot be. Wherever one goes, He is present. However far one may go, it is He Who takes him. Even in committing sin, it is He Who breaths within the sinner. The person can even forget Him, but there is no way to lose Him. One cannot even lose Him by mistake, because He *is* the person.

Sant Kabir says that the drop is in the Ocean and the drop is a part of the Ocean. The drop knows the Ocean because the Ocean is not different from the drop, but yet again the drop cannot truly know the Ocean for the very fact that it remembers only a part of the Ocean, and the part cannot know the Whole. When the drop becomes again *into* the Ocean, only then can the drop 'know' the Ocean. The Ocean is not separate from the drop. So, man can know God, and yet say that he does not know Him at all. If he feels that he knows God, it is an Illusion, because God is Immeasurable and Unknowable. Only when the soul is totally absorbed in the constant, sweet remembrance of God, can one actually 'know' God!

The person begins to be aware of God's various works and also His beneficence. Sant Kabir says that God's works are manifested in all Creation and yet people remain blind to this. Seeing Creation, they remain blissfully unaware of the Creator. The Hand of God is all around, within and without. The Cause is subtle, but the effect is gross. One cannot see the Cause, just like one cannot see electricity; yet when the switch is pulled, the lamp is lit. An unseen Hand provides the purpose for each event, and makes all things happen orderly.

A prayer rises in the heart. "O Almighty God, Lord of all compassion, come close to me and let me meet You!" Kabir Sahib says, "This kind of lover lives in his own private world inhabited by no other, with only himself and his Beloved.

Those who remember Almighty God develop a restless yearning to meet Him. That deep and heartfelt longing seeks fulfilment through constant sweet remembrance, and it is eventually accomplished."

Sant Kabir says that Simran of the Holy Names of God is a very important part of this Sweet Remembrance. If the Simran is done with full attention and the tongue of the soul (the tongue of thought), then the heart of that person becomes tuned to the Lord. A Connection is made and it reacts in the heart of that person. This constant remembrance helps him to achieve the Goal, and opens the Spiritual Way. Worldly thoughts vanish, to be replaced by thoughts of Almighty God. Conscious effort gradually becomes an unconscious effort. When one's effort and God's compassion meet, that person's efforts end, and only Divine Grace remains. When the search changes from a conscious effort to the unconscious, then ego is no more, because the ego is a product of the conscious mind.

Whenever the person sits down for meditation, all the worldly thoughts and affairs about his home, children, employment, family, and friends, come in front of him. Either he does Simran of them, or they think about him, and due to a combination of both, this world stays alive in him. Worldly thoughts keep coming and going in his mind all the time due to this constant association. Thoughts and impressions of the world do affect the person. In order to be safe from this influence, Sant Kabir suggests that one should always have Simran, so much so that these impressions will be erased, and any new thoughts will be of God.

As one travels through time, dust and dirt gather on the mind. The body can be cleansed with the external water, but the mind and its dirt remain within. Therefore, some other type of cleaner is required. Dirt is gathering on the mind every moment which, no matter how many times one bathes during the day, cannot be cleansed by the outside water. Simran relates to this cleaning water within. It is, therefore, priceless.

Sant Kabir advises that if one wishes to obtain inner bliss, he must sit down in meditation as instructed by the Master, turn within, and contact the Holy Naam Current resounding from the Higher Spiritual Planes. He explains, "With the Simran of the Lord, one can feel peace in his heart and mind. When Almighty God gives the Grace to get out of this whirlpool of the world, then the soul gets dipped into the colour and bliss of this sweet Elixir. By doing this Simran, one becomes totally absorbed into the Lord. This will bring forth not only Inner, but also outer peace."

Remembrance does not require a separate effort. That which permeates every hair of the body is what is called 'unremembered remembrance.' It saturates every pore of the body, and whatever the person does or speaks or thinks about all day long, His Sweet Remembrance should reverberate like a soft melody within. In the constant remembrance that God is in all, one forgets his own little self. One sees the Almighty all around, in all directions.

The Simran which is given by the Master, vanquishes the deadly five passions and they run away. Sant Kabir describes these cravings to be 'robbers who deprive one of the Spiritual Wealth.' Only when they are completely destroyed does one truly become attached to Simran. When they are at last driven out, the joy of Simran invests the soul with a previously unknown peace, and the Way Godward opens up. The mind and heart become full of harmony and tranquillity.

"Within each person lies dormant the sweetest notes of unplayed Music and ravishing Symphonies which are incessantly reverberating. This Music never stops. It goes on day and night."

Sant Kabir advises, "O foolish person! Why don't you turn your mind inwards where you will find a bounty of Divine Nectar. Become intoxicated with that Stream of Elixir, which will easily quench your Spiritual Thirst!" The person wastes his whole lifetime outside the eye focus and thus the priceless Jewel, which the ever-merciful Lord has bestowed on the person, remains untouched because the person has never entered within.

If one were to find a precious jewel on the roadside, he would wrap it carefully in a handkerchief, lest it be lost. While going home, he would continually be feeling that handkerchief to be certain that the jewel was still there. Similarly, one's remembrance of God should be constantly nurtured within, in the same manner. Is the thread of remembrance still intact? Is the flow of Love continuous? Eventually, the remembrance will continue in sleep, as well. In this case, when one's eyes are closed, he becomes absorbed completely in God.

Kabir Sahib is requesting people to pray and praise, and do Simran of the Creator, so that their own coming and going in the world will finally be ended. He says that whoever has Love and devotion for God's sweet remembrance on his tongue is saved from the Agent of Death, who will not appear at the time of that person's departure from the physical body.

Again and again, Sant Kabir Lovingly advises that people constantly engage in the Simran (Sweet Remembrance) of the Master. "O Man! As long as you are in the body, you must have the Simran of your Master all the time, so that while doing so, the Life-Impulse of your Master will take you to a stage of intense longing, combined with great passion and zeal. That, in turn, will ultimately lead you to be One with God."

He points out that some people do a particular practice of remembering the various gods and goddesses of their religion, and they worship idols, photographs, and religious Books. They recite from the Scriptures and then they repeat the names of those gods, goddesses and avatars. "However, those who do Simran in this fashion are wasting their efforts because first of all, they have not physically seen those gods, goddesses and avatars to whom they are worshipping. One cannot 'remember' something or someone whom he has never met. Those who worship the stone idols cannot converse with them."

Sant Kabir explains that if somebody recites from the Holy Books (which were written either by avatars, gods or goddesses, or even those written by a Perfect Master), he might receive some inspiration to study more deeply. "If the seeker, however, got the gist out of the religious Books, and then acted upon it, then those Books could be of some benefit. Most people only read them as a ritual or as a duty, or sing songs from them and remember them in that way, but these people don't try to bring those very Teachings into their own life practice. As a result, they achieve nothing in the way of knowing the Creator; rather they just waste the precious life given to them by Almighty God."

One will receive Special Words, Charged with Divine Love and attention, when he comes to the Living Master. With these Holy Names, the devotee can then remember the God-Power working in the Master, and these Words will have full Charging, not only of the attention of the Master, but also of Almighty God Himself, because the Master is One with God. These Words are 'Electrified', so to say in the worldly way.

Sant Kabir tells us that the Special Names never lose their Godly Power because they have the Godman's own Life-Impulse (His Divine Attention) put on them. There are very, very few lucky souls who receive this Divine Charging that Sant Kabir is describing. If His verses are carefully read, it will be noticed that every four or six stanzas, He always ends with the same affirmation, "...*when the True Master gives you, with His Grace, these Charged Words.*"

Sant Kabir clearly points out that when one does constant repetition of these particular Charged Words (the Holy Names of God), they are of great benefit because one then knows the One Whom he is reciting them for. "The devotee has met the Living Master, he has seen Him and he has talked with Him. If he has any questions or doubts about Spirituality, he can clear them with the Godman right away, because of the God-manifested Charging in Him. That Godman has total compassion and unbounded Grace for His devotee."

In the initial stages of discipleship, when one begins to practice the Simran, the soul keeps ascending and descending in the attention, until it can become attached and absorbed into something in the Inner Spiritual Realms. But when it contemplates on the Master's Radiant Form, thereafter that Resplendent Form keeps the disciple company, constantly offering protection and guidance in the Higher Spiritual Regions.

Kabir Sahib says, "The most delicious Nectar is streaming down constantly from the Lord within, but people are engrossed in the outer, sensual pleasures and so remain deprived of this Heavenly Amrit." Naturally, if one wishes to detach the mind from worldly pleasures, he must give it something superior. That 'something' is the Simran of God's Holy Names.

In one of His verses, Kabir Sahib repeats three times, *"Remember the Lord, remember the Lord, remember the Lord!"* He is emphasizing the great, great significance of Simran. Through this Sweet Remembrance of the Supreme Father, one obtains the Godly attention of the Master.

One single Glance of compassion from the Saint is enough to liberate a soul from the endless Cycle of births and deaths. Through this Simran, one can catch hold of the Shabd (the Holy Sound Current), and then his soul can rise on it to reach back to its Origin in Sach Khand. When the remembrance becomes constant and uninterrupted, the thread of thought remains ever connected with Him.

Sant Kabir emphasizes that this is the only Way to obtain Divinity. "To do the Simran of God, one begins by putting more and more attention towards this." In other words, the person is thinking constantly and ceaselessly about the Supreme Father with his whole heart, mind, and soul. The devotee becomes a part of God.

It is a very simple rule: "As you think, so you become." If one thinks about any person with full heart and soul, that person will also be thinking about him. What a wonderful thing that if one constantly remembers the Creator, then Almighty God, the Supreme Creator, will also be thinking about him! Kabir Sahib tells us that "The end result is that God will become that devotee, and the devotee will become God! Once the devotee knows Almighty God, then he will be knowing of all His Creation and will have the full knowledge of Divinity."

Kabir Sahib explains that the body becomes cleansed by this discipline of the Simran of the Lord's Holy Names. "The devotee who repeats the Simran of God's Holy Names, asks for nothing but God." He says that the devotee seeks God for the sake of God alone, and this is his crowning glory. Simran is like a tonic for the soul.

Sant Kabir gives the example of a bride (which is the soul), waiting for her Eternal Groom (the Supreme Lord). She stays fully decorated, anxiously waiting for Him. Shyness and modesty are considered the highest qualities, a lack of ego. No one wants to reveal himself before God. One tries to hide weaknesses as best he can, for what has one got to show Him? There is nothing worthy of His Attention. One has nothing to offer that is worthy of Him. Modesty is a state of utter humility. Only when a person is humble, is he accepted in the Court of the Lord. The more a person reveals his devotion by proclaiming his worship, shouting his prayers, boasting of his fasts and acts of penance, the further removed he is from God.

This worldly example shows that when one cleanses the heart through Simran, there is nothing but one desire to see the glory of God inwardly. Then one should rest assured that *He will appear!* And after His glorious appearance, all the doubts and suspicions of this world immediately vanish. "When the bride leaves the petty, temporary pleasures of this world, she gains permanent happiness with her Immortal Groom (Almighty God)."

When the Simran goes on by itself, it is known as *'true and complete'*. It becomes an effortless effort, because it goes on automatically. "That type of continuous remembrance, which goes on without any effort, will take one to the Goal. The Simran at this time is strong and constant."

He further says, "Simran should be done Lovingly, with full attention. Simran done in this way helps to still the mind, and the *Nirat* (the soul's Power to see inside at the Third Eye) becomes still. If you make your body and mind still, and don't talk, then the attention and the Nirat also become motionless. There is no comparison for one moment of that bliss with any other. When the Simran and the Nirat become as One, the Veil will be removed. The soul of the devotee then 'wakes up', and the disciple starts seeing Spiritual beauty inside."

Sant Kabir teaches that Simran is the most basic step to progress in Spirituality. He says, "There are many types of Japs, but any type of Simran which is spoken is less fruitful. For example, the Yogis do Simran with the attention focused at the different lower Chakra Centres, but unfortunately the mind tends to run uncontrolled here and there. None of these types of practices are successful at all. The practice of Simran done with the aid of beads, such as a rosary, is only temporary and of no value. *Simran is to be done with the tongue of thought*, and not with the physical tongue. It is entirely a mental process. The passing of the fingers over the wooden beads on a rosary leads one nowhere. However, if one were to turn the beads of the mind, he would see God's Light within."

Sant Kabir teaches the practice of Simran done with the tongue of the attention, which gives energy and life to the body, the mind, and the senses. By doing this *Simran of the soul*, the mind becomes stilled and concentrated.

Sant Kabir says, "I do the Simran of the Lord, the Creator, Almighty God with the rosary of my tongue. All the Saints and true devotees from the beginning of time have dwelt in the unbounded peace, ecstasy and tranquillity of this Spiritual practice."

A Connection with the Divine is made, which reacts in the heart of the recipient. This constant remembrance helps one to achieve the Goal and opens up the Spiritual Way. All worldly deliberations vanish, to be replaced by thoughts of God. The devotee feels God's Divine Presence everywhere. Sant Kabir says that when a person has so much remembrance of God in his heart that no other thought enters his mind, he can be truly called a Perfect Person.

Sant Kabir cautions that daily routine and worldly obligations should not interfere with one's Simran. "While engaged in worldly pursuits, one should not forget the Aim and Objective in life, which is God realization. One must Love Simran as the very Breath of his life, whether awake or asleep, in sickness or in health."

Sant Kabir advises us to never forget the Grace of the Master Who has given this Simran. "Embed it in your heart and *never, ever forget Him*, because He is the One Who is going to take you across this Ocean of Worldly Existence with His Guru Parshad, and you will become totally engrossed in the Ocean of all Love. When you Drink the Nectar of Simran, its sweetness will permeate every pore of your body."

He reminds the seekers that this Simran of the Charged Words of God is only to be had from the Sat Guru alone. With every breath one must remember His Divine Presence. "This Simran will take one to all the Higher Stages of Spirituality. This Simran is vibrating throughout the whole of Creation. It makes this life and the hereafter filled with boundless bliss and ecstasy. Then one's coming and going in this world, will be forever finished."

"Those are the Blessed ones who do the Simran of God. Not only their body, but the whole atmosphere around them becomes Charged with the Blessed radiation of God's Holy Name. That person makes everything near him as pious and blissful."

#9-3 Dhyan (Contemplation of the Master's Radiant, Effulgent Form)

Sant Kabir urges the devotee to daily engage in contemplation upon He Who has so kindly bestowed the Divine Light. *'Dhyan'* means contemplation of someone. Simran and Dhyan naturally go hand in hand. If one is doing Simran of someone, he will naturally have that person's Dhyan. One automatically thinks about that form whose Simran he is doing. One practice cannot be separate from the other.

Dhyan is the second part of reciting Simran, but this only comes when the Simran is complete and continuous. At this stage, one is not consciously doing Simran, but the Simran tends to continue itself automatically. This condition only comes when one has fully accomplished the goal of Simran. Sant Kabir says that Dhyan is like two-sided contemplation, and He gives the example that when one thinks about God, God also thinks about that person. "This is the secret of Spirituality, because as one remembers and thinks about his Spiritual Master, the Master is also remembering His devotee a hundred-fold!" It needs fierce courage to keep this constant remembrance.

Sant Kabir explains that there are two faculties working in the body:

1. *Surat* (the attention of hearing inside).
2. *Nirat* (the attention of seeing inside).

As the person focuses his attention with the Power of the Simran of God's Holy Names, he can see God with the Nirat. This is the true effect of Dhyan. "Without Nirat, the soul is blind. Tell me where can it go?" The Nirat is the gazing faculty of concentration, and it is with this aspect that one can see the Spiritual Realms inside.

With the practice of Simran, the soul gathers behind the eyes at the Tenth Gate, and if it is done with full attention, then the soul rises into the Higher Realms of Spirituality. Sant Kabir says, "Unless the Nirat is awakened, however, the attention remains closed and without value, even if it has gathered at the Tenth Gate. One cannot go further into the Higher Realms. The True Master, with His unbounded mercy and Grace, opens up this Nirat at the very first Spiritual Sitting."

It is known that the Yogis labour for years to open this, but the True Master unlocks it right at the time of Spiritual Initiation. "In the beginning of the Inner Spiritual Journey, the Nirat leads and the Surat follows. By this method, the Third Eye opens up into the Higher Spiritual Regions, at which time the Surat then takes the lead, with the Nirat following."

Sant Kabir stresses the value of contemplation on the Form of the Master. "To have the Dhyan of the Living Master is the highest Dhyan in Spirituality that one can have." One cannot expect to have any result from gazing at a picture of the Sat Guru, because only Life can pull up the other life.

Kabir Sahib tells us of many benefits one receives when he has his Dhyan towards the Sat Guru. "The Master's purity of heart and countless attributes enter into the devotee. The mind becomes stilled and concentration develops. By contemplating on the Sat Guru, one increases his power to remember God, and the Sat Guru creates in the devotee a continuous remembrance of God."

"The Master is *Akaal* (free of Kaal; free of birth and rebirth). He is the Light of all Truth and He is made of Truth. God's Light shines forth from His body. He is the only One to put the devotee's attention towards God."

He comments, "If you are praying to God to have the knowledge of Truth, you can have it only through the Master. Thereafter, all the sickness of the deadly five Passions vanishes, as the mind reaches its True Home."

He assures that if one does this type of meditation, he won't have to take another birth to do it again. There is no return to another physical body, because one is freed from the Cycle of birth and rebirth. "One can obtain the kingdom of God with this practice!"

Thinking about someone and contemplating on someone are very different processes. In thinking, the mind goes from one thought to another; in contemplation, one goes into the depths of someone. The process of thinking is linear, but in contemplation, the Inward Journey begins. Contemplation is the true revelation and concentration of the Simran. In thinking, one uses the mind, but in contemplation, the mind is not used. The mind is no more, and when it is gone, then true contemplation begins. Contemplation means the absence of the mind. Contemplation goes deeper than thinking. The doer becomes lost and contemplation eventually brings about an end to the mind.

As long as one is immersed in his own desires, lost in the demands of the mind, he remains blind and ignorant. The mind is another name for this 'blindness'. Contemplation is the opening of the eyes. Through contemplation alone does one become aware of all the worlds. Then one sees God's Holy Name on every leaf, and hears His Divine Melody in the winds. Through contemplation, one ceases to bear the burden of life itself.

In the verses of Sant Kabir, there are three types of Dhyan:
1. On the Physical Form of the Master.

2. On the Radiant Light which appears when the Nirat is awakened by the Master at the time of Spiritual Initiation.
3. On the Inner, Effulgent Form of the Master, which appears within this Radiant Light during meditation, and takes the soul of the devotee into the Higher Spiritual Regions.

Sant Kabir tells us that this third form of Dhyan is the highest in Spirituality. When this *Noor-e-Saroop* (Resplendent Form) manifests inside, and the devotee puts his full attention on it, then he himself becomes totally engrossed with the Master. The worshipper and the object of worship become One. This is the highest stage of Mysticism, and a Person Who is able to practice this, is called **a Godman**.

#9-4 Shabd (The Divine Sound Current)

Sant Kabir says that there is an unending *Kirtan* (Divine Music) playing inside, a continuous rapture of enduring harmonies. "Listening to it gives one unrivalled Powers, for it can liberate the soul from the endless Cycle of birth and death. *There are five worlds encased in the forehead, and a particular melody is playing in each!* Five Divine Sounds are arising from within, and can grant salvation to the soul. *To contact this Inner Life Current* is *the highest form of worship.* The

Word of God is an unwritten Law and an unspoken Language, and it is the same throughout all Creation. **Meditation is the art of listening to God.** One can realize this when he ascends the body's house of the Nine Doors (the two eyes, two ears, two nostrils, one mouth, and two openings below)."

The Shabd is present in every living being, whether he be Hindu, Muslim, Christian, Jain, Zoroastrian, or Jewish. At the time of Spiritual Initiation, the devotee is given a Direct Contact with this Sound Current. Sant Kabir says that one has to only direct the attention inward in order to hear it. "People, however, generally remain satisfied with outer music, due to a lack of Spiritual leaders to grant a Demonstration of the Inner Sounds."

All religions have emphasis on music, such as Kirtan. In this connection, Sant Kabir says that outer music helps to some extent to achieve concentration, but He emphasizes that only doing this outer Kirtan with musical instruments will not take the soul to any Inner Stage. "Outer music awakens the mind, while at the same time, it dulls the soul. The Jiva develops a fondness for this outer music, and the life goes wasted, because the real Aim of the human birth is missed." This is why Sant Kabir does not approve of the outer singing of hymns, or the playing of musical instruments and dancing.

"The Inner Music on the other hand, awakens the soul and puts the mind to sleep. Unless a person doesn't leave the outer music, he has no place in God's kingdom."

He continues, "This Inner Music is ever resounding within, and is without end. This Divine Melody has purifying and uplifting effects on the mind and the soul. It has great ennobling power and is of infinite worth. It is God-inspired, as *it is the means by which the Supreme Lord is in contact with the soul!*" Sant Kabir says that by communion with this Music, one can attain the Eternal Truth, for it grants the much-awaited liberation from repeated birth and death.

He uses examples of several musical instruments to describe the sounds of these Inner Melodies. "The Supreme Lord's lyre plays by itself!" and "The Unstruck Melody of God's trumpet resounds in its fullness!" Again, "When the body is full of Light, the Unstruck Melody of the veena (a stringed instrument) vibrates throughout!"

Actually Sant Kabir is describing the heavenly Inner Sounds in terms of the musical instruments that exist in the outer world and which are familiar to everyone, but in reality these Inner Sounds are nowhere close. These labels only assist in describing them to the best of the human ability. The Inner Sounds only somewhat resemble such instruments as small bells, a big church bell, a conch, a huge drum or thunder sound, a trumpet or siren, water falling or running, crickets or stringed instruments, the bagpipe, and the flute.

Sant Kabir beautifully describes this Eternal Symphony as a great Spiritual Current continually flowing down from Heaven in waves of energy that constantly vibrate throughout the whole Universe. "It is the Life-Support of every tiny atom throughout all Creation. This Divine Sound Current is ultimately the means by which each and every soul will eventually return back to the Creator."

Sant Kabir has even pointed out its location, saying that "It manifests on the Inner Forehead of the person. The Tenth Door is the only place where the Sound Current can be heard. The other Nine Doors only lead to the outer physical world. When one turns inward, the mind becomes still."

He compares the Holy Shabd Power of God to a true Inner Diamond, vibrating in each and every atom in the whole of Creation. "The True Master has manifested this Secret Jewel of the Holy Naam within me. It remains, however, a Divine Secret until one sees the God Power working everywhere and through everyone."

Sant Kabir says that the Celestial Music from Heaven not only can be heard, but also can be *seen* as Radiant Light, drawing the attention upwards, purifying the mind and the heart. In many verses, He describes the Sound Current that enables the soul to rise into the Spiritual Regions, above and beyond the Physical Region. He says that the soul is accompanied and guided by the Master, for the Master has made these Inner Journeys Himself many times, and is fully competent to assist the devotee.

"I have finished with my intellect and clever scheming. God cannot be known by the outer senses. I have focused my attention into the Sound Current, which has made me fearless and unaffected by the false pleasures and comforts of this world. When one sees God first-hand, all doubts vanish because this Sound Current grants Eternal Life."

He says that the mind, "which was always moving like the wind, now becomes stilled. My mind is now my obedient servant. My Divine Thirst has been quenched forever by the Water of this Godly bliss."

Using some very powerful analogies, Sant Kabir has described some characteristics of the Holy Sound Current. "The stroke of the sword draws out the breath of the person it strikes. However, *He who endures the 'blow' of the Holy Shabd is the True Sat Guru,* and I am His disciple."

This is an indication that the force of the Sound Current can only be *absorbed and digested* by a true devotee. The Master makes the disciple progressively ready, and 'fit' in stages to 'hear' these rapturous Inner Sounds.

Sant Kabir says that at first one listens to the water sounds, or the cricket sounds. Gradually, as the Sound becomes louder (actually, the devotee's attention is growing more and more focused), it seems to become more like the stringed instruments, then perhaps like a drum or a whistle, until it becomes a flute-like sound or a bagpipe sound.

At this point, it is so loud that the devotee's full attention is absorbed into it, as it commands the entire concentration. "The Sound acts like a sort of magnet, and it is upon this Divine Orchestra that the soul can speedily soar ever upwards and onwards. The Inner Sound is definitely more absorbing than the Inner Light, and exerts more of a precise 'pull' to attract the soul towards it, and into it."

When Sant Kabir discusses the Lord's Music, He praises the Master, saying that it is the True Saint Who makes the devotee turn towards the Lord, and Who bestows this Holy Sound. In gratefulness He says, "What would be the life without this?"

This Eternal Kirtan of God is the True Master's Parshad, and Sant Kabir points out that this Eternal Amrit is only bestowed on one who has this good fortune recorded on his forehead. "These Heavenly Strains cannot be heard in the Churches, Temples, and Mosques of the outside world. It is a Continuous Sound, the means of uniting the soul with the Lord. If one does the Simran of the Sound Current with Love and full faith, he will definitely cross over the Ocean of this worldly existence."

He continues in His unbounded praise of the Master Who has bestowed such Grace on the devotee. "In the Holy Company of the Master, one listens to the Celestial Music and sees the Light of God. The Lord is continuously in my thoughts and my heart."

He offers such praise, "O Lord! I am Yours! I have surrendered to You! I am Your *unbought slave!* In past lives, I was Your worshipper. This relationship will never change. The Holy Sound Current which resounds at Your Threshold, You have put on my forehead, at the Third Eye. Let Thy Holy Name come forth from my mouth, and Thy Lotus Feet stay forever within my heart!"

He continues, "I have met the True Sat Guru, Who shot the Arrow of God's Name (the Holy Shabd) at me. That struck me and made a hole in my heart forever. I hear where the Celestial Music, this Divine Melody of God, is coming from. I listen to it as I progress upwards on the Spiritual Journey.

Ultimately the Sound pulls me ever onward and back to my Original Home."

When the devotee has developed the habit of listening continuously to the Sound Current, the Eternal Divine Melody flows continuously without end. "With the Grace of the True Master, I have received the Internal, true knowledge, the Light and Sound of God, and with that bliss, I am forever dyed in the Colour of the Holy Naam!"

Verse after verse is devoted to the praise of the Holy Sound Current. "This Effulgent Harmony does not cease. It plays on forever. It is unending and limitless. It is the Voice of God, an imperishable Song and the true Word of the Master. For this reason, it is known as the *Unhad Shabd*, the unlimited, unbounded Music of God."

"Within the centre of a person's being are innumerable Songs, the hearing of which can break the chains of life and death."

Sant Kabir makes the reader appreciate the importance of this Gift of the Master, by reminding him of the endless time that the soul has remained imprisoned in the Physical Region. "Many thousands of lives in different forms and species have I spent in Illusion. Now I am tired. The True Master has taken away all my sorrows. It is a great and rare Boon that the Master has bestowed on me this Nectar of Godly Love, and I have reached the Spiritual Goal! This Divine Elixir has saved me, and finished my coming and going in this world!"

Kabir Sahib directs some verses to the Preachers and Ministers, trying to make them wake up and see these things for themselves. "O Pundit! Listen to me, O Learned One! When you leave this physical body, then the Divine Sound also goes along with your soul. The soul rises further and further with the Sound Current."

He tells them that the life is passing so quickly and not much time is left. "Only in the physical body can the soul awaken to the stage of the Third Spiritual Plane, which I have attained with God's Grace. I have received the Inner knowledge of Truth. Now I know the Light of God and its Source, the Creator. With this Divine knowledge, I have received the whole knowledge of God's Creation."

Giving the example of a metal pot, that makes a sound when it is struck, He says that the same pot, if broken into pieces, cannot make any noise. He is explaining that when the body dies, it can no longer talk or function because the real Sound (God's Melody) has left that body.

"There is still time to take advantage of this golden opportunity that God has given, as long as one is alive in the body. O Learned Pundit! Listen carefully! You are still in the physical body, and have time. When the person dies, he can no longer make any kind of sound."

#9-5 The Inner Realms

PART ONE

In describing the Spiritual Experiences of the Glorious Inner Realms, Sant Kabir first makes us aware of the many long and arduous systems of rising above the body consciousness, as taught by the ancient Yogis. Yogic systems, by their very methods alone, imply a course of extremely strict and disciplined activity to free the soul from the limiting aspects of the physical and mental life, and then to connect it with the All-Pervading Power of God. In other words, the soul, which is presently lost in the outgoing activities of mind and matter, must regain union with the Creator.

There are many paths in the Yogic system, but mostly they have to do with the cleanliness and fitness of the body, mental contentment and detachment from the physical, the attainment of certain Supernatural Powers, and the achievement of a state of complete desirelessness. The practitioners of Yoga appear to need Herculean strength and stamina to follow the rigors outlined in the various systems. Strict diet control, an exacting and forced restraint over the mind, extremely well-regulated breathing exercises, arduous physical postures and activities, combined with harsh internal cleansing processes impose an almost 'controlled death' of the body and its various functions.

This is all a result of the Yogis believing that in order to progress Spiritually, peace of mind and heart is an absolute necessity. As long as one is under the influence of the mind and its desires, they say, such contentment is impossible. However, even with all this extremely disciplined exertion, the Yogis *might* somehow reach up to the Sixth Chakra, between and behind the two eyebrows.

Sant Kabir explains the Yogic path of rising through the various Chakras of the body, but He says this method doesn't lead the soul anywhere into the Higher Spiritual Realms. "It ends at the Third Eye, the Sixth Chakra", but *this is the very point where the Sant Mat actually begins!*

All of the outer education, gleaned by the practice of Yoga, is termed by Sant Kabir as *Apra Vidya knowledge*. He says that this is not True knowledge, but rather knowledge that is away from Spirituality and is useful only for mind satisfaction, in order to explain the complex worldly system and its workings.

"To start the first step towards God," reveals Sant Kabir, "one has to clean himself inwardly in the heart and mind." The devotee must exert full discipline and restraint in all areas of life. Casting out the five evil tendencies, the devotee gradually replaces them with the virtues of chastity, patience, generosity, detachment, humility, and Discrimination.

Sant Kabir offers even more constructive advice, saying "Leave off eating all kinds of meat, and don't take intoxicants or alcohol. The intellect will then be awake and one can ride on it, rising above all worldly Illusion and doubt. The mind and heart will become happy and full of peace."

Referring to people like the Rishis, Munis, Yogis, and Sadhus, who would follow the Yogic instructions of the Shastras, Sant Kabir says that those people who practice Hatha Yoga believe that inner cleanliness of the body is necessary in order to commence Spiritual exercises. He says "To accomplish this end, those people would follow a very rigid set of cleansing rituals, combined with strict diet control."

The first act of purification that those people do, is called *Neti Karma* (cleaning of the nose). A long, narrow piece of cloth is twisted into a very thin string. After soaking it in water, they pass it slowly through each of the nostrils in turn, finally taking it out through the mouth.

Their second practice is called *Dhoti Karma* (washing out of the stomach). This entails holding in one hand, the end of a long piece of sheer, cotton cloth, about two or three inches wide, which has been softened by soaking it in water. The other end of the cloth is slowly swallowed by the mouth until only a small length is left to hold in the hand. Then this cloth is pulled very slowly out of the body. This practice cleans the mucous out of the stomach and the throat.

There are other cleansing methods, but these are the two major ones. After doing these, Sant Kabir says that the Yogi sits on the ground in the lotus position, with each foot on top of the opposite thigh, and tries to still the mind in preparation for meditation.

Hatha Yoga deals with the control of the bodily functions, particularly breathing, in order to gain some control over the mind. Part of the complete practice of this Yoga involves a form of breath control known as *Kumbhak*, in which short and long breaths are taken and then retained within for a measured duration. Ultimately, with practice, the Yogis can hold their breath for hours and even days at a time.

Sant Kabir is revealing that the Yogis believe that they can obtain knowledge of the Beyond by remaining concerned with the *Ganglionic*, or Chakra, Centres. They begin their practices by first focusing their attention on the *Guda Chakra* (near the rectum). This Centre has the Power of *Ganesh*, who is the deity residing there. The Yogis recite the Mantra of '*Kah-Ling*'. Eventually and with much practice, they see a four-petalled lotus flower, and a yellow colour. The Darshan of Ganesh is at long last obtained, and they receive the Boons of the *Riddhi-Siddhi* (various Supernatural Powers) of this Power.

Then Sant Kabir discusses the *Indri Chakra* (also known as *Svahd Chakra*), which is close to the regeneration centre. The whole world is created from this Second Chakra. With much practice, a six-petalled lotus flower and a blue colour can be seen in this Centre. This Chakra belongs to *Brahma* and his wife *Savitri*, so the Yogis recite the Mantra of '*Onkara*' in order to obtain their Powers.

As described by Sant Kabir, the *Nabhi Chakra* is the Third Centre, located near the navel. The Powers of *Vishnu* and his wife *Lakshmi* reside here, sustaining and preserving all Creation. The lotus flower here has eight petals and the Mantra to be recited is '*Ha-Ring*'.

The Fourth Centre, in the region of the heart, is called the *Hirdey Chakra*. One recites the Mantra of '*Sohn*' endlessly, in order to obtain Boons from *Shiva* and his wife, *Parvati*, the deities who reside at this place of the twelve-petalled lotus.

The throat area is the Fifth Centre, called the *Kanth Chakra*. The deity presiding here is *Shakti*, which is *Maya* itself, and is the Power spreading throughout the lower six Chakras. The Mantra to be recited here is *'Jah-Sri'*.

The Sixth and last Centre in the physical body below the Third, or Single Eye, is the *Ajna Chakra*, located between and behind the two eyebrows. Immediately above and behind the eyes is a two-petalled lotus flower, where the mind, called *'Borah'*, lives. Further up, there is the *Nij Mun*, or the *Brahmandi Mind*.

In describing these Chakras, Sant Kabir says that the Yogis do all this practice of worshipping the Devis and Devtas at each Centre in order to obtain certain Powers from them. These Boons are called *Riddhi-Siddhi* (the lower Supernatural Powers), and are of eighteen types. Sant Kabir then explains the meaning and description of the eight main Powers:

1. *Anima* is the Power to become invisible and the capacity to penetrate into all things so as to see into their inner structure.
2. *Laghima* is the Power to make one's body light in weight. It is often used in levitation and translevitation.
3. *Garima* is the Power to make the body as heavy as one wishes, and to make any object immovable. It is the opposite of Laghima.

4. *Mahima* is the Power to extend one's body to any size, and to see the working of far-off things, like the solar systems.

5. *Prapti* is the Power to get anything one likes by only wishing for it, as well as the capacity to go anywhere, even to the moon.

6. *Prakamyam* is the Power to fulfill the wishes of others.

7. *Vasitvam* is the Power to bring others under one's influence and control, including such elemental forces as the wind, rain, sun, etc.

8. *Ishitva* is the Power to attain all glories for the self, and to play the role of creator, preserver, and destroyer.

In addition to the above Powers, there are many subsidiary attainments, such as understanding the language of birds and animals, reading the thoughts of others, foretelling future events, healing by touch, knowing about one's previous births, and obtaining physical perfection.

Sant Kabir, however, advises that one ought not to be caught up in the wonders of these Powers. They can only be used to obtain worldly objects, knowledge and possessions, such as name and fame, but they cannot provide any Truth or knowledge of the Beyond. Attaining Supernatural Powers only serves to nourish the ego, and this strengthens one's arrogance.

These Powers are meant to be 'kept in reserve', and not to be used for one's personal or material gain. "If used unwisely, these Powers become a definite hindrance to go into the Higher Spiritual Realms, because they are the very lowest Powers that one can receive with practice on the Simran." Sant Kabir points out that one hankering to attain God does not waste his precious time and energy on them, because they will come to the devotee, automatically.

PART TWO

After all this description, Sant Kabir is ready to explain the esoteric side of Spirituality, known as *Para Vidya* (the Teachings of Inner knowledge). This knowledge of the soul begins at the point where the Physical Region meets with the Astral.

Sant Kabir points out that the Path of Spirituality that He teaches, **begins** at the Sixth Centre, the *Ajna Chakra* (the Third, or Single Eye). This Path of Sant Mat leads through *Khand, Brahmand*, on to *Sach Khand*, and finally to *Sat Naam*, the idyllic Home of Almighty God. He emphasizes, "Those of the higher Order of this Sadhna, *begin* with the Ajna Chakra, behind the eyes."

Sant Kabir says that the soul begins its ascent from the *Pind* (Physical) Region through the *Ajna Chakra* (the Seat of the Soul), and goes into the *Andh* (Astral) Region, and then further into the Beyond.

He then begins the description of the Inner Journey by revealing how the attention of the devotee becomes focused at the Third Eye, with the Grace of the True Master. "Passing through the optic nerve, the attention is focused at a point called the Third Eye. From here the soul enters the *Sukhmana* (the Middle Path), lying between the *Ida* (Left Path) and the *Pingla* (Right Path)."

He emphasizes that the Left and the Right Paths lead into the domain of Kaal, but the Middle Path takes one into the Beyond. "Only the true Sadhu can pass through the Nine Doors and reach to the Tenth (which is also known as *Dhaswan Dwar*)." At this stage, the soul merges totally into the Luminous, Effulgent Form of the Master, Who remains with the soul, to be its ever-faithful Guide in the Inner Spiritual Realms.

As the soul ascends within, it reaches the First Spiritual Stage known as *Sahansdal-Kanwal*, the Region of the thousand candle lights. One feels the bliss of so much radiance and Light, that it appears that this lotus is literally a fountain bursting with Light. Sant Kabir says that here, one hears the Sound of the Big Bell, or the Conch.

Further up, there is a very narrow tunnel, called the *Bunknal*, through which the soul must pass. Its direction leads straight out, then upward, and then straight out again.

Sant Kabir has explained in such a way that the whole Region thereafter appears to be an upside-down well, and the person who is a true Sadhu can drink here in abundance from the Fountain of Divine Nectar. "What a pity that whoever doesn't have a Master, dies in thirst of this Sweet Nectar!"

Sant Kabir carefully explains that as the soul rises upwards from *Sahansdal-Kanwal*, there are numerous tricks played by the Negative Power to attract the soul and keep it engrossed in that Region, the purpose being to deter the soul's progress upwards. For example, He says that there are exquisitely beautiful scenes, people, and music to captivate the soul's attention. However, these distractions all run away when the person recites the Five Charged Names of God given to him by the Master at the time of Spiritual Initiation.

After still more ascension, the soul reaches the Second Stage of Sant Mat, known as *Trikuti*. Sant Kabir describes this place to be a *'Mahal'* or palace. This Region is under the domain of Brahma. The soul here listens to the Sound of thunder, or the sweet melody of a huge drum. This Region is full of the knowledge of the physical world as well as of the Beyond. Sant Kabir says that this place is reached by means of the Mantra *'Om'*, and the colour pervading is that of a red rising sun.

Continuing His description of the Inner Realms, Sant Kabir says that the soul ascends onwards to *Brahmand,* the Third Spiritual Region. He uses the name of *Seth Sunn* to describe this place.

As the soul ascends even higher, it comes across a Pool of Nectar, also known as the True *Amritsar*, or *Mansarover*. The soul joyfully takes a dip in this Holy Pool and drinks of its Divine Nectar, thereby becoming the pure form of the *Hans* (pure soul). The soul has now shed its coverings of the Physical, the Astral, and the Causal bodies, and it attains Eternity in this Region. This is a very high stage in Spirituality and here the soul becomes free, at long last, from Kaal.

The soul now advances upwards to the Fourth Region, known as *Par Brahm*, and the Sound pervading is the sweet melody of a stringed instrument, such as the sitar, or violin. The soul itself is shining with Godly Light equal to twelve outer suns. The Mantra which resounds throughout is *'Rahankara'*, and an eight-petalled lotus flower can be found in this Region.

Sant Kabir says that the soul now continues its upward Journey further in the same Region, coming to a place called the *Maha Sunn*, which is an unbelievably vast void. Because of its extremely intense blackness, it can be crossed only with the assistance of the True Master. Without the Sat Guru, nobody can even enter in this Lane. Even though the soul now has the Light equivalent to twelve outer suns, its Light cannot possibly reach to any great distance in such intensive darkness.

Sant Kabir describes some very enrapturing attractions in this Region, which try to capture the soul and attempt to steal it away. He says, for example, that these forces can assume the form of a python snake that sucks through the air in great, powerful sweeps, so that no one can easily escape from its grasp. Fortunately, the Master quickly takes the soul 'under His wing', so to speak, and both the Master and the soul pass swiftly and easily through this huge Region of blackness. The soul can only travel in this Region with the assistance of the Master's Light. Sant Kabir explains that the soul has to cross altogether twenty-one stages in Par Brahm alone, and can only do so in the Company of the True Master.

As the soul ascends further up in the same Fourth Region, past *Maha Sunn,* it sees on its right side an enormous island, which is a complete world in itself. There is a twelve-petalled lotus flower in this area, which Sant Kabir calls as the *Achat Deep*. On the left side is another island, the *Sehaj Deep*, with a brilliant lotus of ten petals.

Still ascending on the Journey through this vast Fourth Region, the soul sees another place where there are five egg-shaped worlds. Sant Kabir remarks that these are so gigantic that in size comparison, the physical world we live in seems *just like a little hair!* Each of these five worlds also has its own Brahma.

Besides this place, there are another four places which are kept very secret. "A lot of souls are staying in each place," says Sant Kabir, "but they cannot leave, as they can neither ascend nor descend from those places."

At the very top of this same Fourth Region, which is known as *Bhanwar Gupha*, there are two colossal mountains, or gateways. There, the soul can at last see itself in its true form, and it recognizes itself as being made of the same Essence as God.

An amazing sight awaits the soul here in *Bhanwar Gupha*. In this place, there are *eighty-eight thousand huge worlds*, each complete in itself and dazzling with lights, literally bursting with diamonds, rubies, emeralds, and other precious gems! Here the Divine Sound Current reminds the soul of the earthly flute, and the word *'Soh'* is recited as the Mantra. Sant Kabir has used words to describe things in a manner that everyone might understand, but the items that are described are only similarities. They might appear to be diamonds, rubies, and emeralds, but they are actually something else!

As the soul leaves this place it reaches, with the Guidance of the Master, to the Door of *Sat Lokh*, also described as *Sach Khand*, the Fifth Spiritual Region of All Truth. In this Region, the soul encounters a fragrance so Divine that there is no equal in this physical world. Sant Kabir says that the soul becomes wonder-struck with the beauty of the sights that it can behold in this Region.

In Sach Khand, the soul now attains the Light equal to sixteen outer suns, and has the true, pure form of the Hans. Kabir Sahib reveals that it is these lucky Hans who are Blessed with the Seva of fanning Sat Purush in His magnificent Court! Sant Kabir says that there is the inebriating Sound of the bagpipe resounding throughout. He also discloses that *a million* suns and moons rising up together could not possibly be equal to one hair of Sat Purush in this wonderful, scintillating Region of unbounded radiance!

Still further up in the Kingdom of the Creator, is the Sixth Region known as *Alakh Lokh*. Sant Kabir says that this place can hardly contain the Light of *a billion* outer suns, but still this cannot stand against the dazzling Light emitted by one hair of *Alakh Purush*, the Lord of this Region.

More further up, is Agam Purusha, the Lord of the Region of Agam Lokh. Sant Kabir says that this Region is beyond description, but He hints that *a trillion* outer suns illuminate this huge, vast palace.

The Highest Spiritual Region, the Eighth, is known as *Anami Lokh*, where the presiding Lord *Anami Purush* resides. This is the ultimate, and last Stage in Sant Mat. This is the abode of Almighty God, the Supreme Being, the One God and Only God, called as *Anami*.

Sant Kabir reveals that this place can only be known by the souls who are able to reach here. This Region is above any description, because there are no equivalent words to even make some semblance or similarity to anything worldly. Almighty God, in this Place, is indescribable. Sant Kabir says that neither is the Region light nor dark, neither heavy nor light, neither is there Sound nor is it soundless. *It just is!*

Sant Kabir explains that this sum total of Sant Mat dwells right within the human body, above the eye-focus! The entirety of Almighty God's Creation, everything that Sant Kabir has described, *is within*, but Maya and Illusion have spread out such a very large, complicated, subtle net to ensnare and trap the poor soul, keeping it ignorant as to its rightful inheritance.

Kabir Sahib further explains how Maya and Illusion have created these traps with such cunning and cleverness so as to put the shadow of Brahmand into the Andh, and further from the Andh into the Pind. These are only shadows of each other, but this plan is so brilliantly created that everything looks unbelievably real, although it is not. It is only *an Illusion of Reality!*

In this connection, Sant Kabir says, "My *Desh* (my True Home) is far away from the Pind and Andh. It starts from the Fourth Spiritual Region and goes upward." He says that when He wants to invert and reach to the described places, He can do so in the blink of an eye. The true devotee also can travel from Pind to Andh to Brahmand and to Sat Lokh, and then further to Anami, riding on the Divine Sound Current. Sant Kabir emphasizes that "This is the only Way that the student of Sant Mat travels. In order to progress on the Spiritual Path, *everyone has to follow this same Way!*"

#9-6 How This Science Can Be Obtained

One has to search for that True Godman, wherever He might be, and follow His Teachings carefully. If one sincerely prays to Almighty God, the devotee will be guided to the Living Master. When that devotee comes under His Sharan, he will have all Grace to follow the Master's Instructions. The Master will tell that devotee to finish with the attachments and desires of this body. The only thing left to be concerned about, then, will be the soul.

The Master will grant the devotee the Way to go into the Higher Spiritual Realms, and He will go along with him. One should have the Holy Company of He Who can awaken the sleeping soul, and take it far, far away from the clutches of mind, matter, and Illusion.

Sant Kabir is describing that the Path of Sant Mat is such that one has to have the good fortune of previous Karmas in order to come to the True Master. Without this Teacher, one cannot cross the Ocean of Illusion, matter, and Deception. The human body is so deeply engrossed in the three worlds of the Physical, the Astral, and the Causal. The Master will help him to cross over these and to enter the other very high worlds, the Super-Spiritual Stages of Khand, Brahmand, and Sach Khand.

The True Master teaches one how to slowly rise up to see the Light of God. Right now, the total Consciousness is all over the body. When one practices regularly day by day in this field and does more and still further more practice, then he sees the Light of God. Sant Kabir is praising that kind of diligent person, that he is a true fighter, a true warrior, with the Grace of the Master. The true hero in the Lane of Love is one who knows himself and the Truth, and sees the Light of God. He is the true warrior that he has not left this Practice in between stages. He finishes the Journey right up to the Third Eye.

Sant Kabir says that there are three ways to find happiness and bliss forever here and in the hereafter:
1. If the person comes into the Holy Company of the Sat Sangat (the Company of Truth, a Godman).
2. If, after coming into His Company, faith, devotion and Love are created in the person towards the God Who is always within him and permeating in every atom.
3. After having these things in his heart and mind, then God's Light manifests in that soul.

By realizing himself and knowing the Oversoul, the person's direction will always be towards God. Once he has obtained that knowledge of the ultimate Goal of the human birth, he will be guided to come to a Competent Master Who will Graciously end his coming and going in this world of life and death.

That person does not come again in this existence of sorrows to suffer the pangs of physical life.

Once he becomes One with God, then that lucky soul sustains all tranquillity and ecstasy from God. People who think that God is far away have not attained this Stage, but he who has achieved the Blessing to be One with God, for him God is the Nearest of the near, nearer than his own breath.

Sant Kabir is explaining the condition of a person when he has the great good fortune to come to a Sat Guru, or a True Master, and then he obeys the Commandments of the Sat Guru while living in this body. He recognizes his own self with the God in him, and he also identifies the Negative Power and all of his tricks. That soul praises the True Master, Who has taken him as His own, and made him to realize what is right and what is wrong. This is the condition that a very rare soul obtains. It is the greatest Boon that a human can ever achieve, and he fulfills his true desire of meeting God. He becomes a Perfect and True human being.

Sant Kabir describes that the devotee now says, "My fear of life and death has vanished. The Beloved Master has given me His own Life-Impulse, the Spiritual Initiation and has dyed me in His own Colour, which He has manifested in me. I have seen the Light of God, and the darkness which I had before has been dispelled at the Seat of the Soul. I have obtained that Priceless Jewel, the Holy Naam, from my True Master, and I am engulfed in it. I have continuous remembrance and meditate upon it. My Third Eye has opened with the Grace of my Master, and I have seen His Effulgent Form. I have received that Precious Gem which my Master has embedded in me, and I think about it day and night."

We are reminded that there is nothing to compare with being taken aboard the shelter of the Godman, the True Sadhu. He will stay with the devotee even beyond the physical death. The devotee should surrender to Him and have His Holy Company, for the Master is One with God, and God is within Him. He is the only True Friend. He is the One Who will become the Guide here and also afterward. He is the One Who will reveal the Light and Sound of God. The devotee will solve the mystery of life and death in His Holy Company.

All Saints, in all times, have taught this age-old Way. This Way came along with the soul when it entered the world. It is made by Almighty God, and therefore it has never, and will never, change.

Sant Kabir strongly advises, "This body will perish one day! Go to the Living Master to have His Holy Company, and obtain true liberation. Have the Assembly only of the Saint, Who will grant salvation. It is a great Boon to have the

Society of a True Master. He is the One Who will take care of the soul, now and in the hereafter."

By way of explanation, He continues, "With the Light of the Divine knowledge of the Sat Guru, my heart became full of Light. He is the One Who made me focus my concentration at the Third Eye. My attention went steadily upwards in stages. All my sickness, attachments, and the five deadly enemies ran away. My mind, full of peace and heavenly bliss, then reached its True Home in Sach Khand. The Lord is continuously in my thoughts and my heart."

He adds, "Without the Grace of the True Master and His *Mool Mantra* (Spiritual Initiation), nobody can reach the Lap of God."

Sant Kabir has written many verses in which He illustrates what happens when the soul finally obtains this salvation of Almighty God. Using the allegory of a wedding party, He says, "The soul is as the wife who is being married to God in a full wedding ceremony." Not only the soul is in attendance, but many, many guests are present. These guests are all the various gods and goddesses who live within the soul's physical body. Sant Kabir then proceeds to describe the many celebrations that happen when the soul finally marries to Almighty God, and He also tells about the various attendants at these ceremonies.

The soul (represented as the spouse) says, "O my Friends! Sing the happy wedding songs. In my house (my body), my God (the Groom), has arrived. Now He is living in my body along with my soul. I am so lucky and Blessed. The utmost Grace from Almighty God has provided me with a Husband Who is the Emperor of emperors, the Supreme Lord, the Divine King! My wedding altar, in the shape of the Lotus Flower, is being decorated by Brahma, and praises of the Lord are being sung."

Sant Kabir continues, "There is nothing to compare in the Physical Region to the place where this Sacred Marriage takes place. It is described as the merging of the soul with the Beloved. This union is the highest, and only happens once in a lifetime."

Sant Kabir explains it in the best possible way, so that the people can understand that in this marriage all the gods and goddesses shower their good wishes, and Brahma and Vishnu sing praises of the Lord.

Continuing the description, He says that 330,000,000 deities (such as Rishis, Munis, devis, and devtas) come to see this amazing ceremony! What a sight to be witnessed! When the meeting finally takes place, the soul who has yearned for aeons and aeons to become One with the Lord, knows that forever and ever she is going to stay with Him!

This happy scene of marriage has been created just to show the worldly people how enticing, charming, and attractive is that moment of union with God. It is so much so appealing that one cannot find words from the vocabulary of the intellect. Sant Kabir so Lovingly makes everyone understand and appreciate this spectacular scene. He says, "When the devotee is attached to his Master, and receives this Nectar from Him, then all other worldly pleasures have no flavour. They seem insipid, compared to the taste of that Treasure of Divine Love."

He repeats, "The condition of true liberation is when one has the wealth of Holy Naam, and lives continuously in the Celestial Music. When one becomes dyed in the Colour of God, becomes totally engrossed in Him and has His Grace, then he is fully contented inwardly and outwardly. He has become One with God."

He says, "I am very Blessed by my Sat Guru, by Whose Grace I have obtained access with God. Blessed and very wise is my True Master, by Whose Grace I have thus realized."

Sant Kabir says that the aim of the Saint is to free the soul from the bondage of the body, and to connect it with the Creator. When the soul gets out from the clutches of the mind, matter, and Illusion, that is called True Salvation. He says that by doing Simran and rising above, one gets out of the clutches of Kaal, and will reach to the Highest Spiritual Realms. "An ordinary person, even an atheist, can be granted salvation by doing Simran."

The knowledge of how to obtain this freedom is given out only by the Master. Therefore, the first step in obtaining salvation is the practice of Gurbhakti, which means to surrender oneself, or to be devoted to, the Master. Then one does Spiritual Practice on the God-given Gift of the Holy Naam (the Divine Light and Sound). As a result, the person receives the state of being *Jivan Mukt* (a truly liberated soul), because this is the condition of being liberated from the bondage of the Cycle of life and death.

The soul is then free to go to its true Home, becoming One with God. Sant Kabir says that person who has learned this art of *Dying While Living* is now the true living person. When the devotee is fully contented inwardly and outwardly, 'dyed' in the Colour of Almighty God and full with the Master's Grace, it means that the devotee has achieved the state of True Salvation. That person forever 'lives' and will not be reborn again. He will never return to this Physical World.

Sant Kabir says, "Now You are my Sat Guru, my True Master, and I am Your disciple. Our union will be from beginning to end. I am Yours now, and I have come to your Shelter. My birth and death, my coming and going, in this terrible Ocean of worldly existence has finished."

Sant Kabir has used some very descriptive imagery, portraying the Master as the Captain of one's ship (the soul) that has to cross over the Ocean of terrible worldly storms. With Love and mercy, the Master guides that ship safely across to the other Shore.

Sant Kabir advises, "Die that type of death that you don't have to come again (be reborn) into this world and die again. When you meditate on the Supreme Lord, you can obtain that State from which there is no return to this world. The Creator takes that person's ship across the Ocean of Life to the other Shore."

The meaning of Mukti is 'freedom'. It implies an affinity only with the Master, and receiving the Holy Nectar from Him. All worldly attachments are released from the clutches of the heart. When one has this treasure of Divine Love, and lives in the Celestial Music, then the condition of true Mukti develops in him. When the devotee is fully contented inwardly and outwardly, dyed in the Colour of God and having the Master's Grace, it means that the devotee has achieved the stage of true Salvation.

Sant Kabir says, "Those who have communed with the Holy Naam according to the instructions of the Master, and have fulfilled the Spiritual Path up to Sach Khand, their faces shall shine with the Glory and Light of Almighty God, and be like a Guiding Beacon in this world of darkness. They shall radiate peace and Light to the whole world!"

Sant Kabir says, "Those who have communed with the Holy Naam according to the instructions of the Master, and have fulfilled the Spiritual Path up to back Khand, their faces, shall shine with the Glory and Light of Almighty God, and be like a Guiding Beacon in this world of darkness. They shall radiate peace and Light in the whole world."

CHAPTER 10

SANT KABIR'S VERSES
ORIGINAL HINDI-PUNJABI TEXT

#1. INTRODUCTION
Jo jan aisee karee kamaaee, tinkee failee jag rosnaaee.
Asht prmaan jageh sukh paaee. KSS p.71

#4-1. THE FORMATION OF CREATION
Naa ohu badhai na ghattaa jaa-e.
Akul niranjan ekai bhaa-e. GGS p.343

Oohaan sooraj naahee chand.
Aad niranjan karai anand. GGS p.1162

Kumaarai ek ju maatee goondhee bahu bidh baanee laaee.
Kaahoo mah motee muktaahal kaahoo biaadh lagaaee. GGS p.479

Khorras bhaan hans ko roopaa.
Beenaa Sant Dhun bajai anoopaa. KV p.149

Brahmaa nahen jab topee deena.
Bishan nahee tab jeekaa.
Shiv saktee ke janmou naahee.
Jabai jog ham seekhaa. KV p.313

Satjug me hum pehre paavree.
Tretaa jhoree jhandaa.
Dvaapar me hum arrband pehraa.
Kaloo firou nav khandaa. KV p.313

#4-2. AKAAL AND KAAL
Kaal Akaal khasam kaa keenaa ihu parpanch badhaavan.
Kah Kabir te ante mukte jin hirdai Raam rasaa-in. GGS p.1104

#4-3. DHARAM RAI
Jaopai Raam Raam rat naahee.
Te sabh Dharam Rai kai jaahee. GGS p.324

Dharam Rai jab lekhaa maagai baakee niksee bhaaree.
Panch krisaanvaa bhaag gae lai baadhio jeeo darbaaree.
GGS p.1104

Kabir gahgach pario kutamb kai kaanthai rah ga-i-o Raam.
Aa-e parai Dharam Rai-e ke beechah dhoomaad haam.
GGS p.1372

Kabir jete paap kee-e raakhe talai duraa-e.
Pargat bhae nidaan sabh jab poochhe Dharam Rai. GGS p.1370

Lakh churaasee dhaar ma tahaa jeev diyvaas.
Choudah jam rakhvaariyaa chaar beid vishvaas. KV p.90

#4-4. HOW KAAL RULES OVER HIS DOMAIN
Chaar din apnee naobat chale bajaae.
Itnak khateeaa gatheeaa mateeaa sang na kachh lai jaa-e.
GGS p.1124

But pooj pooj hindoo mooe turak mooe sir naaee.
Oe le jaare oe le gaade teree gat duhoo na paaee. GGS p.654

Jo paathar kao kahte dev.
Taa kee birthaa hovai sev.
Jo paathar kee paan-ee paa-e.
Tis kee ghaal ajaanee jaa-e. GGS p.1160

Kahat Kabir sunah re praanee pare kaal gras kooaa.
Jhoothee Maya aap bandhaa-i-aa jio nalnee brahm sooaa.
GGS p.654

Lakh churaasee dhaar ma tahaa jeev diyvaas.
Choudah jam rakhvaariyaa chaar beid vishvaas. KV p.90

#4-5. KARMA - THE LAW OF ACTION AND REACTION
Kabir maanas janam dulamb hai ho-e na baarai baar.
Jio ban fal paake bhue girhei bahur na laagei daar. GGS p.1366

Lakh churaasee jeev janto me.
Maanukh param anoop.
So tan paay na chethoo.
Khaa rank ka bhoop. KV p.254

Lakh churaasee dhaar ma tahaa jeev diyvaas.
Choudah jam rakhvaariyaa chaar beid vishvaas. KV p.90

Jit ko laa-i-aa tit hee laagaa taise karam kamaavai. GGS p. 476

Kabir dee-ee sansaar kao leenee jis mastak bhaag.
Amrit ras jin paa-i-aa thir taa kaa sohaag. GGS p.970

Gaaree hi sal oopjai kalh kashat aur meech. KV p.62

*Ka*ṛ*m kareem ju kar rahe met na saakai ko-e. GSS p.1366*

Kabir jor keeaa so julam hai le-e jabaab Khudaa-e.
Daftar lekhaa neekasai maar muhai muah khaa-e. GGS p.1375

Pahilai praalbadh banee, peechai banaa sareer.
Kabir achambaa hai yahee, mun nahi baandhai dheer. KSS

Karam karam sabh koe kahai, karam na cheenai koe.
Jo mun ka bundhan banai, karam kahaavai soe. KSS

#5. THERE IS A GREAT NEED OF SPIRITUALITY
Sukheeaa sabh sansaar hai khaavai aour sovai.
Dukheeaa daas Kabir hai jaagai aour rovai. KG p.11

#5-1. ILLUSION: THE LONG SLEEP OF THE SOUL
Harakh badaaee dekh kar bhagat karai sansaar.
Jab daikhai kuch heentaa aougan tharai gavaar. SKV

Maarag chaltai jo girai taakou naahee dos.
Kahai Kabir baithaa rahai ta sir karrai kos. KV p.33

Kabir ih tan jaa-i-gaa sakah ta leh bahor.
Naange paavah te ga-e jin ke laakh karor. GGS p.1365

Kabir garb na keejeeai dehee dekh surang.
Aaj kaal taj jaahuge jio kaanchuree bhuyang. GGS p.1366

Kabir garb na keejeeai chaam lapete haad.
Haivar oopar chhatar tar te fun dharnee gaad. GGS p.1366

Kiaa maagao kichh thir na rahaaee.
Dekhat nain chalio jag jaaee. GGS p.481

Kabir parbhaate taare khisah tio ih khisai sareer. GGS p.1373

Din te pahar pahar te ghareeaa aav ghatai tan chheejai.
Kaal aheree phirai badhik jio kahah kavan bidh keejai.
GGS p.691

Upjai nipjai nipaj samaaee.
Nainah dekhat ih jag jaaee. GGS p.325

Jaopai Raam Raam rat naahee.
Te sabh Dharam Rai kai jaahee. GGS p.324

Kabir martaa martaa jag mooaa mar bhee na jaaniaa koe.
Aise marne jo marai bahur na marnaa ho-e. GGS p.1366

Kahat Kabir sunah re praanee pare kaal gras kooaa.
Jhoothee Maya aap bandhaa-i-aa jio nalnee brahm sooaa.
GGS p.654

Kabir jao grih karah ta dharm kar naahee ta kar bairaag.
Bairaagee bandhan karai taa ko bado abhaag. GGS p.1377

Kabir bhaang maachhulee suraa paan jo jo praanee khaahe.
Teerath bart nem kee-e te sabhai rasaatal jaahe. GGS p.1377

Kabir har kaa simran chhaad kai paalio bahut khutamb.
Dhandhaa kartaa rah ga-i-aa bhaaee rahiaa na bandh.
GGS p.1370

Kabir hasnaa door kar ronai sai kar chit.
Bin roaie kioo paaeai prem piaaraa mit. KG p.9

Lankaa gadh sone kaa bha-i-aa.
Moorakh raavan kiaa le ga-i-aa. GGS p.1158

Pandit raaje bhoopatee aavah kaone kaam. GGS p.1365

Kabir deen gavaa-i-aa dunee sio dunee na chaalee saath.
Paa-e kuhaaraa maariaa gaafal apunai haath. GGS p.1365

Kaam krodh maa-i-aa mad matsar e-e sampai mo maahee.
Da-i-aa dharam ar gur kee sevaa e-e supanantar naahee.
GGS p.971

Jih ghar kathaa hot har santan ik nimakh na keeno mai pheraa.
Lampat chor doot matvaare tin sang sadaa baseraa. GGS p.971

Marna hai mar jaaingei koee na laigaa Naam.
Oojarr jaai basaaengei chaadkai bastaa gaam. Kabir Vani p.79

Kabir gaagar jal bharee aaj kaal jaihai foot.
Gur ju na chetah aapno adh maajh leejahige loot. GGS p.1368

Kabir sant moo-e kiaa ro-eeai jo apune girh jaa-e.
Rovah saakat baapure ju haatai haat bikaa-e. GGS p.1365

Raam Naam kee gat nahee jaanee bhai doobe sansaaree.
GGS p.332

In Maya jagdees gusaaee tumre charan bisaare.
Kinchat preet na upjai jan kao jan kakaa karah bechaare.
GGS p.857

Kabir paapee bhagat na bhava-ee har pooja na suhaa-e.
Maakhee chandan parharai jah bigandh tah jaa-e. GGS p.1368

Kahat Kabir chhod bikhiaa ras it sangat nihchao marnaa.
Ramaeeaa japah praanee anat jeevan baanee in bidh bhavsaagar
tarnaa. GGS p.92

Kabir oojal pahirah kaapare paan supaaree khaa-he.
Ekas har ke Naam bin baadhe jampur jaanhe. GGS p.1366

Kabir jag kaajal kee kotharee andh pare tis maahe. GGS p.1365

Honhaar so ho-e hai saakat sang na jaao. GGS p.1369

Kiaa jap kiaa tap kiaa brat pooja.
Jaa kai ridai bhaao hai doojaa. GGS p.324

Kabir jaa ghar saadh na seveeah har kee sevaa naahe.
Te ghar marhat saarkhe bhoot basah tin maahe. GGS p.1374

Bhoolee maalanee hai eo.
Satguru jaagtaa hai deo. GGS p.479

Keh Kabir kartaa me sabh hai kartaa sakal samaanaa.
Bhed binaa sabh bharam pare kou bujhai sant sujaanaa. KV p.111

Yugan yug beechure milai tum aaei kai.
Prem kar ang so ang laai. KV p.124

Gaanjaa afeeso postaa.
Bhaang aou sharaabe peevtaa.
Eik prem ras chaakhaa nahee.
Amlee hooaa to kyaa hooaa. KV p.287

Jo dekhaa so dukhiyaa dekhaa.
Tan dhar sukhee na dekhaa.
Udya asat kee baat kehat houn.
Taakar karhoo bibekhaa. KV p.298

#5-2. THE FUTILITY OF OUTER WORSHIP
Kabir Bahman Guru hai jagat kaa bhagtan kaa gur naahe.
Arjh urjh kai pach mooaa chaarao beidhoo maahe. GGS p.1377

Baavan achhar Lokh trai sabh kachh in hee maahe.
Ai akhar khir jaahige oe akhar in mah naahe. GGS p.340

Re jan mun maadhao sio laaeeai.
Chaturaaee na chaturbhuj paaeeai. GGS p.324

Kabir sansaa door kar kaagad deh bihaa-e. GGS p.1373

Kabir preet ik sio kee-e aan dubidhaa jaa-e.
Bhaavai laanbe kes kar bhaavai gharar mudaa-e. GGS p.1365

Jo paathar kao kahte dev.
Taa kee birthaa hovai sev.
Jo paathar kee paan-ee paa-e.
Tis kee ghaal ajaanee jaa-e. GGS p.1160

But pooj pooj hindoo mooe turak mooe sir naaee.
Oe le jaare oe le gaade teree gat duhoo na paaee. GGS p.654

Raag raagnee dimbh hoe baithaa aun har pah kiaa leenaa.
GGS p.654

Kaa-i-aa maanjas kaon gunaa.
Jao ghat bheetar hai malnaa.
Laokee athsath teerath naaee.
Kaoraapan taoo no jaaee. GGS p.656

Na paathar bolai naa kichh de-e.
Fokat karm nihfal hai sev. GGS p.1160

Devee devaa pooja dolah paarbrahm nahee jaanaa.
Kahat Kabir akul nahee chetiaa bikhiaa sio laptaanaa. GGS p.332

Sarjeeo kaatah nirjeeo pooja ant kaal kao bhaaree. GGS p.332

Jal kai majan je gat hovai nit nit mendak naavah.
Jaise mendak taise oe nar phir phir jonee aavah. GGS p.484

Kiaa jap kiaa tap sanjamo kiaa bart kiaa isnaan.
Jab lag jugat na jaaneeai bhaao bhagat bhagwaan.
GGS p.337

Kabir bhaang maachhulee suraa paan jo jo praanee khaahe.
Teerath bart nem kee-e te sabhai rasaatal jaahe. GGS p.1377

Laokee athsath teerath naaee.
Kaoraapan taoo no jaaee. GGS p.656

Baavan akhar jore aan.
Sakiaa na akhar ek pachhaan. GGS p.343

Pario kaal sabhai jag oopar maahe likhe brahm giaanee.
Kah Kabir jan bhae khaalse prem bhagat jih jaanee. GGS p.654

Mala pairat mun khushi tate kachu na hoe.
Mun mala ke fairte katt ujiaro hoe. KSS

Mala ferat jug bhaia fira na mun kar fer.
Kar ka manka darke too manka manka fer. KV p.19

Mala mosei larr parree kahai perat hai mohe.
Mun mala ke perte gur se mela hoe. SKV

Kaha kare angori gine mun taave chahu or.
Jeh faire saaee milei so baiaa kaath kathor. KG p.42

Jantar mantar sabh jhooth hai.
Mot bharmo jug koei.
Saar shabad jaanai binaa.
Kaagaa hans na hoei. KR p.5

Din ko rojaa rehat hai raat ha nat hai gaay.
Yeh to khoon vej bandagee kaho kyo khusee kudaay. KV p.87

Chaar ved Brahmaa nij thaanaa.
Mukat ka maram unhoo nahin jaanaa.
Daan pun un bahut bakhaanaa.
Apne maran kee khabar na jaanaa. KV p.314

Kaheh Kabir suno ho Gorakh.
Chalo Shabad ke sangaa. KV p.314

#5-3. THE MIND AND ITS DESIRES
Guru maanush kar jaantai, te nar kaheeai andh.
Mahaa dukhee sansaar mai, aagai jam ke bandh.
Guru maanush kar jantai, charanaamrit ko paan.
Te nar narkai jaainge, janam janam hoai savaan.
Kabir te nar andh hai, guru ko kehtai aur.
Har roothai gur thor hai, guru roothai nahi thor.
Guru ko manukh jante charan amrit ko paan.
Te nar narke jaaenge janam jan mohe suaan. KSS

Maya tajee to kiyaa huaa maan tajaa nahi jae.
Maan vadai munivar gale maan sabhan ko khaae. KV p.70

Jeh aapaa teh aapdaa, jeh sansaa teh sogh.
Kahai Kabir yeh kioo mitai, chaaron deerag rogh. SKV

Parna Likhna chatori eh to baat sahal.
Kaam dahan mun bas karan gagan charan mushkal. SKV

Jab lag aas sareer kee mirtak hoa na jai.
Kaaeaa Maya mun tajai toorai rahai bijaai. SKV

Has has kant na paaeiaa jin paaeiaa tin roei.
Haasee khailai peeaa milai to koun duhaagan houei. KG p.9

Chah gaee chintaa mitee manuaa bai parvaah.
Jin ko kachoo na chaahiai soee shaahanshaah. KV p.80

Go dhan, gaj dhan, baaj dhan, aur ratan dhan khaan.
Jab aavai santosh dhan sabh dhan dhool samaan. KV p.80

Tun mun diyaa to kayaa hooaa nij mun diyaa na jaay.
Keh Kabir ta daas so kaise mun patiyaay. KV p.42

Kaamee krodhee laalchee insai bhagat na hoy.
Bhagat karai koee soormaa jat baran kul khoy. KV p.67

Kot param laage rahai eik krodh kee laar.
Kiyaa kraayaa sabh gayaa jab aayaa hankaar. KV p.67

Daso disaa ke krodh kee oothee aparbal aag.
Seetal sangat saadh kee tahaa ubreai bhaag. KV p.67

Kutil bachan sabh se buraa jaar karai tan chaar.
Saadh bachan jal roop hai barsai amrit dhaar. KV p.68

Jab mun laagai lobh so gayaa vishay me soy.
Kahai Kabir bichaari kai kas bhakat dhan hoy. KV p.68

Kabira trisnaa paapinee taaso preeti na jor.
Paind paind paache parai laagou motee khor. KV p.68

Kabira aoudhee khopree kabhoo dhaapai naahi.
Teen Lokh kee sanpdaa kab aavai ghar maahi. KV p.68

Moh fand sabh faandiyaa koei na sakai nirvaar.
Koee,sadhoo jan paarkhee birlaa tatav bichaar. KV p.69

Moh magan sansaar hai kanyaa rahee kumar.
Kaahoo surat jo naakree fir fir le avitaar. KV p.69

Jeh lag sabh sansaar hai mirag saban ko moh.
sur nar naag pataal aur rishee munivar sabh joh. KV p.69

Yuvaa jaraa baalaapan beetyo chouth avasathaa aaee.
Jis musvaa ko takai bilaiyaa tas jam ghaat lagaaee. KV p.70

Maan barraaee jagat men kookark pehchaan.
Meet keeai mukh chaatee bair keeai tan haan. KV p.71

Kabira apnai jeev te ye do baatai dhoy.
Maan barraaee kaarnai aachat mool na khoy. KV p.71

Maya tayaage kayaa bhayaa maan taja nahi jaay.
Jaihi maanai munivar thage saban ko khaay. KV p.71

Mad to bahutak bhaanti ka taah na jaanai koy.
Tan-mad mun-mad jaat-mad maya-mad sabh loy. KV p.77

Vidiaa-mad aou gunhoo-mad raaj-mad unmad.
Etnai-mad ko rad karai tab paavai anhad. KV p.77

Mun paancho ke bas paraa mun ke bas nahi paanch.
Jee dekhoo tit dou lagee jit bhaagoo tit aanch. KV p.91

Kabira mun to eik hai bhaavai tahaa lagaay.
Bhaav guru kee bhakt kar bhaavai bishey kamaay. KV p.92

Paanee he to paatlaa dhooaa ho te jheen.
Pavan ho te at ootlaa dosat Kabira keen. KV p.93

Mun ke haarai haar hai mun ke jeetai jeet.
Keh Kabir pio paaeeai munhee kee parteet. KV p.94

Santo yeh mun hai barr jaalim.
Jaasou mun so kaam paro hai tishee hvai hai maalim. KV p.178

Meraa teraa munuaa kaise eik hoee re.
Mai kehtaa hou aakhin dekhee.
Too kaagad ka lekhee.
Mai kehtaa murjhaavan haaree.
Too raakhyo arjhaaee re. KV p.248

Jaha kaam teh Naam nahi, jaha Naam nahi kaam.
Dono kabhoo na milai, ravir jani ik thaam. KSS

#5-4. FEAR AND FEARLESS

Din te pahar pahar te ghareeaa aav ghatai tan chheejai.
Kaal aheree phirai badhik jio kahah kavan bidh keejai.
GGS p.691

Dharam Rai jab lekhaa maagai kiaa mukh le kai jaahigaa.
GGS p.1106

Chaar din apnee naobat chale bajaae.
Itnak khateeaa gatheeaa mateeaa sang na kachh lai jaa-e.
GGS p.1124

Jaopai Raam Raam rat naahee.
Te sabh Dharam Rai kai jaahee. GGS p.324

Kabir gaagar jal bharee aaj kaal jaihai foot.
Gur ju na chetah aapno adh maajh leejahige loot. GGS p.1368

Ankhiyan setee neer behan laagyo.
Ab kas naah too bolat abhagaa.
Kehat Kabir suno bhaaee saadho.
Oorrego hans toote gayo taagaa. KV p.308

Khand Brahmand mah sinjhee meraa batooaa sabh jag bhasmaadhaaree.
Taaree laagee tripal palteeai chhootai hoe pasaaree. GGS p.334

Bhakti doohelee guru kee, nahi kaaer ka kaam.
Sees otaarai haath se, so laisee Sat Naam. KSS

Guru bhakti at kathin hai jioo khandai kee dhaar.
Bina saach pahunche nahi maha kathan bioohaar. KSS

Jaan bhagat ka nit maran anjaane ka raaj.
Sar aousar samjhe nahi peht bhran sou kaaj. SKV

Jah anbhao tah bhai nahee jah bhaao tah har naahe. GS p.1374

Bhai bich bhaao bhaae ko-oo boojhah har ras paavai bhaaee.
Jete ghat amrit sabh hee mah bhaavai tisah peeaaee. GS p.1123

Anjaane ko narak sarag hai har jaane ko naahee.
Jai dar sabh log darat hai so dar hamre naahee. KV p.179

#5-5. THE EFFECTS OF ASSOCIATION WITH WORLDLY PEOPLE
Saakat kaaree kaambaree dhoe ho-e na set. GGS p.1369

Saakat sang na keejeeai jaa te ho-e binaah. GGS p.1369

Kabir jag kaajal kee kotharee andh pare tis maahe. GGS p.1365

Kabir saakat sang na keejeeai doorah ja-eeai bhaag.
Baasan kaaro parseeai tao kachh laagai daag. GGS p.1371

Kaalaa mukh karai maan ka aadar laae aag.
Maan badaaee chaad kar rahe Naam se laag. KSS

Honhaar so ho-e hai saakat sang na jaao. GGS p.1369

#5-6. UNTRUE MASTERS
Kabir maa-e moondao tih guru kee jaa te bharm na jaa-e.
Aap dube chhau bed mah chele dee-e bahaa-e. GGS p.1370

Galee jinaa japmaaleeaa lote hath nibag.
Oe har ke sant na aakheeah baanaaras ke thag. GGS p.475-6

Kabir Bahman Guru hai jagat kaa bhagtan kaa gur naahe.
Arjh urjh kai pach mooaa chaarao beidoo maahe. GGS p.1377

Kabir jhankh na jhankheeai tumro kahio na ho-e. GGS p.1366

Raas biraanee raakhte khaayaa ghar kaa khet. GGS p.1369

Kabir avarah kao updeste mukh mai par hai ret. GGS p.1369

Karnee bin kathnee kathai agyaani din raat.
Kookar jayon bhoonkat firai sunee sunaaee baat. KV p.33

Footee aankh bibaik kee lakhai na sant asant.
Jaakai sang das bees hai taakaa Naam mahant. KV p.85

Shabd saakhee sikh paaras karhee.
Hoy bhoot pun nar kahin parhee. KV p.186

Binaa bhed kandhaar kahaavai.
Aagil janam savaan ko paavai. KV p.186

#6. THE SOUL'S RELATIONSHIP WITH GOD
Jab ham eko ek kar jaaniaa.
Tab logah kaahe dukh maaniaa. GGS p.324

Kumaarai ek ju maatee goondhee bahu bidh baanee laaee.
Kaahoo mah motee muktaahal kaahoo biaadh lagaaee. GGS p.479

Naa ohu badhai na ghattaa jaa-e.
Akul niranjan ekai bhaa-e. GGS p.343

Puja Raam ek hee devaa.
Saachaa naavan gur kee sevaa. GGS p.484

Kabir taa sio preet kar jaa ko thaakar Raam. GGS p.1365

Kah Kabir ihu Raam kee ans.
Jas kaagad par mitai na mansu. GGS p.871

Sarab sukhaa kaa ek har soami so gur Naam da-io. GGS p.856

Aval Allah noor upaa-i-aa kudrat ke sabh bande.
Ek noor te sabh jag upjiaa kaun bhale ko mande. GGS p.1349

Jal thal maahe aapah aap.
Aapai japah aapna jaap. GGS p.343

Mussalmaan kaa ek Khudaae.
Kabir kaa soami rahiaa samaa-e. GGS p.1160

Hai til ke til ke til bheetar birle sadhu paayaa hai.
Chahoo dal kamal tirkutee saaje unkaar darsaayaa hai. KV p.109

Keh Kabir sabh baajee maahee.
Baajeegar ko cheenai naahee. KV p.178

Jab hum rehal rhaa nahen koee.
Hamarmaah rehal sabh koee.
Kehhoo so Raam koun tor sevaa.
So samujhaay kaho mohen devaa. KV p.310

#6-1. FIRST SEPARATION FROM GOD
Tou jalnidh hau jal ka meenu.
Jal mah rahau jlah bin kheenu. GGS p.323

Jio jal jal mah paise na niksai tio dhur milio julaaho. GGS p.692

#6-2. SWEET IS THY WILL
Kabir dee-ee sansaar kao leenee jis mastak bhaag.
Amrit ras jin paa-i-aa thir taa kaa sohaag. GGS p.970

Jo kichhhau hoaa su teraa bhaana.
Jo iv boojhai su sahaj samaanaa. GGS p.1349

Hukmai boojhai chaopar khelai mun jin dhaale paasaa.
GGS p.793

Jal te thal kar thal te kooaa koop te mer karaavai.
Dhartee te aakaas chadhaavai chadhe aakaas giraavai.
GGS p.1252

Gur sevaa te bhagat kamaaee.
Tab ih maanas dehee paaee.
Is dehee kao simarah dev.
So dehee bhaj har kee sev. GGS p.1159

So sevak jo laa-i-aa sev.
Tin hee paae niranjan dev. GGS p.1159

Harjan ootam bhagat sadaavai aagiaa mun sukh paaee.
Jo tis bhaavai sat kar maanai bhaanaa mane vasaaee. GGS p.480

Hukam pachhaan taa khasmai milnaa. GGS p.92

Jo jan bhaao bhagat kachh jaanai taa kao achraj kaaho.
GGS p.692

Jaa tis bhaavai taa hukam manaavai.
Is bere kao paar laghaavai. GGS p.337

Jaa tis bhavai taa laagai bhaao.
Bharm bhulaavaa vichhu jaae. GGS p.92

#6-3. THE TRUE TEMPLE OF GOD

Guru tamara kaha hai, chela kaha rahai.
Kion karke mmilna paia, kion bichare aavai jae. SKV

Preetam pateeaa tab likhoo, jo tum baso bidesh.
Tan mai mun mai praan mai, vaankoo kiyaa sandesh. KV p.18

Paanee keraa pootlaa raakhaa pavan sanchaar.
Naanaa baanee boltaa jyot dharee kartaar. KV p.84

Moko kaha dhoondho bande mai to tere paas men. KV p.142

Kaayaa bheid kiyaa nirvaaraa.
Yeh sabh rachnaa pind manjhaaraa. KV p.150

Jeev roop yak antar baasaa.
Antar jyot keen par gaasaa. KV p.170

Yeh ghat chandaa yeh ghat soor.
Yeh ghat gaajai anhad toor. KV p.195

Ingalaa pingalaa taanaa bharnee.
Sukhmum taar se beenee chadriyaa.
Aath kanval dal charkhaa dolai.
Paanch tat guhn teenee chaudriyaa.
Saaee ke siyat maas das laagai.
Thok thok ke beenee chadariyaa. KV p.312

Guru tamara kaha hai, chela kaha rahai.
Kion karke mmilna paia, kion bichare aavai jae. SKV

Preetam pateeaa tab likhoo, jo tum baso bidesh.
Tan mai mun mai praan mai, vaankoo kiyaa sandesh. KV p.18

Paanee keraa pootlaa raakhaa pavan sanchaar.
Naanaa baanee boltaa jyot dharee kartaar. KV p.84

Moko kaha dhoondho bande mai to tere paas men. KV p.142

Kaayaa bheid kiyaa nirvaaraa.
Yeh sabh rachnaa pind manjhaaraa. KV p.150

Jeev roop yak antar baasaa.
Antar jyot keen par gaasaa. KV p.170

Yeh ghat chandaa yeh ghat soor.
Yeh ghat gaajai anhad toor. KV p.195

Ingalaa pingalaa taanaa bharnee.
Sukhmum taar se beenee chadriyaa.
Aath kanval dal charkhaa dolai.
Paanch tat guhn teenee chaudriyaa.
Saaee ke siyat maas das laagai.
Thok thok ke beenee chadariyaa. KV p.312

#6-4. SWEET PRAISES OF GOD
Raam ju daataa mukat ko sant japaavai Naam. GGS p.1373

Kabir sevaa kao da-e bhale ek sant ik Raam. GGS p.1373

Jah uh jaae tahee sukh paavai maa-i-aa taas na jholai dev.
Kah Kabir meraa mun maaniaa Raam preet keeo lai dev.
GGS p.85

Maano sabh sukh nao nidh taa kai sahaj sahaj jas bolai dev.
GGS p.857

Jal thal maahe aapah aap.
Aapai japah aapna jaap. GGS p.34

Oohaan sooraj naahee chand.
Aad niranjan karai anand. GGS p.1162

Sarab sukhaa kaa ek har suaamee so gur Naam da-io. GGS p.856

Sabh parbat siahee karo gholu samunder mahei.
Dharti ka kagaz karo guru guhn likha na jae. KG p.59

Guru hamara gagan mah, chela hai ghat maahe.
Surat shabd milna paia. Bicharat kabhu naahe. KSS

Shabd guru ko kee jia bhotak guru labaar.
Apnai apnai saad ko thor thor batmaar. KSS

Mussalmaan kaa ek Khudaae.
Kabir kaa soami rahiaa samaa-e. GGS p.1160

Sankar maolio jog dhiaan.
Kabir ko Soami sabh samaan. GGS p.1193

Hamro bhartaa bado bibekee aape sant kahaavai. GGS p.476

Taa madh adhar singhaasan gaajai.
Purukh Shabd teh adhik biraajai.
Kotin soor rom eik laajai.
Aise purakh deedaaraa hai. KV p.134

#6-5. THE FOUR CATEGORIES OF 'RAM'
Raam ka Naam lai drishti lai raam chand.
Bhai vaasishth guru mantra daanee. KV p.158

#7. TRUE WORSHIP
Sant prasaad bhae mun nirmal har keertan mah andin jaagaa.
GGS p.343

Aval Allah noor upaa-i-aa kudrat ke sabh bande.
Ek noor te sabh jag upjiaa kaun bhale ko mande. GGS p.1349

Pragat pragaas Giaan gur gamit Satgur te sudh paaee.
Daas Kabir taas mad maataa uchak na kabhoo jaaee. GGS p.969

Gur kar giaan dhiaan kar mahooaa bhaao bhaathee mun dhaaraa. GGS p.969

Sukhman naaree sahaj samaanee peevai peevanhaaraa.
GGS p.969

Kah Kabir mai so guru paa-i-aa jaa kaa naao bibeko. GGS p.793

Moond lee-e darvaaje.
Baajeeale anhad baaje. GGS p.656

Nagree ekai nao darvaaje dhaavat barij rahaaee.
Trikutee chhootai dasvaa dar khoolaib taa mun kheevaa bhaaee.
GGS p.1123

Kabira jahaa giaan tah Dharm hai jahaa jhooth tah paap.
Jahaa lobh tah kaal hai jahaa khimaa tah aap. GGS p.1372

Heeraa dekh heere karao aades.
Kahai Kabir niranjan alekh. GGS p.972

Aise Giaan pargatiaa purkhotam kah Kabir rang raataa.
GGS p.92

Kabir mun seetal bha-i-aa paa-i-aa brahm giaan. GGS p.1373

Heerai heeraa bedh pavan mun sahaje rahiaa samaaee.
Segal jot in heerai bedhee Satgur bachnee mai paaee. GGS p.483

Sukhman naaree sahaj samaanee peevai peevanhaaraa.
GGS p.969

Saaee aagai saanch hai sabh kao saanch so haai. KG p.43

Bhaavai laambai kais kar bhaavai ghot monaai. KSS

Choothai sai choothaa milai adhitaa barrai saneh.
Choothai ko saacha milai tarr de tootai neh. KSS

Saachai sraap na laagaee saachai kaal na khaie.
Saachai ko saachaa milai, saachai maahe samaaie. KV p.83

Saach braabar tap nahi chooth braabar paap.
Jaakai hirdai saanch hai taankai hirdai aap. KV p.83

Jah anbhao tah bhai nahee jah bhaao tah har naahe. GGS p.1374

Santaa kao mat koee nindah sant Raam hai eko. GGS p.793

Ab mun ult sanaatan hooaa.
Tab jaaniaa jab jeevat mooaa.
Kah Kabir sukh sahaj samaavao. GGS p.327

Santan sang Kabira bigrio.
So Kabir raamai hoe nibrio. GGS p.1158

Kabira jahaa giaan tah Dharm hai jahaa jhooth tah paap.
Jahaa lobh tah kaal hai jahaa khimaa tah aap. GGS p.1372

Toon jal nidh hao jal kaa meen.
Jal mah rahao jalah bin kheen. GGS p.323

Kah Kabir bhaj saarangpaanee.
Raam udak meree tikhaa bujhaanee. GGS p.323

Allah alakh na jaaee lakhiaa gur gur deenaa meethaa.
Kah Kabir meree sankaa naasee sarb niranjan deethaa.
GGS p.1350

Kabir sant moo-e kiaa ro-eeai jo apune girh jaa-e.
Rovah saakat baapure ju haatai haat bikaa-e. GGS p.1365

Gur kai baan bajar kal chhedee pragtiaa pad pargaasaa.
GGS p.332

E-e du-e akhar naa khise so gah rahio Kabir. GGS p.1373

Kabir surg nark te mai rahio satgur ke parsaad. GGS p.1370

Kabir gaagar jal bharee aaj kaal jaihai foot.
Gur ju na chetah aapno adh maajh leejahige loot. GGS p.1368

Chaar din apnee naobat chale bajaae.
Itnak khateeaa gatheeaa mateeaa sang na kachh lai jaa-e.
GGS p.1124

Puja Raam ek hee devaa.
Saachaa naavan gur kee sevaa. GGS p.484

Bhoolee maalanee hai eo.
Satguru jaagtaa hai deo. GGS p.479

Aval Allah noor upaa-i-aa kudrat ke sabh bande.
Ek noor te sabh jag upjiaa kaun bhale ko mande. GGS p.1349

Kah Kabir heeraa as dekhio jag mah rahaa samaaee.
Guptaa heeraa pragat bha-io jab gur gam deeaa dikhaaee.
GGS p.483

Heerai heeraa bedh pavan mun sahaje rahiaa samaaee.
Segal jot in heerai bedhee Satgur bachnee mai paaee. GGS p.483

Saach braabar tap nahi chooth braabar paap.
Jaakai hirdai saanch hai taankai hirdai aap. KV p.83

Hirde pragaas giaan gur gamit gagan mandal mah dhiaanaanaa.
Bikhai rog bhai bandhan bhaage mun nij ghar sukh jaanaanaa.
GGS p.339

Jab lag mun baikunth kee aas.
Tab lag hoe nahee charn nivaas. GGS p.325

Kahat Kabir chhod bikhiaa ras it sangat nihchao marnaa.
Ramaeeaa japah praanee anat jeevan baanee in bidh bhavsaagar tarnaa. GGS p.92

Dakhan des haree kaa baasaa pachham Allah mukaamaa.
Dil mah khoj dilai dil khojah ehee thaor mukaamaa. GGS p.1349

#7-1. ALL HUMANITY IS ONE
Aval Allah noor upaa-i-aa kudrat ke sabh bande.
Ek noor te sabh jag upjiaa kaun bhale ko mande. GGS p.1349

Jayo nainan me pootree.
Yoh khaalik ghat maahe. KV p.4

Jetaa ghat teta mataa bahu baanee bahu bhekh. KV p.3

Sabh ghat hai rahaa.
Soee aap alaikh. KV p.4

#7-2. HUMAN BODY IS THE GOLDEN OPPORTUNITY TO MEET GOD
Hao balihaaree tin kao pais ju neekis jaahe. GGS p.1365

Saas saas par parakh le ghat meh preetam chab.
Bhook na saathan se kabhi, aoosar paeaa abh. SKV

Simran se mun laeeai jaise naad kurang.
Pran taje pal bichure Sant Kabir keh deen. KV p.17

Kabir kaal karantaa abah kar ab kartaa su-e taal. GGS p.1371

*Kabir maanas janam dulamb hai ho-e na baarai baar.
Jio ban fal paake bhue girhei bahur na laagei daar.* GGS p.1366

*Jab lag jaraa rog nahee aa-i-aa.
Jab lag kaal grasee nahee kaa-i-aa.
Jab lag bikal bhaee nahee baanee.
Bhaj leh re mun saarigpaanee.
Ab na bhajas bhajas kab bhaaee.
Aavai ant na bhajiaa jaaee.* GGS p.1159

Is dehee kao simarah dev. GGS p.1159

*Gur sevaa te bhagat kamaaee.
Tab ih maanas dehee paaee.
Is dehee kao simarah dev.
So dehee bhaj har kee sev.* GGS p.1159

*Upjai nipjai nipaj samaaee.
Nainah dekhat ih jag jaaee.* GGS p.325

*Kabir sant moo-e kiaa ro-eeai jo apune girh jaa-e.
Rovah saakat baapure ju haatai haat bikaa-e.* GGS p.1365

Kabir parbhaate taare khisah tio ih khisai sareer. GGS p.1373

*Kabir haad jare jio laakaree kes jare jio ghaas.
Ih jag jartaa dekh kai bha-i-o Kabir udaas.* GGS p.1366

*Kabir gaagar jal bharee aaj kaal jaihai foot.
Gur ju na chetah aapno adh maajh leejahige loot.* GGS p.1368

*Vai sut vai bit vai pur paatan bahur na dekhai aa-e.
Kaht Kabir Raam kee na simrah janam akaarath jaa-e.*
GGS p.1124

*Kabir guru kee bhakat kar, taj bikhiaa ras choj.
Baar baar nahi paaeeai, maanas janam kee mouj.* KSS

*Kabir soeaa kiaa karai jaagan kee kar chounp.
Eh dam heera laal hai ginn ginn gur ko sounp.* KV p.73

Kaheta hoo keh jaat hoo kahoo bajaavat dhol.
Sooaasaa birthaa jaat hai teen Lokh ka mol. KV p.55

Brich kabhoo nahi fal bhakhai nadi na sanchai neer.
Parmaarath ke kaarne, saadhun dharaa sareer. KV p.46

Raat gavaaee soy kar divas gavaayaa khaay.
Heeraa janam amol thaa kourree badlai jaay. KV p.55

Aachai din paachai gaei guru se kiyaa na het.
Ab paktaavaa kyaa karai chirreeyaa chug gaeen khet. KV p.55

Pancho noubat baajtee hot chateeso raag.
So mandir khaalee parraa baithan laagai kaag. KV p.56

Lakh churaasee jeev janto me.
Maanukh param anoop.
So tan paay na chethoo.
Khaa rank ka bhoop. KV p.254

#7-3. HELPING FACTORS FOR SPIRITUAL PROGRESS

Paannee baado naav mai, ghar mai baado daam.
Dono haath ooleecheeai, yahee sayaano kaam. SKV

Deh deh kachoo deh too jab lag teri deh.
Nischai kar opkaar hi jivan ka fal eh. KSS

Barraa hooaa to keaa hooaa jaise perr khajoor.
Panthi ko chaayaa nahi, fal laagai at door. KV p.71

Tan deeai tan na ghatai nadee ghatai nahi neer.
Apnee aakon dekh lo yo kabh rahai Kabir. KV p.79

Deh, deh, kachoo deh too jab lag teree deh.
Deh kheh ho jaaigee fir kon kahaiga deh. KSS

Deh tarai ka gunn yahee deh, deh, kuch deh.
Kahai Kabira deh too jab lag teri deh. KV p.73

Brich kabhoo nahi fal bhakhai nadi na sanchai neer.
Parmaarath ke kaarne saadhun dharaa sareer. KV p.46

Jeevat marah marah phun jeevah panarap janam na hoee.
GGS p.1104

Jio jal jal mah paise na niksai tio dhur milio julaaho. GGS p.692

Raajaa raana rao rank bara jo simrai Naam.
Kahai Kabir sabh se bara jo simrai nehkaam. KSS

Nar naaree sabh narak hai, jab lag deh sakaam.
Kabir soo bhaave peeo ko, jo simrai nehkaam. KSS

Jo kichh hoaa su teraa bhaanaa.
Jo iv boojhai su sahaj samaanaa. GGS p.1349

Kah Kabir saadhoo ko preetam tis moorat balihaaree. GGS p.1252

Charan kamal jaa kai ridai basah so jan kio dolai dev. GGS p.857

Satgur keeno parupkaar.
Kaadh leen saagar sansaar.
Charn kamal sio laagee preet.
Gobind basai nitaa nit cheet. GGS p.331

Due ser maangao choonaa. Paao gheeo sang loonaa.
Adh. ser maangao daale. Mo kao donao vakhat jivaale.
Khaat maangao chaopaaee. Sirhaanaa avar tulaaee.
Oopar kao maangao kheendhaa. Teree bhagat karai jan theendhaa.
Mai naahee keetaa labo. Ik naao teraa mai phabo. GGS p.656

Kabir saadhoo kee sangat rahao jao kee bhoosee khaao.
GGS p.1369

Kabir jao grih karah ta dharm kar naahee ta kar bairaag.
Bairaagee bandhan karai taa ko bado abhaag. GGS p.1377

Kahai Kabir pooran jag soee.
Jaa ke hirdai avar na ho-ee. GGS p.330

Kabir meraa mujh mah kichh nahee jo kichh hai so teraa.
Teraa jujh kao saopate kiaa laagai meraa. GGS p.1375

Har bha-io khaand ret mah bikhrio hasantee chunio na jaaee.
Kah Kameer kul jaat paant taj cheetee hoe chun khaaee.
GGS p.972

Kabir sabh te ham bure ham taj bhalo sabh ko-e.
Jin aisaa kar boojhiaa meet hamaaraa so-e. GGS p.1364

Kabir jao tuh saadh piram kee sees kaat kar go-e.
Khelat khelat haal kar jo kichh ho-e ta ho-e. GGS p.1377

Gur sevaa te bhagat kamaaee.
Tab ih maanas dehee paaee.
Is dehee kao simarah dev.
So dehee bhaj har kee sev. GGS p.1159

Harjan ootam bhagat sadaavai aagiaa mun sukh paaee.
Jo tis bhaavai sat kar maanai bhaanaa mane vasaaee. GGS p.480

Hukam pachhaan taa khasmai milnaa. GGS p.92

Aise giaan pargatiaa purkhotam kah Kabir rang raataa. GGS p.92

Hukmai boojhai chaopar khelai mun jin dhaale paasaa.
GGS p.793

Pario Kaal sabhai jag oopar maahe likhe Brahm giaanee.
Kah Kabir jan bhae khaalse prem bhagat jih jaanee. GGS p.654

Jin juaalaa jag jaariaa su jan ke udak samaan. GGS p.1373

Kabir khoob khaanaa kheecharee jaa mah amrit lon.
Heraa rotee kaarne galaa kataavai kaon. GGS p.1374

Khinthaa giaan dhiaan kar sooee sabad taagaa math ghaalai.
Panch tat kee kar mirgaanee gur kai maarag chaalai. GGS p.477

Kabir dhudhiaa kookree karat bhajan mai bhang.
Taankai tookeraa daar kar simran karou nisang. KG p.75

Jeevan muktai hai rahai tajai khalak kee aas.
Aagai peechai har firai kayo dukh paavai daas. KV p.49

Kabira saaee mujh ko rookhee rotee dey.
Chopree maangat mai daroo rookhee cheen na ley. KV p.88

Paarai pind meen lai khaaee.
Kahai Kabir log bauraaee. KV p.196

#7-4. DISCRIMINATION (THE FIFTH ELEMENT)
Bhole Bhaa-e mile raghuraa-i-aa. GGS p.324

Heeraa dekh heere karao aades.
Kahai Kabir niranjan alekh. GGS p.972

Jah kee upjee tah rachee peevat mardan laag. GGS p.337

Khinthaa giaan dhiaan kar sooee sabad taagaa math ghaalai.
Panch tat kee kar mirgaanee gur kai maarag chaalai. GGS p.477

Kabir deen gavaa-i-aa dunee sio dunee na chaalee saath.
Paa-e kuhaaraa maariaa gaafal apunai haath. GGS p.1365

#7-5. PRAYER
Karvat bhalaa na karvat teree.
Laag gale sun bintee meree.
Hao vaaree mukh pher piaare.
Karvat de mo kao kaahe kao maare. GGS p.484

Manh prteet na prem ras na kachoo tan mai dhang.
Na jaanoo eis peeo sai kiokar rehsee rang. KV p.27

Ab ki jo saaee milai sabh dukh aakhoo roai.
Charnno oopar sees dhar kahoo jo kehna hoai. KG p.20

Avgun merai baapjee bakash gareeb nivaaj.
Mai tao poot kapoot hao miree baap kao laaj. KV p.27

Saree tum mai bahut gunn avagunn koee naahi.
Jo khojaa dil aapnnaa sabh avgunn mujh maahai. KSS

Mujh mai gunn aiko nahee sunno sant sir mour.
Terai Naam prataap sai paaoon aadar thor. KSS

Mai khottaa saaee kharaa mai agh ka bhan daar.
Mai apraadhi aatmaa saaee sharan oobaar. KSS

Mai apraadhi janam ka nakh shikh bharaa vikaar.
Tum daataa dukh bhanjanaa mairee kardu sambhar. KV p.187

Surat karou mairee saaeeaan main hoo bhojal maahai.
Aapai hi beh jaaoonga jo nah pakrrou baahai. KV p.185

Avar patit too koop hai mai hoo samud samaan.
Ek tek guru Naam kee sunn, guru kripaa nidhaan. KSS

Ridhi sidhi maangoo nahi, maangoo tum sai eh.
Nis din darshan saadh ka kahai Kabir mohe deh. SKV

Baar baar kar jor kar, soneeai karoo pukaar.
Saadh sang mohe daiou nit param guru daataar. SKV

Kabir so din bhalaa, ja din sant milaai.
Ank bhare bhar bheiteeai paap deh kaa jaae. KG p.47

Tai din gaye akaarathi sangat miliou na sant.
Prem bina pashoo jeevnaa bhagat bina bhagwant. KSS

Raam bulaavaa bheijiaa diaa Kabira roei.
Jo sukh saadhu sang mahe so baikunth na hoei. KSS

Ja pal darshan saadh ka ta pal kee baleimaar.
Satnaam rasnaa basei leejai janam sudhaar. KSS

Jo maai bhool bigaarreaa na kar mailaa chit.
Saahib garoovaa chaaheeai nafar bigaarrai nit. KSS

Kabira bhool bigaarreaa kar kar mailaa chit.
Nafar ko deen adheen hai saahib raakhai hit. KV p.27

Saahib tum na bisaario laakh loug mil jaahe.
Ham sai tum kyo bahut hai, tum saum hum kyo nahai. KV p.27

Tumai bisaaraj kiaa banai kis kai sharnnai jaahai.
Shiv baranch mun naarda mairai chit na samaahai. KSS

Kiaa mukh te bintee karoo laaj aavat hai mohai.
tum dekhat avgunn karoo kaisai bhaav tohai. KV p.26

Mujh mai avgunn tujh gunn tujh gunn avgunn mujh.
Jo mal bisroo tujh kaoo too mat bisrai mujh. KSS

Binai karoo kar jor kai sunn guru kripaa ni dhaan.
Sant sang sukh deejeeai dyaa gareebee giaan. KSS

Kabiraa yeh bintee karai charnnan chit basaai.
Maarag saachaa sant ka guru mohai dev bataai. KSS

Avgunn kiai to bahu keeai karat na laagee baar.
Bhaavai bandaa bakhsheeai bhaavai gardan maar.
KV p.27

Tum to samrath saaeeaa drirr kar pakrroo baahai.
Dhur hee lai pahunchaaeeou mat chaadou mag maahai.
KV p.28

Bhagat daan mohai deejeeai guru devan kai dev.
Avar nahee kachu chaaheeai nisdin teree sev. KV p.98

Tum guru deen dayaal ho daataa apranpaar.
Mai boodaou manjhdhaar mai pakarr lagaaou paar. KSS

Antar jaamee aik too sabh jag ke aadhaar.
Jo tum chaadeou haath se kounn ootarai paar. KV p.27

Bhaou saagar hai ate kathan gehraa agam athaar.
Tumhai dayaal daya karou tab paaoon kuch thah. KSS

Avegunnhaaraa gunn nahee nun ka barraa kathor.
Aaisai samrath satguru taahi lagaavai thour. KSS

Kabir dee-ee sansaar kao leenee jis mastak bhaag.
Amrit ras jin paa-i-aa thir taa kaa sohaag. GGS p.970

Kabir mulaa munaare kiaa chadhah saa-ee na bahraa ho-e.
Jaa kaaran too baang deh dil hee bheetar jo-e. GGS p.1374

Kio chhoo-tao kaise tarao bhavjal nidh bhaaree.
Raakh raakh mere beethulaa jan saran tumaaree. GGS p.855

Kabir nain nihaarao tujh kao sarvan sunao tua naao.
Bain uchrao tua Naam jee charan kamal rid thaao. GGS p.1370

#7-6. BHAIRAG (DETACHMENT)
Naa mai jog dhiaan chit laa-i-aa. GGS p.329

Kah Kabir chit chetiaa Raam simar bairaag. GGS p.337

Mohe bairaag bha-io.
Ihu jeeo aae kahaa ga-io. GGS p.870

Khand Brahmand mah sinjhee meraa batooaa sabh jag bhasmaadhaaree.
Taaree laagee tripal palteeai chhootai hoe pasaaree. GGS p.334

Bin bairaag na chhootas maa-i-aa. GGS p.329

Kabir jao grih karah ta dharm kar naahee ta kar bairaag.
Bairaagee bandhan karai taa ko bado abhaag. GGS p.1377

Jah kee upjee tah rachee peevat mardan laag. GGS p.337

#7-7. HUMILITY
Kabir meraa mujh mah kichh nahee jo kichh hai so teraa.
Teraa jujh kao saopate kiaa laagai meraa. GGS p.1375

Yeh to ghar hai prem ka, khaalaa na ghar naahi.
Sees utaarai bhooai dharei, tab paithe ghar maahi. KV p.15

Sees utaarai bhooai dharei, oopar rakhe paao.
Daas Kabira yo kame, aisaa hoe ta aao. KV p.15

Yih to ghar hai prem ka, maarag agam agaadh.
Sees kaat pag tal dhare, tab nikat prem ka saadh. KSS

Sabh se laghtaaee bhalee laghtaa se sabh hoai.
Jas doteeaa kai chandermaa sees navai sabh loai. KV p.82

Deen lakhai mukh saban ka, deen lakhai nahee koai.
Lakhai jo koee deen ko, nar se devtaa hoai. KSS

Dayaa dil mai raakhiai nirdaee kabhi na hoai.
Saaee ke sabh jeev hai keerree kanjoor soai. KSS

Oochai paanee na tikai, neechai hi thehraai.
Neechaa hoai so bhar peeai, oonchaa piaasaa jai. KV p.81

Kanchan tajnna sahej hai sahej taiyaa ka neh.
Maan vadaaee eerkha dorlabh tajnni yeh. KSS

Peeyaa chahai prem ras raakhaa chahai maan.
Ek miaan mei do kharag dekha soona na kaan. KV p.17

Har bha-io khaand ret mah bikhrio hasantee chunio na jaaee.
Kah Kameer kul jaat paant taj cheetee hoe chun khaaee.
GGS p.972

Kabir sabh te ham bure ham taj bhalo sabh ko-e.
Jin aisaa kar boojhiaa meet hamaaraa so-e. GGS p.1364

#7-8. DIVINE LOVE
Kabir jao tuh saadh piram kee paake setee khel.
Kaachee sarsao pel kai naa khal bha-ee na tel. GGS p.1377

Prem chupaaeaa na chupe. Ja ghat pargat hoi.
Jo pai sukh bolai nahi aankh det hai roei. KSS

Jab mai thaa tab guru nahee, jab guru hai mai naahe.
Prem gali aet saakaree, ta mahe do na samaahe. KV p.15

Prem na baaree upjai prem na haat bikaaei.
Raaja raanaa jo roochai sees diai le jaaei. KV p.15

Prem piaalaa jo piai, sees dakhshana daie.
Lobhi sees na de sakai, Naam prem ka laie. KV p.15

Jaha prem taha nem nahi, taha na budh bioohaar.
Prem mangan jab mun bhaiaa kaun ginai tith vaar. KSS

Jogee jangam jeeoora sanyasi darvesh.
Binaa prem pahunche nahi doorlabh satguru desh. SKV

Peeyaa chahai prem ras raakhaa chahai maan.
Ek miaan mei do kharag dekha soona na kaan. KV p.17

Kabir taa sio preet kar jaa ko thaakar Raam. GGS p.1365

Kabir jao tuh saadh piram kee sees kaat kar go-e.
Khelat khelat haal kar jo kichh ho-e ta ho-e. GGS p.1377

Karvat bhalaa na karvat teree.
Laag gale sun bintee meree.
Hao vaaree mukh pher piaare.
Karvat de mo kao kaahe kao maare. GGS p.484

Kabir preet ik sio kee-e aan dubidhaa jaa-e.
Bhaavai laanbe kes kar bhaavai gharar mudaa-e. GGS p.1365

Jahaa bhakat teh nem nahi, tahaa na budh biouhaar.
Prem magan jab mun bhaeaa, koun ginai tith vaar. SKV

Prem prem sabh ko kahai, prem na cheenai koei.

Aath paher bheena rahei, prem kahaavai soei. KG p.397

Aaeaa prem kahaa giaa, dekhaa thaa sabh koei.
Chin rovai chin mai hasai, yeh to prem na hoei. KSS

Deen gareebee bandgee sabh se aadar bhaou.
Kahai Kabir taiee barraa ja meh barraa subhaou. KV p.81

Ja ghat prem na sancharai so ghat jaan masaan.
Jaisei khaal luhaar kee saas let bin praan. KSS

Ja ghat preet na prem ras pun rasnaa nahi Naam.
Te nar pasu sansaar mae opaj marai bedaas. KSS

Kabir rekh sandhoor aur kaajal deeaa na jaaie.
Nainee preetam mil rahaa, doojaa kahaan samaai. KV p.41

Aath paher chousath gharri mairai aour na hoai.
Nainaa maahi too basai neend ko thour na hoai. KV p.41

Patbartaa tab jaaneeai, ratou na ooghrai nain.
Antar gat sakuchee rahai, bolai madhurai bain. KV p.39

Kabir bhathee prem kee bahut jo baithai aaie.
Sir daivai so peeangai, aour se peeaa na jaaie. KSS

Kabir piaalaa prem, peevat adhik rasaal.
Eis kaa peenaa kathan hai, maangai sees kalaal. KG p.521

Prem bina jo bhagat hai so nij dinbh vichaar.
Oodar bharan ke kaarnai janam gavaaeoou saar. KSS

#8. THE TRUE MASTER

Bhai reh kioe Sat Guru Saant kahavei.
Nano Alakh lakhavei. KV p.184

Kabir saadhoo daras te sahib aavai yaad.
Laikhai mai soee gharree baakee kai din baad. KSS

Sukh devai dookh ko harai metai door karai apraadh.
Kahai Kabir kab eh milai param sanehi saadh. KSS

Kabir ih tan jaa-i-gaa kavnai maarag laa-e.
Kai sangat kar saadh kee kai har ke guhn gaa-e. GGS p.1365

Bastoo kahee toondai kahee kah bidh aavei haath.
Kahai Kabir tab paeaai jo pedee leeje saadh.
Pedi liaa saath kar deenee bastoo lakhae.
Kot janam ka panth tha pal mahe pahunch jai. KV p.44

Sadhu sadhu sabh barai apni apni thor.
Shabad vivaike paarkee te mathe ko mor. KV p.86

Guru guru mahe paidh hai guru guru mahe bhau.
Soi guru nit bundia jo Shabd batave dau. KSS

Kah Kabir heeraa as dekhio jag mah rahaa samaaee.
Guptaa heeraa pragat bha-io jab gur gam deeaa dikhaaee.
GGS p.483

Hoegaa khasam ta le-egaa raakh. GGS p.329

Heerai heeraa bedh pavan mun sahaje rahiaa samaaee.
Segal jot in heerai bedhee Satgur bachnee mai paaee. GGS p.483

Kiaa jap kiaa tap sanjamo kiaa bart kiaa isnaan.
Jab lag jugat na jaaneeai bhaao bhagat bhagwaan. GGS p.337

Chal re baikunth tujhah le taarao.
Hichah ta prem kai chaabak maarao. GGS p.329

Allah alakh na jaaee lakhiaa gur gur deenaa meethaa.
Kah Kabir meree sankaa naasee sarb niranjan deethaa.
GGS p.1350

Kah Kabir hum aise lakhan.
Dhann Gurdev at roop bichakhan. GGS p.873

Singho ko lahindai nahi hanso kee nahi path.
Laalo kee nah boreeaa saadh na chalai jamaat. KV p.45

Jete ghat amrit sabh hee mah bhaavai tisah peeaaee. GGS p.1123

Kabir surg nark te mai rahio satgur ke parsaad. GGS p.1370

Kio chhoo-tao kaise tarao bhavjal nidh bhaaree.
Raakh raakh mere beethulaa jan saran tumaaree. GGS p.855

Hamro bhartaa bado bibekee aape sant kahaavai. GGS p.476

Toon satguru hao naotan chelaa.
Kah Kabir mil ant kee belaa. GGS p.324

Har ke sant sadaa thir pooja ko har Naam japaat.
Jin kao kirpaa kart hai gobind te satsang milaat. GGS p.1251

Hirde pragaas giaan gur gamit gagan mandal mah dhiaanaanaa.
Bikhai rog bhai bandhan bhaage mun nij ghar sukh jaanaanaa.
GGS p.339

Kah Kabir jis Satguru bhetai punrap janam na aavai. GGS p.476

Kah Kabir mai so guru paa-i-aa jaa kaa naao bibeko. GGS p.793

Panche sabad anaahad baaje sange saaringpaanee.
Kabir daas teree artee keenee nirankaar nirbaanee. GGS p.1350

Kabir sangat kareeai saadh kee ant karai nirbaah. GGS p.1369

Gur kar giaan dhiaan kar mahooaa bhaao bhaathee mun dhaaraa. GGS p.969

Raam ju daataa mukat ko sant japaavai Naam. GGS p.1373

Har ke sant sadaa thir pooja ko har Naam japaat.
Jin kao kirpaa kart hai gobind te satsang milaat. GGS p.1251

Hamro bhartaa bado bibekee aape sant kahaavai. GGS p.476

Chal re baikunth tujhah le taarao.
Hichah ta prem kai chaabak maarao. GGS p.329

Bhoolee maalanee hai eo.
Satguru jaagtaa hai deo. GGS p.479

Maano sabh sukh nao nidh taa kai sahaj sahaj jas bolai dev. GGS p.857

Aayaa thaa sansaar men, Dekhan ko bahu roop.
Kahai Kabira Sant ho, Par gayaa najar anoop. KV p.9

Satguru mil sat Shabd lakhaavai saar Shabd bilgaavai.
Keh Kabir soee jan pooraa jo nayaaraa kar gaavai. KV p.108

Jab lag pooraa Guru na paavai.
Tab lag bhev jal fir fir aavai. KV p.187

Eik baar jiya parchou paavai.
Bhavjal tarai baar nahi laavai. KV p.187

Kahai Kabir pooran jag soee.
Jaa ke hirdai avar na ho-ee. GGS p.330

Bhai bich bhaao bhaae ko-oo boojhah har ras paavai bhaaee.
Jete ghat amrit sabh hee mah bhaavai tisah peeaaee. GGS p.1123

Tan mun taako deejia jaankei vikhiaa nahe.
Aapa saari chaandh kar raakhai sabhhi mahe. KV p.42

Mun ke haare har hai, mun ke jeete jeet.
Kah Kabir peeo paaeai, munhee kee parteet. KSS

Tan mun dia to pal kia sirka tal gaya bhar.
Jo kabhu kahe mai dia bahut sahega maar. SKV

Tan mun dia to kia hua nij mun dia na jaie.
Kahai Kabir ta das sion kaise mun patiaie. KV p.42

Tan mun dia aapna nij mun taake sang.
Kahai Kabir abhe bhaya sun satguru parsang. SKV

Nij mun to arpan kia charan kamal kee thor.
Kahai Kabir gurdev bin najar na aave aor. SKV

Jo too peeaa kee piaaranee apnaa kar lei ree.
Kalhe kalpana mait kar charnou chit de ree. SKV

#8-2. THE UNBOUNDED GRACE OF THE MASTER
Heerai heeraa bedh pavan mun sahaje rahiaa samaaee.
Segal jot in heerai bedhee Satgur bachnee mai paaee. GGS p.48

Sut apraadh karat hai jete.
Jananee cheet na raakhas tete. GGS p.478

Kabir dee-ee sansaar kao leenee jis mastak bhaag.
Amrit ras jin paa-i-aa thir taa kaa sohaag. GGS p.970

Sarab sukhaa kaa ek har Soami so gur Naam da-io.
Sant Prahlaad kee paij jin raakhee harnaakhas nakh bidrio.
GGS p.856

In maa-i-aa jagdees gusaaee tumre charan bisaare.
Kinchat preet na upjai jan kao jan kakaa karah bechaare.
GGS p.857

Chal re baikunth tujhah le taarao.
Hichah ta prem kai chaabak maarao. GGS p.329

Jo jan bhaao bhagat kachh jaanai taa kao achraj kaaho.
GGS p.692

Gur kai baan bajar kal chhedee pragtiaa pad pargaasaa.
GGS p.332

So dhiaan dharah je bahur na dharnaa. GGS p.327

Toon satguru hao naotan chelaa.
Kah Kabir mil ant kee belaa. GGS p.324

Dhaavat jon janam brahm thaake ab dukh kar ham haario re.
Kah Kabir gur milt mahaa ras prem bhagat nistaario re.
GGS p.335

Hirde pragaas giaan gur gamit gagan mandal mah dhiaanaanaa.
Bikhai rog bhai bandhan bhaage mun nij ghar sukh jaanaanaa.
GGS p.339

Kah Kabir jis Satguru bhetai punrap janam na aavai. GGS p.476

Kabir sangat kareeai saadh kee ant karai nirbaah. GGS p.1369

Jako Guru ne rang deeah kabhi na hoi kurang.
Kot kaal chajkolee kabhi na ho chit bhang. SKV

Jeevat mirtak ho rahai tajo khalak kee aas.
Rakhshak samrath satguru mat dookh paai daas. SKV

Bastoo kahee toondai kahee kah bidh aavei haath.
Kahai Kabir tab paeaai jo pedee leeje saadh.
Pedi liaa saath kar deenee bastoo lakhae.
Kot janam ka panth tha pal mahe pahunch jai. KV p.44

Sukh devai dookh ko harai metai door karai apraadh.
Kahai Kabir kab eh milai param sanehi saadh. KSS

Ridhi sidhi maangoo nahi, maangoo tum sai eh.
Nis din darshan saadh ka kahai Kabir mohe deh. SKV

Baar baar kar jor kar, soneeai karoo pukaar.
Saadh sang mohe daiou nit param guru daataar. SKV

Kabir so din bhalaa, ja din sant milaai.
Ank bhare bhar bheiteeai paap deh kaa jaae. KG p.47

Tai din gaye akaarathi sangat miliou na sant.
Prem bina pashoo jeevnaa bhagat bina bhagwant. KSS

Raam bulaavaa bheijiaa diaa Kabira roei.
Jo sukh saadhu sang mahe so baikunth na hoei. KSS

Ja pal darshan saadh ka ta pal kee baleimaar.
Satnaam rasnaa basei leejai janam sudhaar. KSS

Sona kaee na laage loha kun nahi khae.
Boora bhala jo guru bhagat kabhu narak na jai. SKV

Jeevat marah marah phun jeevah panarap janam na hoee.
GGS p.1104

Pragat pragaas giaan gur gamit Satgur te sudh paaee.
Daas Kabir taas mad maataa uchak na kabhoo jaaee. GGS p.969

Sukhman naaree sahaj samaanee peevai peevanhaaraa.
GGS p.969

Satgur keeno parupkaar.
Kaadh leen saagar sansaar.
Charn kamal sio laagee preet.
Gobind basai nitaa nit cheet. GGS p.331

Kah Kabir bhai saagar tarn kao mai satgur ot la-io. GGS p.336

Jit ko laa-i-aa tit hee laagaa taise karam kamaavai. GGS p.476

Tan rainee mun pun rap karihao paachao tat baraatee.
Raam raae sio bhaavar laihao aatam tih rang raatee. GGS p.482

Charn kamal kee maoij mah rahao ant ar aad. GGS p.1370

Nah sheetal hai chandrma him nah sheetal hoy.
Kabira sheetal sant jan Naam saanehi soy. KV p.47

Jaat na poochou saadh kee pooch leejiai gayaan.
Moul karo tarvaar ka parree rahen do mayaan. KV p.47

Saadhoo bhukhaa bhaav ka dhan ka bhookhaa naahe.
Dhan ka bhookhaa jo firai so to saadhoo naahe. KV p.47

Saadhoo samundar jaaneeai maahee ratan bharaay.
Mand bhaag muthee bharai kar kankar charr jay. KV p.48

Had chalai so maanvaa behad chalai so saadh.
Had behad donou tajai taako mataa agaadh. KV p.48

Sonaa sajan saadh jan toot jurai sou baar.
Durjan kumbh kumhaar ke aikay dhakaa daraar. KV p.48

Kahat Kabir soee santjan jouhree.
Karam kee rekh par mekh maarai. KV p.143

Mahaa Suhn sindh bikhmee ghaatee.
Bin Satguru paavai nahi baatee. KV p.148

Bhagat beej paltai nahee, jo jug jaaei anant.
Oonch neech ghar janam lei, tau sant ka sant. KSS

#8-3. SHARAN (SURRENDER TO THE MASTER'S WILL)
Tun mun taako deejia jaankei vishiya nahe.
Aapa saari chaandh kar raakhai sahib mahe. KV p.42

Mun ke haare har hai, mun ke jeete jeet.
Kah Kabir peeo paaeai, munhee kee parteet. KSS

Tan mun dia to pal kia sirka tal gaya bhar.
Jo kabhu kahe mai dia bahut sahega maar. SKV

Tan mun dia to kia hua nij mun dia na jaie.
Kahai Kabir ta das sion kaise mun patiaie. KV p.42

Tan mun dia aapna nij mun taake sang.
Kahai Kabir abhe bhaya sun satguru parsang. SKV

Nij mun to arpan kia charan kamal kee thor.
Kahai Kabir gurdev bin najar na aave aor. SKV

Kah Kabir saadhoo ko preetam tis moorat balihaaree. GGS p.1252

Amrit Naam japao jap rasnaa.
Amol daas kar leeno apnaa. GGS p.331

Kabir jao tuh saadh piram kee paake setee khel.
Kaachee sarsao pel kai naa khal bha-ee na tel. GGS p.1377

Kabir jao tuh saadh piram kee sees kaat kar go-e.
Khelat khelat haal kar jo kichh ho-e ta ho-e. GGS p.1377

Toon satguru hao naotan chelaa.
Kah Kabir mil ant kee belaa. GGS p.324

Bhagatee mun te hout hai, mun de keejai bhaaou.
Parmaarath parteet mai yeh tan jaaei ta jaaou. SKV

Kabir piaalaa prem, peevat adhik rasaal.
Eis kaa peenaa kathan hai, maangai sees kalaal. KSS

Saahib kai darbaar mai kamee kee naahai ai.
Bandaa mouj na paavaee chook chakree mahai. SKV

#8-4. SATSANG (THE MASTER'S HOLY DISCOURSE)

Kabir sangat kareeai saadh kee ant karai nirbaah. GGS p.1369

Kahe Kabir hum tur keh peidee lai hukam hazooree. SKV

Leh aartee ho purkh niranjan satgur poojah bhaaee.
Thaadhaa Brahmaa nigam beechaarai alakh na lakhiaa jaaee.
GGS p.1350

Kahat Kabir sunah re santah saadh sangat tir jaahigaa.
GGS p.1106

Kabir sangat saadh kee din din doonaa het. GGS p.1369

Kabir saadhoo kee sangat rahao jao kee bhoosee khaao.
GGS p.1369

KABIR SAHIB'S VERSES • 645

Kabir ek gharee aadhee gharee aadhee hoo te aadh.
Bhagtan setee goste jo keene so laabh. GGS p.1377

Har ke sant sadaa thir pooja ko har Naam japaat.
Jin kao kirpaa kart hai gobind te satsang milaat. GGS p.1251

Kabir chandan kaa birvaa bhalaa berio dhaak palaas.
O-e bhee chandan ho-e rahe base ju chandan paas. GGS p.1365

It sangat naahee marnaa. GGS p.92

Heerai heeraa bedh pavan mun sahaje rahiaa samaaee.
Segal jot in heerai bedhee Satgur bachnee mai paaee. GGS p.483

Kahat Kabir sunah re santah saadh sangat tir jaahigaa.
GGS p.1106

Kabir baisnao kee kookar bhalee saakat kee buree maa-e.
Oh nit sunai har Naam jas oh paap bisaahan jaa-e. GGS p.1367

Kabir sadhoo kee sangat rahao jao kee bhoosee khaao.
GGS p.1369

Santan sang Kabira bigrio.
So Kabir raamai hoe nibrio. GGS p.1158

Kabira sangat saadh kee jayon gandhee ka baas.
Jo kach gandhee de nahee tou bhe baas subaas. KV p.52

Mathuraa bhaavai dvaarika bhaavai ja jagnaath.
Saadh sangat har bhajan bin kachoo na aavai haath. KV p.52

Daso disaa ke krodh kee oothee aparbal aag.
Seetal sangat saadh kee tahaa ubreai bhaag. KV p.67

Satsang kee aadhee gharee, simran baras pachaas.
Barkhaa barsai ik gharee, rahat firai baaraah maas. KSS

Kabir darsan saadh ka, saahib aavai yaad.
Laikhai me soee gharee, baakee kai din baad. KSS

#8-5. FAITH IN THE MASTER

Guru maanush kar jaantai, te nar kaheeai andh.
Mahaa dukhee sansaar mai, aagai jam ke bandh.
Guru maanush kar jantai, charanaamrit ko paan.
Te nar narkai jaainge, janam janam hoai savaan.
Kabir te nar andh hai, guru ko kehtai aur.
Har roothai gur thor hai, guru roothai nahi thor.
Guru ko manukh jante charan amrit ko paan.
Te nar narke jaaenge janam jan mohe suaan. KSS

Charan kamal jaa kai ridai basah so jan kio dolai dev. GGS p.857

Kabir jao tuh saadh piram kee paake setee khel.
Kaachee sarsao pel kai naa khal bha-ee na tel. GGS p.1377

Chet achet moor mun mere baaje anhad baajaa.
Kah Kabir sansaa brahm chooko dhroo prahilaad nivaajaa.
GGS p.856

#8-6. SEVA (SELFLESS SERVICE TO THE MASTER)

Kabir sevaa kao da-e bhale ek sant ik Raam. GGS p.1373

Kabir jaa ghar saadh na seveeah har kee sevaa naahe.
Te ghar marhat saarkhe bhoot basah tin maahe. GGS p.1374

Gur sevaa te bhagat kamaaee.
Tab ih maanas dehee paaee.
Is dehee kao simarah dev.
So dehee bhaj har kee sev. GGS p.1159

Kaam krodh maa-i-aa mad matsar e-e sampai mo maahee.
Da-i-aa dharam ar gur kee sevaa e-e supanantar naahee.
GGS p.971

Satguru poojau sadaa sadaa manaavao.
Aisee sev dargah sukh paavao. GGS p.1158

Puja Raam ek hee devaa.
Saachaa naavan gur kee sevaa. GGS p.484

Jab lag bhagat sakaam hai, tab lag nihfal sev.
Kahai Kabir vai kioou milai, nehkaamee nardev. KV p.14

Bhagat daan mohai deejeeai guru devan ke dev.
Avar nahi kachu chaaheeai nis din teree sev. SKV

#8-7. BHAKTI (DEVOTION TO THE MASTER)
Dookh mahe simran sabh kare, sukh nahe kare na koe.
Sukh mahe simran jo kare, to dookh kahai hoe. KV p.19

Sukh mahe simran na keeaa, dookh me keeia yaad.
Kahai Kabir tan daas kee kaun sonei feriaad. KV p.19

Har roothai guru thor hai, guru roothai nahi thor. KV p.43

Bhring jayo keet ko palat bhringai kiyaa aap sum rang dai lai urraaee. SKV

Bhakti doohelee guru kee, nahi kaaer ka kaam.
Sees otaarai haath se, so laisee Sat Naam. KSS

Guru bhakti at kathin hai jioo khandai kee dhaar.
Bina saach pahunche nahi maha kathan bioohaar. KSS

Jaan bhagat ka nit maran anjaane ka raaj.
Sar aousar samjhe nahi peht bhran sou kaaj. SKV

Bhagat bhekh bahu antaraa, jaisai dharan akaas.
Bhagat leen guru charan mei, bhekh jagat kee aas. KV p.13

Jehaa bhagat teh bhekh nahi, barnasharam teh naahe.
Naam bhagat jo prem so, so durlabh jag maahe. KSS

Jab lag naataa jaat kaa, tab lag bhagat na hoei.
Naataa taj bhagatee karai, bhagat kahaave souei. KV p.14

Bhagat ka than aite dulabh hai, bhaikh soogam nij soei.
Bhagat jo niaaree bhekh se, yeh jaanai sabh koei. KSS

Bhagat padaarath jab milai, tab guru hoei sahaaei.
Prem preet ki bhagat jo, pooran bhaag milaaei. KSS

Kabir guru kee bhakat kar, taj bikhiaa ras choj.
Baar baar nahi paaeeai, maanas janam kee mouj. KSS

Kabir guru kee bhagat ka maun mei bahut hoolaas.
Mun mansaa maanjai nahi, yohe kehat hai daas. KSS

Bhagat bhaaou ke reet kee nah aaee pehchaan.
Tan de mun de sees de jag se rahai amaan. SKV

Bhagat daan mohai deejeeai guru devan ke dev.
Avar nahi kachu chaaheeai nis din teree sev. SKV

#8-8. PUJA (WORSHIP OF THE MASTER)
Jab lag mun baikunth kee aas.
Tab lag hoe nahee charn nivaas. GGS p.325

Akaal purakh kee aarsee saathon kee hai deh.
Alakh ko jo lakha chaahai inhee meh lakh leh. SKV

Panche sabad anaahad baaje sange saaringpaanee.
Kabir daas teree artee keenee nirankaar nirbaanee. GGS p.1350

Akaal purakh kee aarsee saathon kee hai deh.
Alakh ko jo lakha chaahai inhee meh lakh leh. SKV

Kahio Kabir bichaar kai sant sunahu mun maahe. GGS p.1374

Kabir jao tuh saadh piram kee paake setee khel.
Kaachee sarsao pel kai naa khal bha-ee na tel. GGS p.1377

Kah Kabir ab jaaniaa santan ridai majhaar.
Sevak so sevaa bhale jih ghat basai muraar. GGS p.337

#8-9. BIREH (THE LONGING AND PINING OF SEPARATION)
Kabir bireh bhuyangam mun basai mant na maanai ko-e.
Raam biogee naa jeeai jeeai ta baoraa ho-e. GGS p.1368

Karvat bhalaa na karvat teree.
Laag gale sun bintee meree.
Hao vaaree mukh pher piaare.
Karvat de mo kao kaahe kao maare. GGS p.484

Kabir chakaee jao nis beechhurai aa-e milai parbhaat.
Jo nar bichhure Raam sio naa din mile na raat. GGS p.1371

Kabir ambar ghanhar chhaa-i-aa barkh bhare sar taal.
Chaatrik jio tarsat rahai tin ko kaon havaal. GGS p.1371

Nainou kee kar kotharree putlee palangh bichaaei.
Palkou kee chik daal kar piya ko leeaa richaei. KV p.17

Nainou andar aaou too nain chaap tohei lev.
Na mai dekhoo aour ko, na tohai dekhan dev.
Jaagoo tab pargat lakhoo, souoo tab ghat maahai.
Lochan raat sabh gharree, kabhoo bisroo naahe. KV p.39

Birhin de sandaisarra suno hamaarai peev.
Jal bin machalee kioou jeeai paanee mei ka jeev. KV p.22

Bireh tej tan mei tapai ang sabhi akulaaei.
Ghat soona jiv peev mai mout dhoondh fir jaaei. KSS

Kabir sundaree yo kahai suneeou kant sujaan.
Baig milo tum aaei kar nahi to tajhoo pran. KSS

Kai birehn ko meech de kai aapaa dikh laaei.
Aath pahar ka daajhnaa so pai sahaa na jaaei. KSS

Bireh kamandal kar leeai bairaagee do nain.
Maangai daras mathookarri chakai rahai din rain. KV p.23

Eh tan ka divlaa karoon baatee mailoo jeebh.
Louhoo seenchoo tel joiu kab mukh daikhoo peev. SKV

Nain hamaarai baavrai chin chin lourai tujh.
Na tum milo na mai sukhee aisee vedan mujh. KG p.70

Maas gayaa pinjar rahaa taakan laagai kaag.
Sahib ajhoo na aayaa koee mand hamara bhaag. KV p.23

Behar setee mat arrai rai mun mor sujaan.
Haad maas sabh khaat hai jeevan karai masaan. KSS

Bireh prabal dal saajkai gher leeo mohai aaei.
Na maarai chaadai nahee tarraf tarraf jeea jaai. KSS

Peeaa bin jeea tarsat raheai pal pal birhe sataae.
Rain divas mohe kal nahee sisak sisak jeh jaae. KV p.24

Nagravaa hamai na bhaavai. Smee kee nagree ate sundar.
Jaha koee aavai na jaavai. Chand sooraj jaha paounn na paanee.
Koee sandesh pahunchaavai. Darad eh saaee ko sunaave. SKV

Peer puraanee bireh kee pinjar peer na jaae.
Ek peer hai preet kee rahee kalaijai chaaei. KSS

Chot sataai bireh kee sabh tan jaajar hoai.
Maaran haaraa jaanhee kai jis laagee soeai. KSS

Bireh bhavgam bas nahi keeaa kalaijai ghaav.
Birehn ang na morrhee jioo bhaavai tioo khaav. KG p.56

Dekhat dekhat din gaieh nis bhi dekhat jaae.
Birehn piya paavai nahee baikal jeeoo ghabrae. KV p.25

So din kaisaa hoeigaa guru gaheng baah.
Apnaa kar baithaavahee charan kaval kee chaah. KV p.25

Naam biyogee bikaal tan taahei na cheenai koei.
Tanbolee ke paan jeeoou din din peelaa hoei. KSS

Hirdai bheetar dou jalai dhuvaa na pargat hoei.
Jaakei laagee so lakhai kai jin laaee souee. KV p.24

Tan bheetar mun maaniaa baahar kahoo na laag.
Jvaalaa te fir jal bhaeeaa buchee jalanti aag. SKV

Saaee sevat jal gaee maas na rahiaa deh.
Saaee jab lag seveeah eh tan hoei na kheh. KV p.24

#8-10. SWEET PRAISES OF THE MASTER
Bhoolee maalanee hai eo.
Satguru jaagtaa hai deo. GGS p.479

Kabir chot suhelee sel kee laagat le-e usaas.
Chot sahaarai sabad kee taas guru mai daas. GGS p.1374

Kah Kabir hum aise lakhan.
Dhann Gurdev at roop bichakhan. GGS p.873

Kabir aisaa ek aadh jo jeevat mirtak ho-e.
Nirbhai ho-e kai guhn ravai jat pekhao tat so-e. GGS p.1364

Hamro bhartaa bado bibekee aape sant kahaavai. GGS p.476

Ab tao jaae chadhe singhaasan mile hai saaringpaanee.
Raam Kabira ek bhae hai koe na sakai pachhaanee. GGS p.969

Kah Kabir mai so guru paa-i-aa jaa kaa naao bibeko. GGS p.793

Santaa kao mat koee nindah sant Raam hai eko. GGS p.793

Kabir saachaa satguru mai miliaa sabad ju baahiaa ek.
Laagat he bhu-e mil ga-i-aa pariaa kaleje chhek. GGS p.1372

Guru hai baro Gobind te mai mahe dekh vichar.
Har simrei so vaar hai Gur simrei so paar. KV p.43

Jaaki saachee soorat hai taaka saachaa khel.
Aath pahar chosath gharree saaee saitee miel. KSS

Aavat gaaree ek oolt hoai anek.
Kahai Kabir na oolteeai vahi ek ki ek. KV p.62

Gaar angaar krodh chal nindaa dhooaa hoai.
In teeno ko parharai saadh kahavai soai. KV p.62

Mun mera panchi bhaeaa ourr kar chalaa akaas.
Swarg Lokh khaali parraa sahib santan paas. KSS

Sukh devai dookh ko harai metai door karai apraadh.
Kahai Kabir kab eh milai param sanehi saadh. KSS

Kabir har kaa simran jo karai so sukhaeeaa sunsaar.
It aut katah na dolaee jis raakhai sirjanhaar. GGS p.1375

Gur Gobind doouo kharrai kaakai laago paay.
Balhaaree guru aapnai Gobind diyo bataay. KV p.42

Teen Lokh nou khand mai guru te barraa na koei.
Karta karai na kar sakai guru karai so hoei. KV p.43

Satguru sum koee nahi, saat deep nou Khand.
Teen Lokh na paaeeai, aur ik-is Brahmand. K Vani p.6

Indramatee sun bachan adheenee.
Bolee madhur giaan gun bheenee.
Mohai adham ko tum sukh deenhaa.
Tum prasaad aagaumgum keenhaa.
Tum Sat Purush daas kehlaaye.
Yeh shobhaa kas uhaa chapaaye.
Morai chit yeh nishchey aaee.
Tum supurush doojaa nahi bhaaee.
So mai aay dekh yeh thaaee.
Dhan samrath mohai liyaa jagaaee. AS p.58-59

#9. THE HOLY NAAM
Kah Kabir nirdhan hai so-ee.
Jaa kai hirdai Naam na ho-ee. GGS p.1159

Bavan achhar Lokh trai sabh kachh en hee maah.
Eay akhar khir jahgay oie akhar en mah nahi. GGS p.340

Bhagat ka than aite dulabh hai, bhaikh soogam nij soei.
Bhagat jo niaaree bhekh se, yeh jaanai sabh koei.
Bhagat padaarath jab milai, tab guru hoei sahaaei.
Prem preet ki bhagat jo, pooran bhaag milaaei. KSS

Kabir addhee saakh yeh, kot garanth kar jaan.
Naam sat jag jhooth hai, surat sabad pehchaan. KSS

#9-1. DYING WHILE LIVING
(RISING ABOVE BODY CONSCIOUSNESS)
Parna Likhna chatori eh to baat sahal.
Kaam dahan mun bas karan gagan charan mushkal. SKV

Martaa martaa jag muaa saachaa muaa na koei.
Daas Kabira yon muaa bahur na marna hoai. KV p.36

Oonchaa tarvar gagan pal birla pakshi khaai.
Eis pal ko to veh phakhai jo jeevat mar jaai. KSS

Jeevat mirtak ho rahai tajo khalak kee aas.
Rakhshak samrath satguru mat dookh paai daas. SKV

Mareeai to mar jaaeeai foot parrai sansaar.
Aisaa marna ko marai din mai so so baar. KV p.28

Jab lag aas sareer kee mirtak hoa na jai.
Kaaeaa Maya mun tajai toorai rahai bijaai. SKV

Jeevat marah marah phun jeevah panarap janam na hoee.
GGS p.1104

Sukhman naaree sahaj samaanee peevai peevanhaaraa.
GGS p.969

Hirde pragaas giaan gur gamit gagan mandal mah dhiaanaanaa.
Bikhai rog bhai bandhan bhaage mun nij ghar sukh jaanaanaa.
GGS p.339

Ab mun ult sanaatan hooaa.
Tab jaaniaa jab jeevat mooaa.
Kah Kabir sukh sahaj samaavao. GGS p.327

Nagree ekai nao darvaaje dhaavat barij rahaaee.
Trikutee chhootai dasvaa dar khoolaib taa mun kheevaa bhaaee.
GGS p.1123

Kabir kasaotee Raam kee jhoothaa tikai na ko-e.
Raam kasaotee so sahai jo mar jeevaa ho-e. GGS p.1366

Kabir martaa martaa jag mooaa mar bhee na jaaniaa koe.
Aise marne jo marai bahur na marnaa ho-e. GGS p.1366

Kabir jis marne te jag darai mere mun aanand.
Marne hee te paaeeai pooran parmaanand. GGS p.1365

Kabir aisaa ek aadh jo jeevat mirtak ho-e.
Nirbhai ho-e kai guhn ravai jat pekhao tat so-e. GGS p.1364

Jeevat marai marai fun jeevai aise sun samaa-i-aa.
Anjan maah niranjan raheeai bahur na bhavjal paa-i-aa.
GGS p.332

Pind mooai jeeo kih ghar jaataa.
Sabad ateet anaahad raataa. GGS p.327

Aise marah je bahur na marnaa. GGS p.327

Parbrahm ke taj ka kaisaa hai unsaan.
Hahibai ki shaibhaa nahee daikhai hee parmaan. KR p.9

Asmaan ka aasraa chorr pyaare.
Ult dekho ghat apnaa ji.
Tum aap me aap tehkeek karo.
Tum chorro mun kee kal panaa ji. KV p.203

Sugvaa pinjaruaa chor bhaagaa.
Es eis pinjare me das darvaajaa. KV p.307

Martaa martaa jag muaa aur muaa na koei.
Daas Kabira yo muaa bahurna marnaa hoai. KV p.36

Conchaa tarvar gagan fal birlad pakshee khaae.
Is fal ko to veh bhakhe jo jeevatmar jai. KSS

Pragat pragaas giaan gur gamit Satgur te sudh paaee.
Daas Kabir taas mad paataa uchak na kab-hoo jaaee. GGS p.969

Allah alakh na jaaee lakhiaa gur gur deenaa meethaa.
Kah Kabir meree sankaa naasee sarb niranjan deethaa.
GGS p.1350

Charn kamal kee maoi mah rahao ant ar aad. GGS p.1370

Yeh karnee ka bhaid hai, naahi budh bichaar.
Kathnee chad karnee karou, tou kuch paavo saar. SKV

Jeevat marah marah phun jeevah panarap janam na hoee.
GGS p.1104

Kabir sangat kareeai saadh kee ant karai nirbaah. GGS p.1369

Hirde pragaas giaan gur gamit gagan mandal mah dhiaanaanaa.
Bikhai rog bhai bandhan bhaage mun nij ghar sukh jaanaanaa.
GGS p.339

Satgur keeno parupkaar.
Kaadh leen saagar sansaar.
Charn kamal sio laagee preet.
Gobind basai nitaa nit cheet. GGS p.331

Kah Kabir jis Satguru bhetai punrap janam na aavai. GGS p.476

Kabir ih tan jaa-i-gaa kavnai maarag laa-e.
Kai sangat kar saadh kee kai har ke guhn gaa-e. GGS p.1365

Dhaavat jon janam brahm thaake ab dukh kar ham haario re.
Kah Kabir gur milt mahaa ras prem bhagat nistaario re.
GGS p.335

Kahat Kabir sunah re santah saadh sangat tir jaahigaa.
GGS p.1106

Is dehee kao simarah dev. GGS p.1159

Toon satguru hao naotan chelaa.
Kah Kabir mil ant kee belaa. GGS p.324

Kio chhoo-tao kaise tarao bhavjal nidh bhaaree.
Raakh raakh mere beethulaa jan saran tumaaree. GGS p.855

Nij pad oopar laago dhiaan.
Raajaa Raam Naam moraa brahm giaan. GGS p.1159

Jeevat marai marai fun jeevai aise sun samaa-i-aa.
Anjan maah niranjan raheeai bahur na bhavjal paa-i-aa.
GGS p.332

Aise marah je bahur na marnaa. GGS p.327

Kahai Kabir niranjan dhiaavao.
Tit ghar jaao je bahur na aavao. GGS p.327

Jaa tis bhaavai taa hukam manaavai.
Is bere kao paar laghaavai. GGS p.337

Kabir surg nark te mai rahio satgur ke parsaad. GGS p.1370

Kah Kabir hum aise lakhan.
Dhann Gurdev at roop bichakhan. GGS p.873

Bhagvat bheer sakat simran kee katee kaal bhai faasee.
Daas Kameer chario gar oopar raaj leeo abnaasee. GGS p.1162

Mool mantr Sat Guru dayaa bin.
Kaise utrai paaraa. KV p.160

Naagin darpai sant se uhvaa nahi jaavai.
Keh Kabir Gur Mantr se aapai mar jaavai. KV p.168

#9-2. SIMRAN (REPETITION OF THE NAMES OF GOD)
Simran se mun laeeai jaise naad kurang.
Pran taje pal bichure Sant Kabir keh deen. KV p.19

Simran se sukh hot hai simran se hukh jae.
Kahe Kabir simran keeai saae mahe samae. KV p.19

Kah Kabir bhaj saarangpaanee.
Raam udak meree tikhaa bujhaanee.
Is dehee kao simarah dev.
So dehee bhaj har kee sev. GGS p.1159

Vai sut vai bit vai pur paatan bahur na dekhai aa-e.
Kaht Kabir Raam kee na simrah janam akaarath jaa-e.
GGS p.1124

Kah Kabir chit chetiaa Raam simar bairaag. GGS p.337

Bhagvat bheer sakat simran kee katee kaal bhai faasee.
Daas Kameer chario gar oopar raaj leeo abnaasee. GGS p.1162

#9-3. DHYAN (CONTEMPLATION
    OF THE MASTER'S EFFULGENT FORM)
Gur kar giaan dhiaan kar mahooaa bhaao bhaathee mun
dhaaraa. GGS p.969

Nirat bina surat aanthri kaho kahan ko jae.
Duaar na paave shabd ke pheir kaie bhaka. SKV

Hirde pragaas giaan gur gamit gagan mandal mah dhiaanaanaa.
Bikhai rog bhai bandhan bhaage mun nij ghar sukh jaanaanaa.
GGS p.339

Nij pad oopar laago dhiaan.
Raajaa Raam Naam moraa brahm giaan. GGS p.1159

So dhiaan dharah je bahur na dharnaa. GGS p.327

Kahai Kabir niranjan dhiaavao.
Tit ghar jaao je bahur na aavao. GGS p.327

#9-4. SHABD (THE DIVINE SOUND CURRENT)

Guru hai baro Gobind te mai mahe dekh vichar.
Har simrei so vaar hai Gur simrei so paar. KV p.43

Pragat pragaas giaan gur gamit Satgur te sudh paaee.
Daas Kabir taas mad maataa uchak na kabhoo jaaee. GGS p.969

Sukhman naaree sahaj samaanee peevai peevanhaaraa.
GGS p.969

Gur kar giaan dhiaan kar mahooaa bhaao bhaathee mun dhaaraa. GGS p.969

Baavan akhar jore aan.
Sakiaa na akhar ek pachhaan. GGS p.343

Kabir saachaa satguru mai miliaa sabad ju baahiaa ek.
Laagat he bhu-e mil ga-i-aa pariaa kaleje chhek. GGS p.1372

Panche sabad anaahad baaje sange saaringpaanee.
Kabir daas teree artee keenee nirankaar nirbaanee. GGS p.1350

Satgur keeno parupkaar.
Kaadh leen saagar sansaar.
Charn kamal sio laagee preet.
Gobind basai nitaa nit cheet. GGS p.331

Amrit Naam japao jap rasnaa.
Amol daas kar leeno apnaa. GGS p.331

Moond lee-e darvaaje.
Baajeeale anhad baaje. GGS p.656

Har ke sant sadaa thir pooja jo har Naam japaat.
Jin kao kirpaa kart hai gobind te satsang milaat. GGS p.1251

Dhaavat jon janam brahm thaake ab dukh kar ham haario re.
Kah Kabir gur milt mahaa ras prem bhagat nistaario re.
GGS p.335

Khand Brahmand mah sinjhee meraa batooaa sabh jag bhasmaadhaaree.
Taaree laagee tripal palteeai chhootai hoe pasaaree. GGS p.334

Nagree ekai nao darvaaje dhaavat barij rahaaee.
Trikutee chhootai dasvaa dar khoolaib taa mun kheevaa bhaaee.
GGS p.1123

Ree kalvaar gavaar moodh mat ulto pavan firaavao.
Mun matvaar mer sar bhaathee amrit dhaar chuaavao.
GGS p.1123

Ab ham tum ek bhae hah ekai dekhat mun pateeaahee. GGS p.339

Toon jal nidh hao jal kaa meen.
Jal mah rahao jalah bin kheen. GGS p.323

Kah Kabir bhaj saarangpaanee.
Raam udak meree tikhaa bujhaanee. GGS p.323

Bin bairaag na chhootas maa-i-aa. GGS p.329

Kabir nain nihaarao tujh kao sarvan sunao tua naao.
Bain uchrao tua Naam jee charan kamal rid thaao. GGS p.1370

Allah alakh na jaaee lakhiaa gur gur deenaa meethaa.
Kah Kabir meree sankaa naasee sarb niranjan deethaa.
GGS p.1350

Pind mooai jeeo kih ghar jaataa.
Sabad ateet anaahad raataa. GGS p.327

Kabir oojal pahirah kaapare paan supaaree khaa-he.
Ekas har ke Naam bin baadhe jampur jaanhe. GGS p.1366

Sant prasaad bhae mun nirmal har keertan mah andin jaagaa.
GGS p.343

E-e du-e akhar naa khise so gah rahio Kabir. GGS p.1373

Sarab sukhaa kaa ek har soami so gur Naam da-io. GGS p.856

Kah Kabir jo Naam samaane sunn rahiaa liv soee. GGS p.1104

Aadit karai bhagat aarambh.
Kaa-i-aa mandir mansaa thambh.
Ahinis akhand surhee jaa-e.
Tao anhad ben sahj mah baa-e. GGS p.344

Aaor dunee sabh bharm bhulaanee mun Raam rasaa-i-n maataa.
GGS p.92

Jis kao sabad basaavai antar chookai tisah piaasaa. GGS p.793

Kahat Kabir chhod bikhiaa ras it sangat nihchao marnaa.
Ramaeeaa japah praanee anat jeevan baanee in bidh bhavsaagar tarnaa. GGS p.92

Baavan achhar Lokh trai sabh kachh in hee maahe.
Ai akhar khir jaahige oe akhar in mah naahe. GGS p.340

Satguru poojao sadaa sadaa manaavao.
Aisee sev dargah sukh paavao. GGS p.1158

Khinthaa giaan dhiaan kar sooee sabad taagaa math ghaalai.
Panch tat kee kar mirgaanee gur kai maarag chaalai. GGS p.477

Kaal Akaal khasam kaa keenaa ihu parpanch badhaavan.
Kah Kabir te ante mukte jin hirdai Ram rasaa-in. GGS p.1104

Kabir dee-ee sansaar kao leenee jis mastak bhaag.
Amrit ras jin paa-i-aa thir taa kaa sohaag. GGS p.970

Poorab janam ham tumre sevak ab tao mitiaa na jaaee.
Tere duaarai dhun sahaj kee maathai mere dagaaee. GGS p.969

Chet achet moor mun mere baaje anhad baajaa.
Kah Kabir sansaa brahm chooko dhroo prahilaad nivaajaa.
GGS p.856

Kabir chot suhelee sel kee laagat le-e usaas.
Chot sahaarai sabad kee taas guru mai daas. GGS p.1374

Sarab sukhaa kaa ek har Soami so gur Naam da-io.
Sant Prahlaad kee paij jin raakhee harnaakhas nakh bidrio.
GGS p.856

Kah Kabir akhar due bhaakh. GGS p.329

Nao ghar dekh jo kaaman bhoolee baste anoop na paaee.
Kaht Kabir navai ghar moose dasvai tat samaaee. GGS p.339

Heerai heeraa bedh pavan mun sahaje rahiaa samaaee.
Segal jot in heerai bedhee Satgur bachnee mai paaee. GGS p.483

Kah Kabir heeraa as dekhio jag mah rahaa samaaee.
Guptaa heeraa pragat bha-io jab gur gam deeaa dikhaaee.
GGS p.483

Raja Raam anhad kinguree baajai. GGS p.92

Jab kumbhak bharpur leenaa.
Tah baaje anhad beenaa. GGS p.972

Nirbhao kai ghar bajaavah toor.
Anhad bajah sadaa bharpoor. GGS p.971

#9-5. THE INNER REALMS
Kar nainou deedaar mehal men, pyaaraa hai tek.
Kaam krodh madd lobh bisaaro, seel santosh chimaa sat dhaaro.
Madd maans mithyaa taj daarou.
Ho gyann ghorrai asvaar bharam se nayaaraa hai. KSSV p.67

Dhotee netee bastee paaou, aasan padam jugat se laaou.
Kumbhak kar rechak karvaaou.
Pahilai mool sudhaar kaaraj ho saaraa hai. KSSV p.67

Mool kanval dal chatur bakhaano.
Kaling jaap laal rang maano.
Dev ganes teh ropaa thaano.
Ridh shradh sidh chanvar dhoolaaraa hai. KSSV p.67

Savaad chakr shatdal bistaarou.
Brahma saavitree roop nihaarou.
Oult naaginee ka sir maaro.
Tahaan Shabad ounkaaraa hai. KSSV p.67

Naabhi arshat kanval dal saajaa.
Seth singhaasan bisun biraajaa.
Hiring jaap taasu mukh gaajaa.
Lachmi siv aadhaaraa hai. KSSV p.67

Dvaadas kanval hrideh ke maahi.
Jang gaur siv dhayaan lagaaee.
Soh Shabad taahaan dhum chaaee.
Gan karai jaijaikaaraa hai. KSSV p.67

Do dal kanval kanth kei maahee.
Tohei madh abi baaee.
Haree har Brahma chanvar dhuraaee.
Jeh shring Naam ochaaraa hai. KSSV p.67

Ta par kanj kanval hai bhai.
Bang bhounraa dui roop lakhaaee.
Nig mun karat tahan thakurai.
So nainan pichvaaraa hai. KSSV p.68

Kavlan bhaid kiyaa nivaaraa.
Yeh sabh rachnaa pind manjhara.
Satsang kar Sat Guru sir dhaaraa.
Veh Sat Naam uchaaraa hai. KSSV p.68

Aankh kaan mukh band karaaou.
Anhad jeenga Shabad sunaaou.
Dono til ik taar milaaou.
Tab daikho guljaaraa hai. KSSV p.68

Chand soor aikai ghar laaou.
Sushmun saiti dhyaan lagaaou.
Tirbeni kesung samou.
Bhor utar chal paaraa hai. KSSV p.68.

Ghantaa sankh suno dhun douee.
Saehas kanval dal jagmag hoi.
Ta madh karta nirkho soui.
Banknaal gaas paraa hai. KSSV p.68

Daakini saakini bahu kilkaarai.
Jam kinkar dharm doot hakaare.
Sat Naam sunn bhaagai saarai.
Jab Sat Guru Naam uchaaraa hai. KSSV p.68

Gagan mandal bich udharmukh kuiyaa.
Gurmukh saadhu bhar bhar piyaa.
Nigurai pyaas marai bin kiyaa.
Jaa ke hiyai andhiyaaraa hai. KSSV p.68

Trikuti mehal me bidhaa saaraa.
Ghanhar garjai bajai nagaaraa.
Laal baran suraj oujiyaaraa.
Chaturkanyal manjhaar Shabad aoukaaraa hai. KSSV p.68

Saadh soee jin yeh garr leenhaa.
Nou darjaajai pargat cheenha.
Dasvaan khol jaay jin deenhaa.
Jahaa kuluf raha maaraa hai. KSSV p.69

Aigai seth sunn hai bhai.
Maansrovar paith anhaaee.
Hansan mili hansaa hoee jaee.
Milai jo ami ahaaraa hai. KSSV p.69

Kingree saarang bajai sitaaraa.
Achchar Brahm sunn darbara.
Dvadas bhanu hans ujiyara.
Khat dal kanval manjhaar Shabad rarankara hai. KSSV p.69

Mahaa sunn sindh bishmi ghatee.
Bin Sat Guru paavai nahi baati.
Byaaghar sindh sarap bahu kaati.
Teh sahaj achint pasaaraa hai. KSSV p.69

Ashat dal kanval Paar Brahma bhai.
Dahine dvadas achint rahaaee.
Baayai das dal sahaj samaaee.
Yon kavlan nirvaaraa hai. KSSV p.69

Paanch Brahm paancho undh beeno.
Paanch Brahm ni-achar cheenho.
Chaar mukaam gupt teh keenho.
Ja madh bandeevaan purush darbaaraa hai. KSSV p.69

Do parbat kai sandh nihaaro.
Bhavar gufaa te sant pukaaro.
Hansa karte kel apaaro.
Tahaa guran darbaaraa hai. KSSV p.69

Sahas athaasi deep rachai.
Heerai panyai mahel jarrai.
Murlee bajat akhand sadaai.
Teh soh chankaaraa hai. KSSV p.69

Soh had taji jab bhaaee.
Satr Lokh kee had puni aaee.
Udhat sugandh maha adhikaaee.
Ja ko vaar na paaraa hai. KSSV p.70

Shordas bhaanu hansaa ko rupaa.
Beenaa Sat Dhun bajai anupaa.
Hansaa karat chanvar sir bhoopaa.
Sat Purush darbara hai. KSSV p.70

Kotin bhaanu uday jo hoee.
Aitai hi puni chandr lakhoee.
Purush rom sum aik na hoee.
Aisaa Purush didaaraa hai. KSSV p.70

Aaigai Alakh Lokh hai bhaiee.
Alakh Purush kee teh thukraaee.
Arban soor roum sum naahee.
Aisaa Alakh nihaaraa hai. KSSV p.70

Ta par Agam mahel ik saajaa.
Agam Purush taahi ko raajaa.
Kharban soor roum ik laajaa.
Aisaa Agam apaaraa hai. KSSV p.70

Ta par akeh Lokh hai bhaaee.
Purush Anaamee tahan rahaaee.
Jo pahunchaa jaanegaa vaahee.
Kehan sunan te nayaaraa hai. KSSV p.70

Kaayaa bheid kiyaa nirbaaraa.
Yeh sabh rachnaa pind manjhaaraa.
Maya avgatee jaal pasaaraa.
So kaareegar bhaaraa hai. KSSV p.70

Aadh Maya keenhi chaturaaee.
Jhoodhee baajee pind dikhaaee.
Avgate rachan rache and maahee.
Ta ke pratibib daaraa hai. KSSV p.70

Simran se sukh hot hai simran se hukh jae.
Kahe Kabir simran keeai saae mahe samae. KV p.19

Pragat pragaas giaan gur gamit Satgur te sudh paaee.
Daas Kabir taas mad maataa uchak na kabhoo jaaee. GGS p.969

Jah uh jaae tahee sukh paavai maa-i-aa taas na jholai dev.
Kah Kabir meraa mun maaniaa Raam preet keeo lai dev.
GGS p.857

Amrit Naam japao jap rasnaa.
Amol daas kar leeno apnaa. GGS p.331

Ab mun ult sanaatan hooaa.
Tab jaaniaa jab jeevat mooaa.
Kah Kabir sukh sahaj samaavao. GGS p.327

Ree kalvaar gavaar moodh mat ulto pavan firaavao.
Mun matvaar mer sar bhaathee amrit dhaar chuaavao.
GGS p.1123

Ab ham tum ek bhae hah ekai dekhat mun pateeaahee. GGS p.339

Tan rainee mun pun rap karihao paachao tat baraatee.
Raam raae sio bhaavar laihao aatam tih rang raatee. GGS p.482

Kabir aisaa ek aadh jo jeevat mirtak ho-e.
Nirbhai ho-e kai guhn ravai jat pekhao tat so-e. GGS p.1364

Sant prasaad bhae mun nirmal har keertan mah andin jaagaa.
GGS p.343

Paanchao larikaa jaar kai rahai Raam liv laag. GGS p.1366

Sarab sukhaa kaa ek har soami so gur Naam da-io. GGS p.856

Kah Kabir jo Naam samaane sunn rahiaa liv soee. GGS p.1104

Kabir dee-ee sansaar kao leenee jis mastak bhaag.
Amrit ras jin paa-i-aa thir taa kaa sohaag. GGS p.970

Kathnee meethee khand si karnee bish ki loy.
Kathnee taj karnee karai bish so amrit hoy. KV p.32

BIBLIOGRAPHY

                                                                   CODE

1. Sri Guru Granth Sahib

2. Kabir Granthavali
   Ed. by Mataprasad Gupta
   1969 Lokabharati Prakashan
   Allahabad, India

3. Kabir Sagar
   by Bihari Yugalananda
   1914 Shrivenkateshvar Steam Press
   Bombay, India

4. Kabir Granthavali (Doha)
   Charlotte Vaudeville
   1957 Institut Francais
   D'Indologie Pondichery France

5. Kabir Vani
   Charlotte Vaudeville
   1982 Institut Francais
   D'Indologie Pondichery France

6. Kabir Sahib Shabdavali First Part   KSSV
   1970 Belvedere Printing Press
   Allahabad India

7. Kabir Vachanavali 2nd Ed.   KV
   Ed. by Agarachanda Nahata
   1963 Rajasthan Oriental Research Institute
   Jodhpur India

8. Kabir Granthavali 5th Ed.   GK
   Introd. by Shyam Sunder Das
   1951 Kasi N.P. Sabha
   India

9. Satya Kabir Sahib Ki Sakhi   KSS
   Ed. Swami Yugalanand
   1908 Shri Venkateshwar Steam Press,
   Bombay India

10. Kabir Vani   Kabir Vani
    Randhir Prakashan
    Hardwar India

11. Anurag Sagar   AS
    Publishers Chatr Singh & Jivan Singh
    Amritsar India

12. Selected Kabir Verses   SKV

13. Janam Sakhi Bhagat Kabir Ji Kee   JSBK
    by Narinder Kaur Bhatia
    1995 Guru Nanak Dev University
    Amritsar India

14. Kabir Legends
    by David Lorenzen
    1991 State University of New York Press
    New York U.S.A.

GLOSSARY

A

AGAM PURUSH - The Inconceivable One; Lord of the Seventh Spiritual Region.

AJNA CHAKRA - Focal point behind and between the eyes, Seat of the Soul during waking state, Third Eye.

AKAAL - Name for the Positive Power.

AKAAL PURUSH - Almighty God.

ALAKH LOK - The Sixth Spiritual Region, two stages before the Absolute.

ALAKH PURUSH - The Indescribable One; Lord of the Sixth Spiritual Region.

AMRIT - Divine Nectar, which makes one immortal.

ANAMI - The Nameless One without attributes; the Absolute Formless God; the Essence before it comes into expression or existence; the Eighth and final Spiritual Stage.

ANAND - Ecstasy, or bliss.

ANDH - The Second Spiritual Region, also known as Trikuti, the Astral Region, and Sahansdal Kanwal.

ANHAD BANI - Sound that is unending and knows no limits; fig. Audible Life-Current originating from the Divine Will, endlessly carrying on the work of creating and sustaining the Universe; interchangeably used with An-hat, meaning 'Unstruck' as it is automatic, and not instrumental.

APRA VIDYA - Knowledge of the material world (observation and experiment) through senses, comprising of religious rites and rituals, fasts, vigils, pilgrimages, with special reference to ethical and moral life which forms the basis for Spiritual Experience.

ASCETICISM - In many yogas, it refers to renunciation of worldly duties for the purpose of spending one's life in meditation.

ASHTANGI - Also known as Maya; wife of Kaal; mother of Brahma, Vishnu, and Mahesh (Shiva).

ASTRAL - Refers to the Region where the soul is covered by the Astral body. It is the first Region to which the soul journeys after transcending the physical body.

ASTRAL BODY - The outer covering of the soul when inhabiting or travelling in the Astral Region.

AVTAR - Incarnation of Vishnu.

B

BANI - Fig. The Holy Word, or Naam. The Eternal Sound Current.

BHAE - To be in awe of someone or something. It is the fear that the goal may not be realized before the end of this life. It is a fear of death which brings one to the True Master. One then wants to know further about Spirituality.

BHAIRAG - Detachment from worldly pleasures, asceticism, renunciation.

BHAIRAGI - One who has given up all attachments for this world for remembrance of the Master.

BHAJAN - One of the three Sadhans (disciplines) in self-realization and God-realization, and means to be in tune with the Holy Sound Current within; also used for holy songs and hymns. In Sant Mat, the practice of listening to the Holy Sound Current.

BHAKTI - Worshipful devotion to the Godman; meditation.

BHAKTI YOGA - One of the three important systems of Yoga; Jnana (The Path of Knowledge), Bhakti (The Path of Devotion), and Karam (The Path of Action).

BHANWAR GUPHA - Fourth Spiritual Region.

BHAU - Affection.

BIJAK - (Lit. A Key) A collection of compositions attributed to Sant Kabir.

BIRHA - Intense pain and longing of separation from the Beloved.

BODY-CONSCIOUSNESS - Awareness of the physical body and the physical world. The Attention, which is the outer expression of the soul, is dragged to and kept aware of only the outer world by the mind and senses. Rising above body consciousness means that the Attention is inverted through meditation to the Spiritual Regions and is temporarily oblivious to the outer world and the physical body.

BRAHM - Lord of the second Spiritual Region.

BRAHMA - The Power in charged of the Creation below the first Spiritual Region of Sahansdal Kanwal.

BRAHMAND - The Third Spiritual Region, also known as the Causal Region, or Dhaswan Dwar.

BRAHMIN - Lit. 'One who knows Brahmn (God)'. In practice, the 'highest' of the four Hindu castes, that of priests and educators.

BUDDHI - Thinking and reasoning faculty--the intellect; the discriminating faculty that reasons right from wrong.

C

CASTE - An inherited socio-religious rank amongst the Hindus and Muslims. Tradition divided its adherents into four basic castes: Brahmins (priestly class engaged in the study and teaching of Scriptures), Ksatriya (warrior race consisting of fighting forces for purposes of defence), Vaisya (merchants and farmers), and Sudra (people serving the foregoing three classes.) The latter of these were known as the low-caste 'untouchables', and were excluded from the general social and religious privileges.

CAUSAL - Refers to Brahmand, the Plane in which the soul sheds the Physical and Astral body, and is covered only by the Causal body. It is the Region from where the mind originates. The ruler of this Region is Brahm.

CHAKRAS - Six ganglionic Energy Centres in the bodily system on which the yogins concentrate in meditation, by controlling which one gains mastery over various processes going on in the body, e.g. physiological, psychological, and respiratory, etc. The six Chakras are: Guda Chakra, located at the base of the spine;

Indri Chakra, near the regenerative organ; Nabhi Chakta, near the navel; Hirday Chakra, near the heart; Kanth Chakra, near the throat; and Ajna Chakra, located between and behind the eyebrows.

CHARAN KAMAL - Shelter, refuge at the Feet of the True Master.

CHARGED - In Sant Mat, refers to the Spiritual Power of the esoteric Names given at the time of Spiritual Initiation.

CHIT - Memory; Inner Attention; that which gives the mind the ability to think; Consciousness.

CYCLE OF TRANSMIGRATION - The law governing the three lower Planes whereby souls continue returning to the world again and again in different species of life to work out their Karmas or fruits of action. There are 8.4 million species of life; hence, the Wheel of Eighty-Four; also known as the Cycle of the 8.4 Million Species.

D

DAN - Service with one's wealth.

DARSHAN - To have a view of the Master's Illustrious Form with Loving devotion, within or without.

DASWAN DWAR - Third Inner Plane, next after the Causal, Region between Brahmand and Par Brahm, both of which form the Second Grand Division in Creation, Plane of Universal Mind, consisting of Pure Spirit and subtle form of matter in varying degrees; there the pilgrim-soul, by a dip in Amritsar (the Sacred Pool within), is washed clean of all impurities regaining its pristine purity, becoming a Hansa, or a royal white swan.

DEADLY FIVE - The five cardinal vices of Lust, Anger, Greed, Attachment, and Ego.

DEVI - Goddess of the lower Regions.

DEVTA - God of the lower Regions.

DHARAM RAI - King-Judge; the Lord of the Astral world who impartially judges all by their actions, the law being 'As you sow, so shall you reap'.

DHARMA - Moral or religious basis upholding and supporting the Universe.

DHUN - Reverberation of the Sound Principle in Creation, the Music of the Spheres.

DHYAN - Concentration, particularly on the Holy Shabd; communion with the Word. Fixing the Attention on some focus within. Meditation; contemplation.

DYING WHILE LIVING - Refers to the process of rising above the body-consciousness through meditation and having the same experience that the soul undergoes at the time of final death.

E

EYE-FOCUS - The seat of the soul in the body. See Single Eye, Third Eye.

G

GIAN - Spiritual knowledge.

GODMAN - Lit. 'God-in-man'. An adept in Shabd, commissioned from Almighty God to take souls back to their Eternal Home.

GOD POWER - Absolute God-into-Expression in the form of Light and Sound.

GOD-REALIZATION - The state in which the soul merges with God, thus attaining Conscious knowledge of God. This state takes place when the soul reaches the Spiritual Plane known as Sach Khand.

GURBANI - Scriptural words as given by the Gurus.

GURBHAKTI - To surrender oneself, or to be devoted to, the Guru.

GURDWARA - A Sikh shrine or temple.

GURMAT - Path of the Guru, both as He preaches without and the one that is revealed within, by following which one reaches the True Eternal Home of God.

GURMUKH - One who by constant and scrupulous practice of the Gurmat, or the Path explained and made manifest, acquires a special status next to the Master (Guru), as His mouthpiece.

GURU - A Spiritual Teacher, treated with the deepest respect and greatest reverence; One Who Lights up the Way Godward; a Torch-Bearer on the Way back to the Mansion of the Lord. Lit. Dispeller of darkness. The Master Power manifesting on the Physical Plane.

GURU DEV - Radiant Form of the Master that meets the disciple as his spirit ascends above the body consciousness.

GURU PRASHAD - The Life-Impulse of the Sat Guru; His Attention.

H

HAJJ - In Islam, the sacred pilgrimage to Mecca.

HATHA YOGA - A form of yoga dealing with the control of the body and bodily activities as a means to good health, and eventually to stilling the mind. The process of purification and rejunvenation is done by means of six purificatory acts, like Neti and Dhoti, etc.

HOLY WORD - The God-into-manifestation Power also known in various Scriptures as Naam, Shabd, Naad, Kalma, Baang-e-Aasmani, Sonorous Light, Sraosha, Voice of Silence.

HUKAM - Denotes the 'Divine Will' that ordains and works out God's plan. An awareness of Divine Will means that the ego has vanished.

I

IDA - In Spirituality, the Left Path.

INITIATION, SPIRITUAL - The process by which an Adept connects a disciple or seeker, with the Inner Light and Sound.

INVERSION - The process of withdrawing the Attention from the outer world, the body, and the senses, and focusing it at the Third, or Single, Eye.

ISHQ - Divine Love; Love, in the Spiritual sense.

J

JAP - Intense repetition, usually orally, of a Mantra.

JIVA - Soul when bound by any or all of the three bodies; Physical, Astral, or Causal.

JIVAN MUKT - Liberated soul.

JIVAN MUKTI - Liberation from the cycle of births and death while living in the physical body; true Salvation.

K

KA'ABA - The place of Muslim pilgrimage in Mecca.

KAAL - The Negative Power, or that aspect of the One God that flows downward and is responsible for the maintenance of the Causal, Astral and Physical Planes. The female aspect of Kaal is known as Maya. Kaal manifests in three ways: Brahma (the Creator), Vishnu (the Preserver), and Shiva (the Destroyer) within the confines of the lower three worlds only. The preservative aspect of Kaal (Vishnu) incarnates (as an avatar) from time to time to maintain the balance of minimum Spirituality and to restore justice. Lit. Time (or darkness), which is measured in terms of events and occurrences that are of impermanent nature, wherein all the embodied souls live, move and have their being, until disrobed of the physical raiment by disease, decay, and dissolution called 'death', a final change in the level of Consciousness.

KAAL NIRANJIN - The full name of the Negative Power.

KALI YUGA - The Age of Time or the Dark Age; the fourth and final time-cycle of the manifestation of the Universe.

KARMA - The term denotes a highly complex system of actions and reactions, based on I-hood, which causes continual wandering in the Cycle of Transmigration weaving a ceaseless chain of cause and effect resulting from a thoughtless thought, an inadvertently uttered word, or an unintended deed, for each of these has a potential to fructify, not only in this lifetime, but even in lives to come.

KIRTAN - Singing of Scriptures with accompaniment of instruments.
KRIYAMAN KARMA - Karma that one performs freely in present earth life, which will make or mar the future; wilful actions.

L

LOKH - Region; world.
LORD OF DEATH - (Also Lord of Judgement, Dharam Rai). For those not under the care of a True Master, they come before the Lord of Death who renders an account of their good and bad deeds, and decides where they should go after death.
LOTUS FEET OF THE MASTER (and Dust of the Master's Holy Feet) - are devotional expressions, which mean the Spiritual Grace and Power that continually emanate or radiate from a True Master. The lotus simile is used because the lotus flower always floats upon the surface of the water. In the same way, the Master's Holy Feet are on the ground, but the True Master is always higher above the earth, and in continuous Inner Communion with the Supreme Lord.

M

MANDIR - Holy Temple of the Hindus.
MANTRA - A series of words given by a Godman to still the mind.
MASTER - In Sant Mat, a True Teacher or Sat guru is commissioned by Almighty God to give Spiritual Initiation into the Holy Naam.
MAT - Path or Teachings.
MAULANA - A Muslim Divine.
MAULVI - Muslim priest. A person learned in Islamic religion.
MAYA (Skt. Illusion or Deception). The feminine aspect of Kaal, which is responsible for the clouding of vision in the lower worlds, so that individual forms appear as real in themselves, and the Power of God which gives them reality and is working through them, is not perceived. To take as real what is unreal, just like a mirage. It is the root cause of suffering and sorrows in the world.

MEDITATION - In Sant Mat, the process of concentration by which the sensory current is withdrawn upward and bodily transcension is achieved. It includes three practices: Simran (q.v.), Bhajan (q.v.), and Dhyan (q.v.).

MIND - According to Sant Mat, the mind refers to the emanation of the Causal or mental Region of existence. It has its reflection in the Astral Plane as the Astral mind, and in the Physical Realm as the Physical mind.

MOKSHA - Salvation; liberation from the cycle of births and death.

MOSQUE - A place of worship of the Muslims.

MUKTI - Salvation, liberation, to be free of bondage.

MULLAH - A Muslim teacher of theology and sacred law.

MUN - The mind.

MUNI - (Lit. One who hears within.) Sage or holy person.

N

NAAM - The Creative Power-of-God, His original Expression, the Essence of the whole manifested Universe and of each individual, variously called Vak-Devi, Sruti or Sraosha by ancients, Naad or Akash Bani by Hindus, the Holy Word by Christians, Kalma or Kalam-I-Qadim by Muslims, and Naam or Akhand Kirtan by Sikh Gurus. Being an emanation from the Supreme Being, it reveals the Divine Will to man--directly to those souls ('Word made flesh') who have become one with it, and through them to others.

NINE APERTURES - Nine openings into the material world: two eyes, two ears, two nostrils, one mouth, and two openings below.

NIRAT - Gazing faculty; that part of the Attention used in seeing. The soul's power to see within.

O

OM - The Sound Current or Naam from the Causal Plane downward; the Creator of the lower words.

P

PANDIT - (Skt. a learned person). A teacher, usually a Brahman, learned in Hindu religious, legal and social lore.

PARAM HANSA - Lit. Great Swan. A purified soul who has dipped in Amritsar, the pool of Nectar in Par Brahm.

PARAM SANT - A veritable Sant; a title bestowed upon Saints of very High Order having access to the Nameless Region.

PARA VIDYA - Knowledge of the Beyond, or Science of the Soul which lies beyond the senses, mind, and the intellect.

PAR BRAHM - The upper part of the Second Grand Division (Brahmand) where spirit predominates over the matter, unlike in the lower part (Dhaswan Dwar), where both are at par; the Region above the Causal Plane.

PARSHAD - Anything, but usually a food item, that is Blessed by a Godman.

PERFECT MASTER - One Who has gone to Sach Khand.

PIND - The Physical Plane; the lowest Plane of all. Included all solar systems, universes, galaxies, etc. Also refers to the physical body up to the focal eye-centre, behind and between the eyes; also the physical body.

PIR - Muslim or Sufi term for Guru or Master.

PRALABDH KARMA - Luck, fate, destiny; that Karma which caused our present life, over which one has no control.

PRANAS - Vital airs pervading in the entire bodily system.

PUJA - Worship.

PUNDIT - A Sanskrit scholar, learned in the Vedas.

PURAN GURU - True Guru; True Master; Perfect Master.

Q

QAZI - A Muslim learned in religious law and theology.

QUR'AN - (Arb. the reading). The sacred book of the Muslims; Also known as Qur'an Shariff.

R

RADIANT FORM OF THE MASTER - The Form of the Master, full of Light and Effulgence, which one sees in meditation.

RIDDHI - Riddhis and Siddhis usually go together and stand for miraculous or supernatural Powers of 18 kinds that one may acquire by developing the mind-force, but such powers prove a definite hindrance in the way of Spiritual growth and development.

RISHI - In Hinduism, an inspired poet or sage or seer. An enlightened one, a Yogi.

S

SACH KHAND - Realm of Truth, the Fifth Inner Plane and First purely Spiritual One, Seat of the Positive Power, the Supreme Father, who at this stage is seen to be one with both the Guru and the individual mind. It is the Goal that Saints of the highest order set for their disciples, as it is not until this stage is attained that true liberation is achieved.

SADHANS - Spiritual discipline for subduing the mind and the senses as preliminary to self-unfoldment.

SADHU - A disciplined soul with inner access as far as the Third Inner Plane.

SAHANSDAL KANWAL - Lit. Region of thousand-petalled lotus. It is the centre of the Astral Plane; the First Region to which a soul travels on its journey back to God.

SAHIB - The Supreme Being. Frequently used as a suffix added to the name of Saints as a mark of respect.

SANCHIT - Stored Karmas; all the fructified Karmas lying to the credit of individuals from time immemorial.

SANGAT - A holy congregation of the True Master.

SANT - Saint; Master of the Highest Order. One with access to the purely Spiritual Realm of Sach Khand, the Fifth Plane (the First Grand Division in Creation). It is the highest rank in the Spiritual heirarchy; One in Whom God is manifested.

SANT MAT - The Path of the Masters. The essence of all religions, it is attached to none and consists of the practice of Surat Shabd Yoga at the Lotus Feet of the True Master.

SANT SAT GURU - A Saint of the Highest Order Who is commissioned by God to lead others back to Him and to show them the Truth within their own selves.

SANYASI - One who has renounced the world and is free from attachments.

SAT - Truth; that which exists.

SAT GURU - Master Power manifesting on the level of Sat Purush. The True Master is a Sant commissioned to teach the Inner Path to the seekers after Truth and to grant them Contact with the saving life-lines within.

SAT LOK - The Region of Truth; the Fifth Inner Plane; another name for Sach Khand.

SAT NAAM - True Name; Expression of Existence; Name given to the Primal Sound Current as emanating from Sat Purush, the first manifestation of the Absolute God.

SAT PURUSH - Almighty God; the True Being; the presiding God-Power (the first and foremost manifestation of the Absolute God) in Sach Khand, the First Grand Division in the Creation, a purely Spiritual Realm. Also called the Supreme Father or the Positive Power, He is the Lord of Sach Khand and is the highest form of God.

SATSANG - Lit. The Company of Truth. The congregation presided over by a True Master.

SATSANGI - Disciple of a True Master; one who comes in contact with Truth.

SCIENCE OF SPIRITUALITY - Sant Mat; Path of the Masters.

SEAT OF THE SOUL - Third Eye, Single Eye.

SEVA - Selfless Service, a labour of Love.

SHABD - The Inner Sound Current that is vibrating in all Creation, and is responsible for the Creation and maintenance of the entire Universe. It is an Expression of God that can be heard by the Inner Ears.

SHAH-RAG - Central Current in the finer body which is traversed by means of Spiritual discipline of a True Master. It is also called Sushmana.

SHARAN - Lit. Under the Master's protection; refuge at the Lotus Feet of the Master; resignation to the Will of the Sat Guru; unconditional surrender to the Master.

SIDDHA - A sect of the yogins, who clam to possess Supernatural Powers, by means of yogic discipline.

SIDDHAS - Higher disciples and souls endowed with Supernatural Powers.

SIMRAN - Constant remembrance. In Sant Mat, it involves the silent repetition of the five charged Names (given by the True Master at the time of Spiritual Initiation) while concentrating the attention at the Third, or Single, Eye.

SINGLE EYE - Seat of the Soul; Third Eye.

SUFI - A Muslim mystic.

SURAT - Attention; the outer expression of the soul; hearing faculty.

SURAT SHABD YOGA - Lit. The yoga of embedding the Surat or Attention in the Shabd or Word. Same as Sant Mat. The Yoga of the Attention, or expression of the soul, with the Holy Word or expression of God. The yoga or union of the Surat (soul) with Shabd (Sound Current); also called Sehaj Yoga because it can easily be practiced by all, young or old, strong or infirm. It leads to full liberation without recourse to the control of the Pranas, and is the essence of all religions.

T

TAP - Austerities, penance.

TEMPLE - Hindu place of worship.

THIRD EYE - Single Eye; the Seat of the Soul located between and behind the two eyebrows. The point at which practitioners of Surat Shabd Yoga concentrate in meditation in order to transcend body-consciousness.

TRANSMIGRATION - The passing of the soul at the time of physical death into new bodies or different forms of life.

TRUE HOME - Sach Khand; Eternal Home.

U

UNHAD SHABD - Lit. Unstruck Music. Continuous Sound, which is not perishable.

UNSTRUCK SHABD - Naam or Word. Music which is Eternal and has no beginning nor end.

W

WHEEL OF LIFE AND DEATH - Cycle of birth and rebirth through which the soul must pass to reap the rewards and punishments of its deeds.

Y

YAMA - The Judge-god administering justice untampered by mercy, according to the Law of Karma.

YAMDOOTS - Agents of death; messengers and assistants of Dharam Rai.

YUGA - One complete Yug has four distinct stages: (1) Sat Yuga, is the Golden Age. (2) Treta Yuga, the second (Silver) Age. (3) Dwapar Yuga, the third (Copper) Age. (4) Kali Yuga, the fourth (Iron or Dark) Age.

BIOGRAPHIES

HAZUR BABA SAWAN SINGH JI MAHARAJ

---

*H*azur Baba Sawan Singh Ji Maharaj, a most munificent personality, was born on 27th of July 1858 in the village of Mehmansingh-Wala, District Ludhiana (Punjab) India. He was Initiated into the Mysteries of the Beyond in 1894 by Hazur Baba Jaimal Singh Ji (Who had brought the Path of the Masters, or Sant Mat, from Agra to the Punjab).

He retired from Government Service as a Civil Engineer in 1911, and lived on His own pension, carrying on the responsibilities of Mastership for 37 years (1911-1948) at Dera Baba Jaimal Singh at Beas, India.

His Teachings drew seekers from all over India, and different parts of the world. He travelled widely in India, including the portion now known as Pakistan, and had pity and compassion for many hundreds of thousands of souls, directing them on the Mystic Path to self-knowledge and God-Realization.

He treated the subject of Spirituality as a subjective Science of verifiable results, whereas other sciences are objective and depend on knowledge and experience gained through the avenues of the senses and the mind.

His religion was the Religion of the Soul, and under His Loving guidance, this Spiritual Science, hitherto confined mostly to the East, now found a ready welcome in the West, attracting a large number of devotees from all walks of life to the Path Godwards.

Throughout His life, He helped the poor and the needy, and during the Partition of India in 1947, in His mercy and compassion, kept safe all His devotees during that horrible holocaust.

Hazur Baba Sawan Singh Ji said that "Of all the Saints Who have visited the world from time immemorial, none has come to found a new religion or a new creed. They have all brought the same Message. They have all preached the same Truth. They have all shown the same Path. Their Message, Their

HAZUR BABA SAWAN SINGH JI MAHARAJ

Hazur Baba Sawan Singh Ji Maharaj, a most munificent personality, was born on 27th of July 1858 in the village of Mehmansingh-Wala, District Ludhiana (Punjab) India. He was Initiated into the Mysteries of the Beyond in 1894 by Hazur Baba Jaimal Singh Ji (Who had brought the Path of the Masters, or Sant Mat, from Agra to the Punjab).

He retired from Government Service as a Civil Engineer in 1911, and lived on His own pension, carrying on the responsibilities of Mastership for 37 years (1911-1948) at Dera Baba Jaimal Singh at Beas, India.

His Teachings drew seekers from all over India, and different parts of the world. He travelled widely in India, including the portion now known as Pakistan, and had pity and compassion for many hundreds of thousands of souls, directing them on the Mystic Path to self-knowledge and God-Realization.

He treated the subject of Spirituality as a subjective Science of verifiable results, whereas other sciences are objective and depend on knowledge and experience gained through the avenues of the senses and the mind.

His religion was the Religion of the Soul, and under His Loving guidance, this Spiritual Science, hitherto confined mostly to the East, now found a ready welcome in the West, attracting a large number of devotees from all walks of life to the Path Godwards.

Throughout His life, He helped the poor and the needy, and during the Partition of India in 1947, in His mercy and compassion, kept safe all His devotees during that horrible holocaust.

Hazur Baba Sawan Singh Ji said that "Of all the Saints Who have visited the world from time immemorial, none has come to found a new religion or a new creed. They have all brought the same Message. They have all preached the same Truth. They have all shown the same Path. Their Message, Their

Teachings, and Their Path hold good for all time and for all mankind."

Sant Kirpal Singh Ji has written, "The relationship of Love between the Master and His Disciple covers many phases and many developments. It begins with respect for One knowing more than oneself. In the beginning when I went to my Master, people asked me, 'How great is Baba Sawan Singh?' I told them, 'I do not know how great He is, but I know He is surely far, far above me--far above that which I wanted.' That is all you can say in the beginning. Only those who are equal to Him can know Him. A Master alone can know what a Master is. We see only that much which He reveals to us."

"Gods, men and angels--greater than these was He;
My emperor was unparalleled in this world and the next
For when the veil lifted, I beheld God Himself in human form
And O Lord, He was so different from what I thought Him to be."

(excerpt from a poem by H.H. Sant Kirpal Singh Ji to His Master Hazur Baba Sawan Singh Ji.)

The Great Master, Hazur Baba Sawan Singh Ji, left the earthly sojourn to become One with the Oversoul on 2nd of April 1948, after appointing Sant Kirpal Singh Ji as His Spiritual Successor.

HIS HOLINESS SANT KIRPAL SINGH JI MAHARAJ

His Holiness Sant Kirpal Singh Ji Maharaj was born on 6th of February 1894 in the village of Sayyad Kasram, District of Rawalpindi, in Punjab, India (now a part of Pakistan). He had Inner Experience from an early age and decided at the tender age of sixteen years that "God first, and the world next!" A lifelong search for God led Him to investigate the claims of many Saints in the various religious traditions.

He had the Inner Vision of His Master, Hazur Baba Sawan Singh Ji of Beas, for seven years before He met Him physically, becoming His Disciple in 1924. He lived the life of a householder with a wife and family, following the career of a Civil Servant in the Indian Government and rising to the position of Deputy Assistant Controller of Military Accounts. He retired from Office on His own Pension in 1947.

Sant Kirpal Singh Ji had sat at the Holy Feet of His Master for a total of 24 years, before He was entrusted with the Guruship by His Master in 1948 when the Latter left the body. He then served as the Spiritual Master for 26 years (1948-1974), residing at Sawan Ashram in Delhi, India, imparting Spirituality to sincere seekers after Truth, giving them a Conscious Contact with their own souls and with God.

Sant Kirpal Singh Ji taught the natural Way to find God while living in this world, and His life was the embodiment of His Teachings. One of His favourite phrases was "Truth is higher than everything; higher still is true living."

He always stressed the importance of firsthand Experience as the basis of True Faith. "Seeing is Above All!" and "Seeing is Believing!" are among His favourite phrases. Nothing is to be taken for granted, as the soul is given a direct Contact with the Oversoul.

For thousands and thousands of sincere seekers after Truth, their meeting with Him was the most significant event in their lives. He linked them to the Divine Principle of the Light and Sound of God, manifesting inwardly as a Manifestation of God, and opened their Inner eyes and Inner ears to enable them to enjoy firsthand knowledge of what previously had been only hearsay for them.

He explained that the Science of the Surat Shabd Yoga is the most natural and the easiest Path for people of all ages, and that religion and education are no bar to Spirituality.

He fulfilled the wish of His Master by establishing *Ruhani Satsang,* a common platform for all sincere seekers after Truth to sit together, irrespective of their caste, colour, creed, or nationality. There they would receive the principles of Spirituality and be encouraged to practice Spiritual discipline, thereby gaining salvation and peace.

This Great Soul undertook three World Tours (1955, 1963, and 1972) during which time He visited the major cities of the United States, Canada, Europe, Central and South America, meeting with political and religious leaders throughout the world.

He was President of the World Fellowship of Religions for seventeen years, the Conferences being held in Delhi in 1957, 1960 (Calcutta), 1965, and 1970. This is an International Organization representing more than two hundred and fifty religious groups from all parts of the world. He was conferred the honour of the Order of St. John of Jerusalem, Knights of Malta in 1962, being the first non-Christian to be so honoured.

In 1970, He established Manav Kendra, or Man Centre, dedicated to man-making, man-service, and land-service. He was the first Spiritual Master invited to address the Parliament of the Indian Government in August 1974.

Sant Kirpal Singh Ji convened the gigantic World Conference on the Unity of Man in 1974 in Delhi, India, in which leaders of half a million sadhus sat together for the first time, as well as social and political leaders from all over the world, bringing the message of hope to every corner of the earth, by declaring at this Conference that the Golden Age of Spirituality had dawned.

In 1935, under the Holy Name of His Master, Baba Sawan Singh Ji, He began publishing the Gurmat Sidhant, a compendium of Spirituality of more than 2,000 pages. He is also the author of about twenty books and numerous articles in English on all aspects of Spirituality, making this Path more accessible to the Western world. His writings were also published in many international as well as Indian languages. He always encouraged us to "Go Jolly!" and we became full with the joyous energy of knowing that this Path of the Masters is one of positive hope.

He left behind Him the Sweet Memory of a Saint Who lived up to what He preached and Who was the absolute Embodiment of peace, truth, Love, and gentleness. He upheld the Truth that the aim of all religions is one and the same.

His Name, KIRPAL, literally means "merciful", "compassionate", "One Who gives His own inspiring Life for the sake of others", and SINGH means "Lion".

Many of us still wonder what we could ever have done to deserve the great good fortune of having had the Company and felt the Love of such a One--a Cosmic Companion of the Great Ones of the past, Who showed us by His life what human beings are supposed to be.

Sant Darshan Singh Ji has written of the greatness of Sant Kirpal Singh Ji: "How does one encompass with words the attributes of a personality so cosmic as Sant Kirpal Singh Ji Maharaj? A Light broke out in the East and spread to the West. A Fragrance sweetened our hearts and minds and penetrated to the inmost depths of our souls. Master of the Tavern, with a heart as large as the ocean, poured out with abandon the Wine of Life, whose intoxication is eternal. A Beauty was born on whom Nature expended its grace and splendor, whose every glance was a transport of bliss, and whose every word was a song of Spiritual awakening."

His Holiness Sant Kirpal Singh Ji Maharaj left the earthly coil on 21st August 1974 in His 81st year, after appointing His Spiritual Successor, Sant Darshan Singh Ji, to carry on the Mission.

SANT DARSHAN SINGH JI MAHARAJ

Sant Darshan Singh Ji Maharaj was the physical son, and also the Spiritual Successor to Sant Kirpal Singh Ji. Born on 14th of September 1921 in the village of Kountrilla, District of Rawalpindi, in the Northern Frontier Province of India (now a part of Pakistan), He was Initiated into the Secrets of the Beyond by His Spiritual Mentor, the Great Saint of Beas, Hazur Baba Sawan Singh Ji, at the young age of five years. After 1948, He continued His Spiritual training with His Illustrious Father, Sant Kirpal Singh Ji. He was appointed by Sant Kirpal Singh Ji in 1974 to continue the Spiritual Mantle.

He took up civil service with the Government of India in 1942 and retired as Deputy Secretary (the third highest post in the Indian Government) after thirty-seven years of distinguished service; thereafter living on His own Pension.

In His fifteen year Ministry (1974-1989), Sant Darshan Singh Ji established over five hundred and fifty Centres of the Sawan Kirpal Ruhani Mission in over forty countries. He presided over the 6th Conference of the World Fellowship of Religions, the Asian Conference of Religions for Peace, and the 15th International Human Unity Conference held in Delhi in November 1988.

He wrote many books, including collections of His Mystic Talks and three volumes of poetry in English, and in addition, He was acclaimed as India's greatest mystic poet writing in the Urdu language, and received four Urdu Academy Awards for His collections. He regarded poetry "at its highest as a cry of the soul". His writings have been translated into more than fifty languages.

He went on four World Tours, was presented with the keys of many cities, was honoured by the Colombian Parliament in 1983 with its Medal of Congress, and by the State Legislature in Michigan and the Congress of the United States with Citations of Merit. He was invited in 1988 to confer with Dr. Robert Muller, former Assistant Secretary General of the United Nations, on the subject of inner and outer peace.

Sant Darshan Singh Ji established Master's Day in 1980, to be held annually on the fourth Sunday in July, providing an opportunity for people of all religions to sit together and share the universal message of their Spiritual Founders, Saints, Masters, and Prophets.

He explained Spirituality as a Path of 'Positive Mysticism', teaching that Spirituality is a matter of 'Inversion', i.e. inverting to the Inner Light and Inner Sound, rather than being a path of 'conversion'. He asked us to remain in our religions, pursuing our Spiritual goals while performing all worldly responsibilities and making positive contributions to society and the world at large.

'Service to Humanity' is one of the principles of His Mission, which has provided aid to victims of natural calamities around the world, serving those people suffering from famine in Ethiopia, the floods in Delhi as well as other parts of India, the volcanic disaster in Colombia (South America), and the earthquake in Mexico City.

He challenged us to "Take Up the Challenge of Inner Space", coining the words 'Soulergy' and 'Innergy' to represent the Divine Power within, the contact of which would bring about a profound metamorphosis.

He resided at Kirpal Ashram in Delhi, India, and discoursed to the thousands of devotees there as well as visitors to India; yet found time to meet privately with any sincere seekers who sought Him out.

He was Love Personified, a warm Father and a Loving Brother to all of us. He would comfort and fill our souls with the Sweet Nectar of His Divine Love, Grace, and Compassion. To sit at His Holy Feet was to imbibe one continuous, eternal moment of Love, a Love which had a beginning, but no end.

Sant Rajinder has written, "Sant Darshan Singh's Message to humanity was that we should develop Love and understanding for each other, on the personal level as well as on the religious, social, and national levels.

"He believed that self-knowledge and God-realization were the birthright of each person. All were welcome to share in the Divine Gifts He had come to distribute. No one was to be excluded from His Spiritual family. He opened His arms and His heart to everyone, no matter what their position in life. His unconditional Love attracted all who met Him, whether rich or poor, lettered or unlettered, young or old.

"We were witnessing the impact of a Love that transcended differences of caste, creed, colour, and nationality. It was a Love so pure and Divine, it inspired and transformed each person who experienced it."

In His boundless Grace and compassion, Sant Darshan Singh Ji Initiated many thousands of lucky souls into the Secret of the Inner Light and Sound during His short, but very Loving Ministry. The Beloved Sant Darshan Singh Ji Maharaj appointed Sant Rajinder Singh Ji as His Spiritual Successor before the Former left the earthly mantle on 30th of May 1989.

SANT RAJINDER SINGH JI MAHARAJ

Sant Rajinder Singh Ji Maharaj was born in Delhi, India, on 20th of September 1946, into a family which was steeped in Spirituality. His Grandfather, Sant Kirpal Singh Ji Maharaj and His Father, Sant Darshan Singh Ji Maharaj were Disciples of Hazur Baba Sawan Singh Ji Maharaj.

His formal training in Spirituality began in July 1962, when He received Spiritual Initiation into the Light and Sound Current from Sant Kirpal Singh Ji.

In 1967, He was directed by Sant Kirpal Singh Ji to continue His further education in the United States. This decision was to have a lasting impact for the future of Sant Mat, and for the Spiritual Teachings to spread further to all the peoples of the Western world.

The two Spiritual Teachers Who had preceded Him had made three or four World Tours, but Sant Rajinder Singh Ji is on a perpetual World Tour, crisscrossing the globe between the East and the West many times a year. One of the goals of His continual travel is to help bring people of diverse cultures closer together. This bonding of fellowship helps to bring about what He calls 'Unity in Diversity'.

During the two, three, or four days that He spends in a city, He conducts an intensive program of Meditation Seminars, public discourses, interviews, and meetings.

Sant Rajinder Singh Ji convenes two annual International Conferences to share this message of peace and unity. Each February, He holds the International Conference of Human Integration, and in September He convenes the Global Conference on Mysticism. The February Conference focuses on the themes of unity and peace, with guest speakers from every continent representing major religions, philosophies, and social organizations. The September Conference is an innovative Conference to help people understand the role of Mysticism in transforming one's life. Sant Rajinder Singh Ji said at the initial Conference, "My purpose is to take the 'mystery' out of Mysticism."

To help centralize the work in the West, Sant Rajinder Singh Ji opened the Science of Spirituality Centre in Naperville (Chicago), Illinois in 1991. Since then, large gatherings and public seminars are held regularly at the Centre.

Sant Rajinder Singh Ji makes Himself accessible to seekers from all over the world who wish to lead a Spiritual life. He personally grants Spiritual Initiation at Kirpal Ashram in Delhi, India; at the Science of Spirituality Centre in the United States; or when He is on Tour throughout the world. He teaches Meditation as a Science that people of all religions, all nationalities, and all ages can practice. The ease and naturalness of this type of Meditation has attracted people throughout the world.

Sant Rajinder Singh Ji has received tributes for His Spiritual and humanitarian work by United States senators, governors, and mayors. He received a special tribute from the Michigan State Legislature and a welcome tribute from the Matsunaga Peace Foundation. In South America He was warmly received and honoured by mayors, presidents of City Councils, governors, and ministers. The Minister of Education in Bogota (Columbia) gave Him the Medal of Cultural Merit in 1990 and the Simon Bolivar award in 1992 on behalf of the Ministry. He was the first non-Columbian to be presented with the Golden Cross, Order of Santiago de Cali, the highest honour that the citizens of Cali bestow.

He was President of the 7th World Religions Conference, was a major presenter at the Parliament of the World Religions held in Chicago in 1993, and the World Conference on Religion and Peace held in Rome and Riva del Garde, Italy, in 1994.

At the 50th Anniversary of the United Nations celebration

held in New York, He opened the program by putting thousands of people into meditation.

In June 1997, Sant Rajinder Singh Ji Maharaj was presented a Peace Award by the Temple of Understanding, an NGO of the United Nations, and the Interfaith Centre of New York.

One of His favourite phrases is "To share His Love, is to attract His Love." If the Master kindly Blesses us with a small part of the Love that He radiates, we will start radiating this Love ourselves.

Maharaj Ji says that our prayer should be to the Master that "Please keep all of us in that state of mind that when we look at You, we realize Who You really are: that You are the God Power, You are the Master Power, You are God-Personified. We pray that we realize that it is only from You that we can receive the Gift of Holy Naam, and it is only with Your Grace that we can go back to God."

Further, He says, "A more Spiritual Age is dawning, and society is moving toward a more enlightened era. We are standing on the threshold of a dawn in which people will be actively pursuing Spiritual growth, and humanity will be working toward a world of peace and unity. It is my hope and prayer that our time together gives you an opportunity to learn more about how to achieve Spiritual growth, personal fulfillment, inner peace, and lasting joy...We spend very little time in trying to find permanent happiness for our soul. Let us spend a few days trying to find inner joy and happiness, trying to solve the mysteries of life, and experiencing peace and bliss."

Sant Rajinder Singh Ji's most significant contribution to modern Spirituality is to present the age-old Teachings in a language clear and understandable to people in the Scientific Age. Using the vocabulary of Science, and the art of communication, He is showing people that there is a practical Way for the soul to reunite with God.

Sant Rajinder Singh Ji understands the pressures humanity now faces, and His Message is clear. As He explains, "By Meditation on the Inner Light and Sound of God within each of us, we can enjoy inner peace. Once we attain this goal, we will radiate love and tranquillity to others. We begin to see the Light of God in all other beings. We realize that we are all children of one Lord, whether our outer labels are from one religion, nationality, or social position. Once we recognize that we are all children of one Creator, that we are brothers and sisters in God, we develop love for all. We seek to help others and we refrain from acts that may hurt others. In this way, we become a source of peace and unity within our individual spheres. If each person were to live in this manner, a time would soon come on earth when world peace would prevail."

LITERATURE ON THE MASTERS' TEACHINGS

Written by Sant Rajnder Singh Ji Maharaj
Ecology of the Soul
Education For a Peaceful World
Inner and Outer Peace Through Meditation
Vision of Spiritual Unity And Peace
Spiritual Fulfillment in Modern Life
Visions of the New Millennium

About Sant Rajinder Singh Ji Maharaj
A Brief Biography of Sant Rajinder Singh Ji Maharaj
Spreading Divine Love
Illumine Every Heart: Tours & Activities of Sant Rajinder Singh
A New Generation of Peacemakers
Beloved Journey
Sant Rajinder Singh at the 1993 Parliament of World's Religions
First Global Conference on Mysticism Souvenir
Science of Spirituality: Vision and Work

Written by Sant Darshan Singh Ji Maharaj
Streams of Nectar: Lives, Poetry, and Teachings of Saints & Mystics
Love At Every Step: My Concept of Poetry
The Wonders of Inner Space
Spiritual Awakening
The Secret of Sectrets: Spiritual Talks
A Tear And A Star
The Cry of the Soul: Mystic Poetry
The Challenge of Inner Space
Soulergy: The Source of All Energy
The Meaning of Christ
Ambassdaors of Peace
Love Has Only A Beginning: Autobiography of Darshan Singh

About Sant Darshan Singh Ji Maharaj
Seeing Is Above All: 1st Indian Tour, Ed. H.C. Chadda
Divine Darshan, by Sharan Malhotra

Written By Sant Kirpal Singh Ji Maharaj
The Crown of Life: A Study in Yoga
Morning Talks
Naam or Word
Godman: Finding a Spiritual Master
A Great Saint--Baba Jaimal Singh: His Life and Teachings
The Jap Ji: The Message of Guru Nanak
The Night is a Jungle and Other Discourses of Kirpal Singh
Portrait of Perfection: A Pictorial Autobiography of Kirpal Singh
Spiritual Elixir, Vols. I and II
Prayer: Its Nature and Technique
Mystery of Death
Wheel of Life
Man! Know Thyself
The Spiritual Path: Anthology of the Writings of Kirpal Singh
The Teachings of Kirpal Singh
Spirituality, What It Is
Heart To Heart Talks, Vols. I and II

About Sant Kirpal Singh Ji Maharaj
The Saint And His Master, by R.K. Khanna
The Eternal Connection, by Hilde Dressel
Divine Darshan, by Sharan Malhotra
Ocean of Grace Divine
Love, Unity, and Peace: Sant Kirpal Singh's Centenary
Kirpal Singh: The Story of a Saint, by J. Scotti & R. Linksman

Sant Rajinder Singh Ji Maharaj may be contacted:

In **India** at Kirpal Ashram, Kirpal Marg, Vijay Nagar, Delhi 110-009, India, Tel 91-11-722-2244, Fax 91-11-721-4040

In **U.S.A.** at Science of Spirituality Centre, 4S. 175 Naperville Road, Naperville, Illinois 60563 U.S.A. Tel 630-955-1200, Fax 630-955-1205
http://www.sos.org